FUSHIGI YÛGI
GENBU KAIDEN

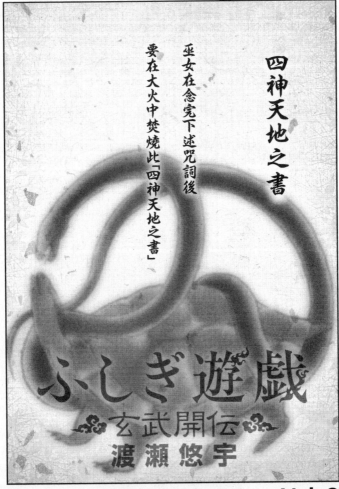

四神天地之書

巫女在念完下述咒詞後

要在大火中焚燒此「四神天地之書」、

ふしぎ遊戯
玄武開伝
渡瀬悠宇

story and art by YUU WATASE　　　**Vol. 9**

CONTENTS

TRANSLATION OF "THE UNIVERSE OF
THE FOUR GODS"

After reciting the following prayer, the Priestess should
throw the scroll into the flames.

Cast of Characters

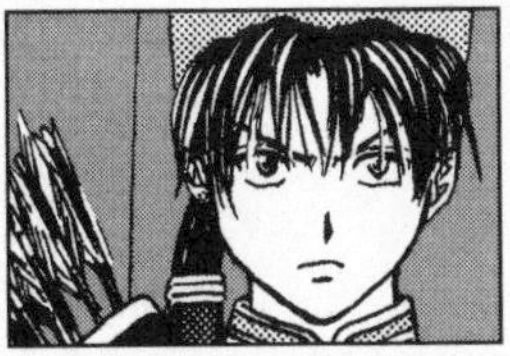

Tomite

A mischievous Celestial Warrior traveling with Takiko.

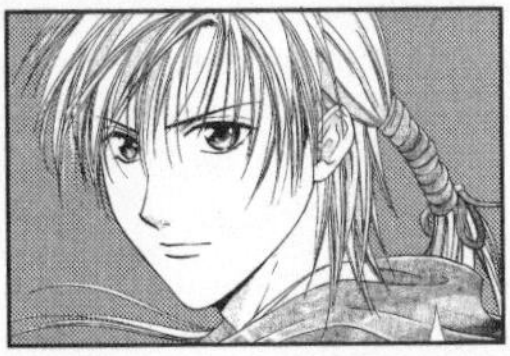

Limdo

"Uruki," a Celestial Warrior. He has the ability to take both male and female form.

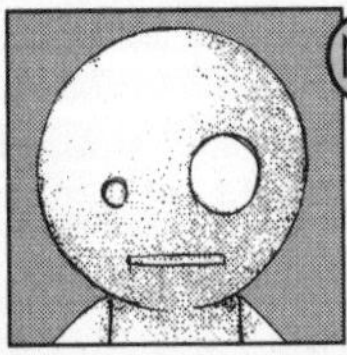

Namame

A spirit of rock made from the Star Life Stone.

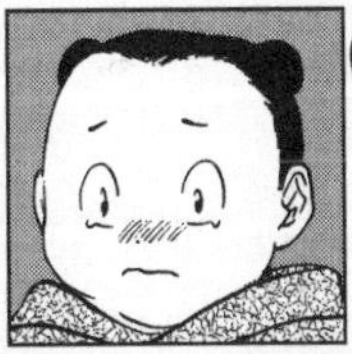

Hatsui

A Celestial Warrior, and a little timid.

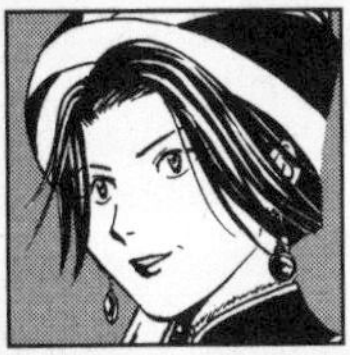

Inami

A Celestial Warrior with elastic, prehensile hair.

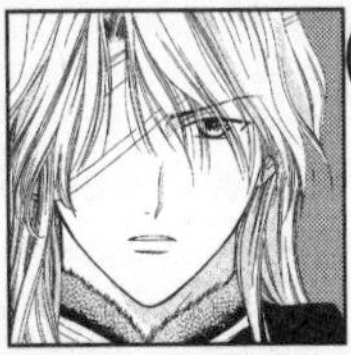

Hikitsu

A Celestial Warrior who cares deeply about his sister Ayla.

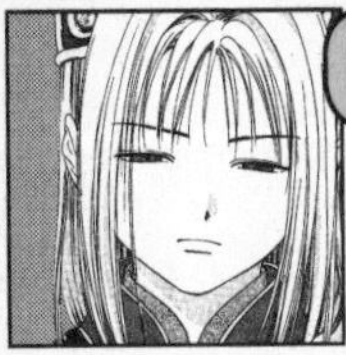

Urumiya (Teg)

A Celestial Warrior held captive in the city of Tèwulán.

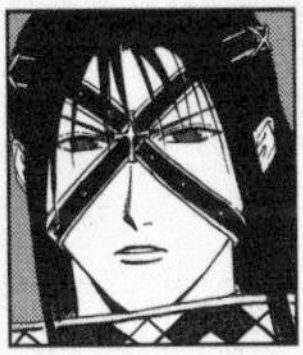

Urumiya (Hagus)

A Celestial Warrior who shares his mark with his imprisoned twin brother.

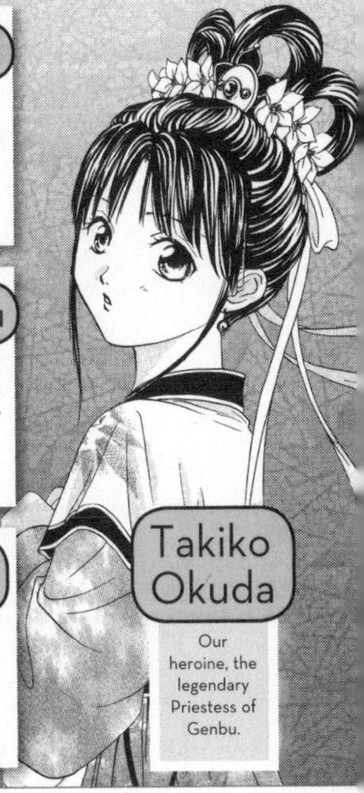

Takiko Okuda

Our heroine, the legendary Priestess of Genbu.

The Story Thus Far

The year is 1923. Takiko is drawn into the pages of *The Universe of the Four Gods*, a book her father has translated from Chinese. There, she is told that she is the legendary Priestess of Genbu, destined to save the country of Bêi-jîa. She must find the seven Celestial Warriors who will help her on her quest.

All the Celestial Warriors have joined Takiko except for Urumiya. But Urumiya turns out to be two people: a pair of twins, Hagus and Teg, who are fighting against Bêi-jîa. Pursued by the Qu-dong army, Takiko and her friends stop in an enchanted forest to rest and heal. While there, the Celestial Warriors discover that, to fulfill the prophecy and save Bêi-jîa, the Priestess must sacrifice her life. For her own good, they drive Takiko away, back to her own world...

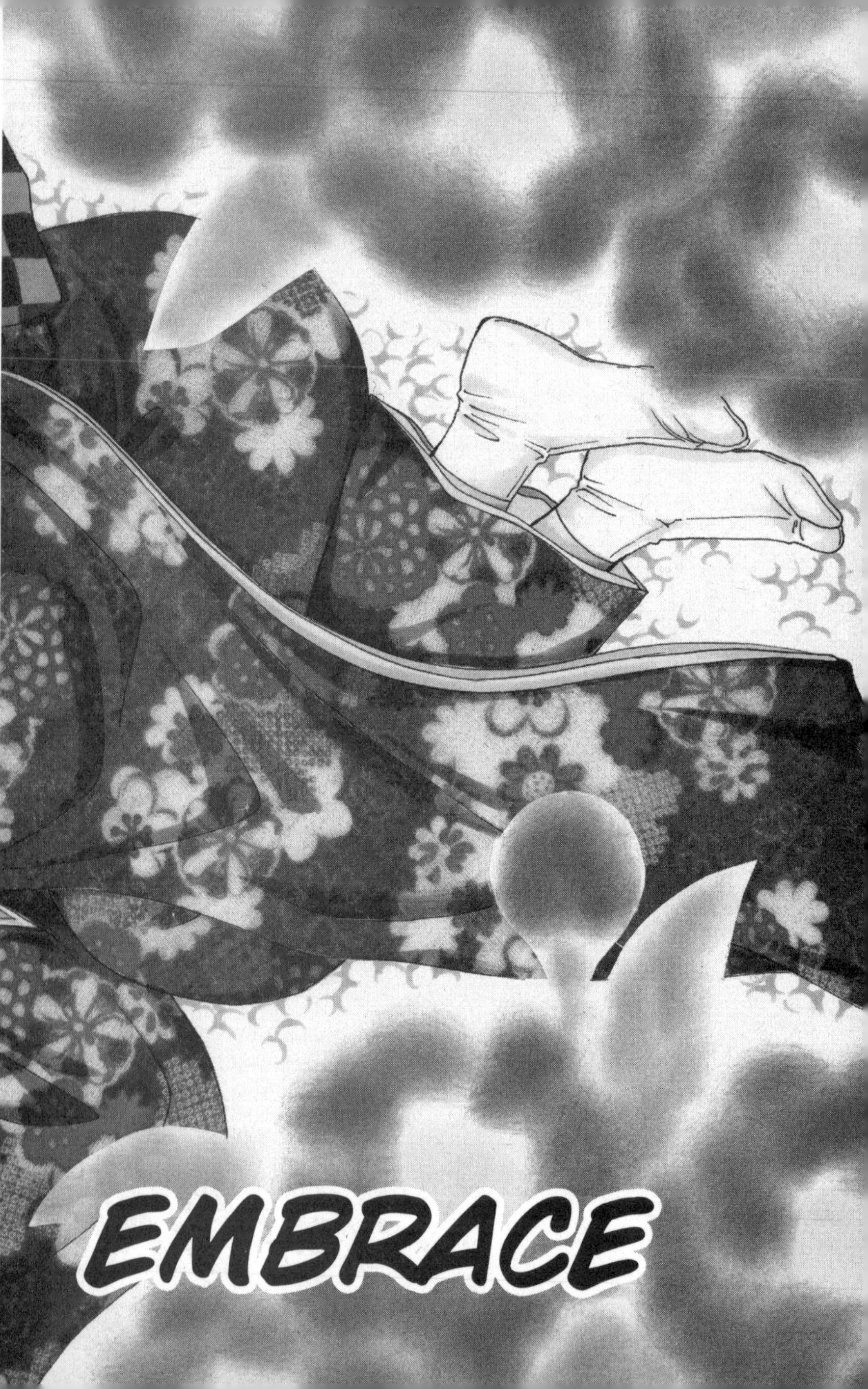
EMBRACE

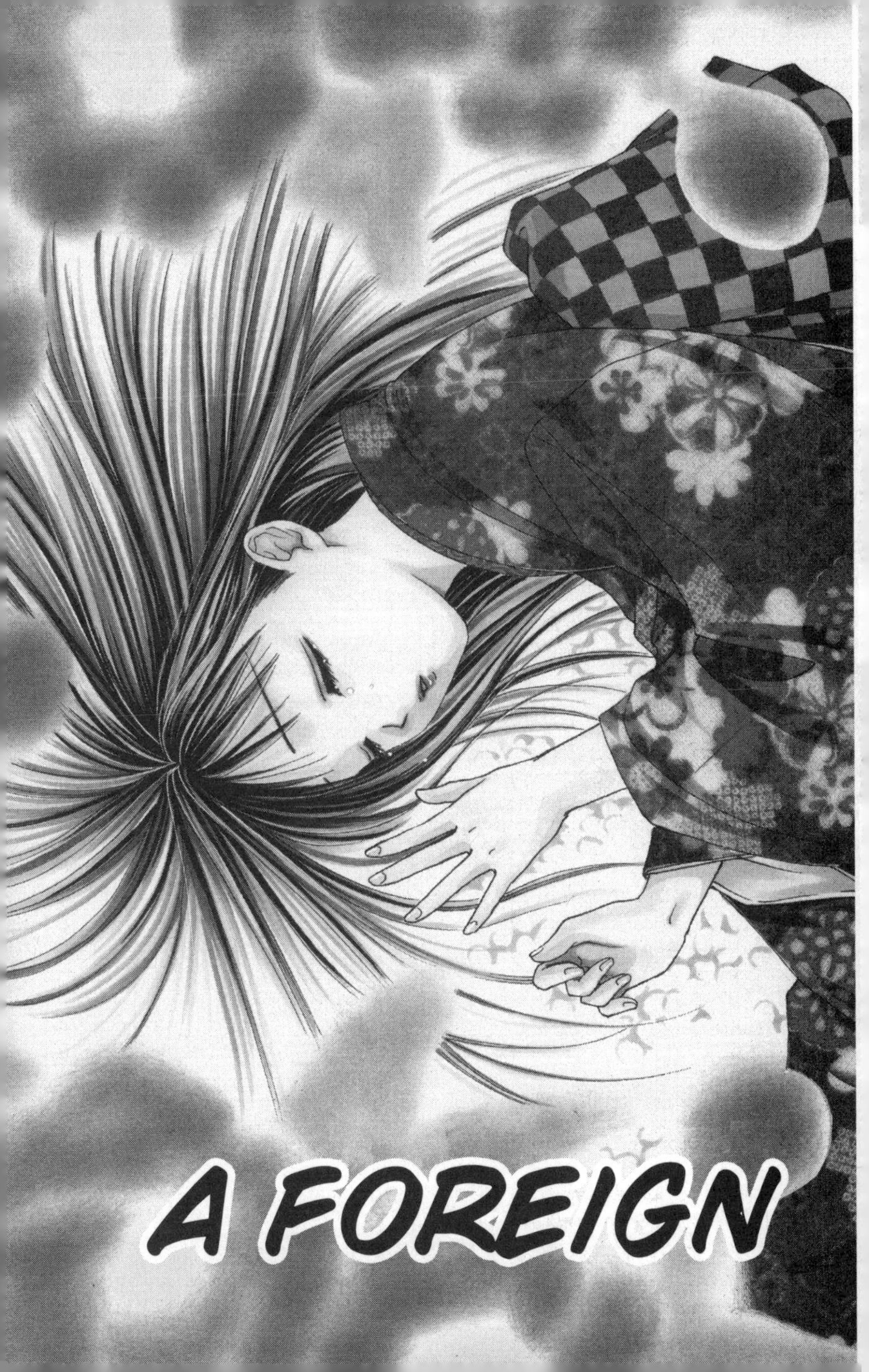
A FOREIGN

1

Hi! It's me, Watase. *Genbu* is finally in its ninth volume!! This is entirely thanks to fans like you! Uh-oh... my arm's starting to hurt already!! It's getting painful to write for long periods of time. I'm fine when I'm drawing. Isn't it weird? Even when I feel too tired to take a bath or eat a meal, I can always draw manga! Was I born to do this or what?

Anyway, we're back in Morioka for Takiko's homecoming (of sorts). Iwate Prefecture, where Morioka is located, has been hit hard by real-life earthquakes recently. I'm sure there will be a lot of hardship until everything is rebuilt. We felt the tremors even in Tokyo. We felt it when an earthquake hit Niigata too. It's so scary. Now I'm worried about whether the Genbu Cave in Morioka has been completely buried. I went there on a research trip five years ago, but even then it had been hit by an earthquake a few days before. And it had already been seriously damaged by an earlier earthquake. It was kept off-limits by a fence. I was disappointed that I couldn't go inside. But at City Hall they gave me some reference pictures and told me stories about it. (Thank you so much!) Takiko supposedly lived in the old village of Shizuku-ishi, where the "Oiwaya of Kakkonda" (a.k.a. Genbu Cave) is.

Too bad they didn't have any period pictures available...

You can take a short hike and see all sorts of rock formations.

2

I walked around the area, imagining events similar to what ended up in this volume. I've mentioned this before, but I brought up Genbu Cave in the manga to match events in the *FY* anime. Tetsuya and Keisuke visited it back when there was no fence. Heh... (The details about Einosuke and some other minor stuff are still different in the anime, but whatever...) I knew of a different cave somewhere else named after all four gods, but this one is bigger. By the way, I heard that the director brought up the cave in the anime because of "a certain suspicion" he had about my upcoming plotlines. I can't confirm whether things will happen exactly as he imagined, of course. Heh heh...

Incidentally, one of the traditional crafts of the Shizuku-ishi region is the "tortoiseshell weave" fabric, which forms a hexagonal honeycomb pattern. A tortoise! That's exactly what Genbu is! I don't know if it's named after the cave or if it's purely a coincidence. Over the years I've seen many so-called coincidences that fit perfectly together. It's fascinating.

Now then... on to an entirely different topic. The magazine *Perfect World*, where *Genbu* has been serialized, is folding. This was sudden news to everyone who's been reading it loyally since the launch, so I apologize. It's actually amazing that a magazine devoted to a single manga artist was able to keep going for so long. The fans deserve a lot of thanks. There were a number of reasons for the discontinuation. After a lot of thought, considering my continuing career as a manga artist, I decided this was the best option.

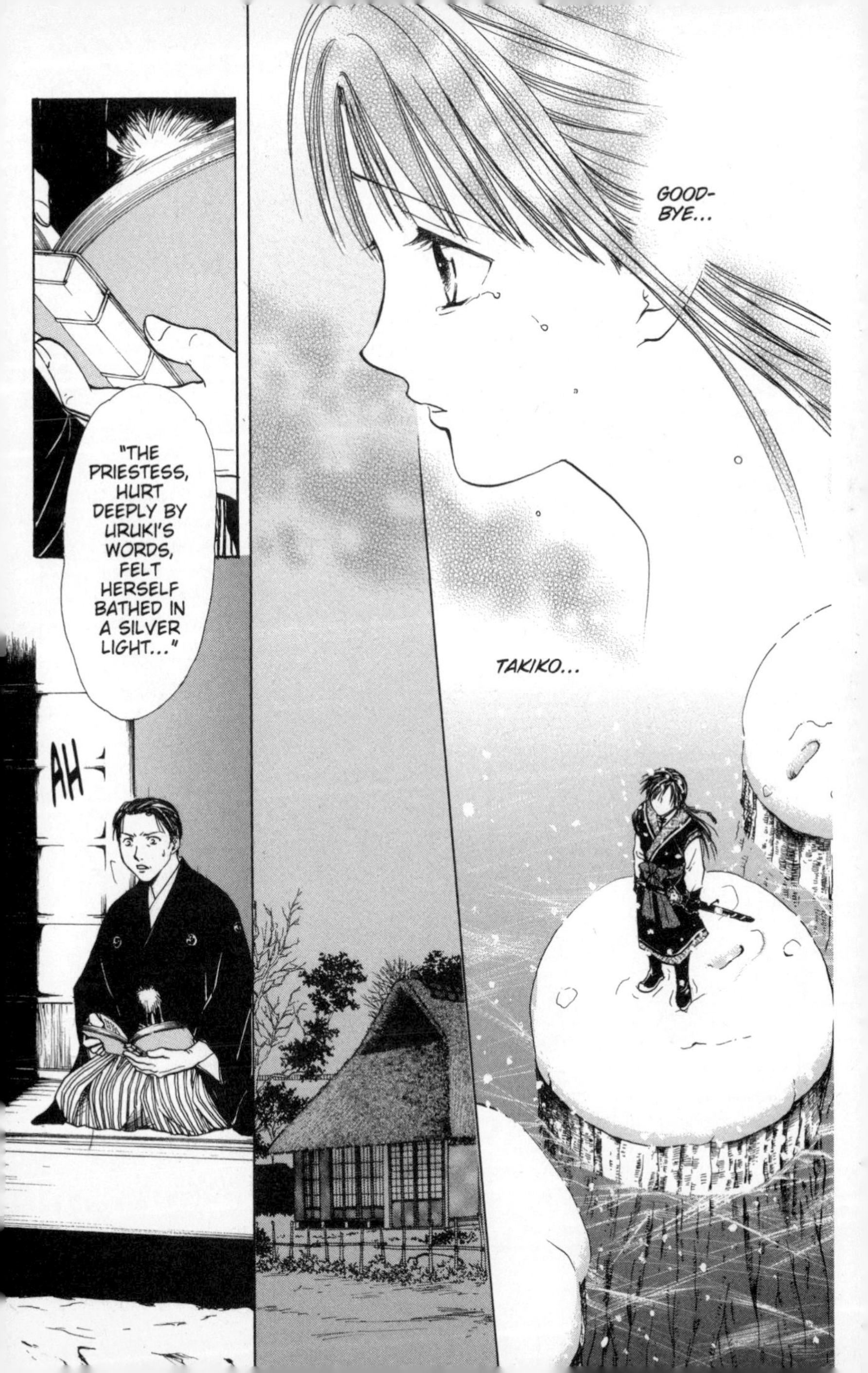
GOOD-BYE...
TAKIKO...
"THE PRIESTESS, HURT DEEPLY BY URUKI'S WORDS, FELT HERSELF BATHED IN A SILVER LIGHT..."
AH

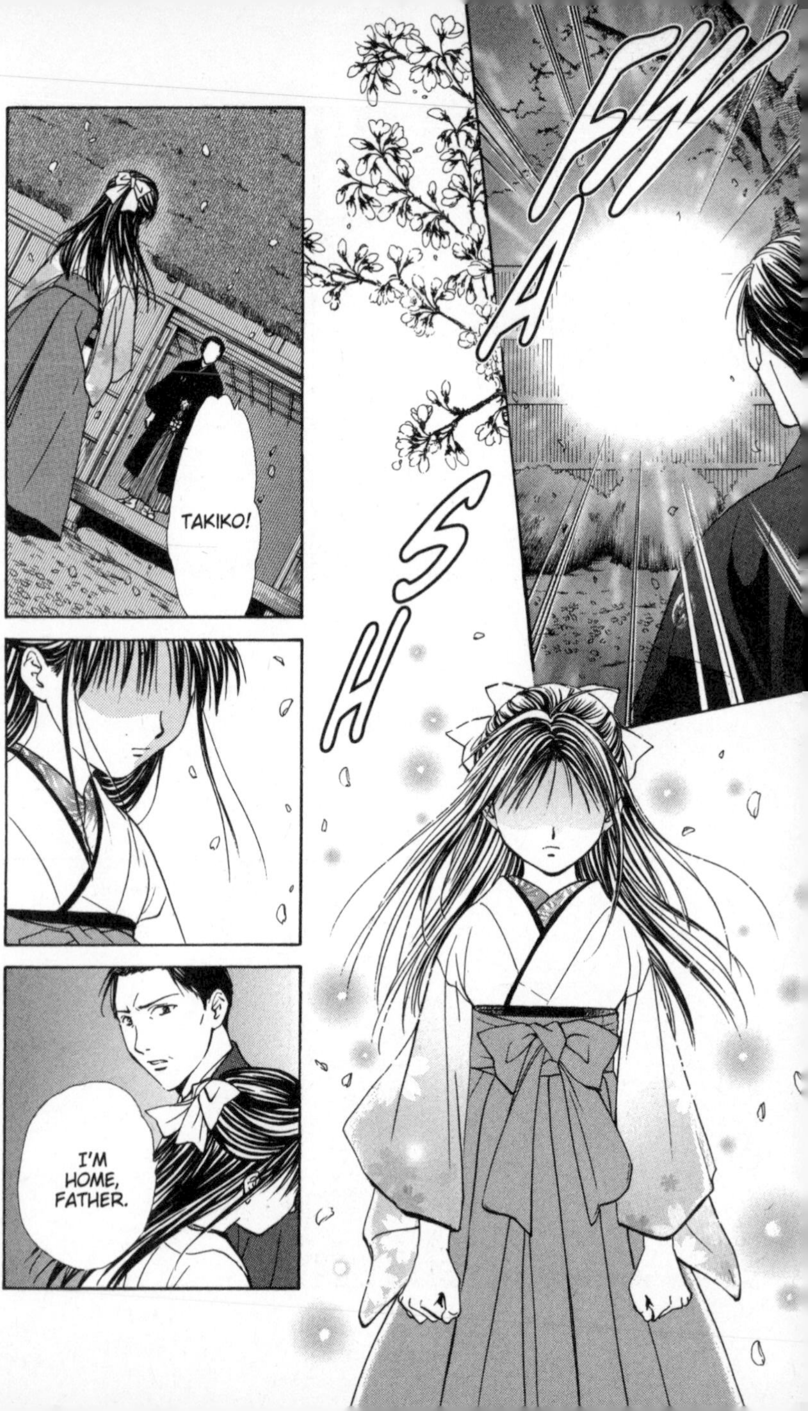
FWASH
TAKIKO!
I'M HOME, FATHER.

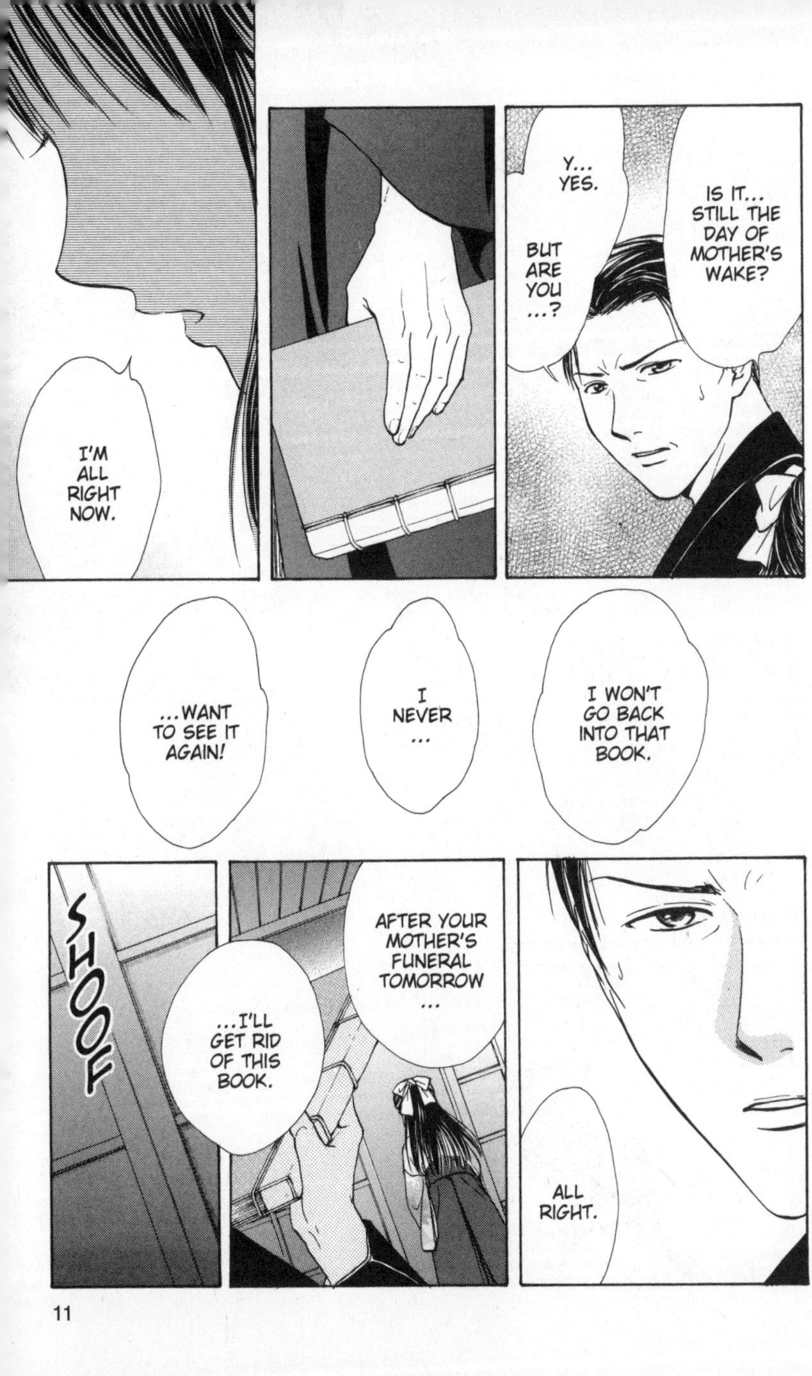
IS IT... STILL THE DAY OF MOTHER'S WAKE?
Y... YES.
BUT ARE YOU ...?
I'M ALL RIGHT NOW.
I WON'T GO BACK INTO THAT BOOK.
I NEVER ...
...WANT TO SEE IT AGAIN!
ALL RIGHT.
AFTER YOUR MOTHER'S FUNERAL TOMORROW ...
...I'LL GET RID OF THIS BOOK.
SHOOF

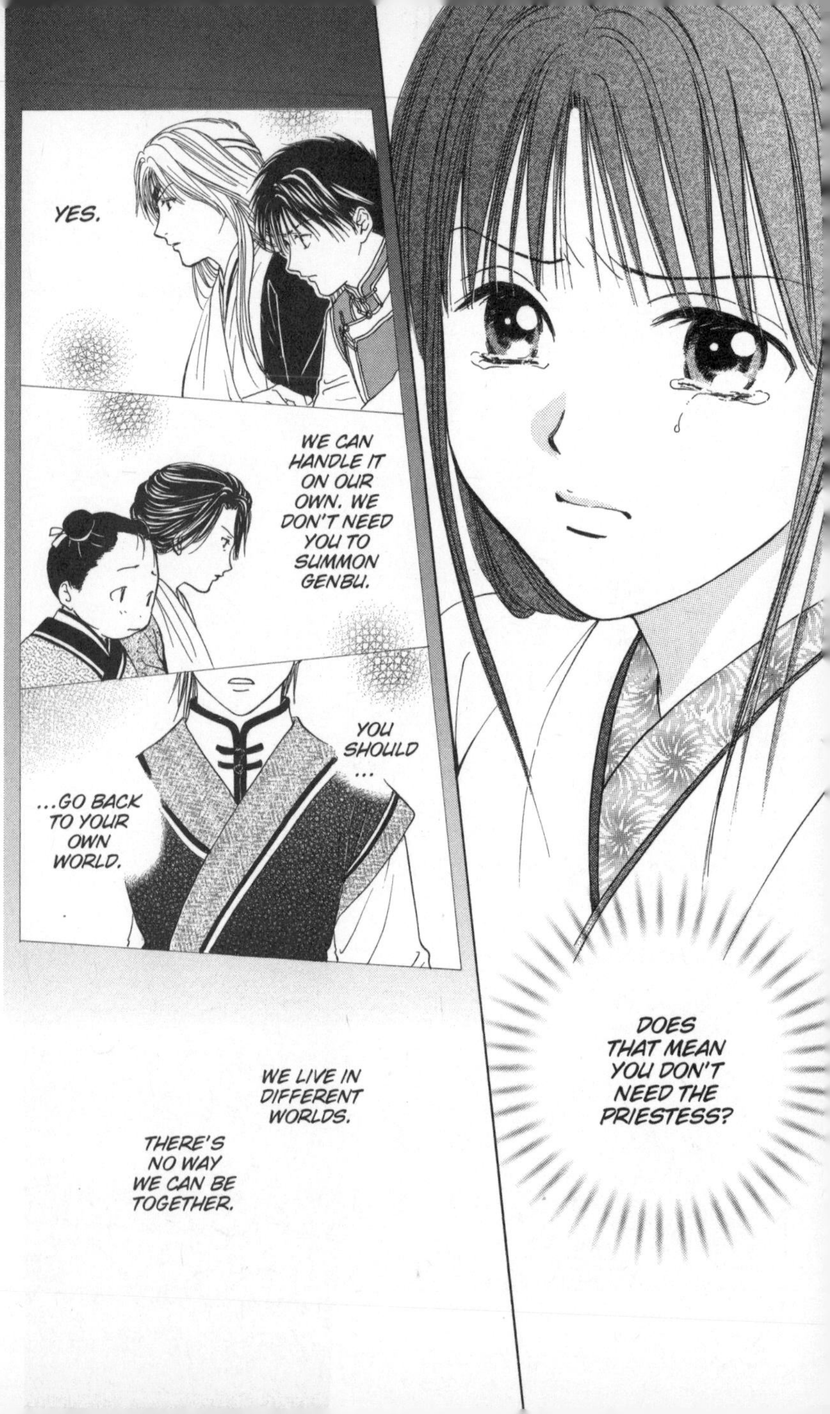
DOES THAT MEAN YOU DON'T NEED THE PRIESTESS?
YES.
WE CAN HANDLE IT ON OUR OWN. WE DON'T NEED YOU TO SUMMON GENBU.
YOU SHOULD ...
...GO BACK TO YOUR OWN WORLD.
WE LIVE IN DIFFERENT WORLDS.
THERE'S NO WAY WE CAN BE TOGETHER.

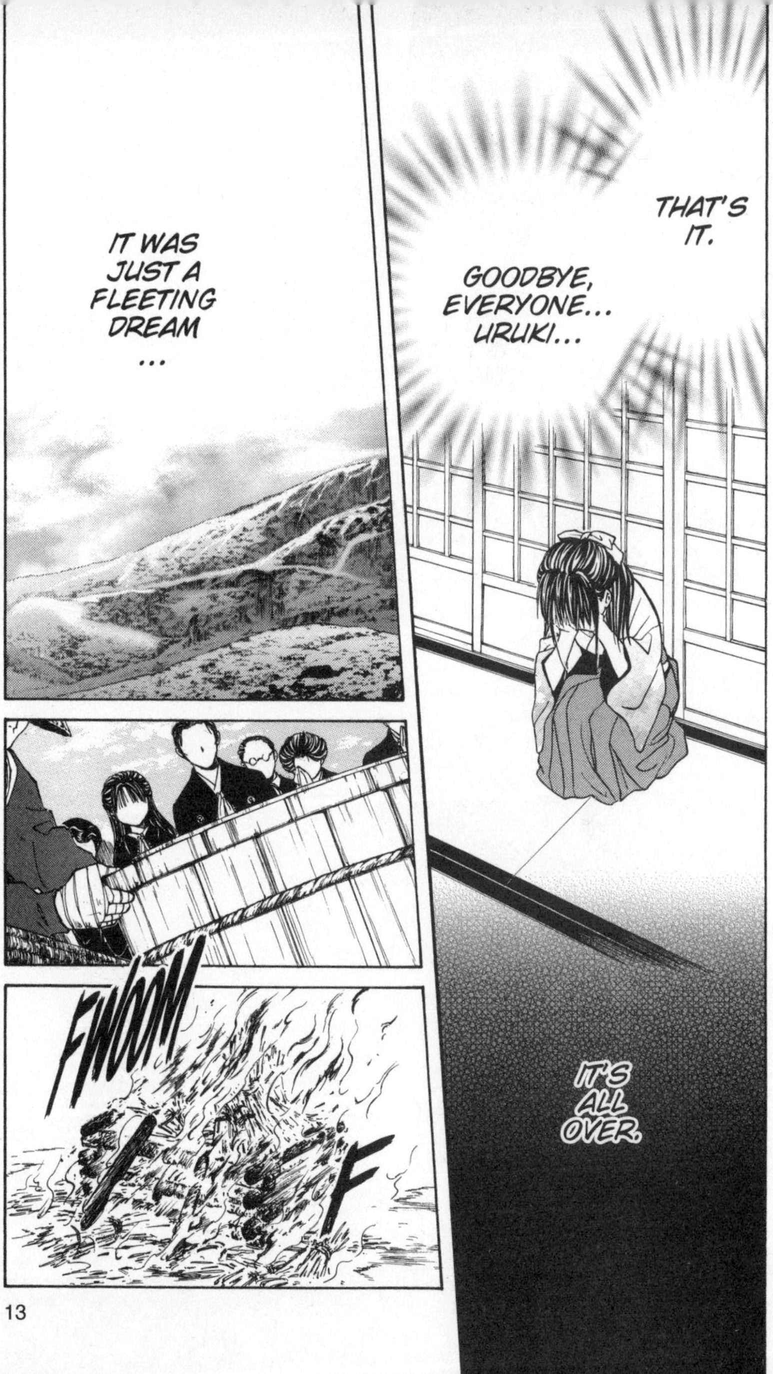
THAT'S IT.
GOODBYE, EVERYONE... URUKI...
IT'S ALL OVER.
IT WAS JUST A FLEETING DREAM...
FWOOM

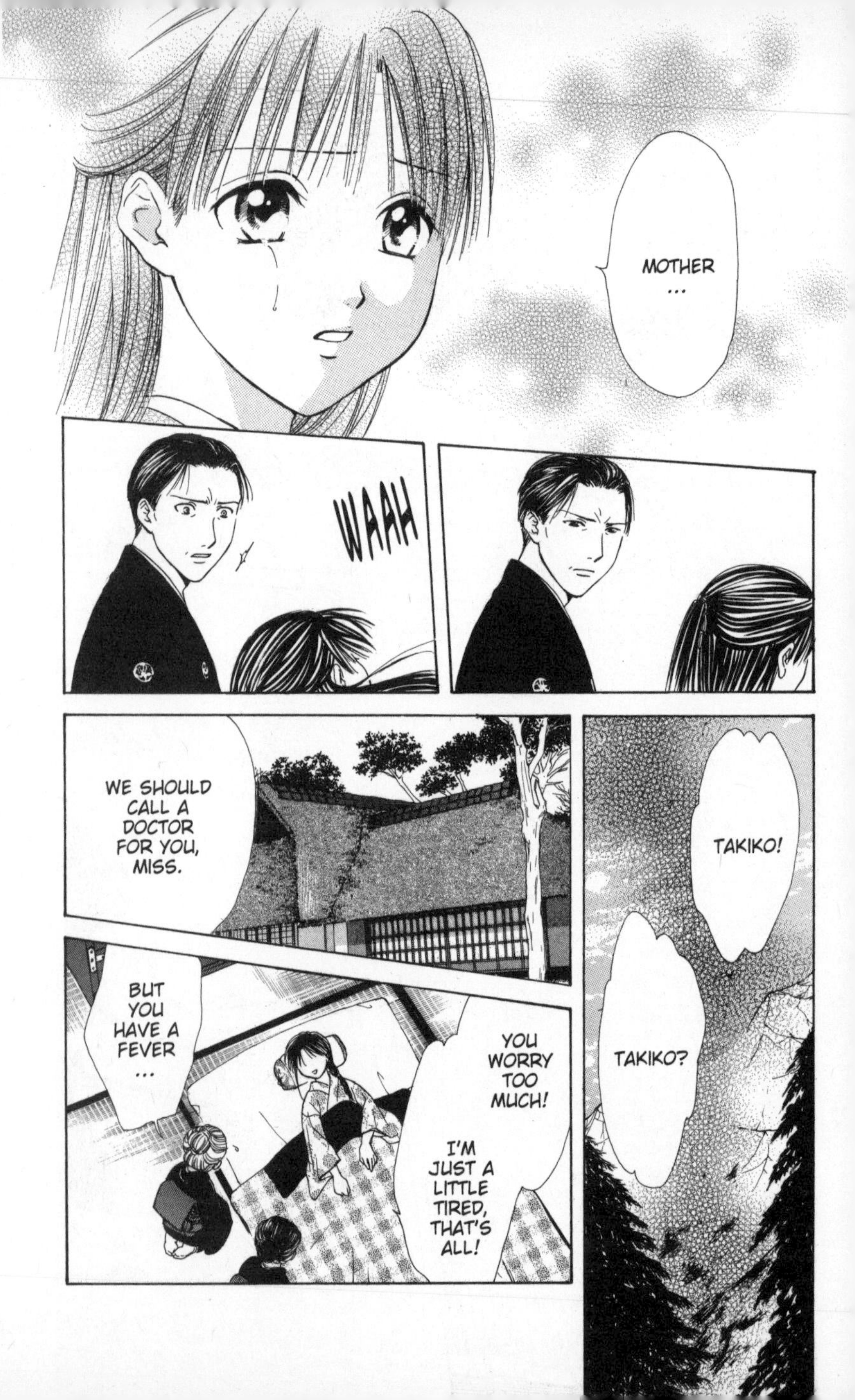
MOTHER ...
WAAH
TAKIKO!
TAKIKO?
WE SHOULD CALL A DOCTOR FOR YOU, MISS.
YOU WORRY TOO MUCH!
I'M JUST A LITTLE TIRED, THAT'S ALL!
BUT YOU HAVE A FEVER ...

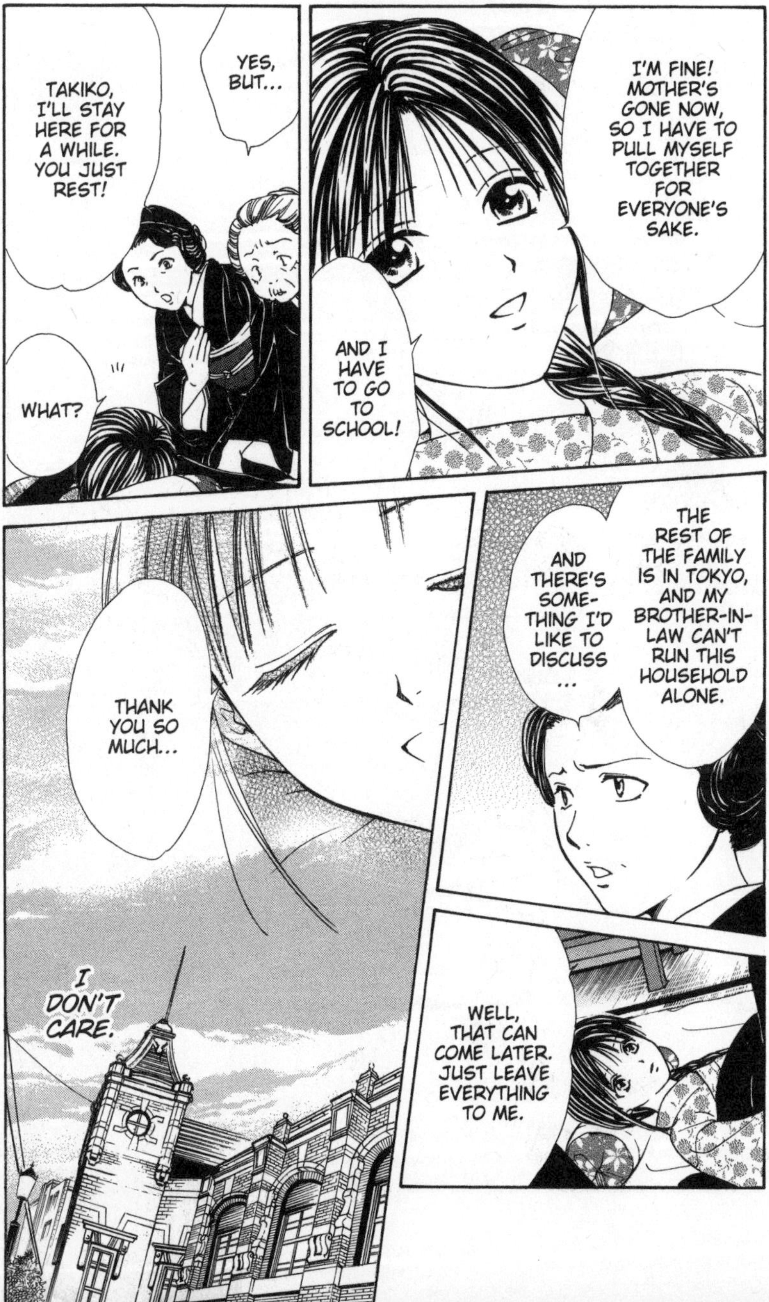
I'M FINE! MOTHER'S GONE NOW, SO I HAVE TO PULL MYSELF TOGETHER FOR EVERYONE'S SAKE.
AND I HAVE TO GO TO SCHOOL!
YES, BUT...
TAKIKO, I'LL STAY HERE FOR A WHILE. YOU JUST REST!
WHAT?
THE REST OF THE FAMILY IS IN TOKYO, AND MY BROTHER-IN-LAW CAN'T RUN THIS HOUSEHOLD ALONE.
AND THERE'S SOME-THING I'D LIKE TO DISCUSS ...
WELL, THAT CAN COME LATER. JUST LEAVE EVERYTHING TO ME.
THANK YOU SO MUCH...
I DON'T CARE.

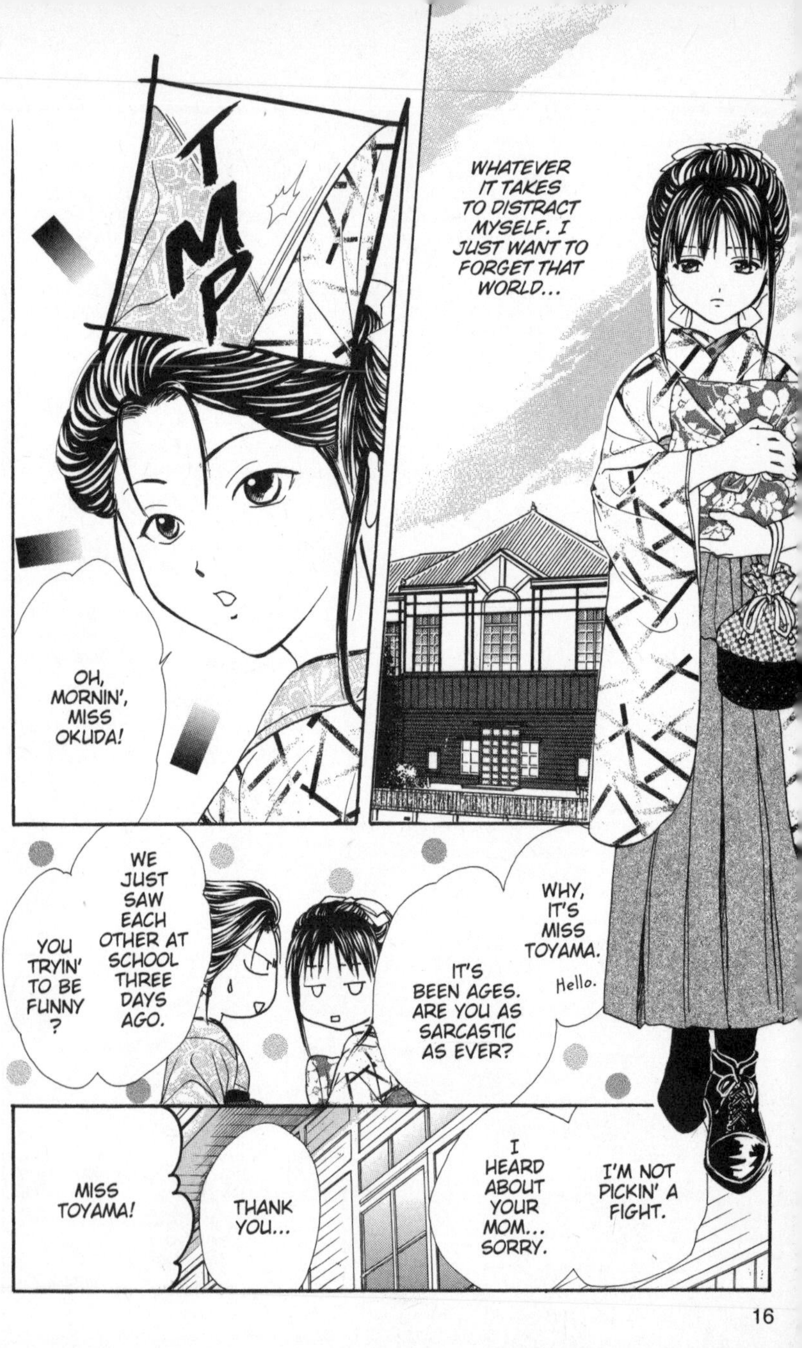
WHATEVER IT TAKES TO DISTRACT MYSELF. I JUST WANT TO FORGET THAT WORLD...
TMP
OH, MORNIN', MISS OKUDA!
WHY, IT'S MISS TOYAMA.
Hello.
IT'S BEEN AGES. ARE YOU AS SARCASTIC AS EVER?
WE JUST SAW EACH OTHER AT SCHOOL THREE DAYS AGO.
YOU TRYIN' TO BE FUNNY?
I'M NOT PICKIN' A FIGHT.
I HEARD ABOUT YOUR MOM... SORRY.
THANK YOU...
MISS TOYAMA!

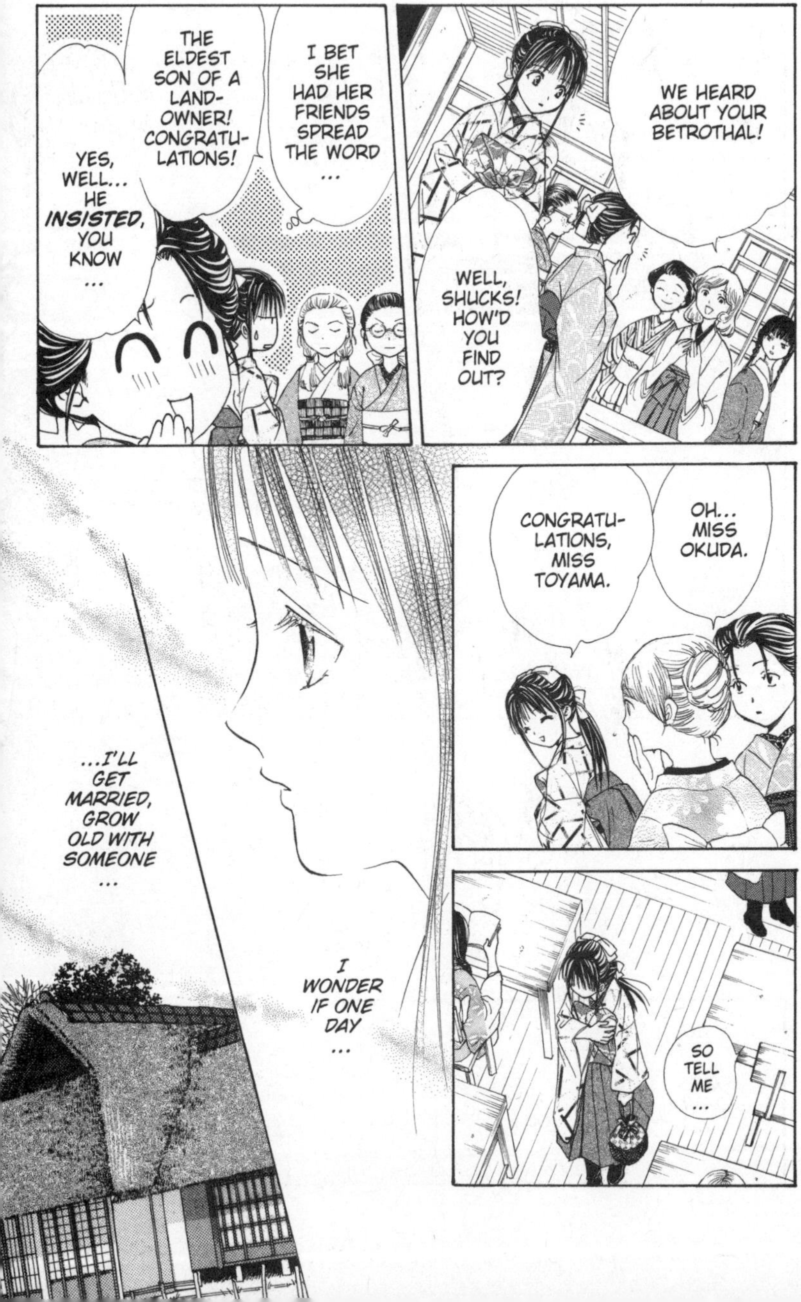
WE HEARD ABOUT YOUR BETROTHAL!
WELL, SHUCKS! HOW'D YOU FIND OUT?
I BET SHE HAD HER FRIENDS SPREAD THE WORD ...
THE ELDEST SON OF A LAND-OWNER! CONGRATULATIONS!
YES, WELL... HE *INSISTED*, YOU KNOW ...
OH... MISS OKUDA.
CONGRATULATIONS, MISS TOYAMA.
SO TELL ME ...
I WONDER IF ONE DAY ...
...I'LL GET MARRIED, GROW OLD WITH SOMEONE ...

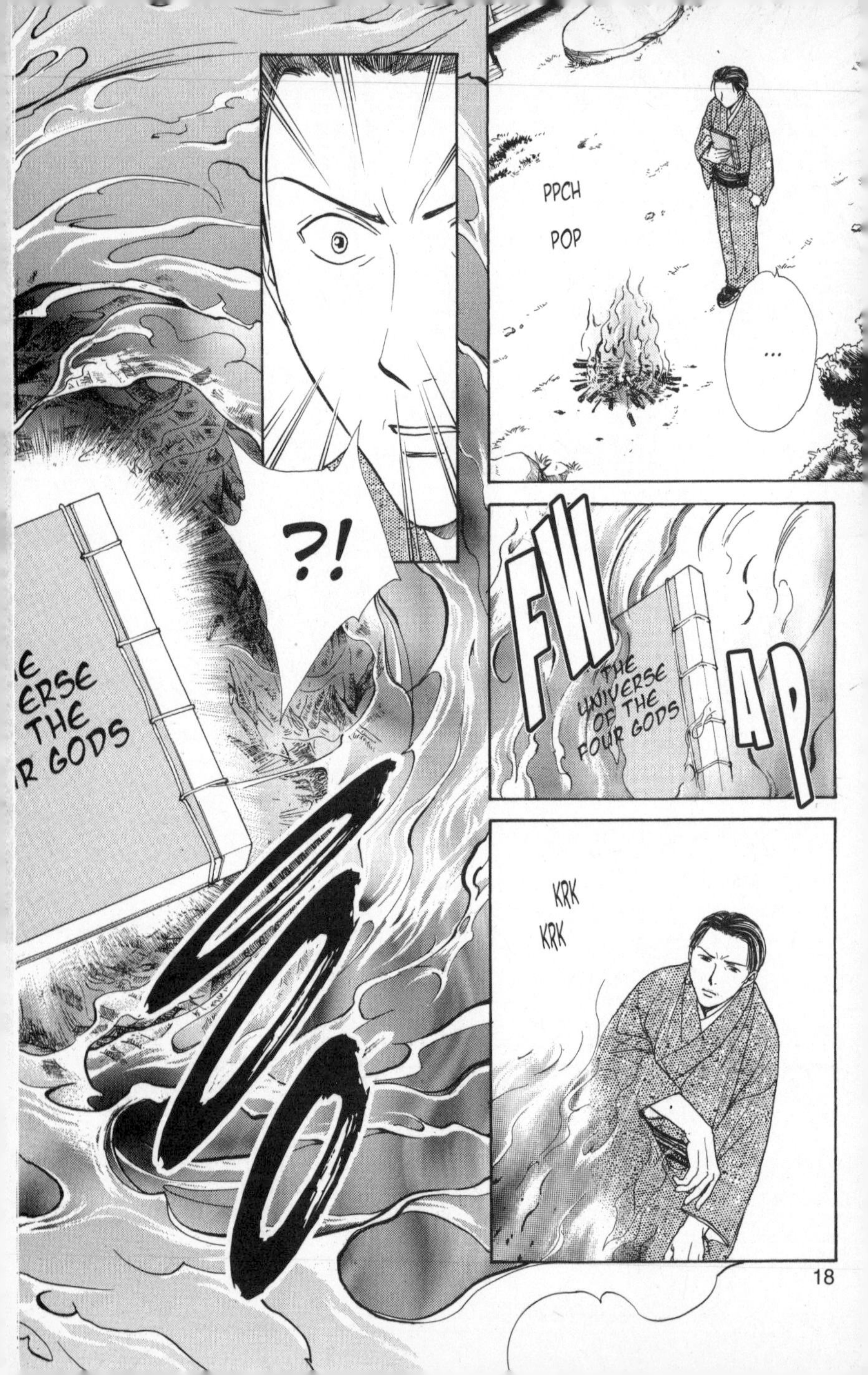
PPCH
POP
...
FWAP
THE UNIVERSE OF THE FOUR GODS
KRK
KRK
?!

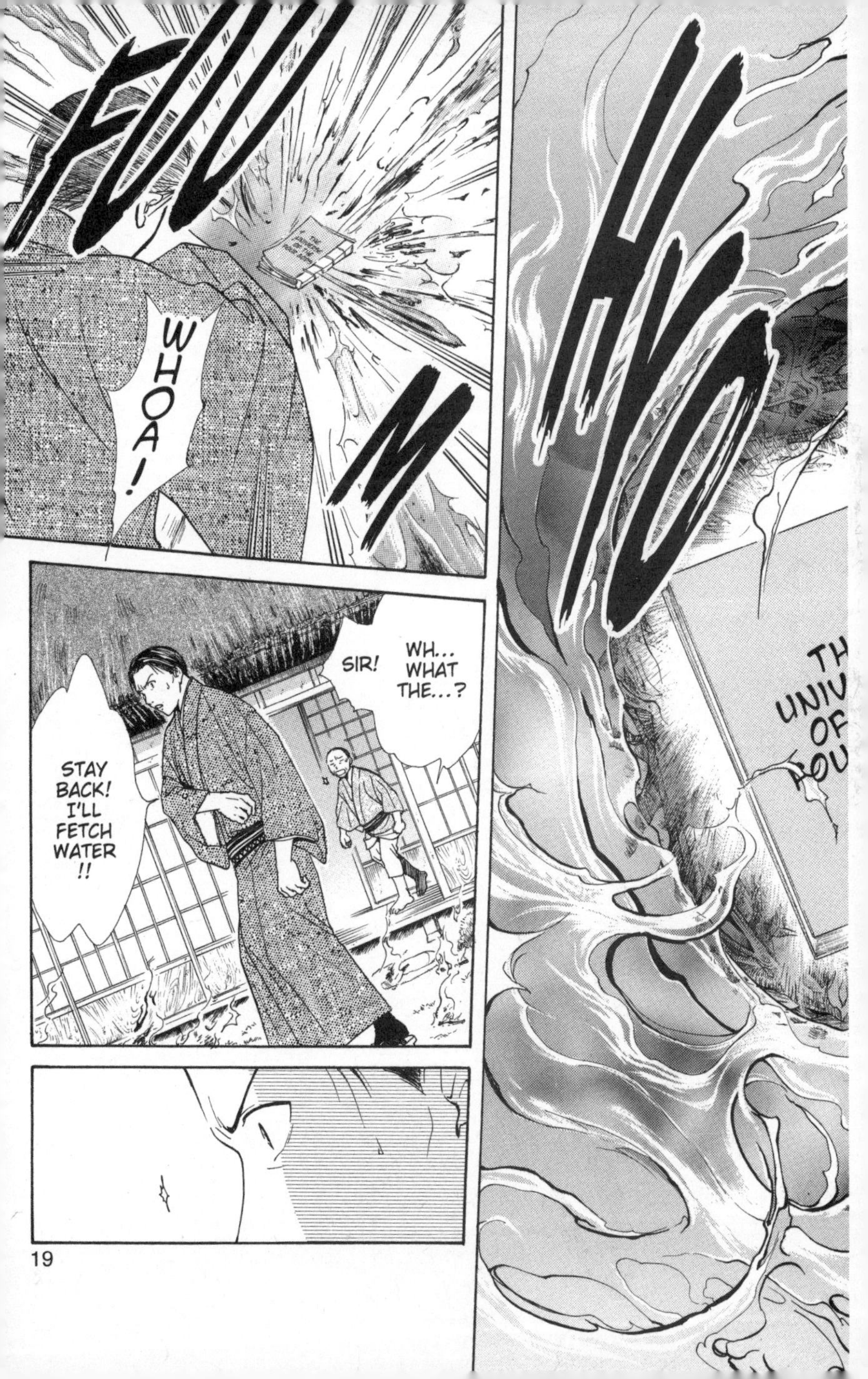
WHOA!
SIR!
WH... WHAT THE...?
STAY BACK! I'LL FETCH WATER!!

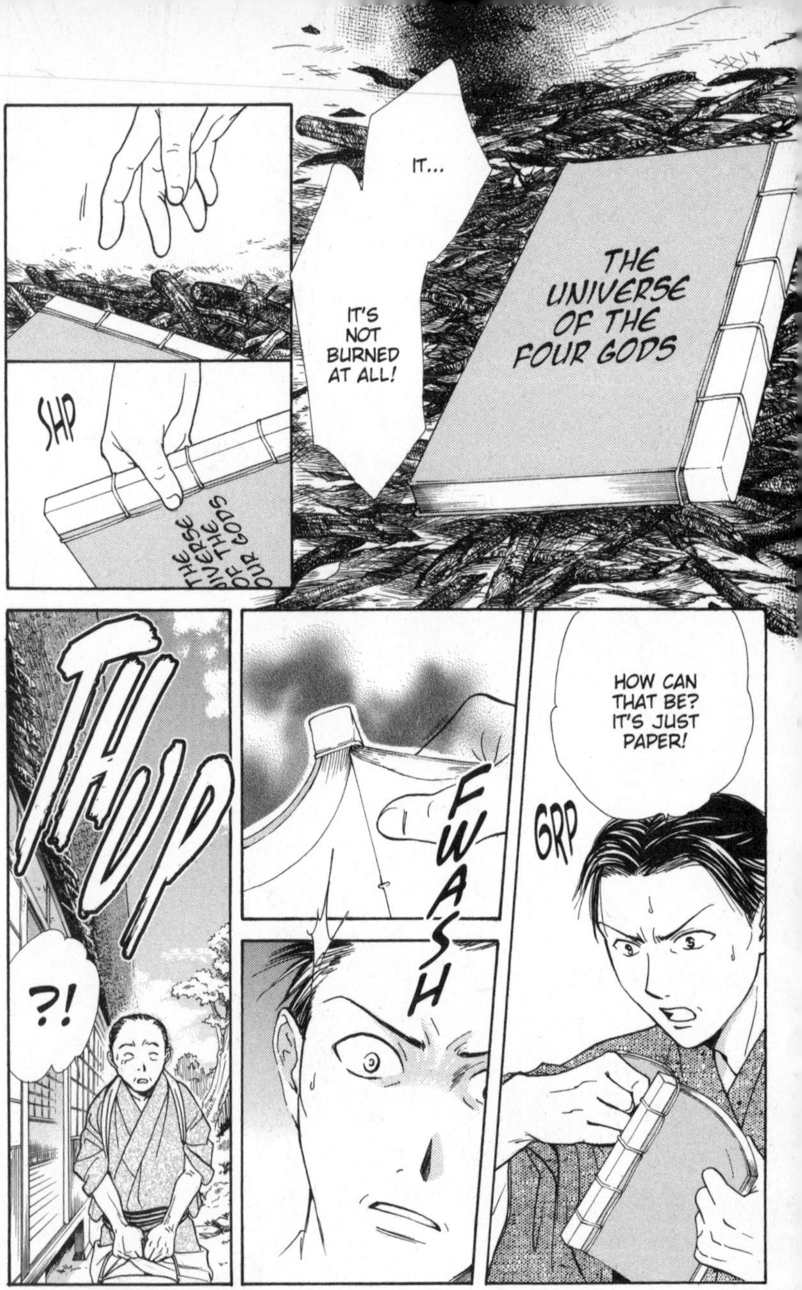
THE UNIVERSE OF THE FOUR GODS
IT...
IT'S NOT BURNED AT ALL!
SHP
HOW CAN THAT BE? IT'S JUST PAPER!
GRP
FWASH
THUP
?!

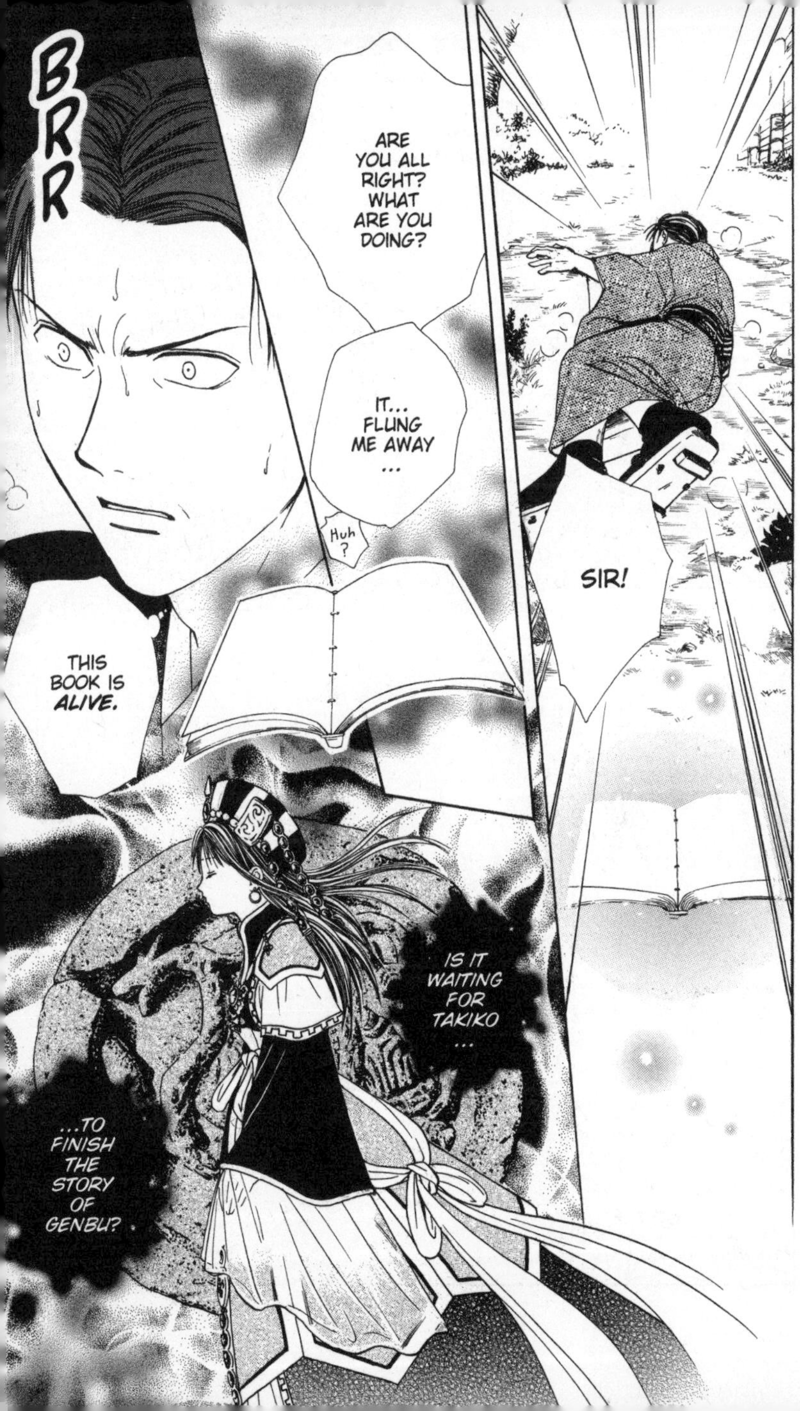
SIR!
ARE YOU ALL RIGHT? WHAT ARE YOU DOING?
IT... FLUNG ME AWAY ...
Huh?
BRR
THIS BOOK IS ALIVE.
IS IT WAITING FOR TAKIKO ...
...TO FINISH THE STORY OF GENBU?

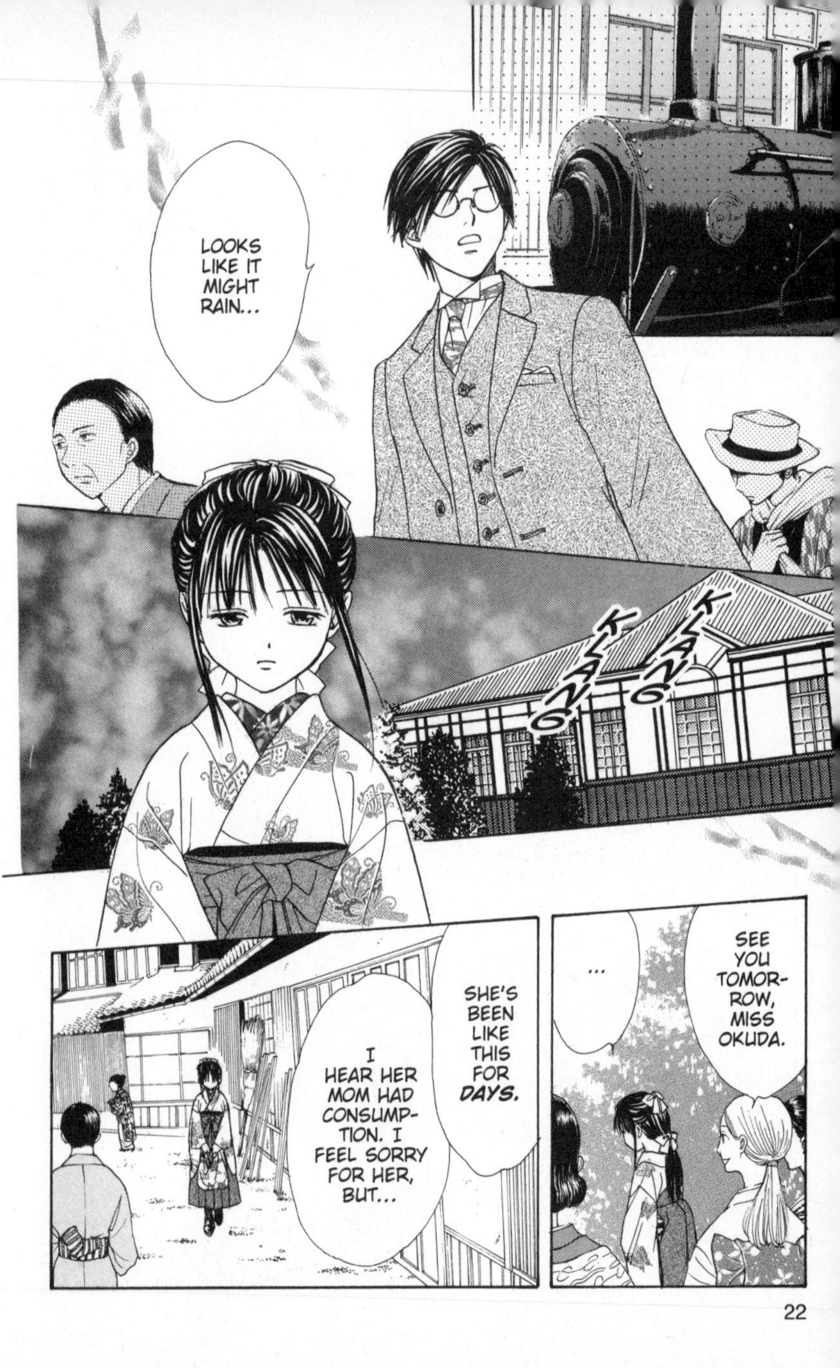
LOOKS LIKE IT MIGHT RAIN...
KLANG
KLANG
SEE YOU TOMOR-ROW, MISS OKUDA.
...
SHE'S BEEN LIKE THIS FOR *DAYS.*
I HEAR HER MOM HAD CONSUMP-TION. I FEEL SORRY FOR HER, BUT...

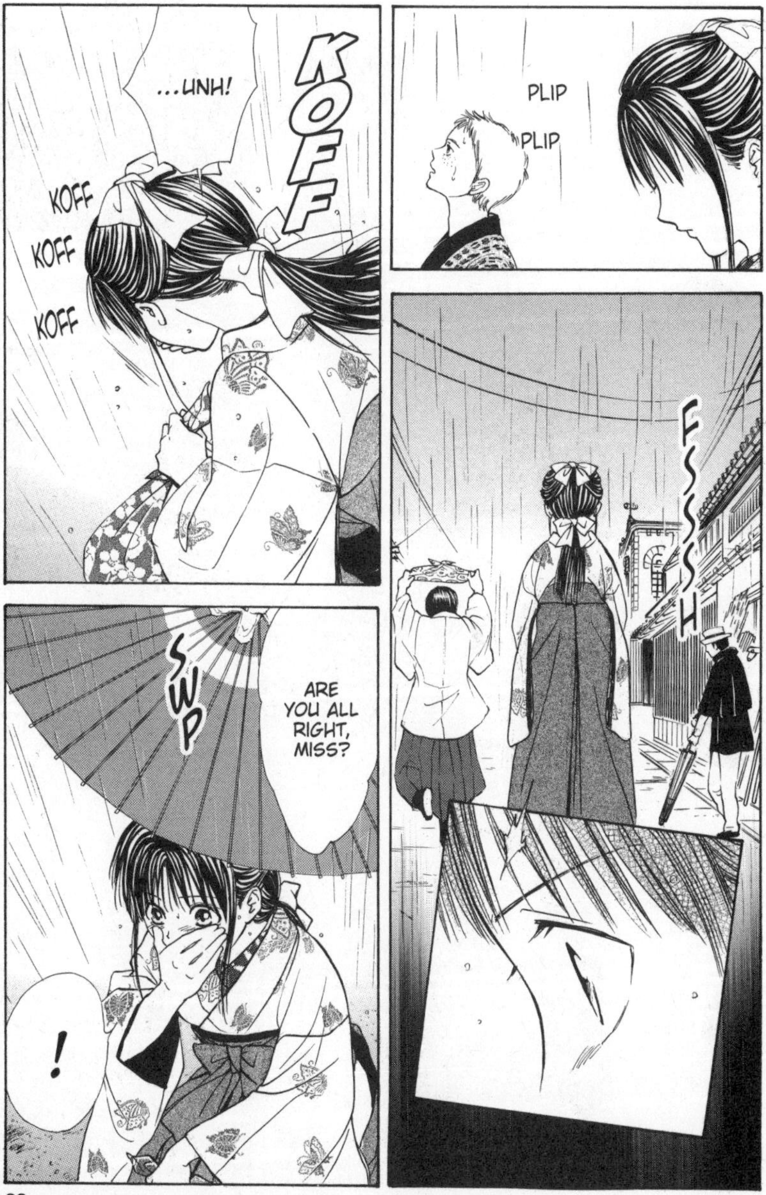
PLIP
PLIP
...UNH!
KOFF
KOFF
KOFF
KOFF
FSSSH
SWP
ARE YOU ALL RIGHT, MISS?
!

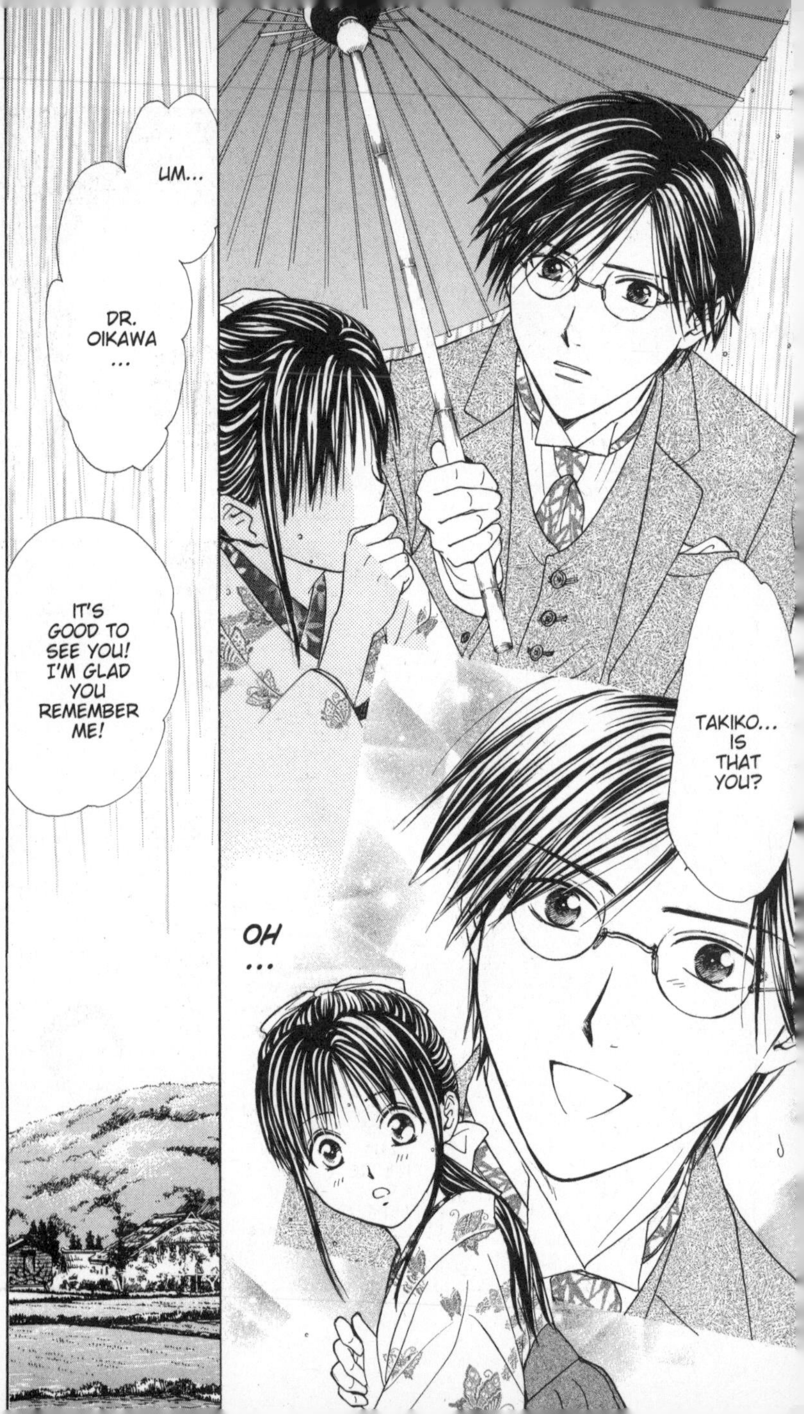
TAKIKO... IS THAT YOU?
OH ...
UM...
DR. OIKAWA ...
IT'S GOOD TO SEE YOU! I'M GLAD YOU REMEMBER ME!

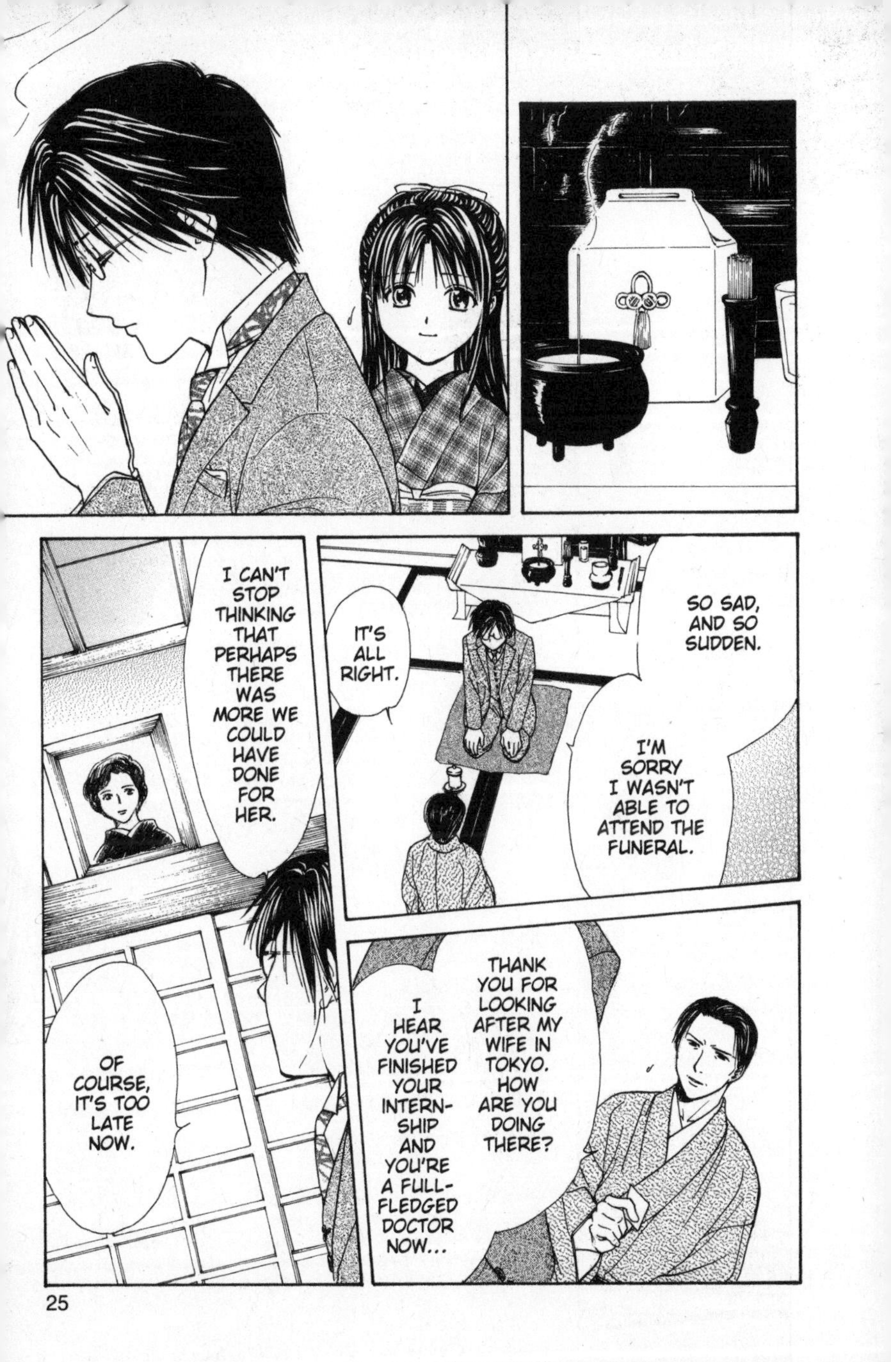
SO SAD, AND SO SUDDEN.
I'M SORRY I WASN'T ABLE TO ATTEND THE FUNERAL.
IT'S ALL RIGHT.
THANK YOU FOR LOOKING AFTER MY WIFE IN TOKYO. HOW ARE YOU DOING THERE?
I HEAR YOU'VE FINISHED YOUR INTERN-SHIP AND YOU'RE A FULL-FLEDGED DOCTOR NOW...
I CAN'T STOP THINKING THAT PERHAPS THERE WAS MORE WE COULD HAVE DONE FOR HER.
OF COURSE, IT'S TOO LATE NOW.

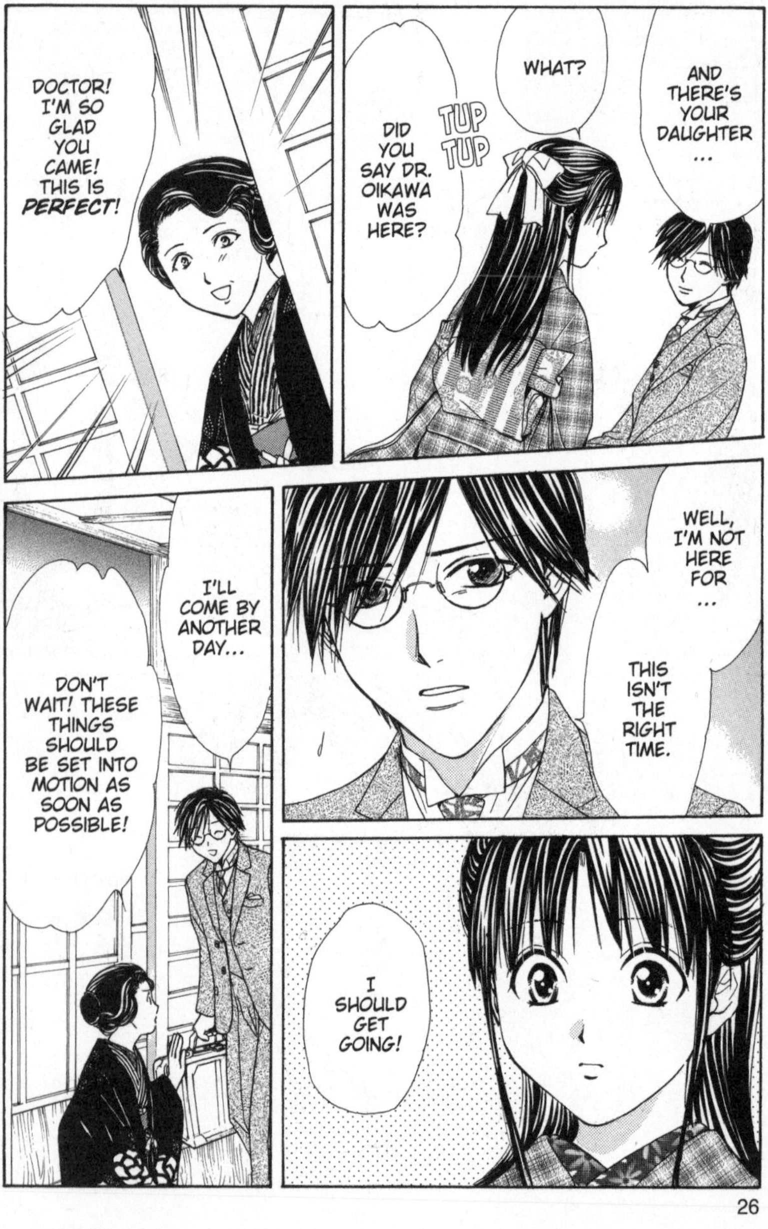
AND THERE'S YOUR DAUGHTER ...
WHAT?
TUP TUP
DID YOU SAY DR. OIKAWA WAS HERE?
DOCTOR! I'M SO GLAD YOU CAME! THIS IS *PERFECT*!
WELL, I'M NOT HERE FOR ...
THIS ISN'T THE RIGHT TIME.
I SHOULD GET GOING!
I'LL COME BY ANOTHER DAY...
DON'T WAIT! THESE THINGS SHOULD BE SET INTO MOTION AS SOON AS POSSIBLE!

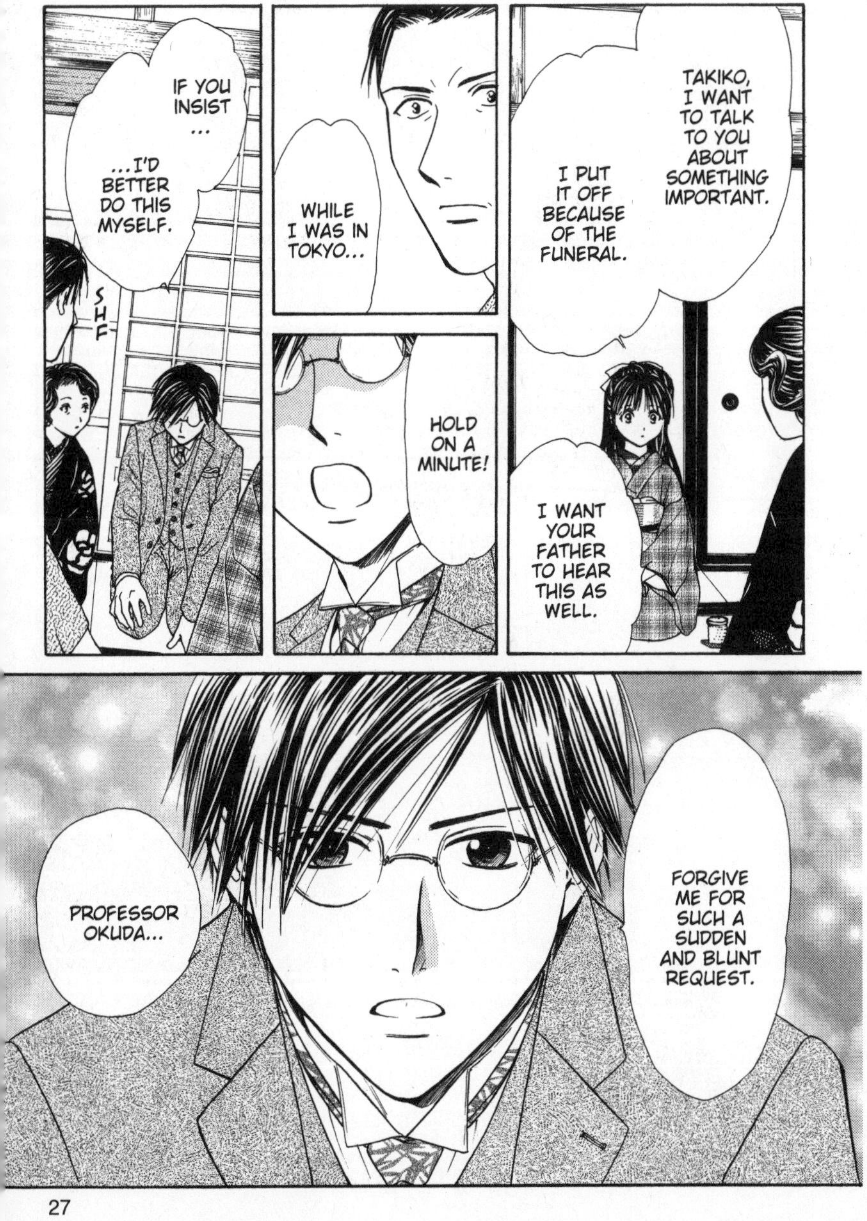
TAKIKO, I WANT TO TALK TO YOU ABOUT SOMETHING IMPORTANT.
I PUT IT OFF BECAUSE OF THE FUNERAL.
I WANT YOUR FATHER TO HEAR THIS AS WELL.
WHILE I WAS IN TOKYO...
HOLD ON A MINUTE!
IF YOU INSIST ...
...I'D BETTER DO THIS MYSELF.
SHF
FORGIVE ME FOR SUCH A SUDDEN AND BLUNT REQUEST.
PROFESSOR OKUDA...

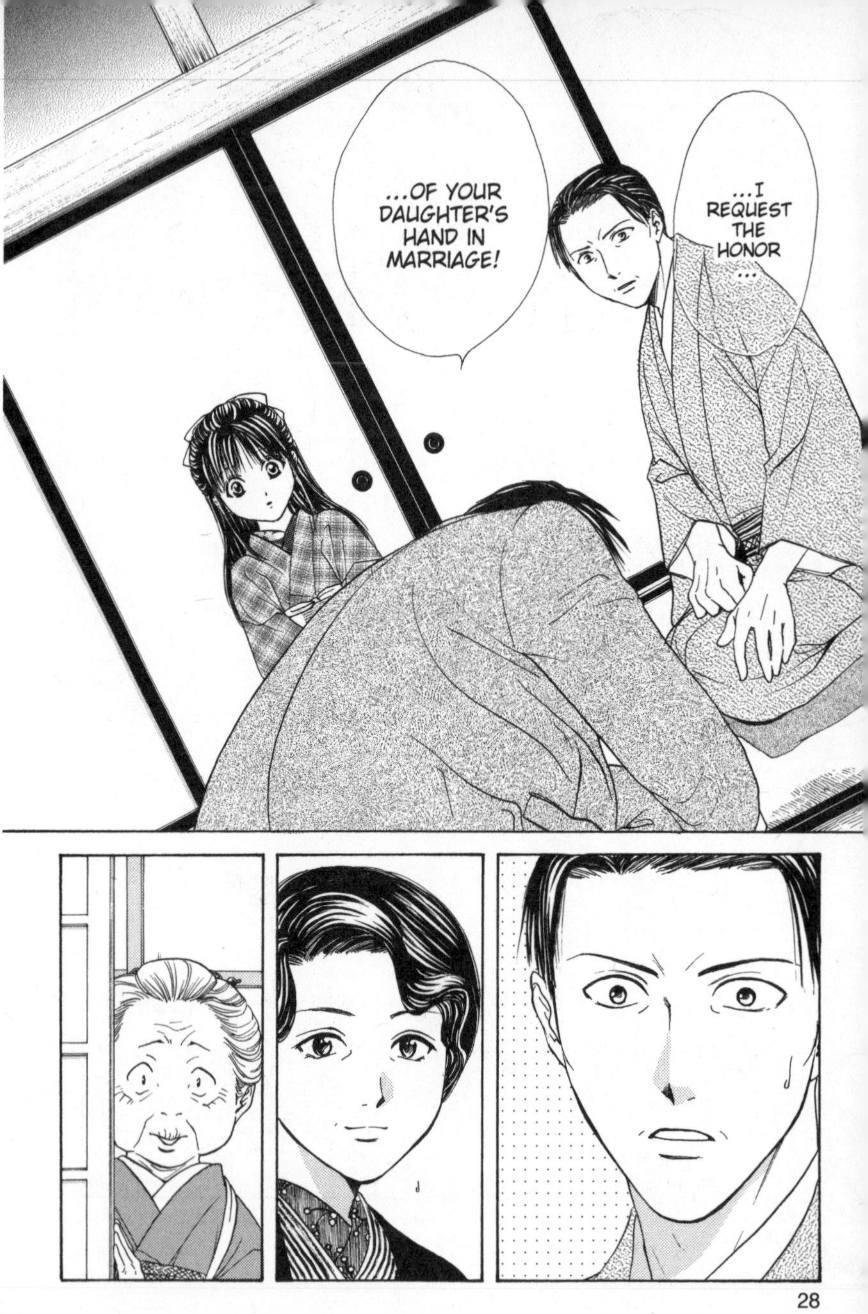
...I REQUEST THE HONOR ...
...OF YOUR DAUGHTER'S HAND IN MARRIAGE!

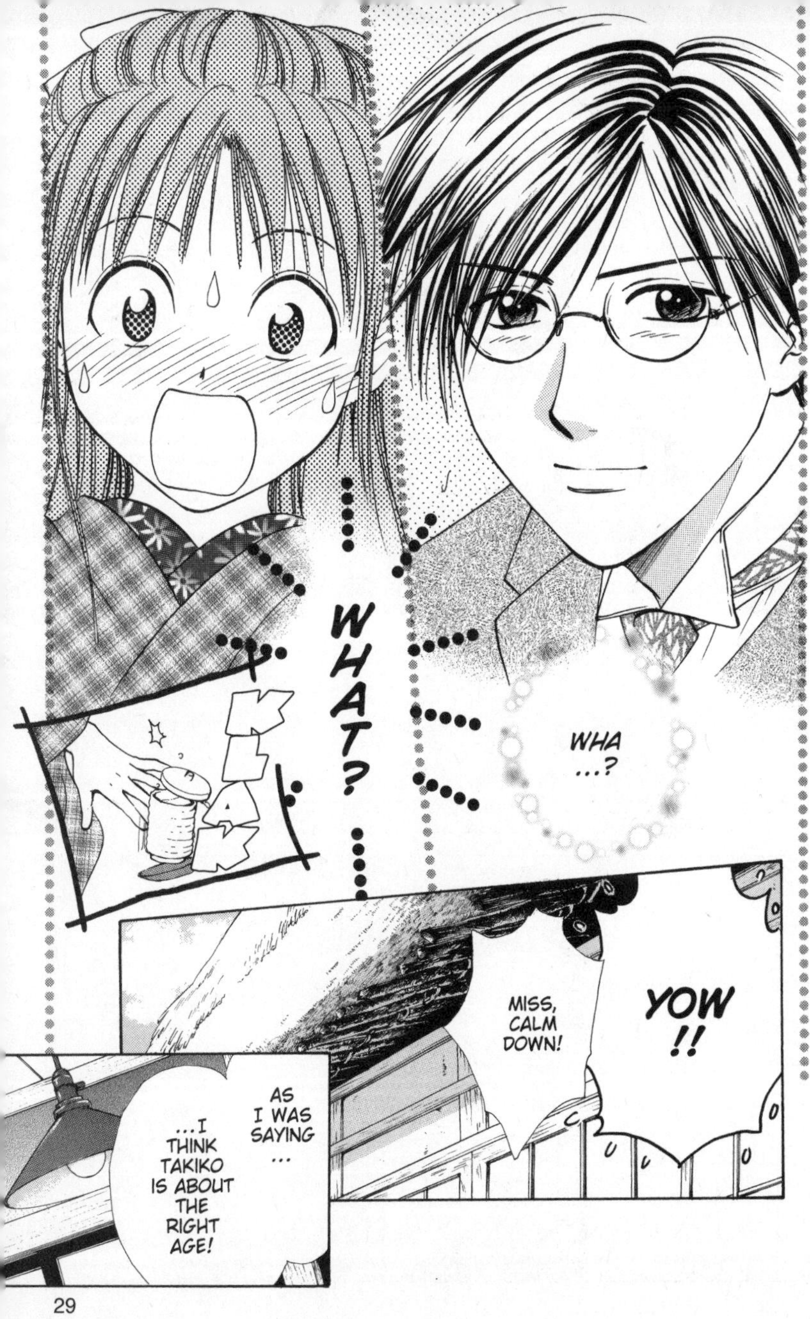
WHA ...?
WHAT?
KLAK
YOW!!
MISS, CALM DOWN!
AS I WAS SAYING ...
...I THINK TAKIKO IS ABOUT THE RIGHT AGE!

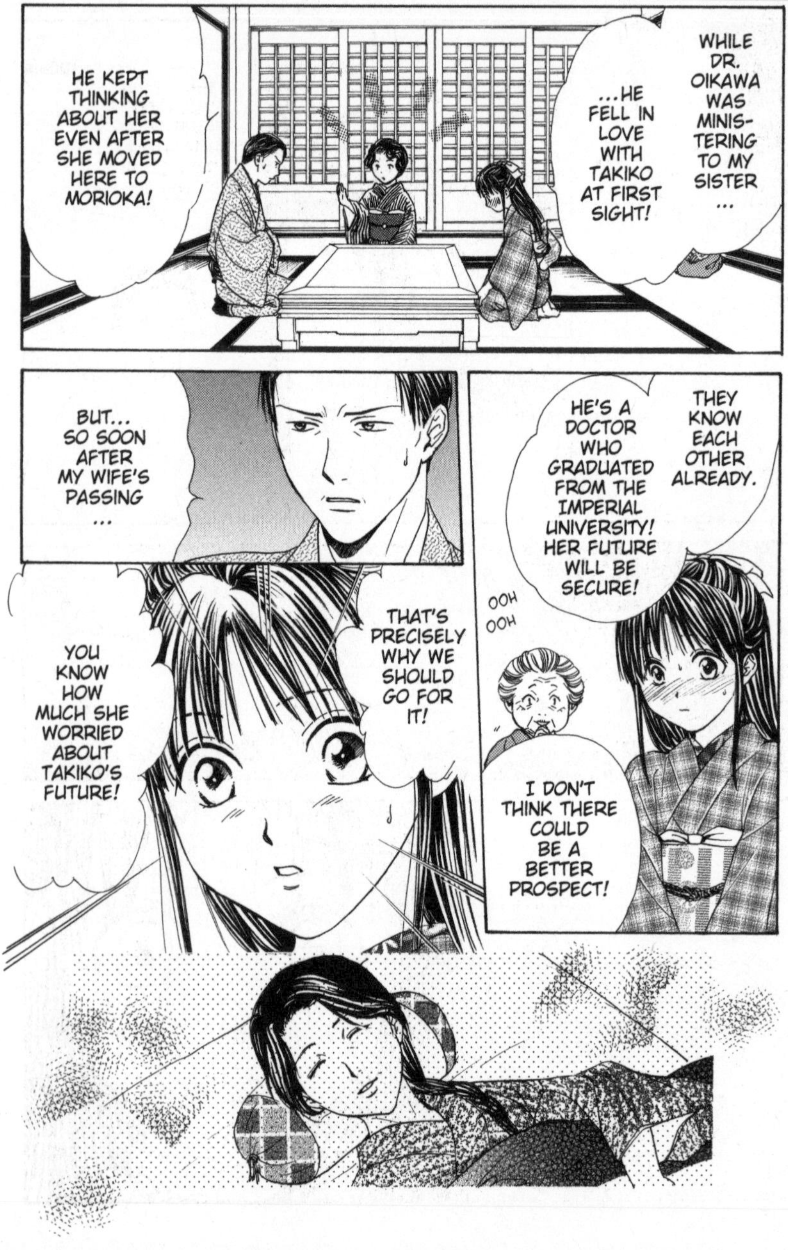
WHILE DR. OIKAWA WAS MINISTERING TO MY SISTER...
...HE FELL IN LOVE WITH TAKIKO AT FIRST SIGHT!
HE KEPT THINKING ABOUT HER EVEN AFTER SHE MOVED HERE TO MORIOKA!
THEY KNOW EACH OTHER ALREADY.
HE'S A DOCTOR WHO GRADUATED FROM THE IMPERIAL UNIVERSITY! HER FUTURE WILL BE SECURE!
OOH OOH
I DON'T THINK THERE COULD BE A BETTER PROSPECT!
BUT... SO SOON AFTER MY WIFE'S PASSING...
THAT'S PRECISELY WHY WE SHOULD GO FOR IT!
YOU KNOW HOW MUCH SHE WORRIED ABOUT TAKIKO'S FUTURE!

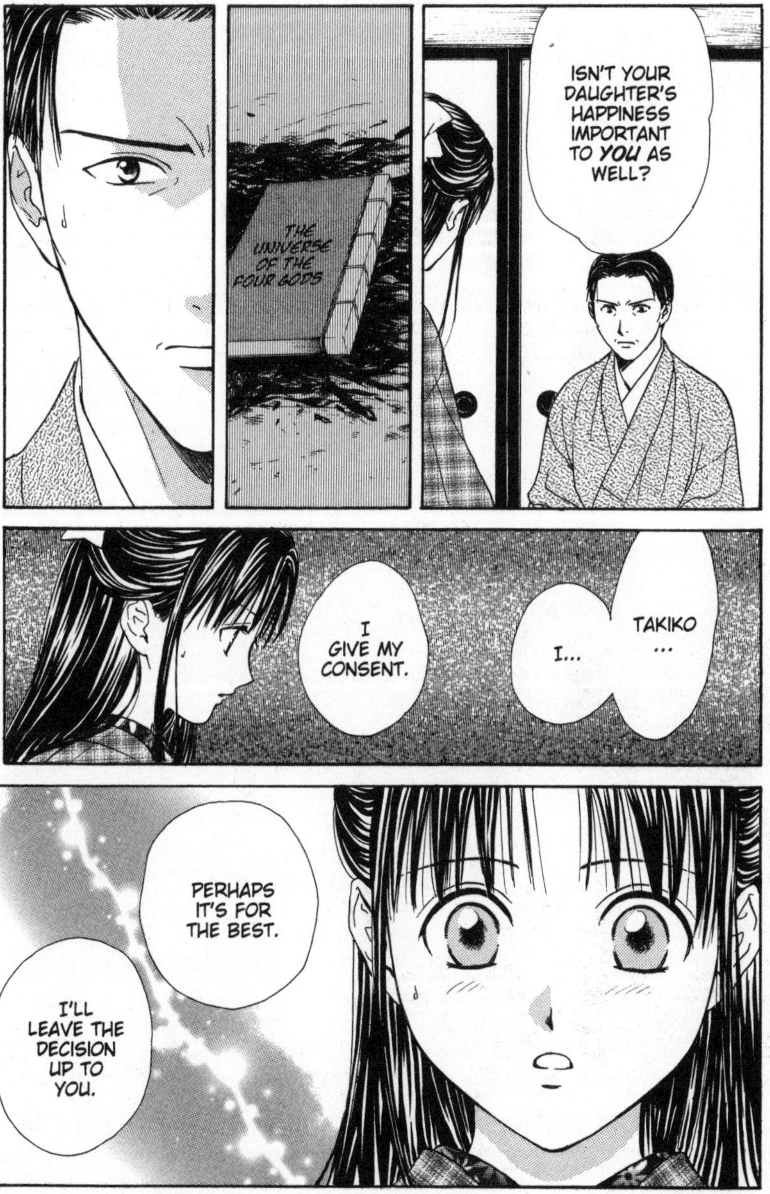
ISN'T YOUR DAUGHTER'S HAPPINESS IMPORTANT TO *YOU* AS WELL?
THE UNIVERSE OF THE FOUR GODS
TAKIKO ...
I...
I GIVE MY CONSENT.
PERHAPS IT'S FOR THE BEST.
I'LL LEAVE THE DECISION UP TO YOU.

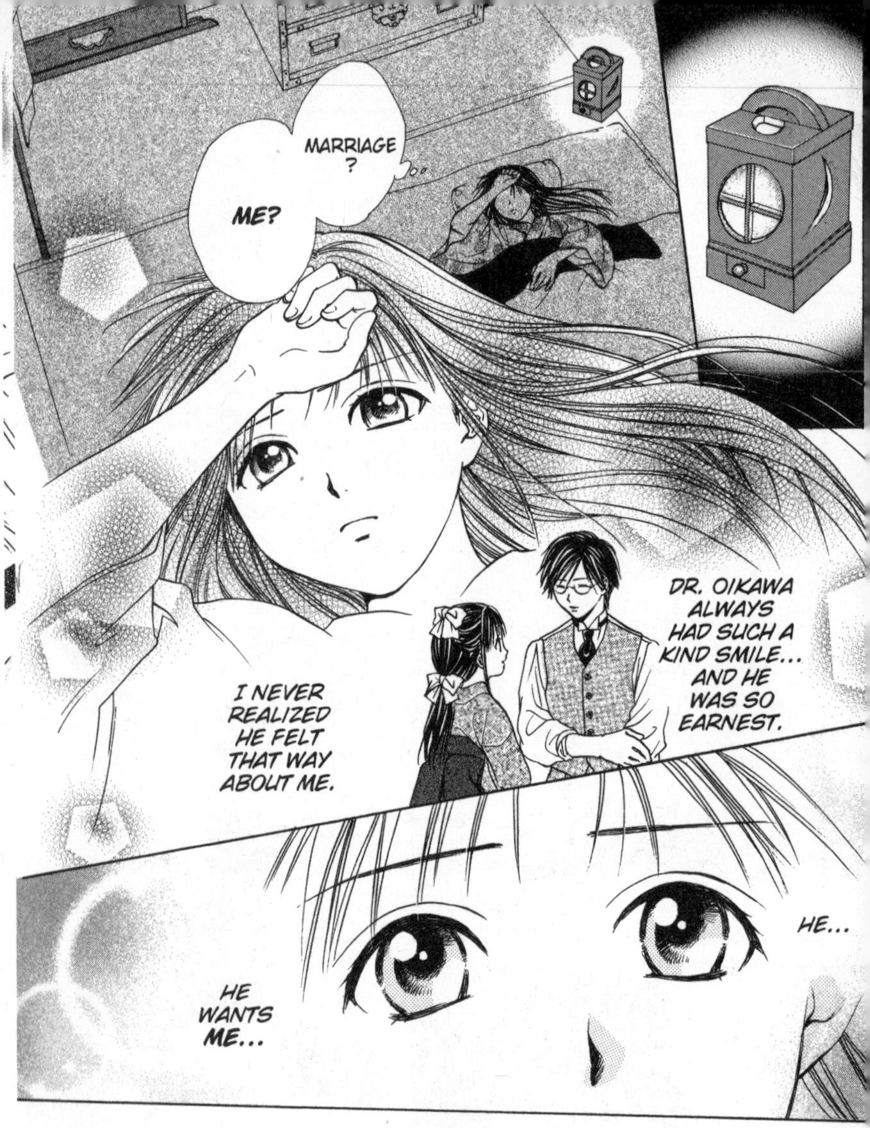
MARRIAGE?
ME?
DR. OIKAWA ALWAYS HAD SUCH A KIND SMILE... AND HE WAS SO EARNEST.
I NEVER REALIZED HE FELT THAT WAY ABOUT ME.
HE...
HE WANTS ME...

NOT THE PRIESTESS. JUST PLAIN **ME.**

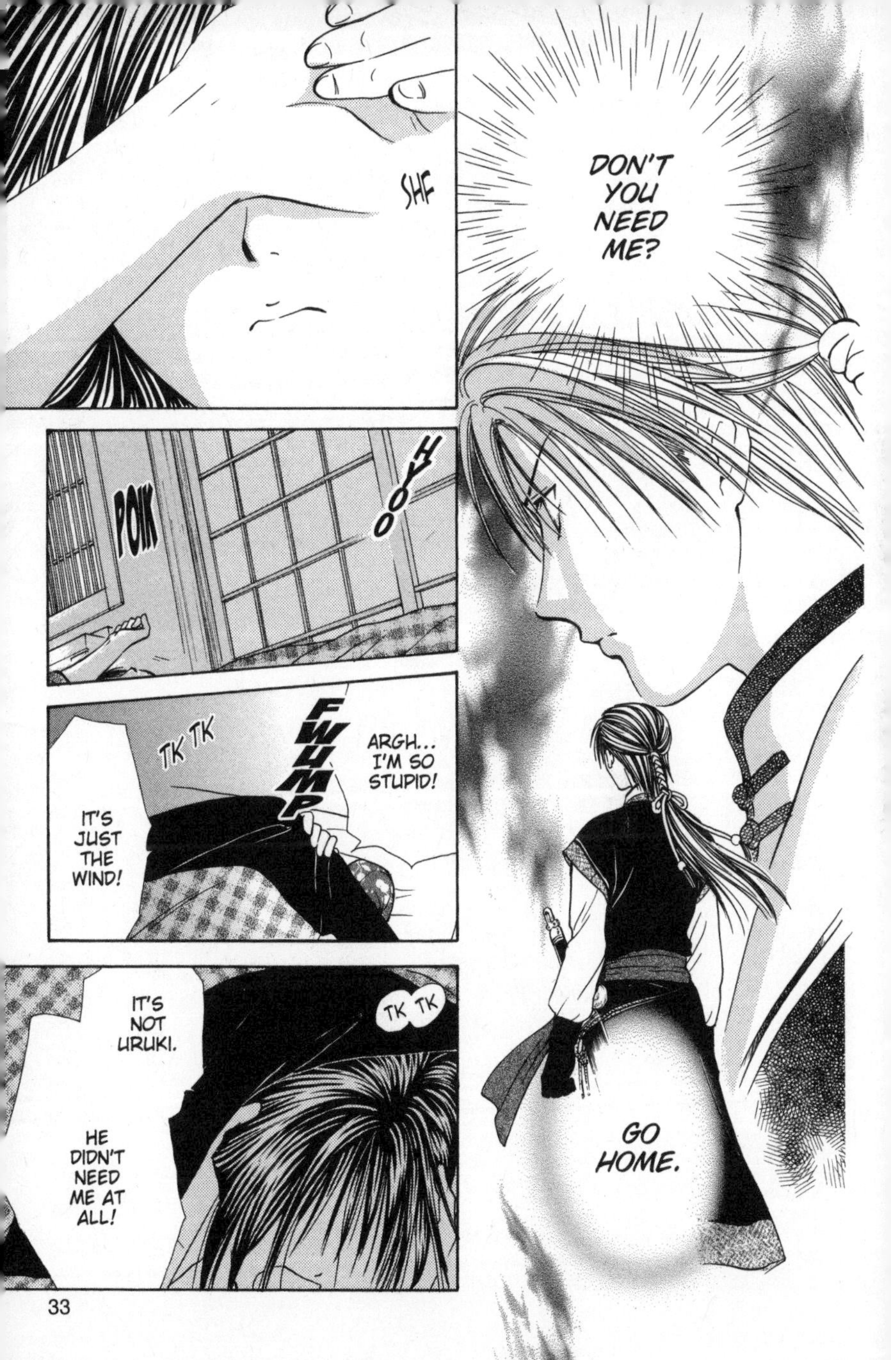
DON'T YOU NEED ME?
GO HOME.
SHF
HYOOO
POIK
ARGH... I'M SO STUPID!
FWUMP
TK TK
IT'S JUST THE WIND!
TK TK
IT'S NOT URUKI.
HE DIDN'T NEED ME AT ALL!

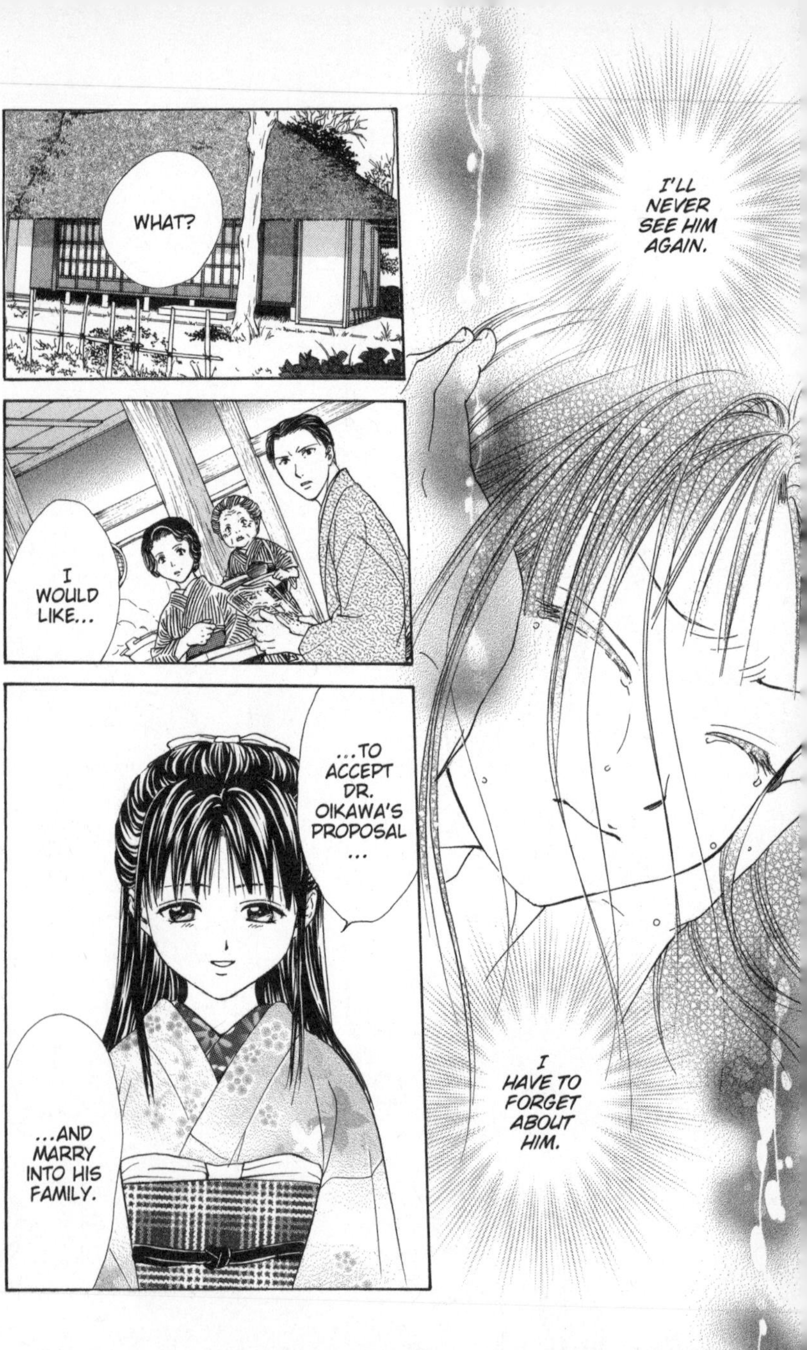
I'LL NEVER SEE HIM AGAIN.
I HAVE TO FORGET ABOUT HIM.
WHAT?
I WOULD LIKE...
...TO ACCEPT DR. OIKAWA'S PROPOSAL...
...AND MARRY INTO HIS FAMILY.

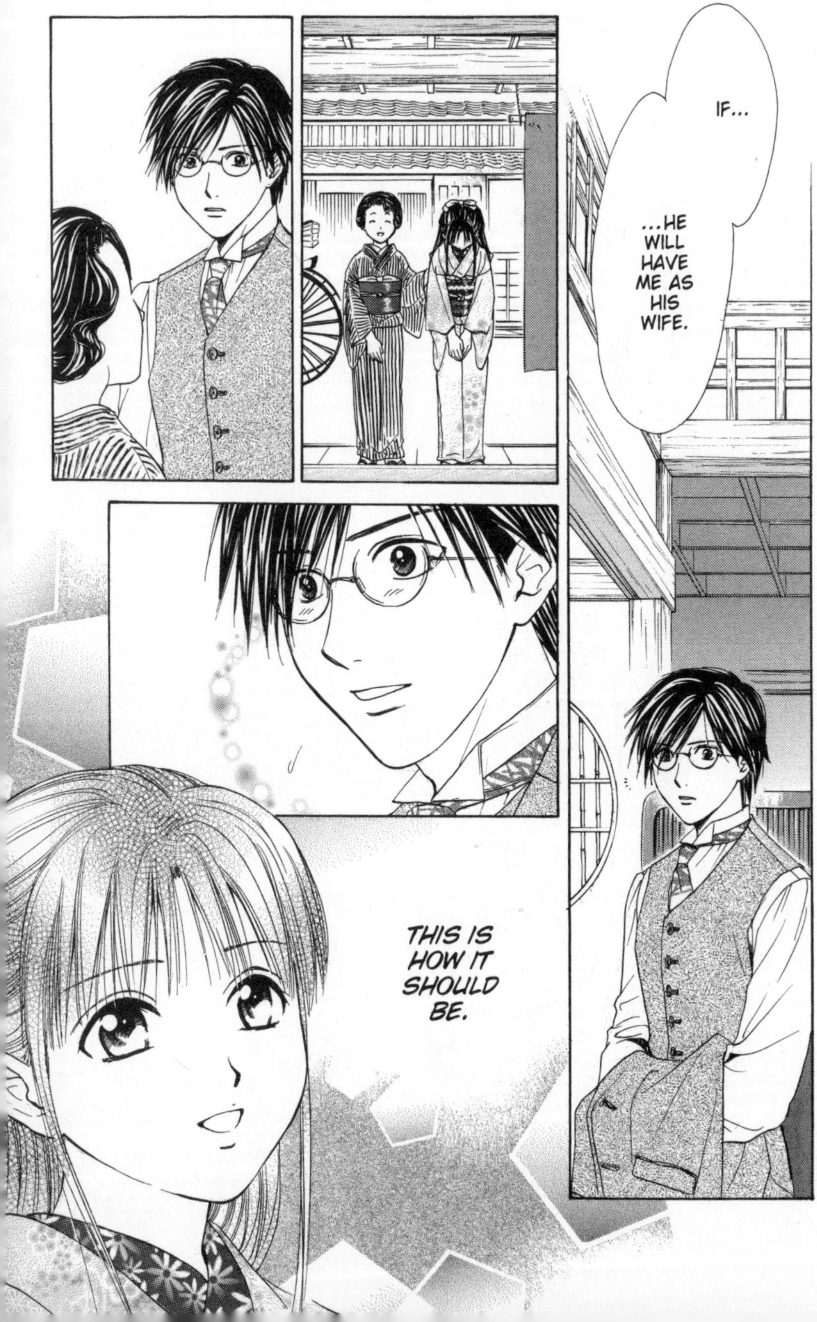
IF...
...HE WILL HAVE ME AS HIS WIFE.
THIS IS HOW IT SHOULD BE.

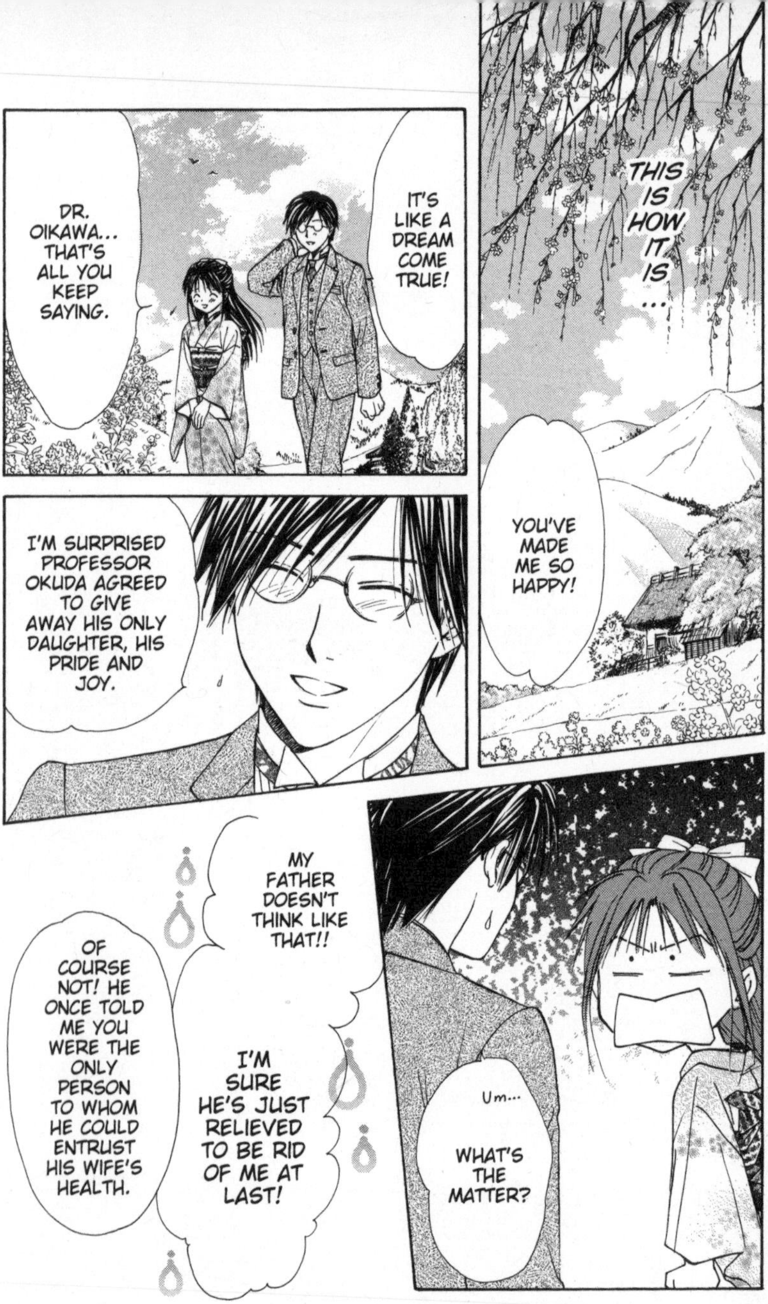
THIS IS HOW IT IS...
YOU'VE MADE ME SO HAPPY!
IT'S LIKE A DREAM COME TRUE!
DR. OIKAWA... THAT'S ALL YOU KEEP SAYING.
I'M SURPRISED PROFESSOR OKUDA AGREED TO GIVE AWAY HIS ONLY DAUGHTER, HIS PRIDE AND JOY.
Um...
WHAT'S THE MATTER?
MY FATHER DOESN'T THINK LIKE THAT!!
I'M SURE HE'S JUST RELIEVED TO BE RID OF ME AT LAST!
OF COURSE NOT! HE ONCE TOLD ME YOU WERE THE ONLY PERSON TO WHOM HE COULD ENTRUST HIS WIFE'S HEALTH.

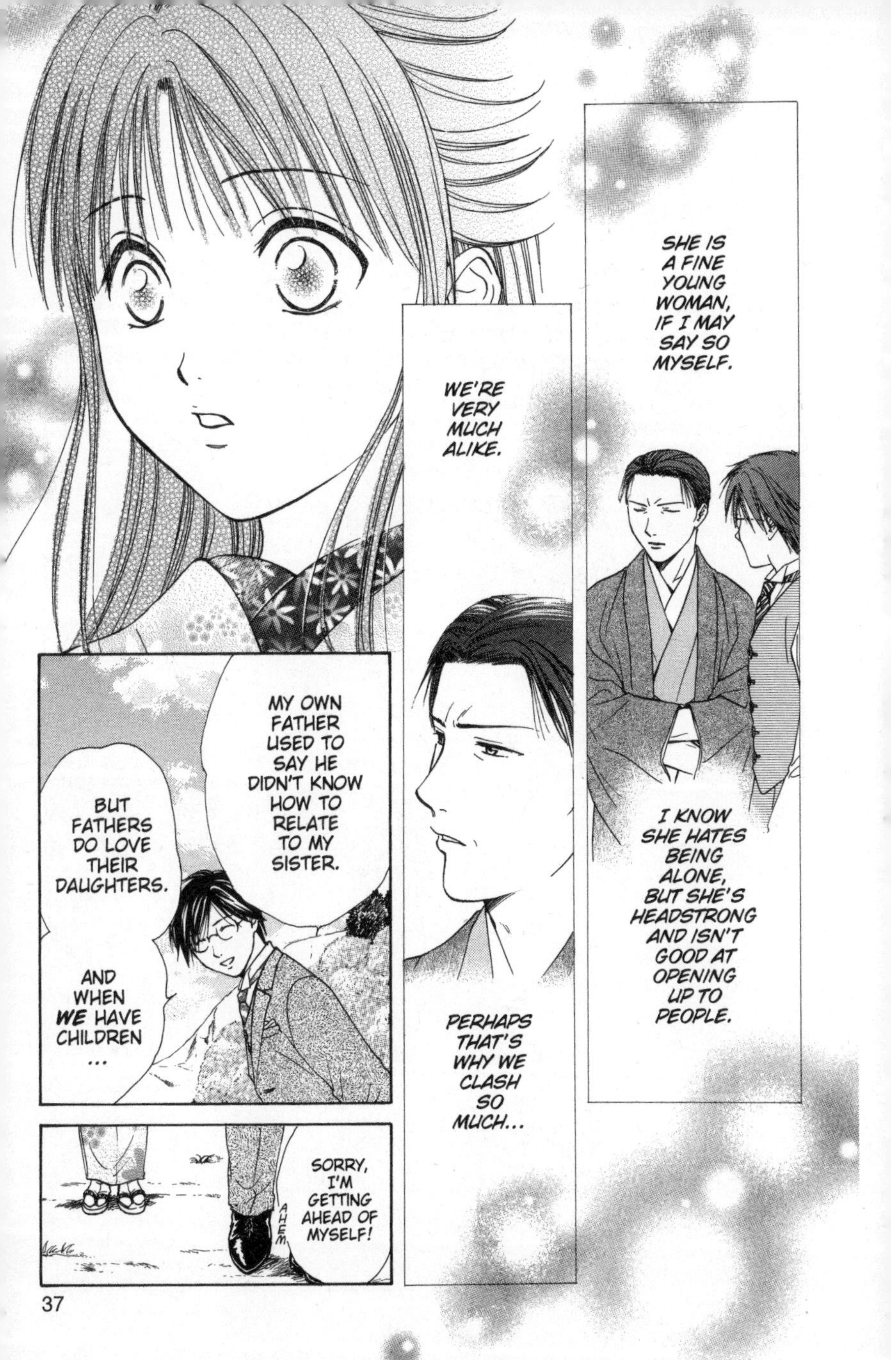
SHE IS A FINE YOUNG WOMAN, IF I MAY SAY SO MYSELF.
I KNOW SHE HATES BEING ALONE, BUT SHE'S HEADSTRONG AND ISN'T GOOD AT OPENING UP TO PEOPLE.
WE'RE VERY MUCH ALIKE.
PERHAPS THAT'S WHY WE CLASH SO MUCH...
MY OWN FATHER USED TO SAY HE DIDN'T KNOW HOW TO RELATE TO MY SISTER.
BUT FATHERS DO LOVE THEIR DAUGHTERS.
AND WHEN **WE** HAVE CHILDREN ...
AHEM
SORRY, I'M GETTING AHEAD OF MYSELF!

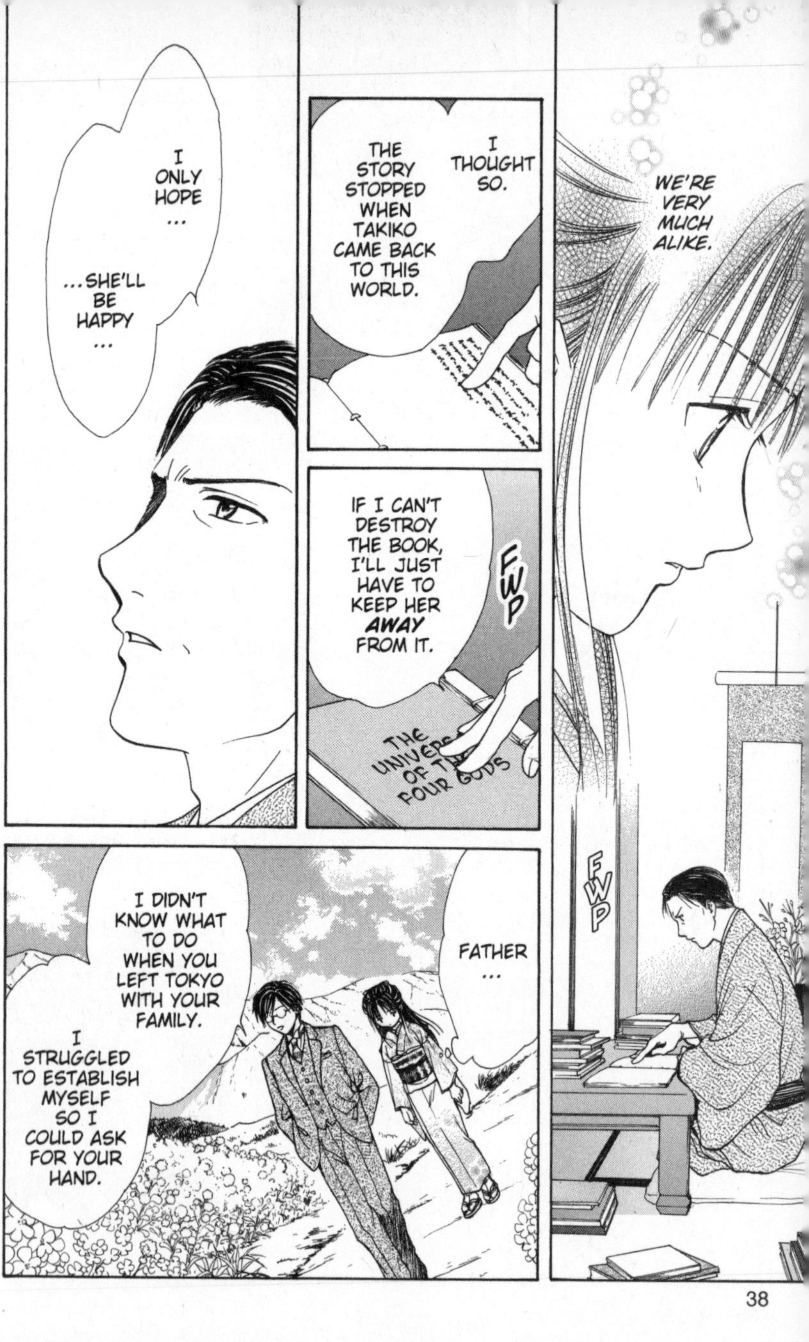
WE'RE VERY MUCH ALIKE.
FWP
I THOUGHT SO.
THE STORY STOPPED WHEN TAKIKO CAME BACK TO THIS WORLD.
IF I CAN'T DESTROY THE BOOK, I'LL JUST HAVE TO KEEP HER *AWAY* FROM IT.
FWP
THE UNIVERSE OF THE FOUR GODS
I ONLY HOPE...
...SHE'LL BE HAPPY...
FATHER...
I DIDN'T KNOW WHAT TO DO WHEN YOU LEFT TOKYO WITH YOUR FAMILY.
I STRUGGLED TO ESTABLISH MYSELF SO I COULD ASK FOR YOUR HAND.

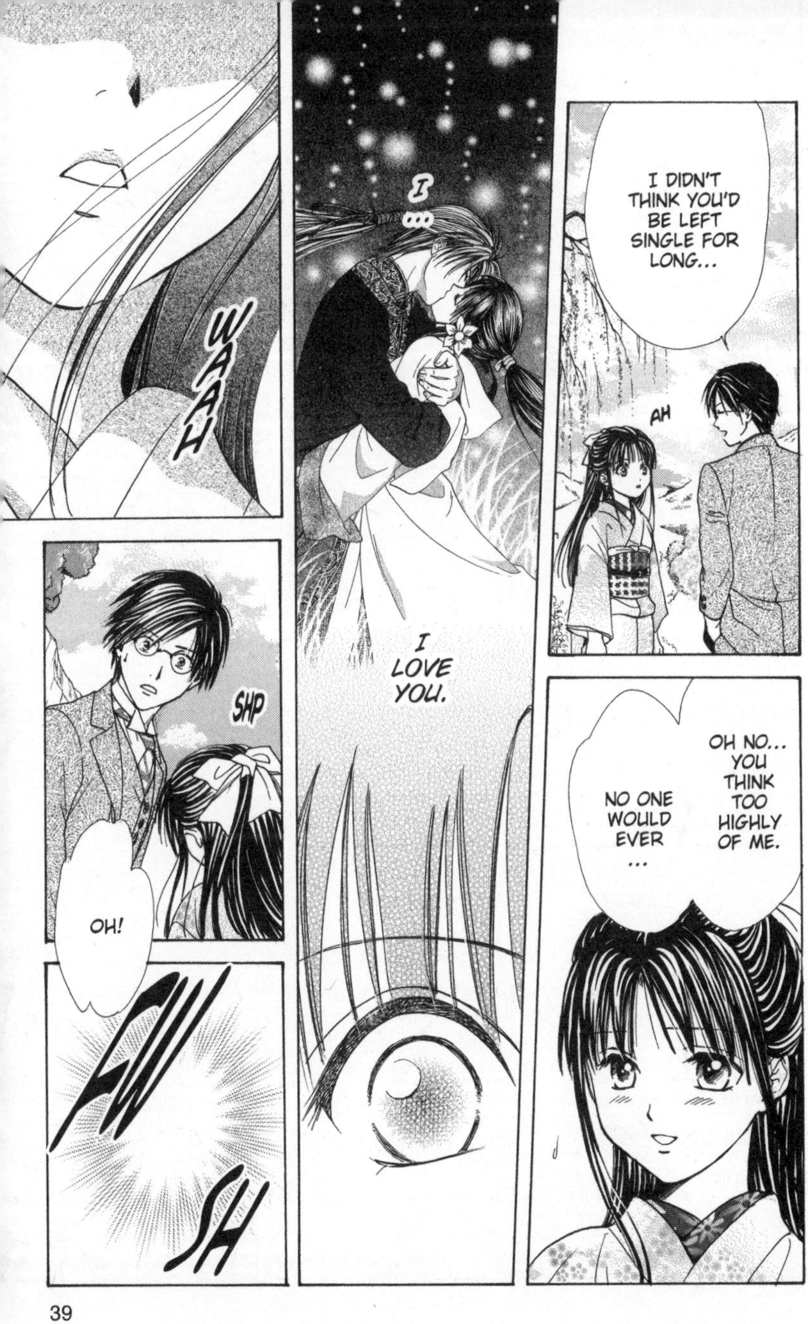
I DIDN'T THINK YOU'D BE LEFT SINGLE FOR LONG...
AH
OH NO... YOU THINK TOO HIGHLY OF ME.
NO ONE WOULD EVER ...
I ...
I LOVE YOU.
WAAAH
SHP
OH!
FWSH

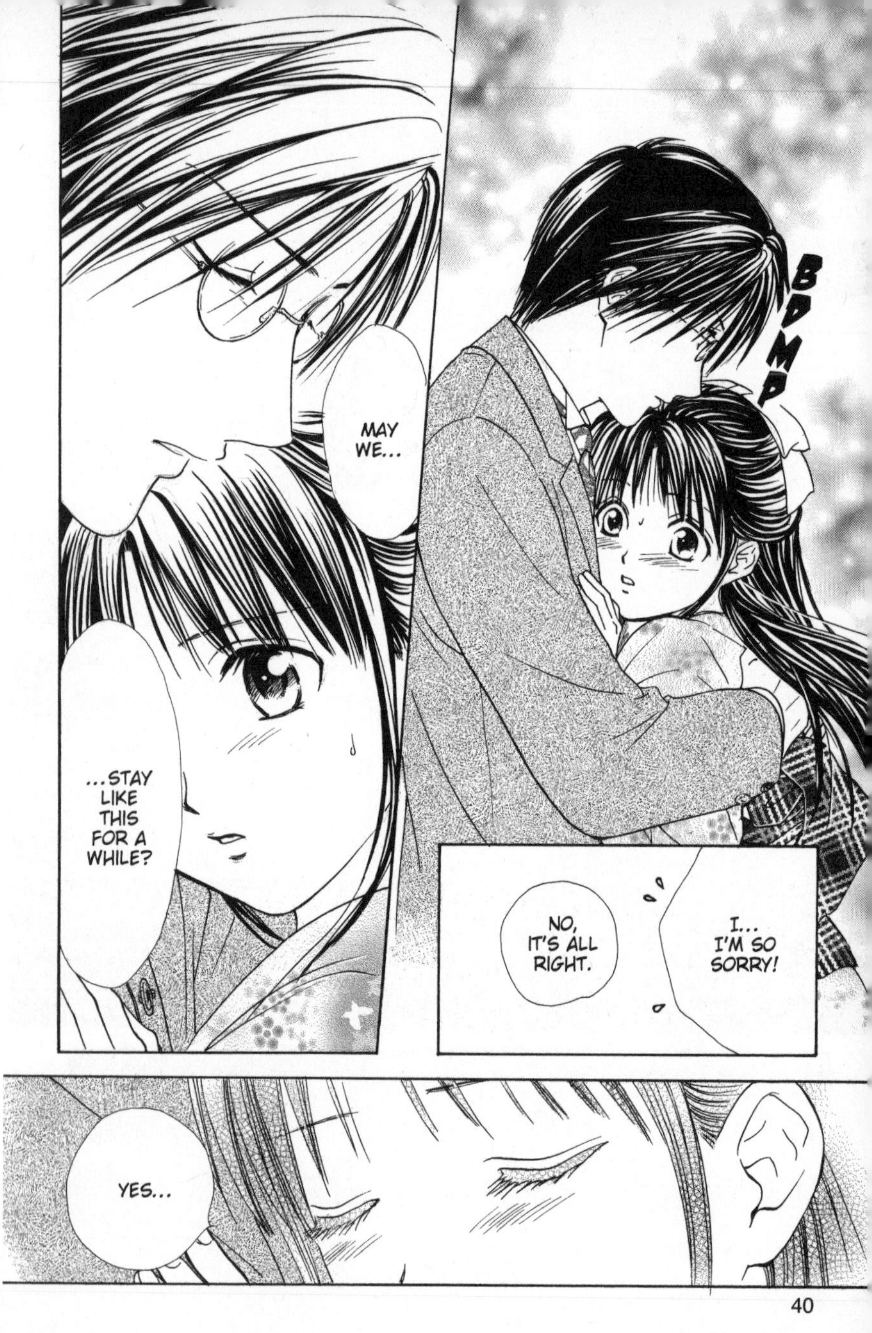
BDMP
I... I'M SO SORRY!
NO, IT'S ALL RIGHT.
MAY WE...
...STAY LIKE THIS FOR A WHILE?
YES...

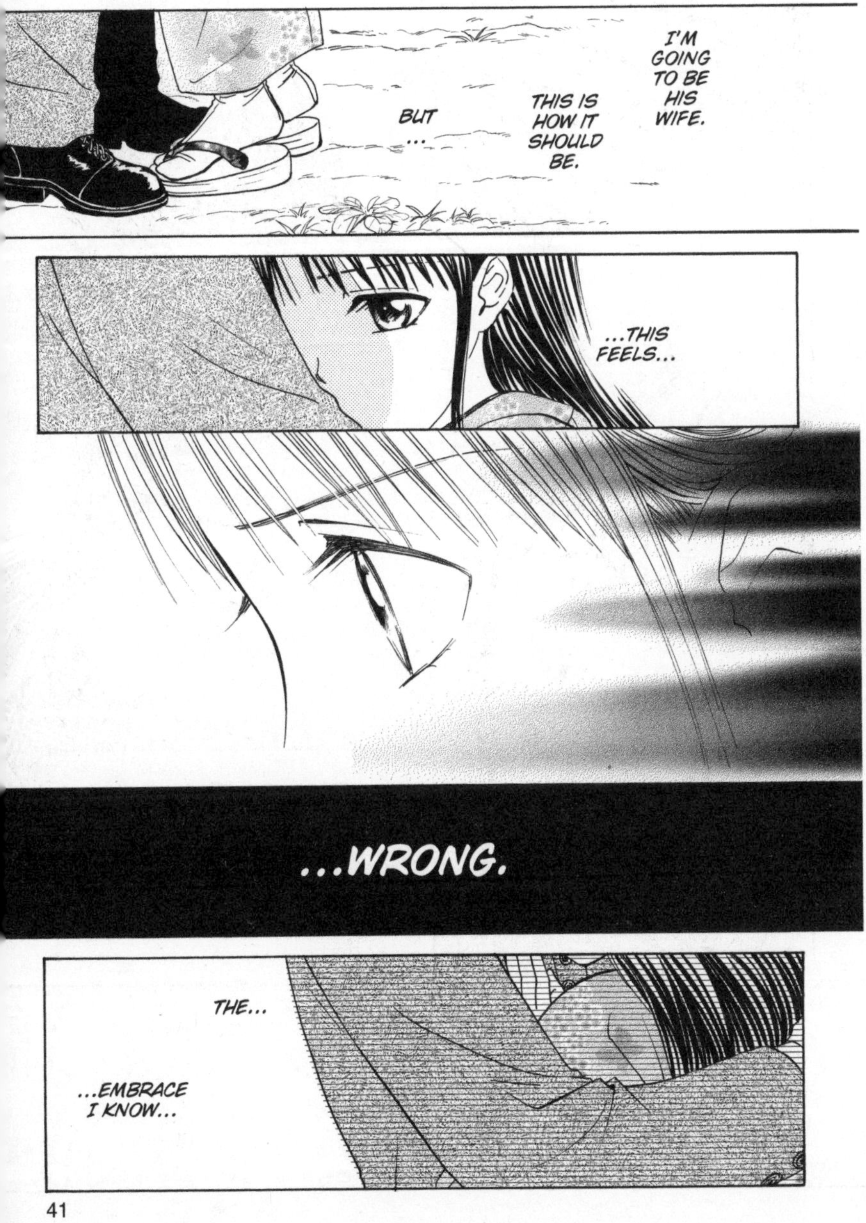
I'M GOING TO BE HIS WIFE.
THIS IS HOW IT SHOULD BE.
BUT ...
...THIS FEELS...
...WRONG.
THE...
...EMBRACE I KNOW...

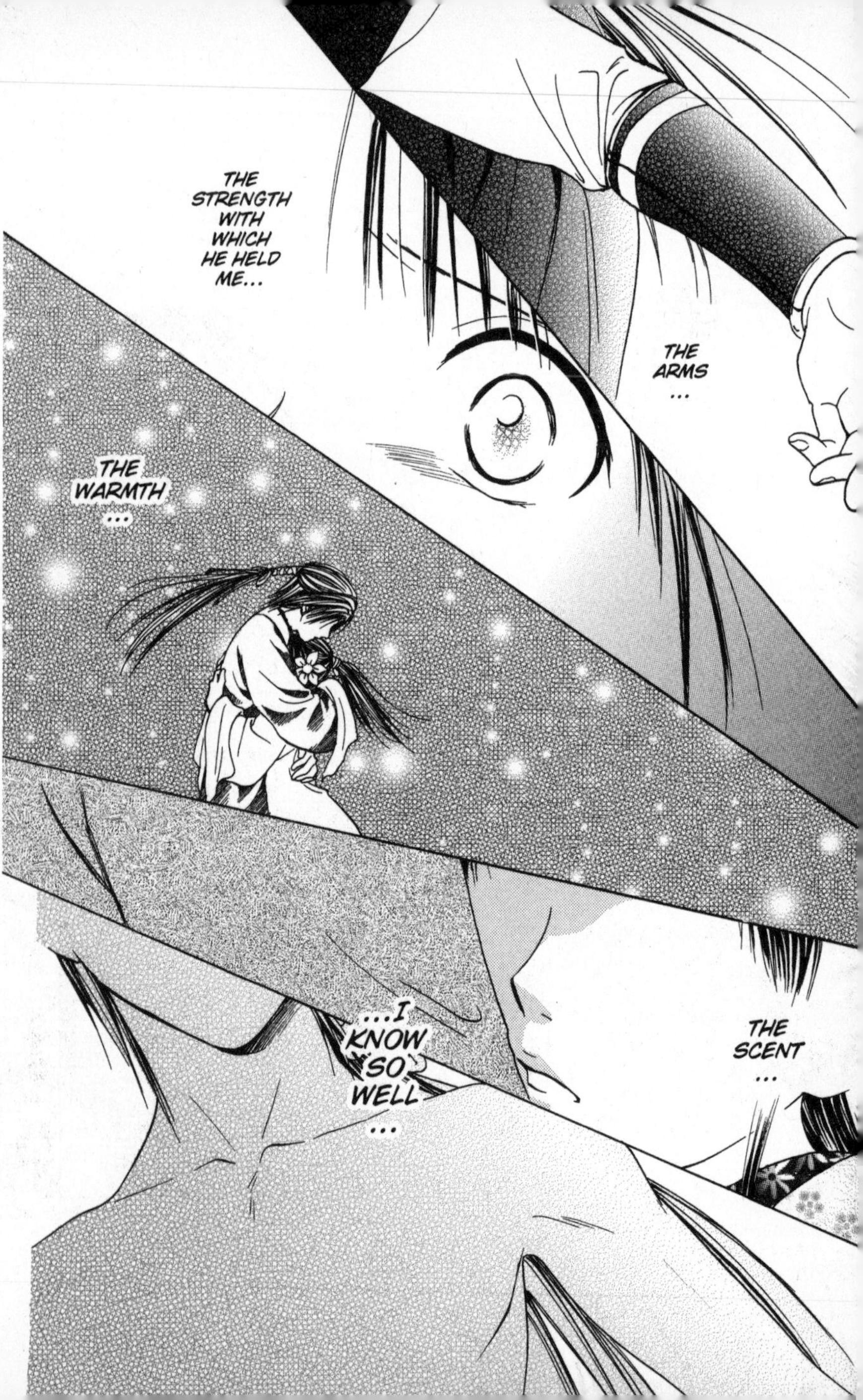
THE ARMS...
THE STRENGTH WITH WHICH HE HELD ME...
THE WARMTH...
THE SCENT...
...I KNOW SO WELL...

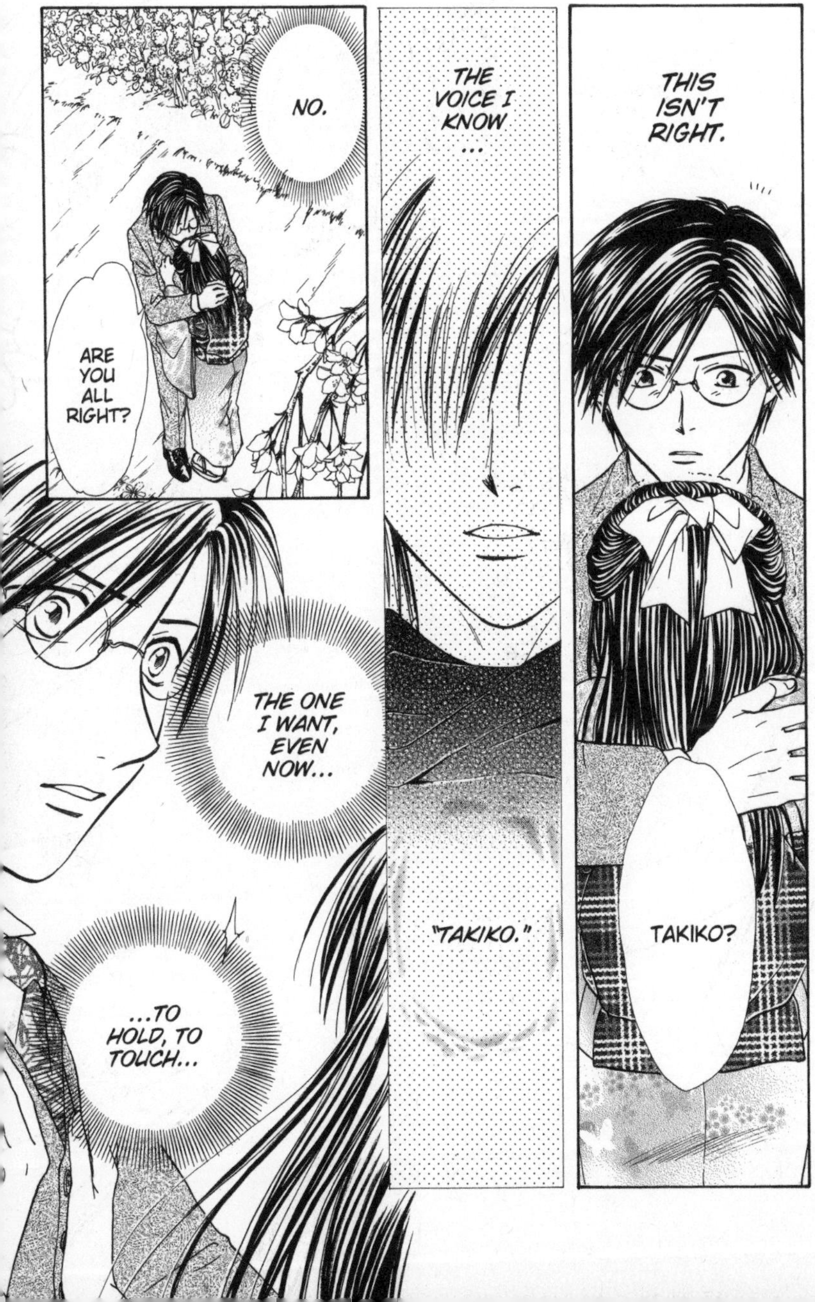
THIS ISN'T RIGHT.
TAKIKO?
THE VOICE I KNOW ...
"TAKIKO."
NO.
ARE YOU ALL RIGHT?
THE ONE I WANT, EVEN NOW...
...TO HOLD, TO TOUCH...

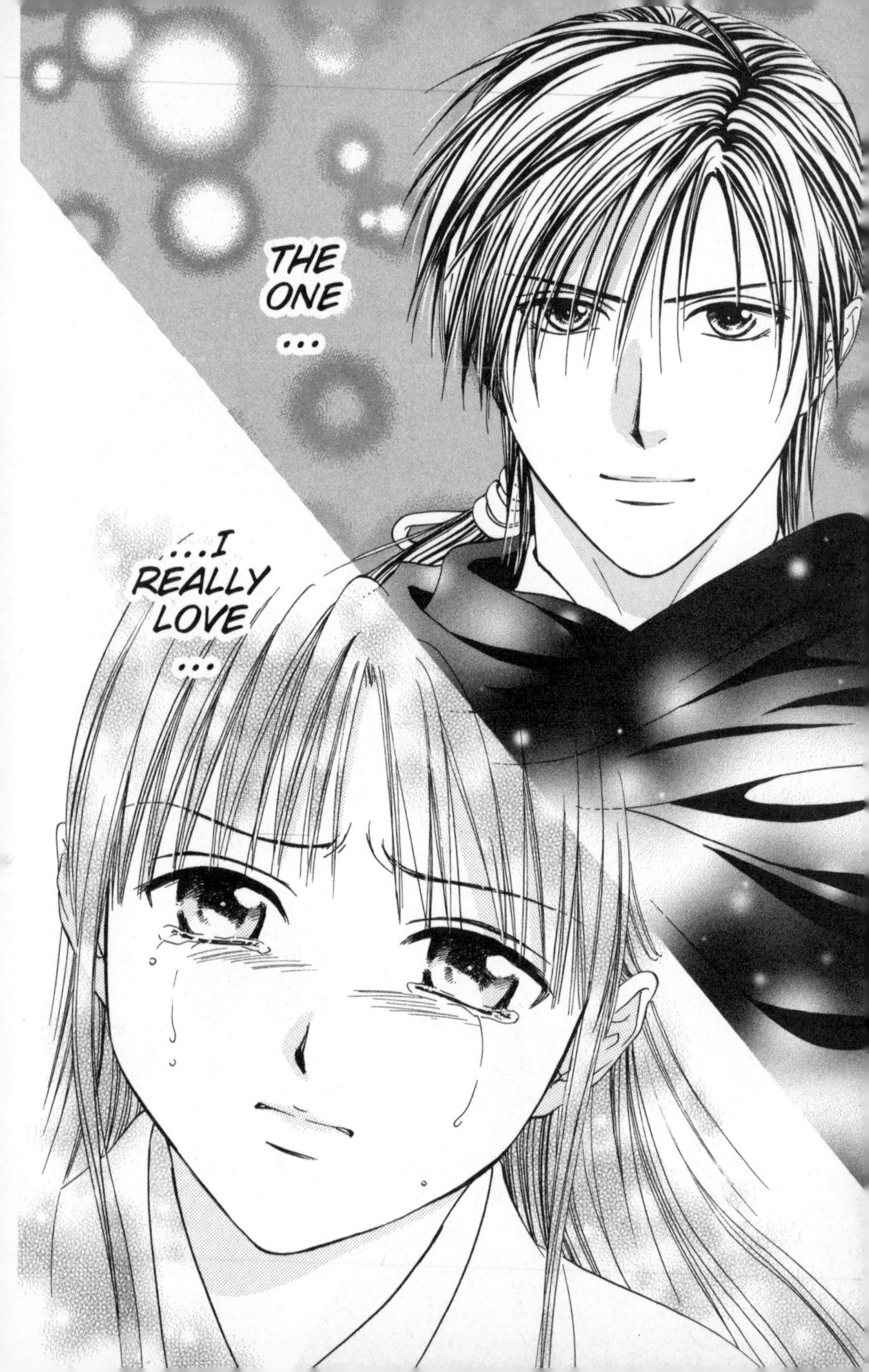
THE ONE ...
...I REALLY LOVE ...

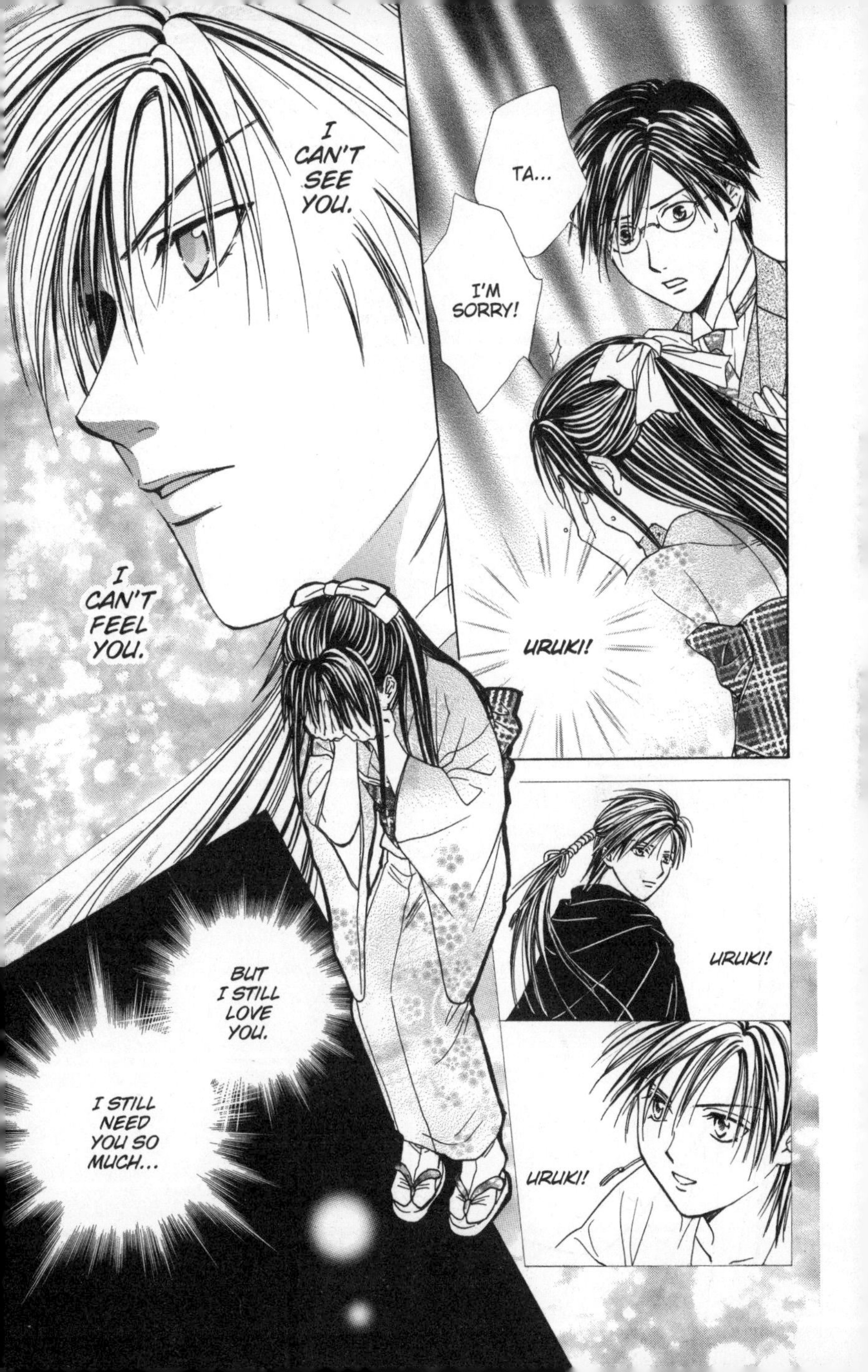
TA...
I'M SORRY!
URUKI!
URUKI!
URUKI!
I CAN'T SEE YOU.
I CAN'T FEEL YOU.
BUT I STILL LOVE YOU.
I STILL NEED YOU SO MUCH...

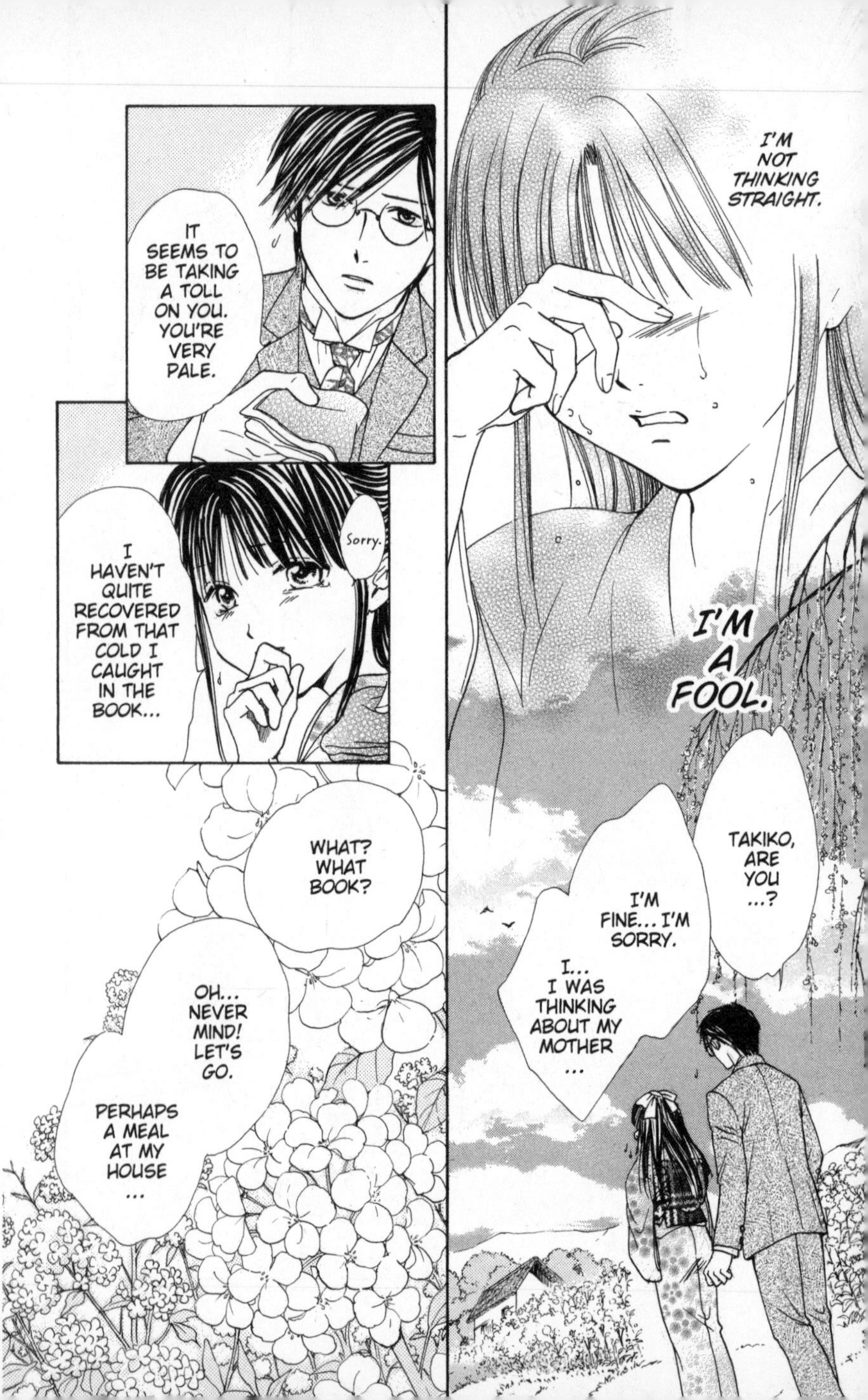
I'M NOT THINKING STRAIGHT.
I'M A FOOL.
TAKIKO, ARE YOU ...?
I'M FINE... I'M SORRY.
I... I WAS THINKING ABOUT MY MOTHER ...
IT SEEMS TO BE TAKING A TOLL ON YOU. YOU'RE VERY PALE.
Sorry.
I HAVEN'T QUITE RECOVERED FROM THAT COLD I CAUGHT IN THE BOOK...
WHAT? WHAT BOOK?
OH... NEVER MIND! LET'S GO.
PERHAPS A MEAL AT MY HOUSE ...

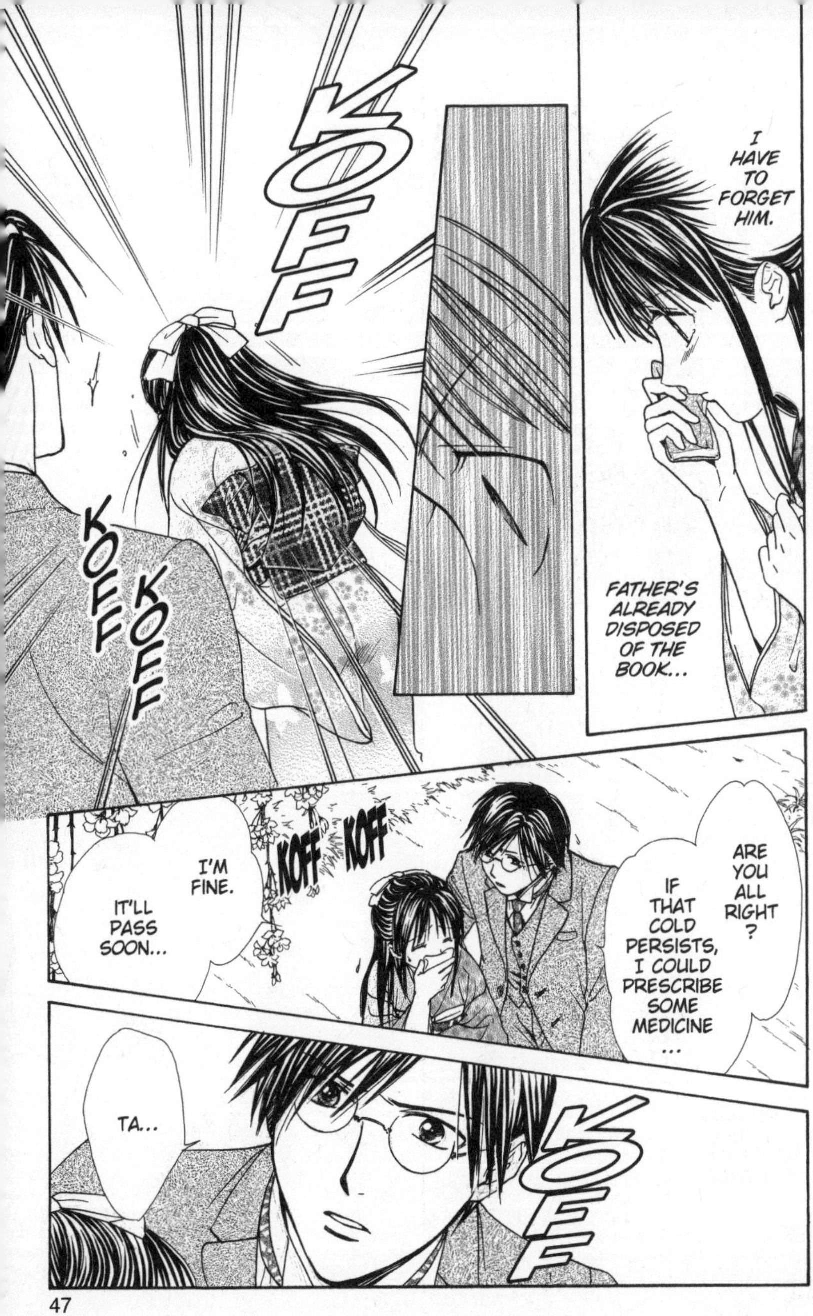
I HAVE TO FORGET HIM.
FATHER'S ALREADY DISPOSED OF THE BOOK...
KOFF
KOFF KOFF
ARE YOU ALL RIGHT?
IF THAT COLD PERSISTS, I COULD PRESCRIBE SOME MEDICINE...
KOFF KOFF
I'M FINE.
IT'LL PASS SOON...
KOFF
TA...

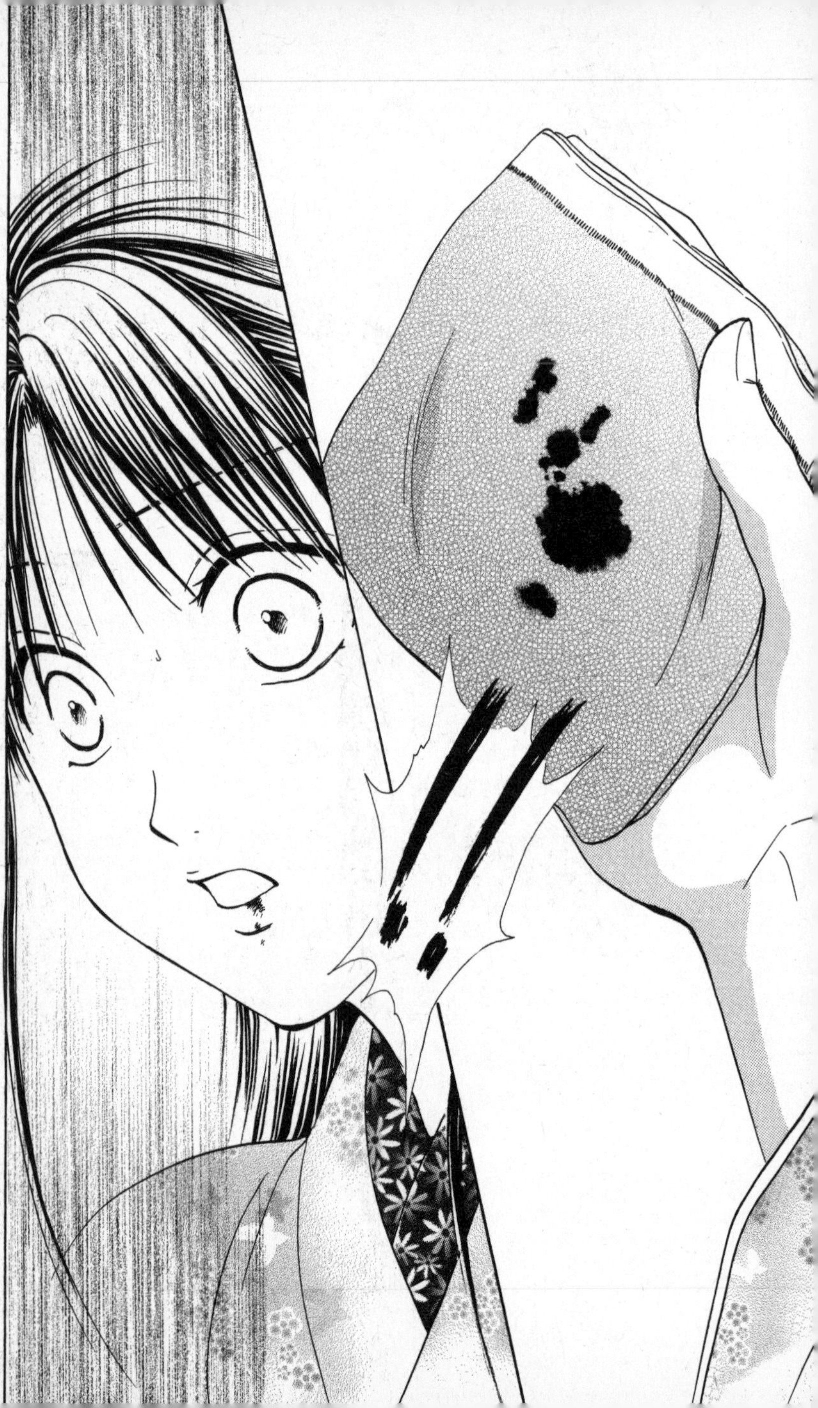

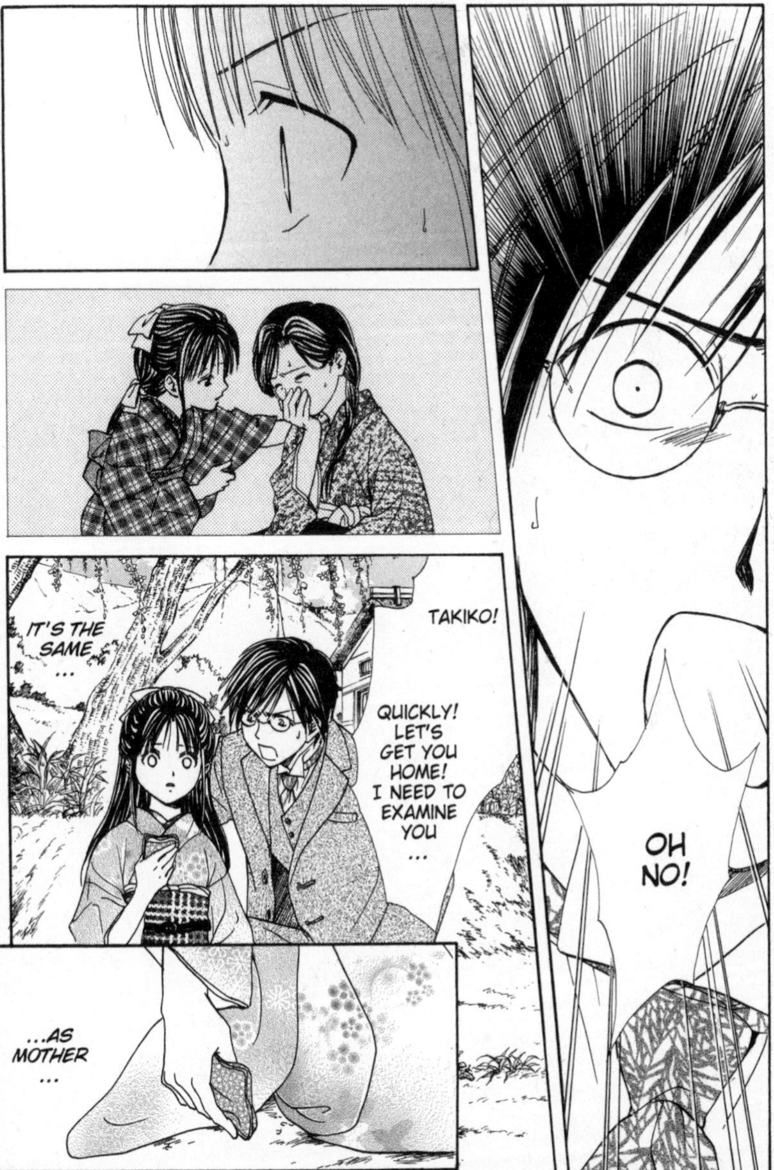
OH NO!
TAKIKO!
QUICKLY! LET'S GET YOU HOME! I NEED TO EXAMINE YOU ...
IT'S THE SAME ...
...AS MOTHER ...

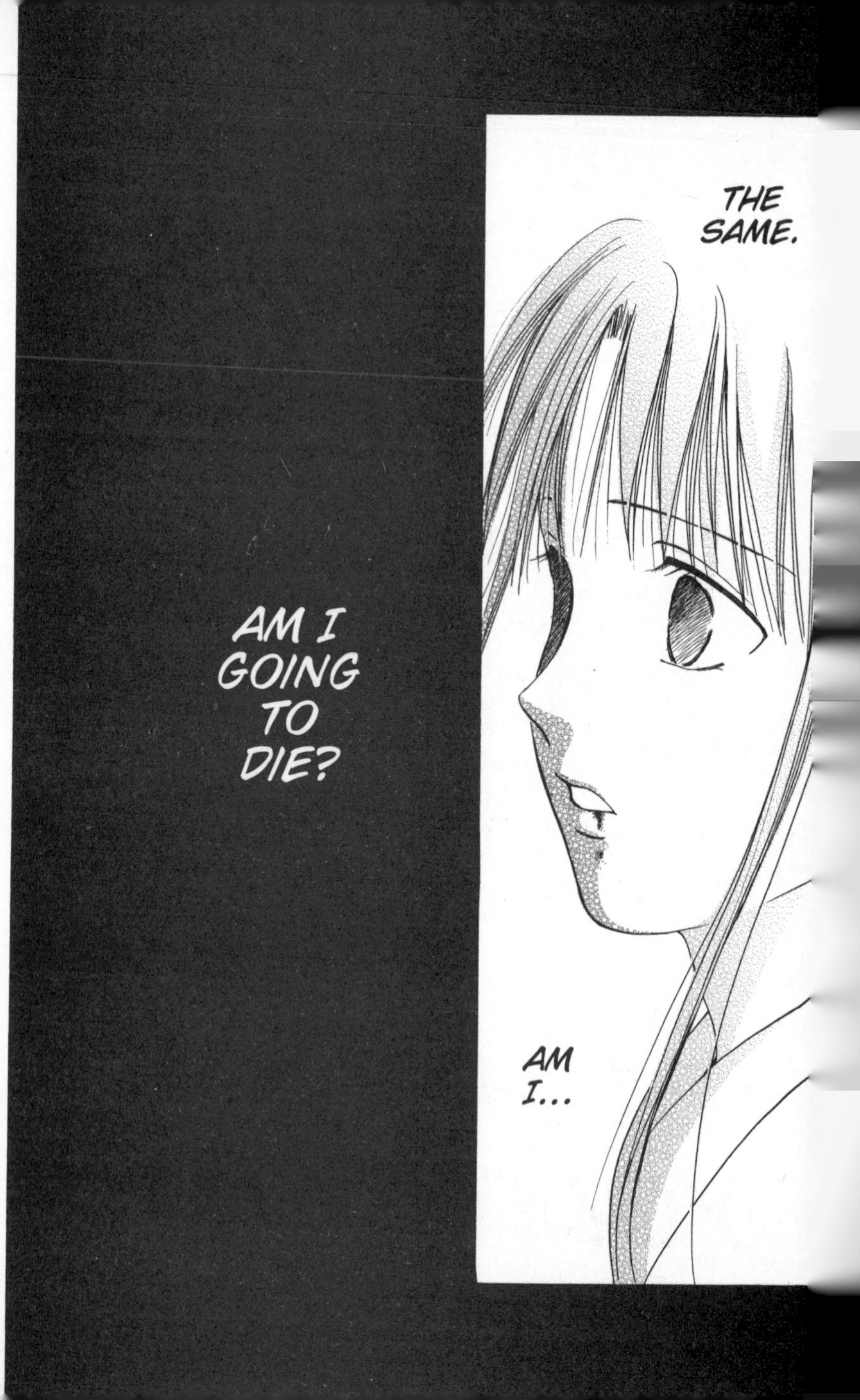
THE SAME.
AM I...
AM I GOING TO DIE?

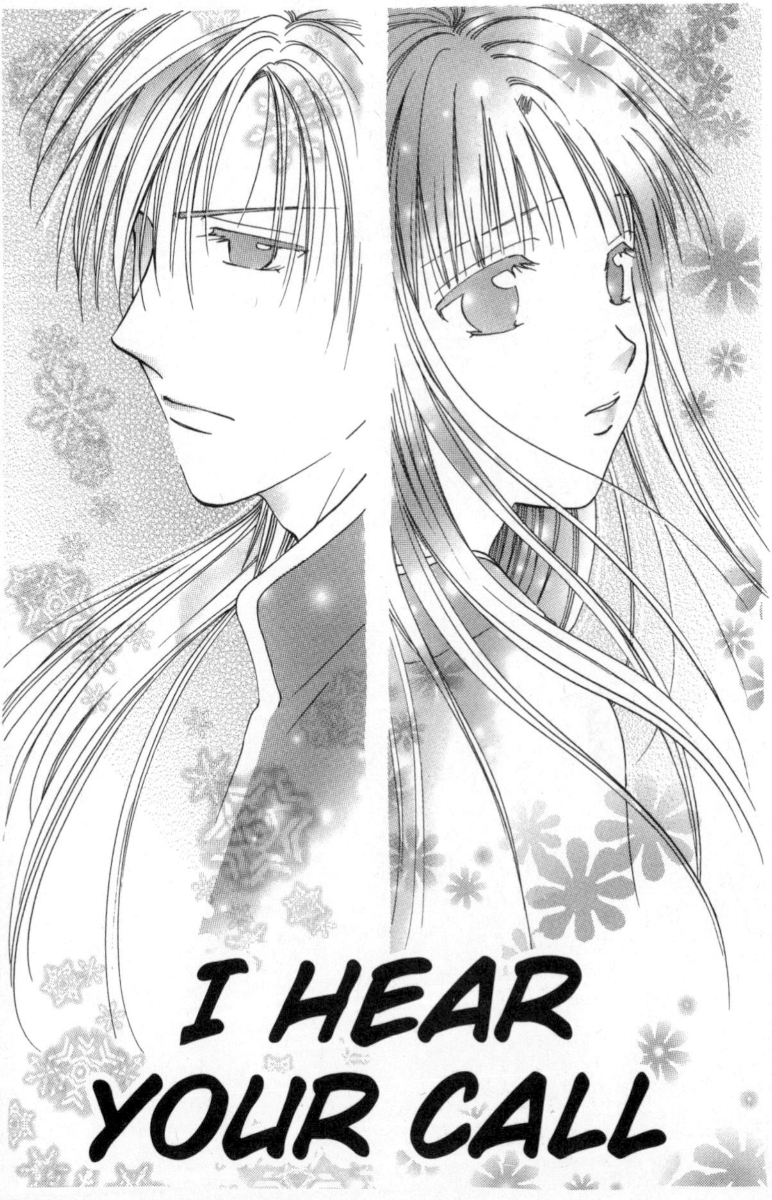
I HEAR
YOUR CALL

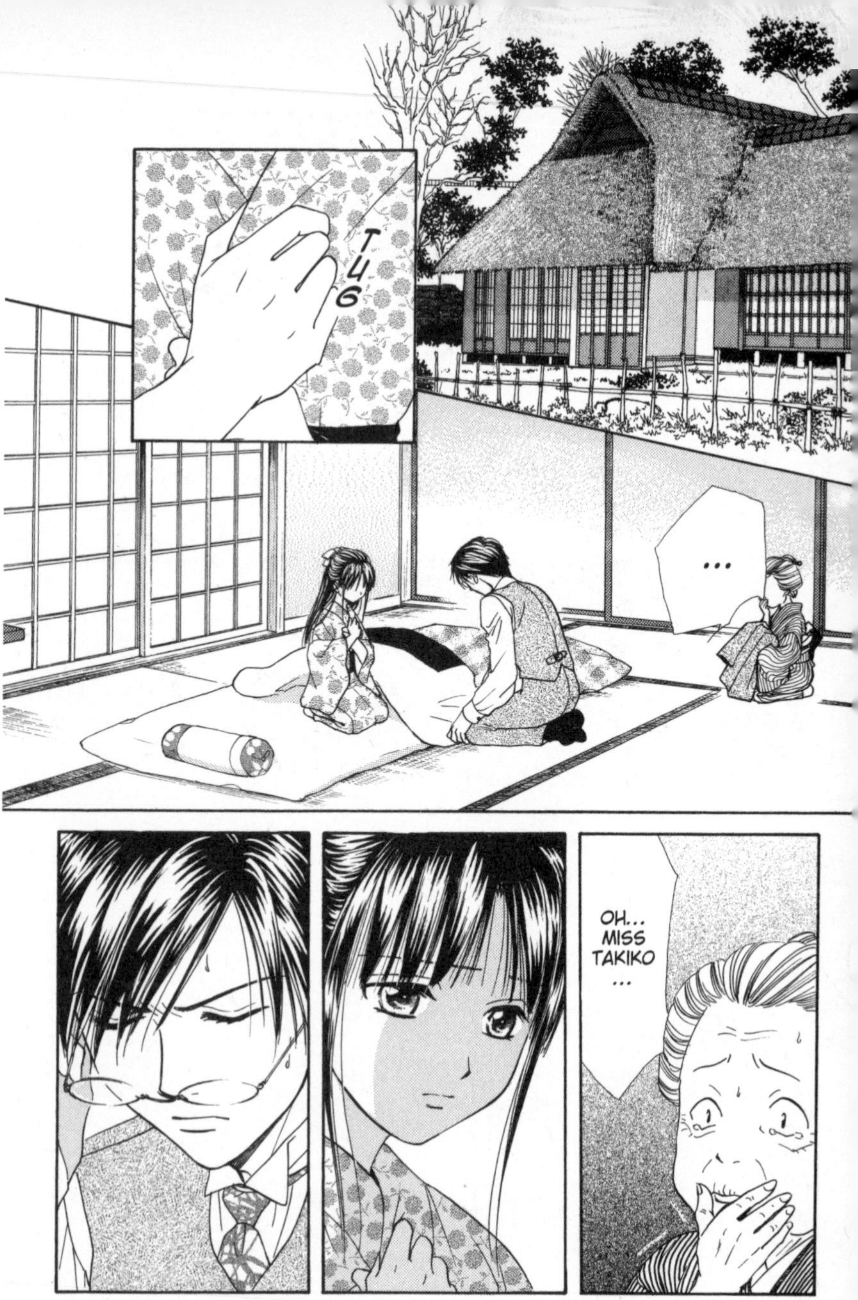
TUG
...
OH... MISS TAKIKO ...

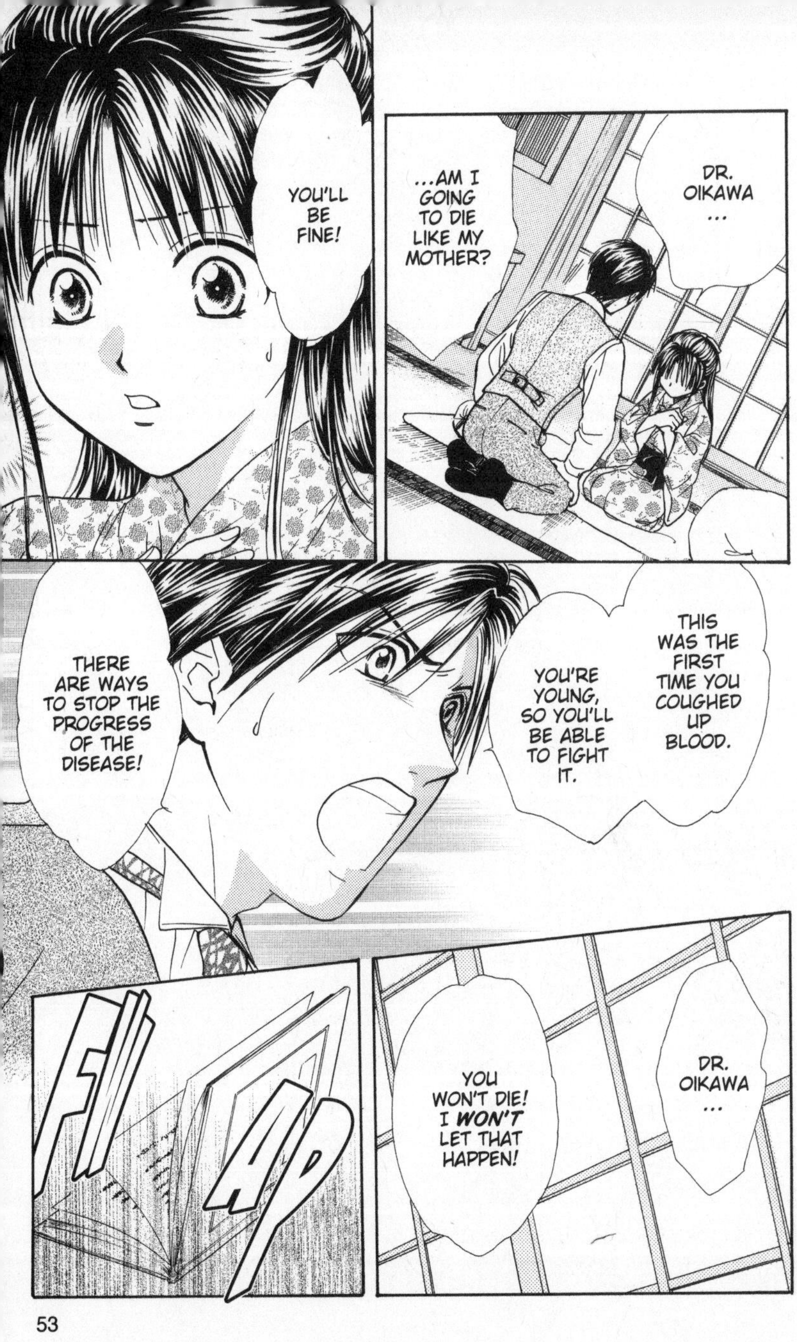
DR. OIKAWA ...
...AM I GOING TO DIE LIKE MY MOTHER?
YOU'LL BE FINE!
THIS WAS THE FIRST TIME YOU COUGHED UP BLOOD.
YOU'RE YOUNG, SO YOU'LL BE ABLE TO FIGHT IT.
THERE ARE WAYS TO STOP THE PROGRESS OF THE DISEASE!
DR. OIKAWA ...
YOU WON'T DIE! I *WON'T* LET THAT HAPPEN!
FLAP

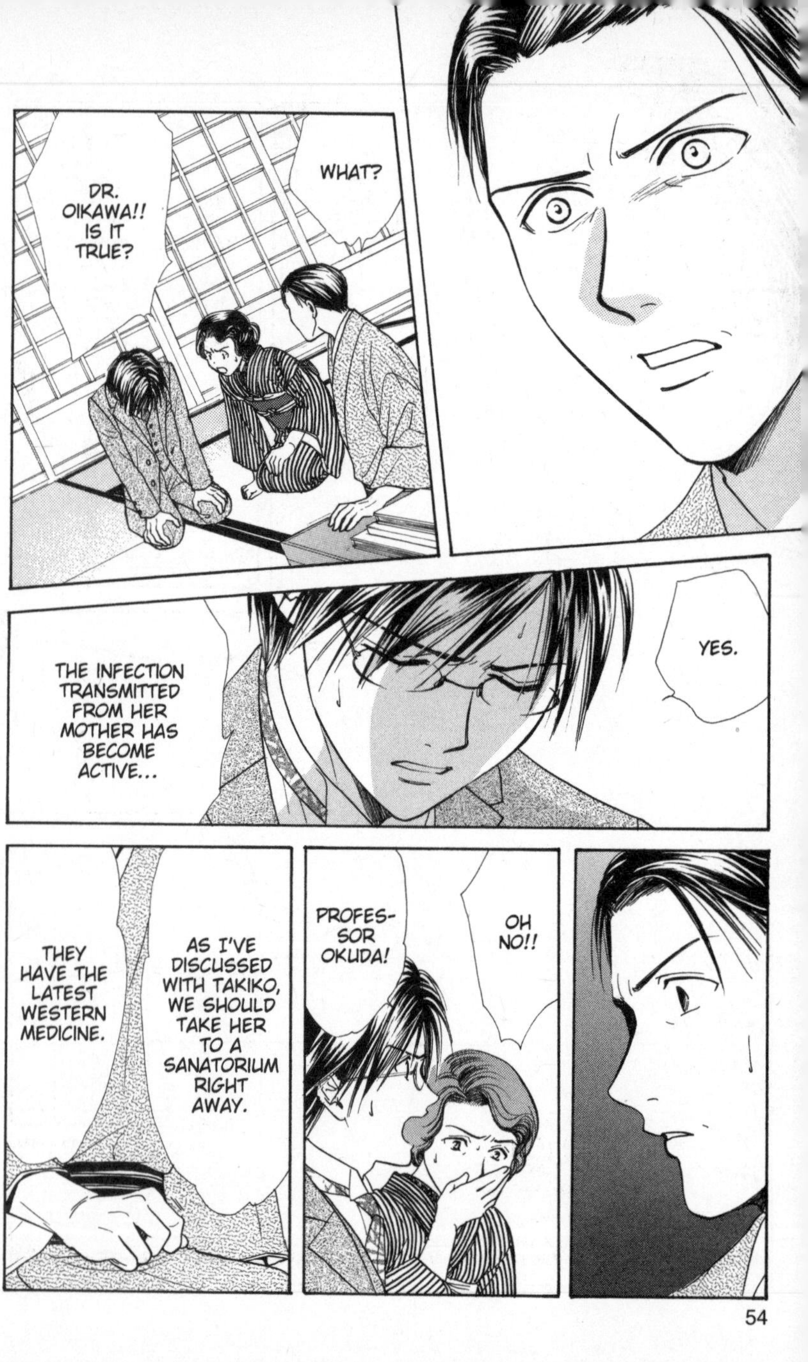
WHAT?
DR. OIKAWA!! IS IT TRUE?
YES.
THE INFECTION TRANSMITTED FROM HER MOTHER HAS BECOME ACTIVE...
OH NO!!
PROFES-SOR OKUDA!
AS I'VE DISCUSSED WITH TAKIKO, WE SHOULD TAKE HER TO A SANATORIUM RIGHT AWAY.
THEY HAVE THE LATEST WESTERN MEDICINE.

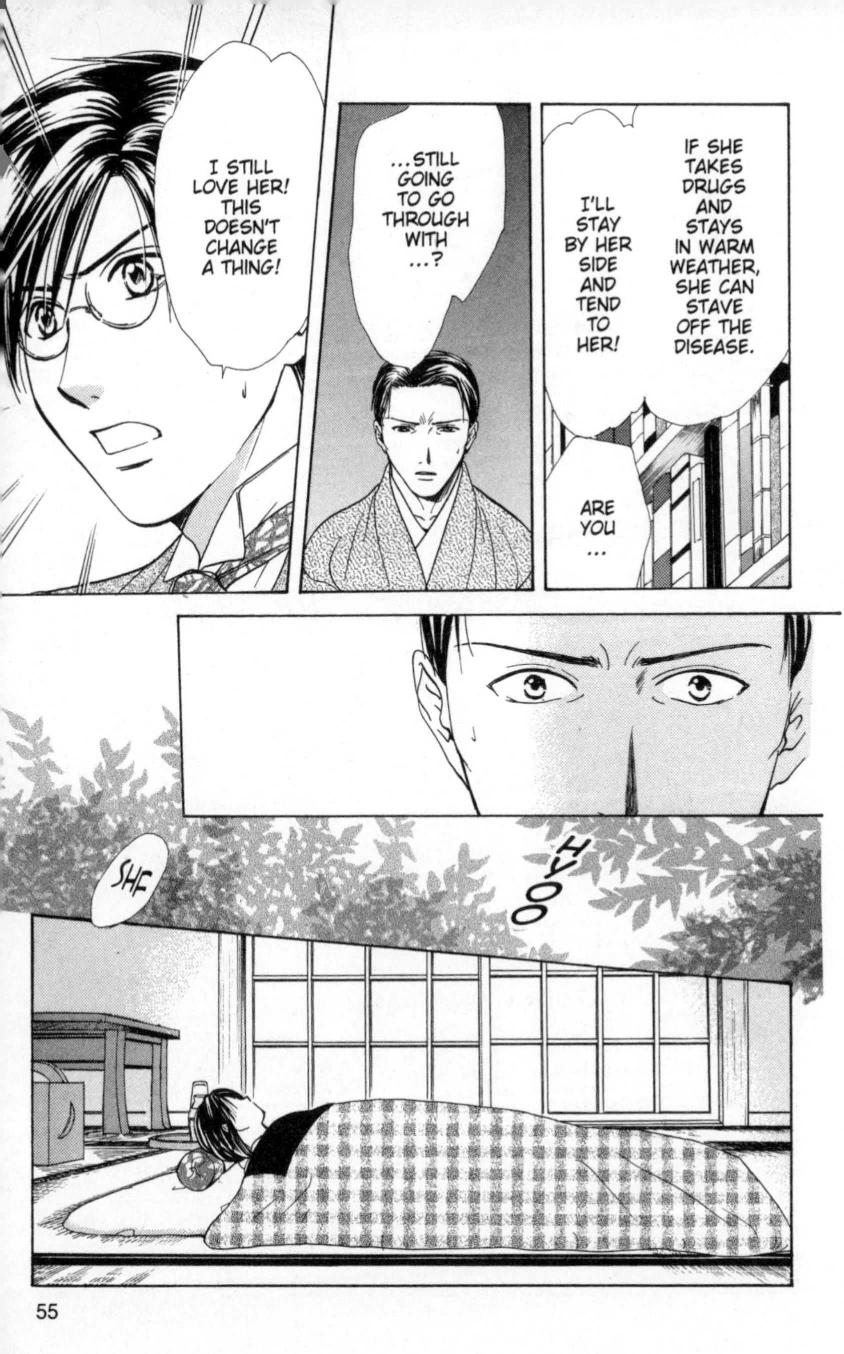
IF SHE TAKES DRUGS AND STAYS IN WARM WEATHER, SHE CAN STAVE OFF THE DISEASE.
I'LL STAY BY HER SIDE AND TEND TO HER!
ARE YOU ...
...STILL GOING TO GO THROUGH WITH ...?
I STILL LOVE HER! THIS DOESN'T CHANGE A THING!
HYOO
SHF

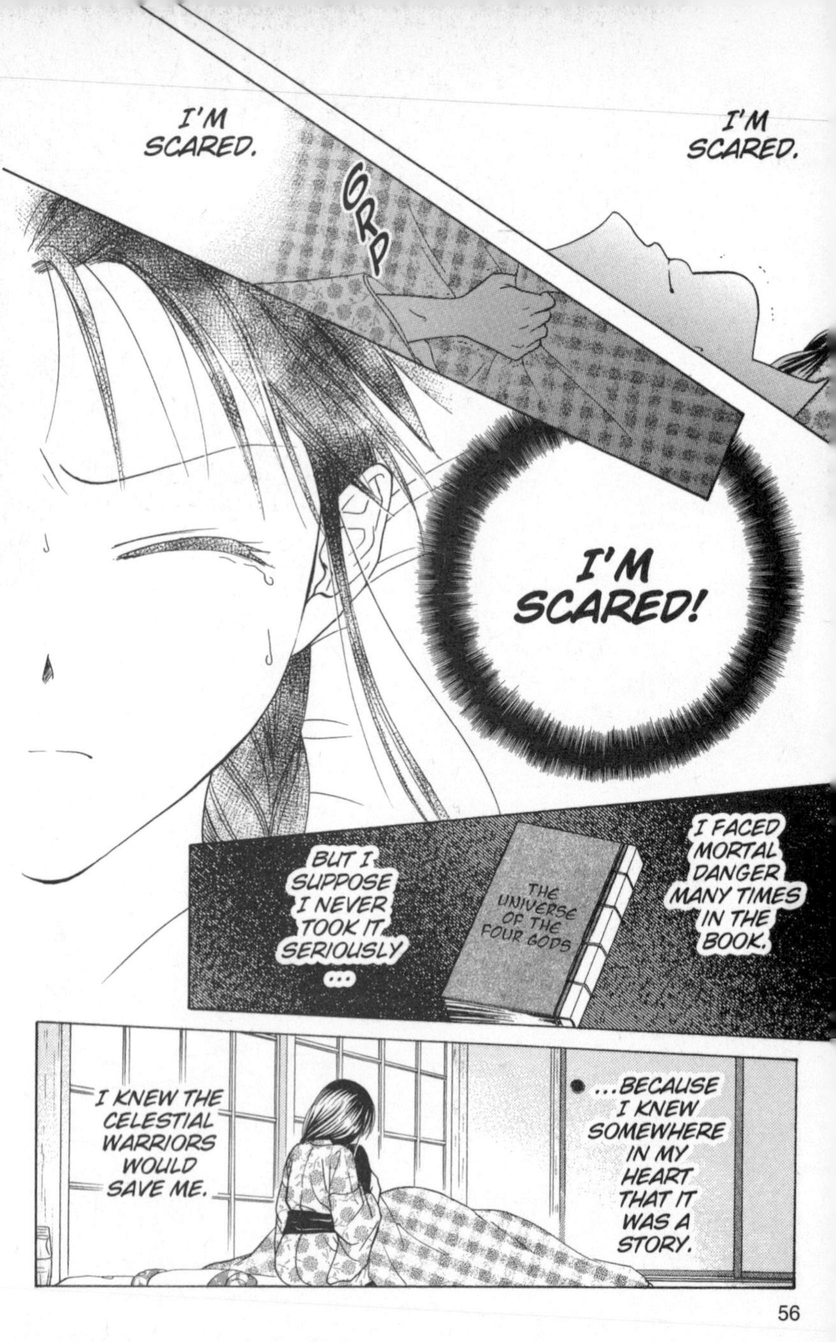

I'M SCARED.
GRP
I'M SCARED.
I'M SCARED!
I FACED MORTAL DANGER MANY TIMES IN THE BOOK.
THE UNIVERSE OF THE FOUR GODS
BUT I SUPPOSE I NEVER TOOK IT SERIOUSLY...
...BECAUSE I KNEW SOMEWHERE IN MY HEART THAT IT WAS A STORY.
I KNEW THE CELESTIAL WARRIORS WOULD SAVE ME.

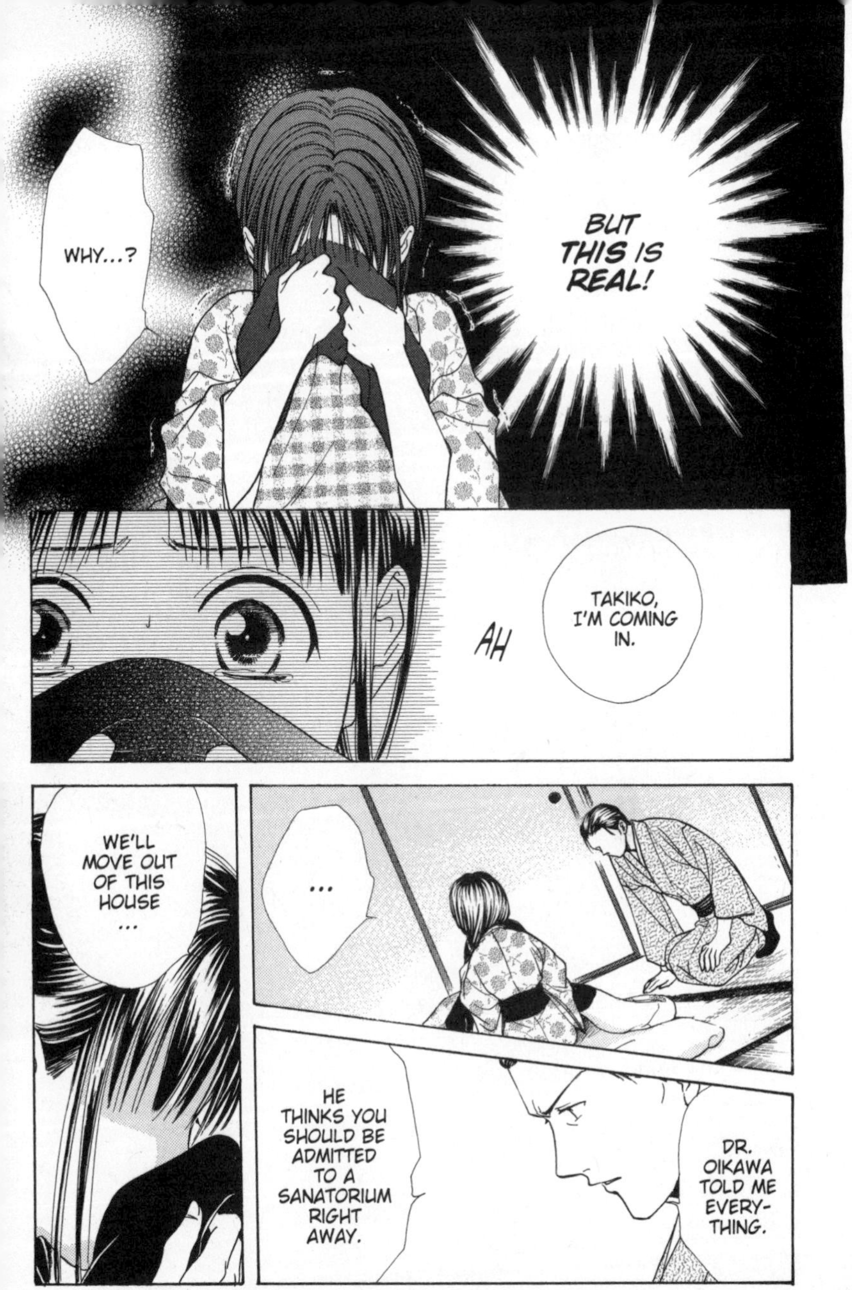
BUT THIS IS REAL!
WHY...?
TAKIKO, I'M COMING IN.
AH
...
DR. OIKAWA TOLD ME EVERYTHING.
HE THINKS YOU SHOULD BE ADMITTED TO A SANATORIUM RIGHT AWAY.
WE'LL MOVE OUT OF THIS HOUSE ...

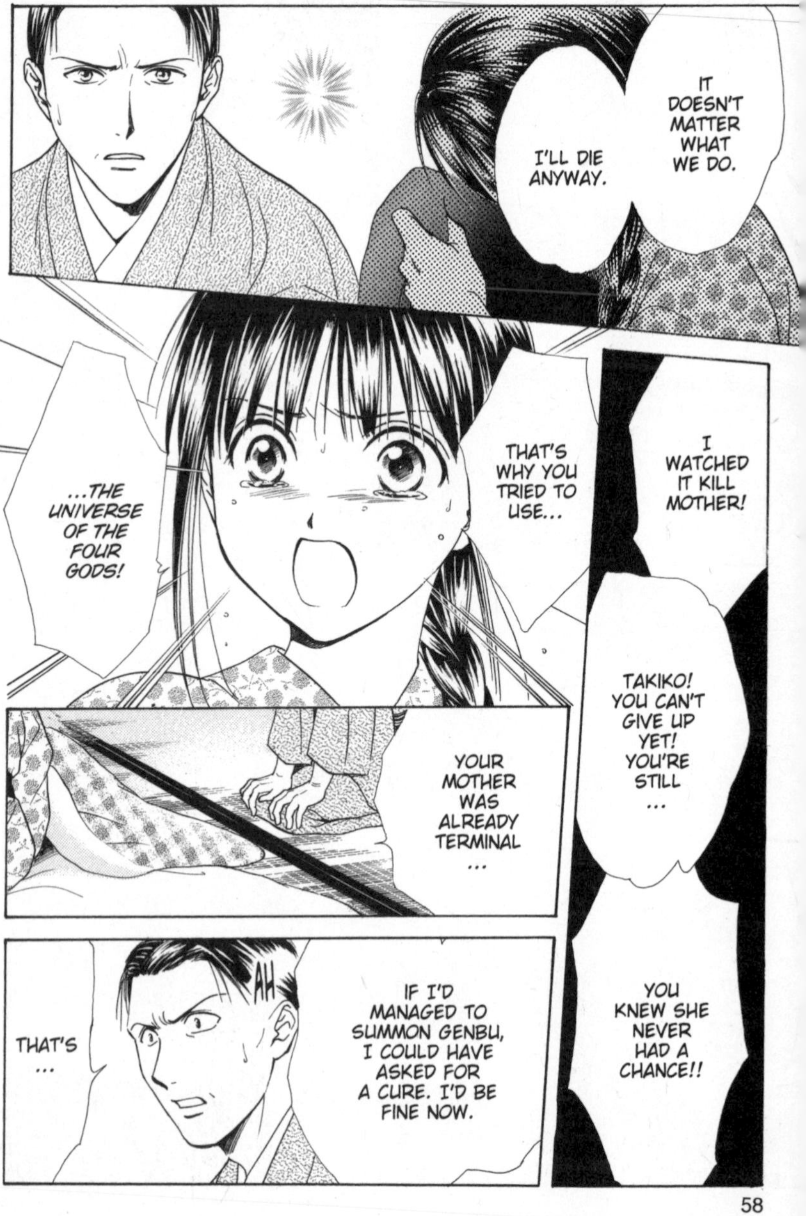
IT DOESN'T MATTER WHAT WE DO.
I'LL DIE ANYWAY.
I WATCHED IT KILL MOTHER!
TAKIKO! YOU CAN'T GIVE UP YET! YOU'RE STILL ...
YOU KNEW SHE NEVER HAD A CHANCE!!
THAT'S WHY YOU TRIED TO USE...
...THE UNIVERSE OF THE FOUR GODS!
YOUR MOTHER WAS ALREADY TERMINAL ...
IF I'D MANAGED TO SUMMON GENBU, I COULD HAVE ASKED FOR A CURE. I'D BE FINE NOW.
AH
THAT'S ...

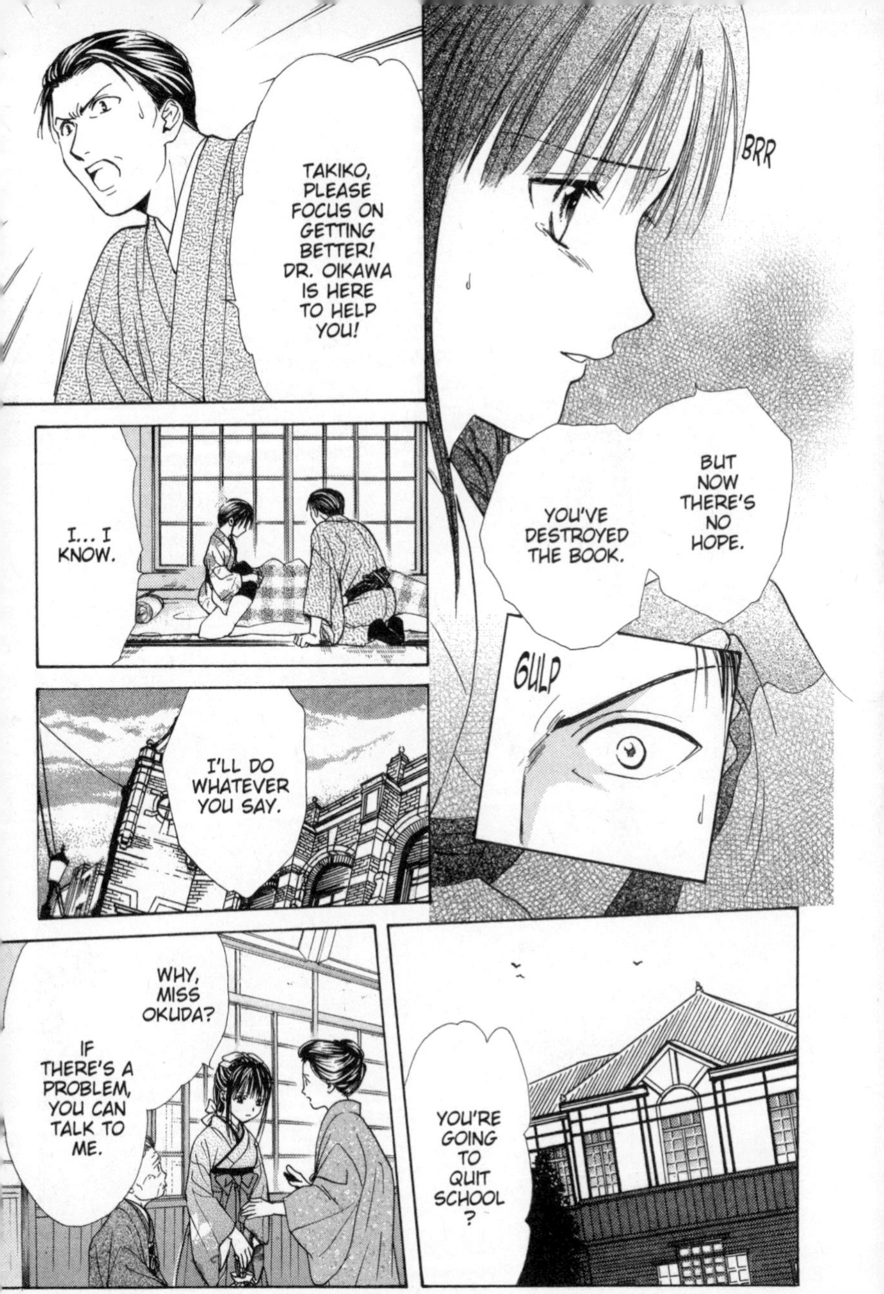
BRR
BUT NOW THERE'S NO HOPE.
YOU'VE DESTROYED THE BOOK.
GULP
TAKIKO, PLEASE FOCUS ON GETTING BETTER! DR. OIKAWA IS HERE TO HELP YOU!
I... I KNOW.
I'LL DO WHATEVER YOU SAY.
YOU'RE GOING TO QUIT SCHOOL?
WHY, MISS OKUDA?
IF THERE'S A PROBLEM, YOU CAN TALK TO ME.

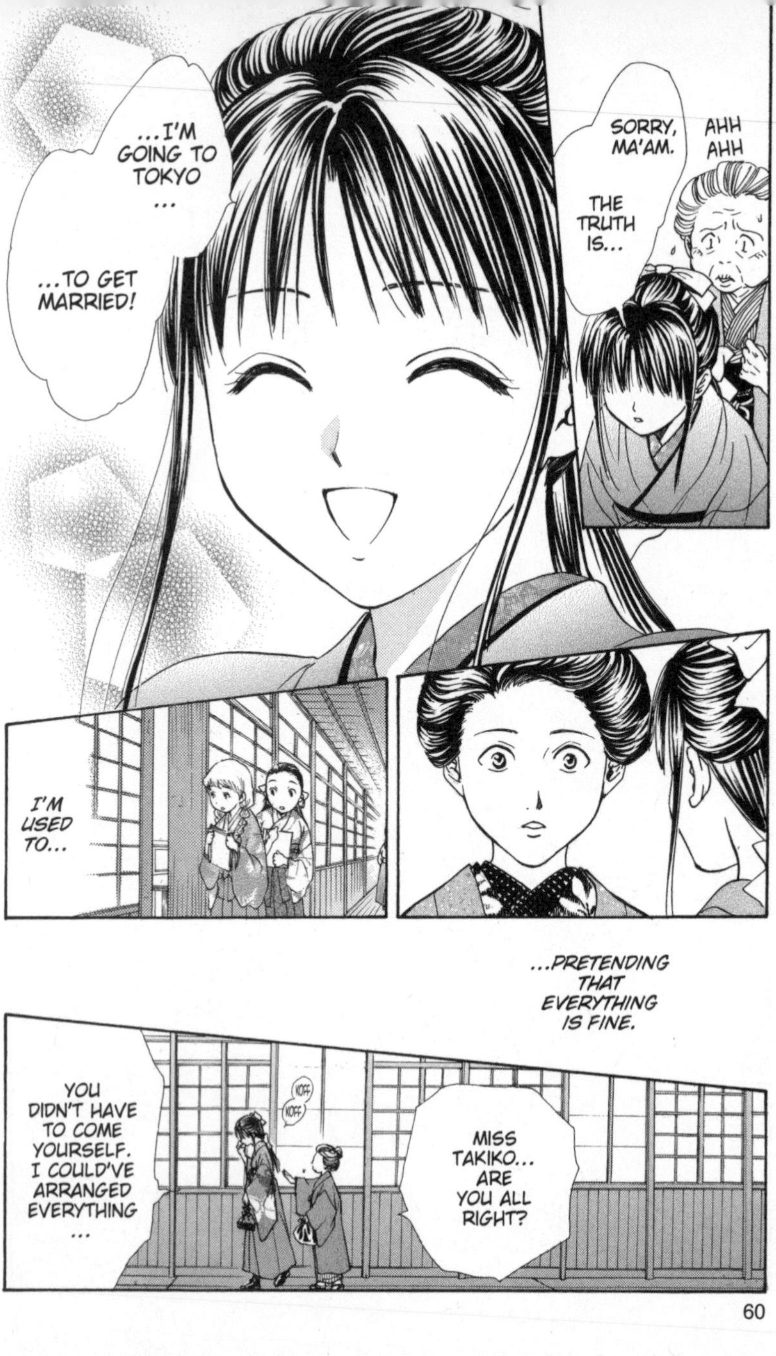
AHH AHH
SORRY, MA'AM.
THE TRUTH IS...
...I'M GOING TO TOKYO...
...TO GET MARRIED!
I'M USED TO...
...PRETENDING THAT EVERYTHING IS FINE.
MISS TAKIKO... ARE YOU ALL RIGHT?
KOFF
KOFF
YOU DIDN'T HAVE TO COME YOURSELF. I COULD'VE ARRANGED EVERYTHING...

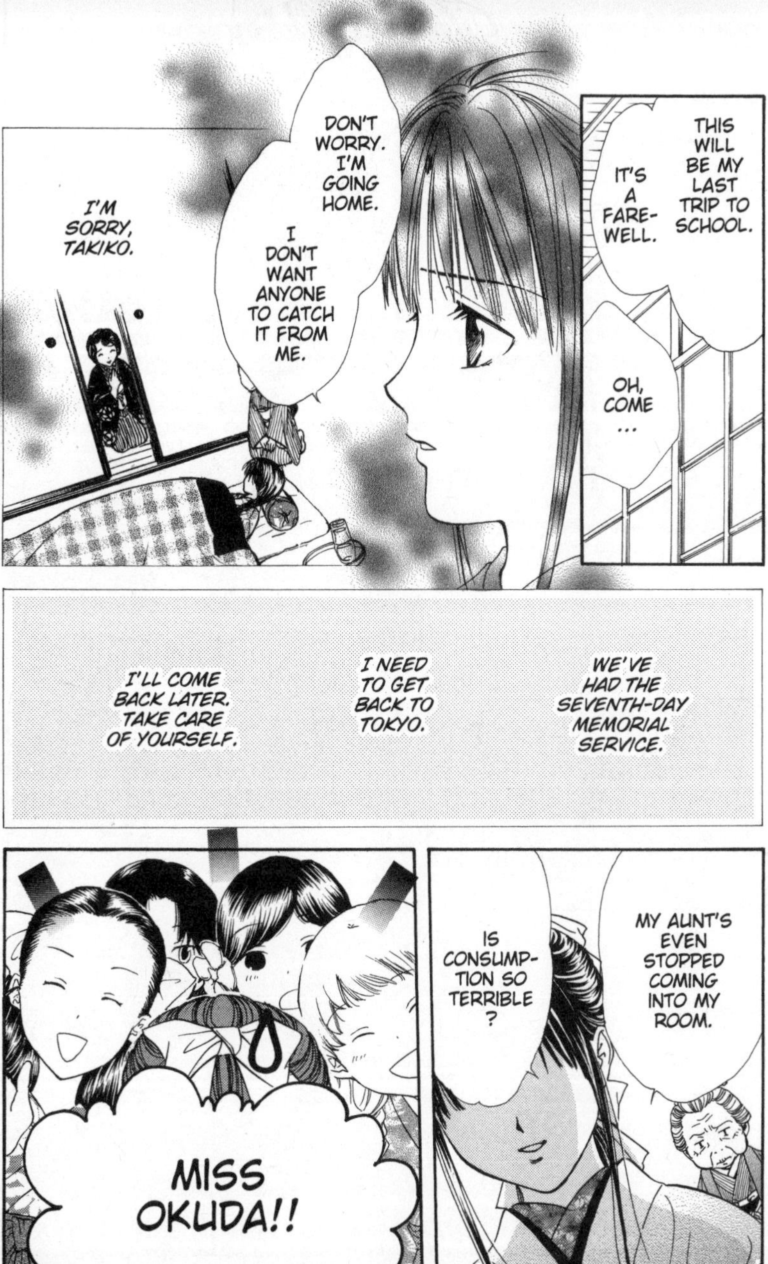
THIS WILL BE MY LAST TRIP TO SCHOOL.
IT'S A FAREWELL.
OH, COME ...
DON'T WORRY. I'M GOING HOME.
I DON'T WANT ANYONE TO CATCH IT FROM ME.
I'M SORRY, TAKIKO.
WE'VE HAD THE SEVENTH-DAY MEMORIAL SERVICE.
I NEED TO GET BACK TO TOKYO.
I'LL COME BACK LATER. TAKE CARE OF YOURSELF.
MY AUNT'S EVEN STOPPED COMING INTO MY ROOM.
IS CONSUMPTION SO TERRIBLE?
MISS OKUDA!!

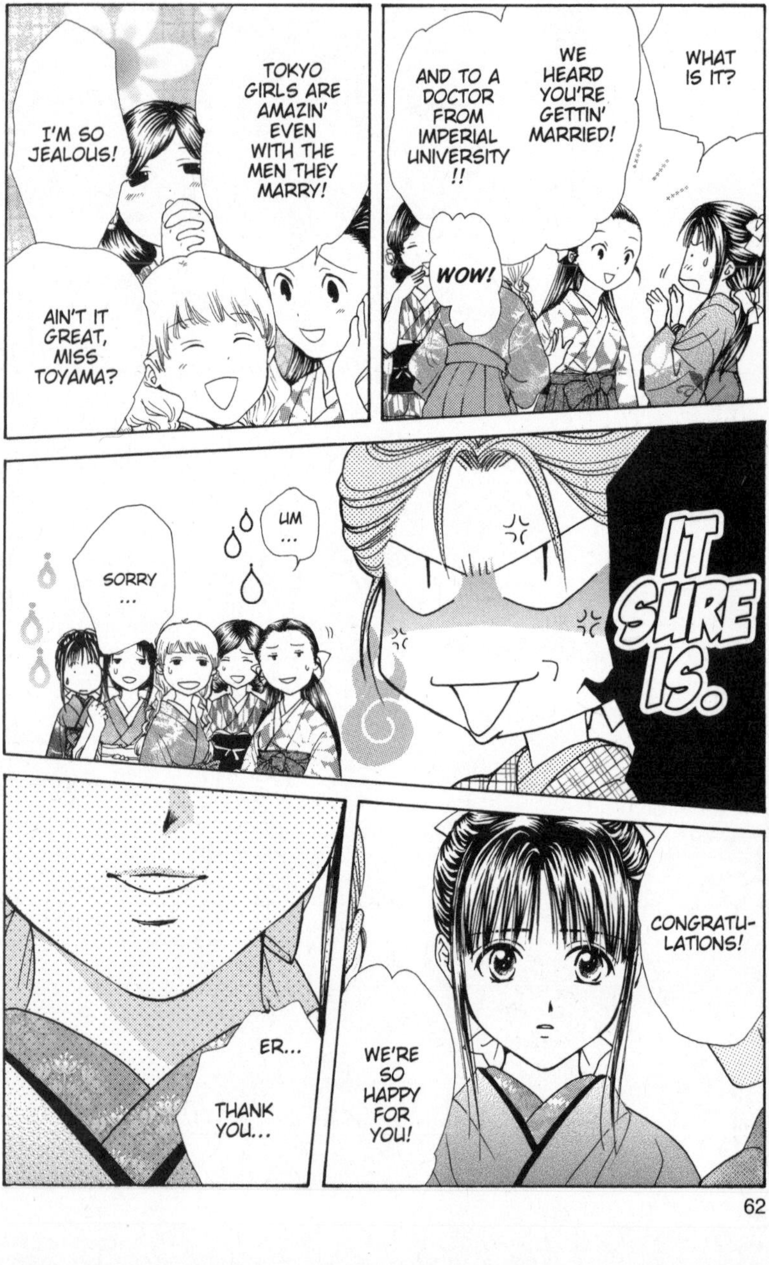
WHAT IS IT?
WE HEARD YOU'RE GETTIN' MARRIED!
AND TO A DOCTOR FROM IMPERIAL UNIVERSITY!!
WOW!
TOKYO GIRLS ARE AMAZIN' EVEN WITH THE MEN THEY MARRY!
I'M SO JEALOUS!
AIN'T IT GREAT, MISS TOYAMA?
IT SURE IS.
UM ...
SORRY ...
CONGRATULATIONS!
WE'RE SO HAPPY FOR YOU!
ER...
THANK YOU...

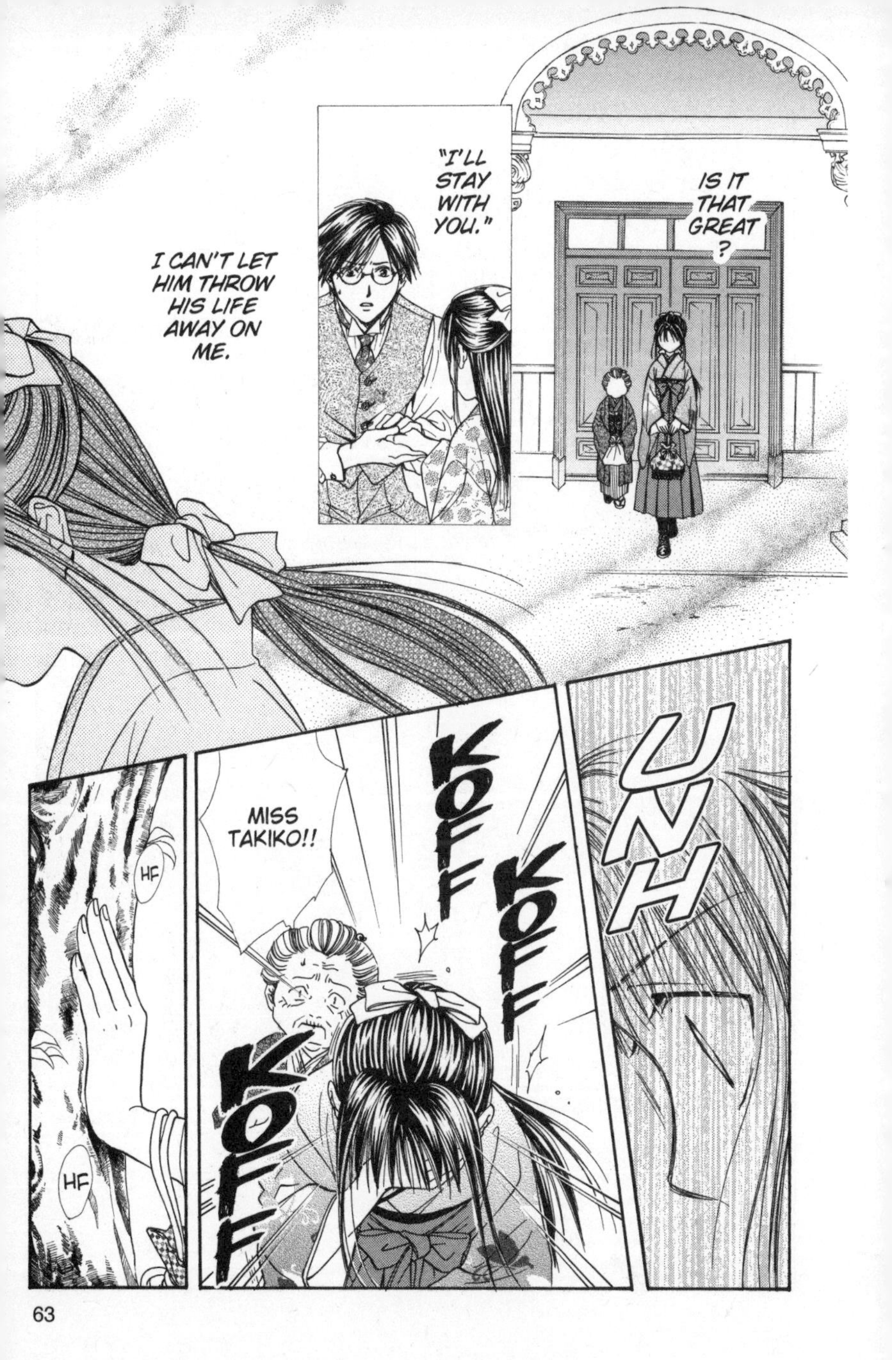
IS IT THAT GREAT?
"I'LL STAY WITH YOU."
I CAN'T LET HIM THROW HIS LIFE AWAY ON ME.
UNH
KOFF
KOFF
MISS TAKIKO!!
KOFF
HF
HF

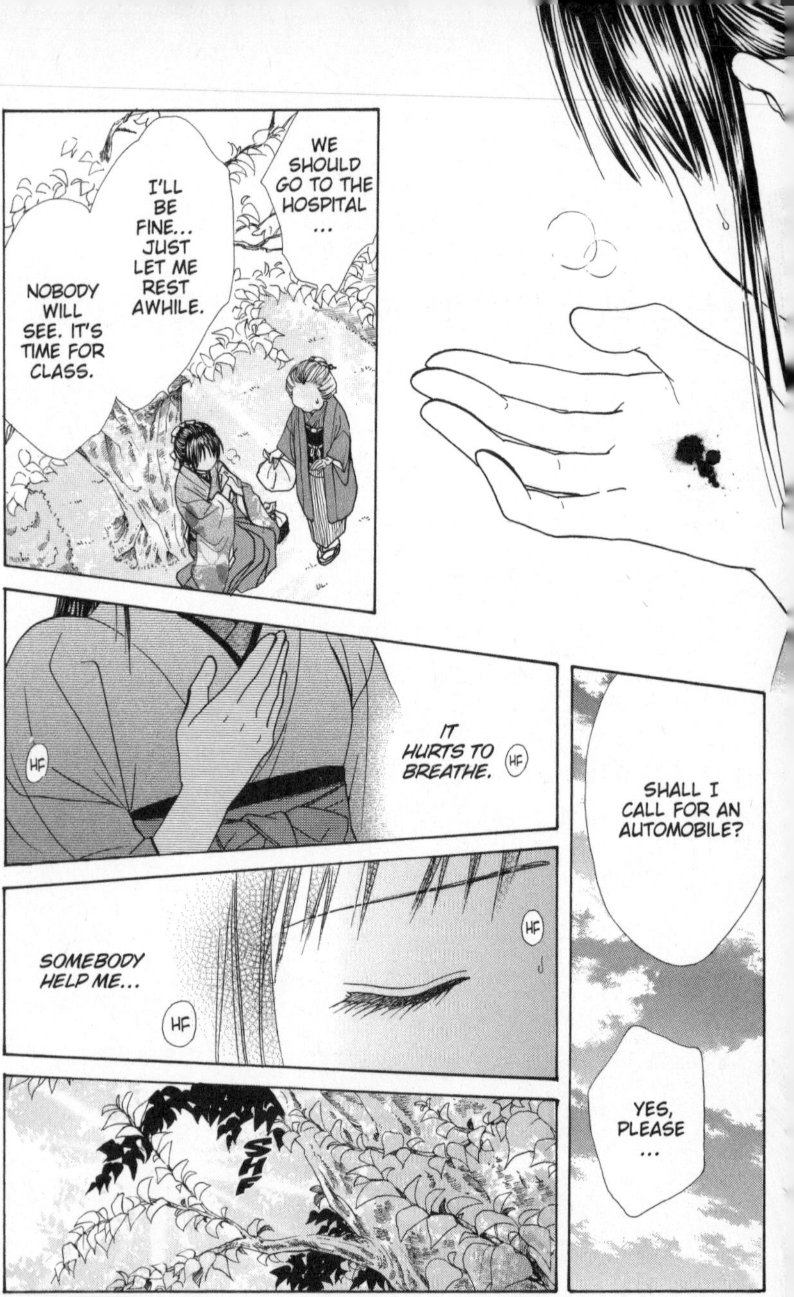
WE SHOULD GO TO THE HOSPITAL...
I'LL BE FINE... JUST LET ME REST AWHILE.
NOBODY WILL SEE. IT'S TIME FOR CLASS.
SHALL I CALL FOR AN AUTOMOBILE?
YES, PLEASE...
HF
IT HURTS TO BREATHE.
HF
HF
SOMEBODY HELP ME...
HF
SHF

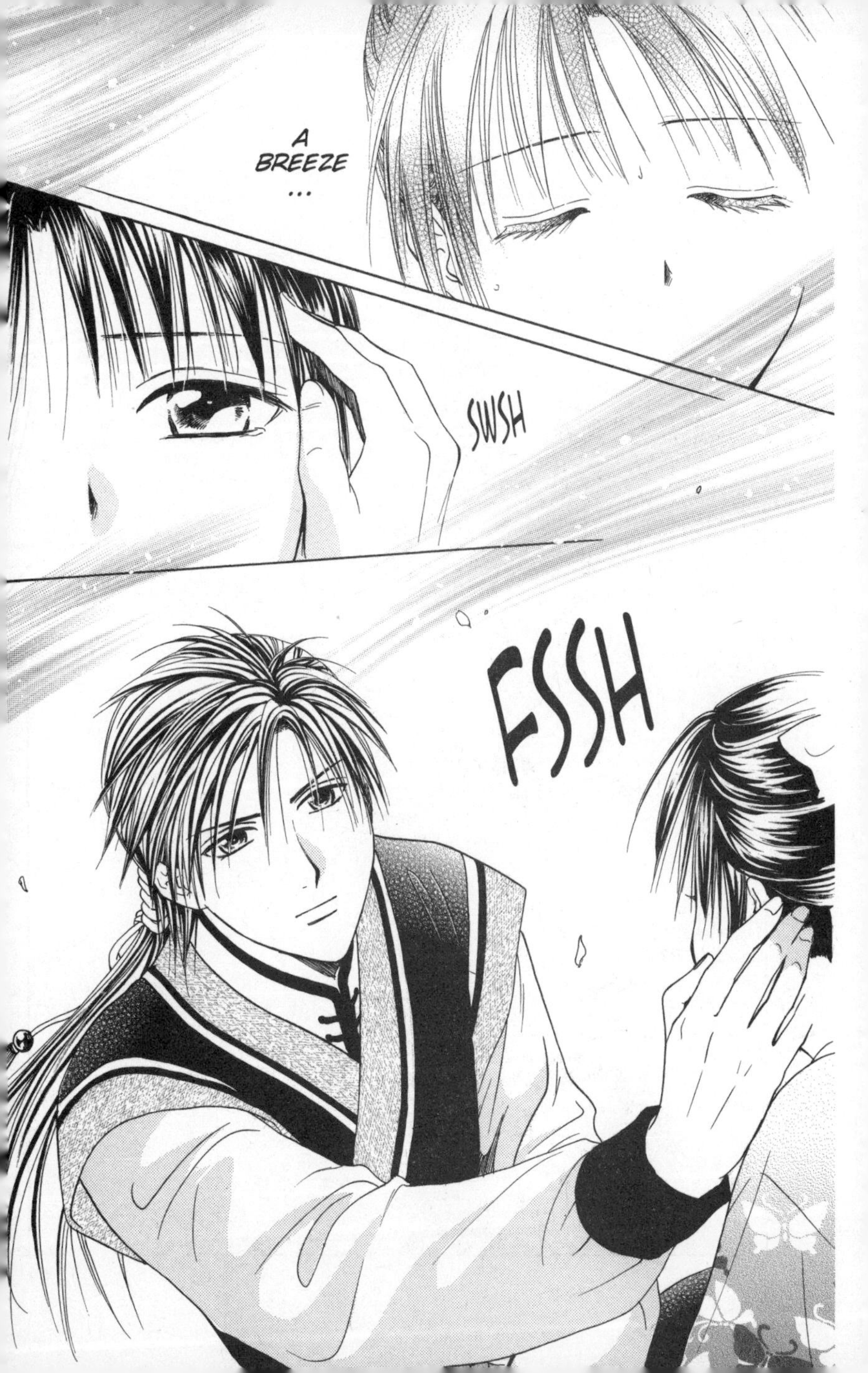
A BREEZE
...
SWSH
FSSH

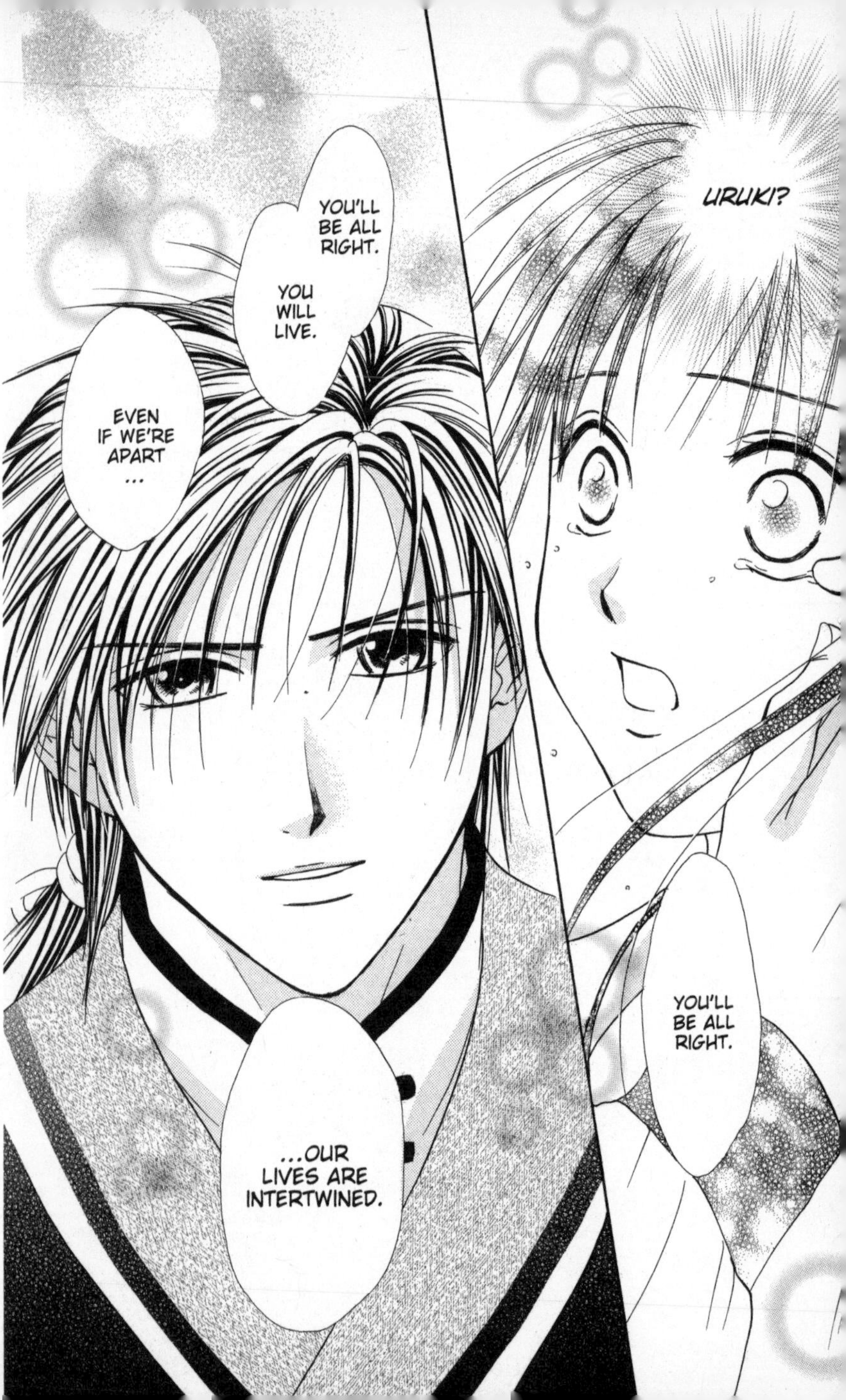
URUKI?
YOU'LL BE ALL RIGHT.
YOU'LL BE ALL RIGHT.
YOU WILL LIVE.
EVEN IF WE'RE APART ...
...OUR LIVES ARE INTERTWINED.

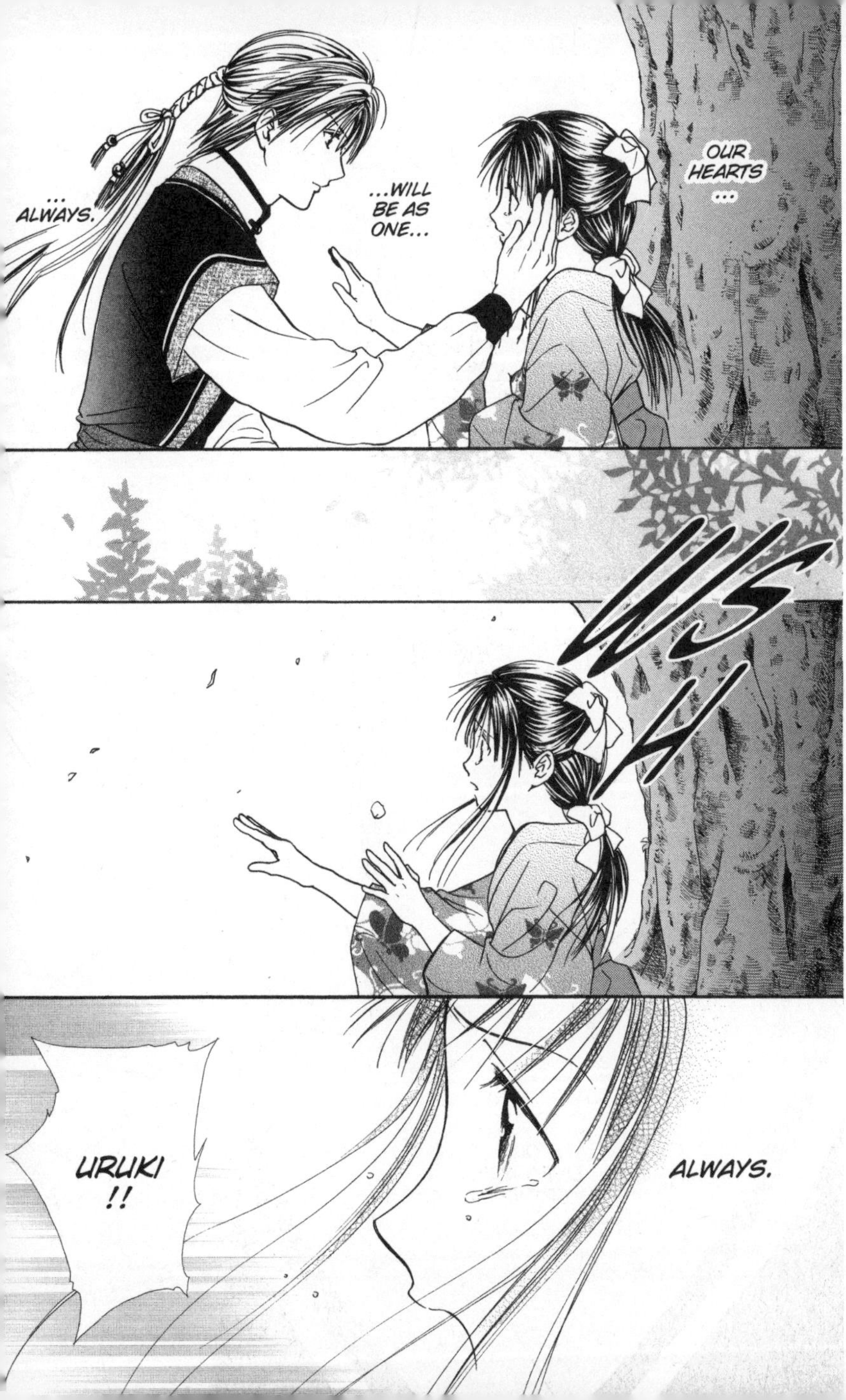
OUR HEARTS...
...WILL BE AS ONE...
...ALWAYS.
WSHH
ALWAYS.
URUKI !!

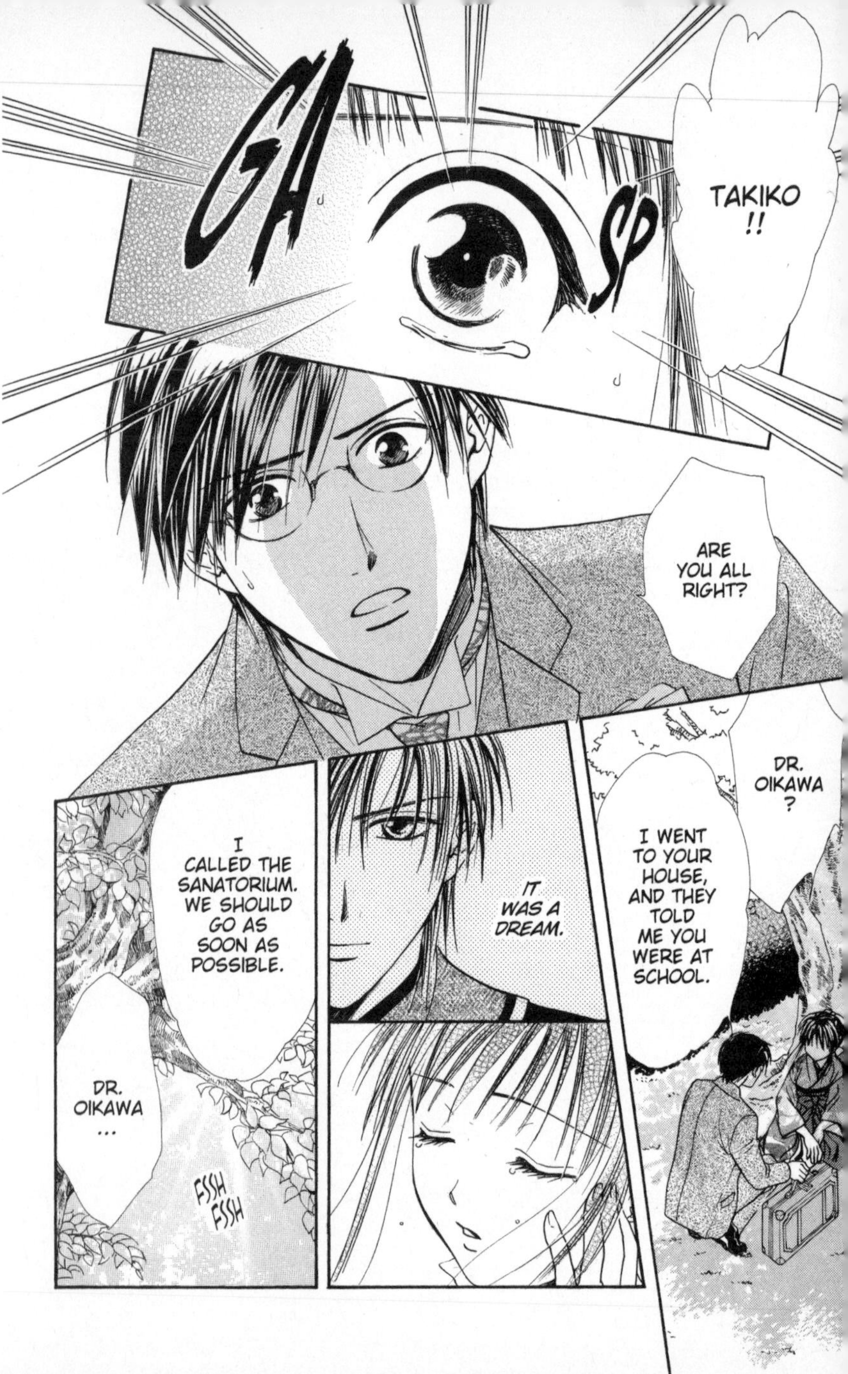
GASP
TAKIKO !!
ARE YOU ALL RIGHT?
DR. OIKAWA ?
I WENT TO YOUR HOUSE, AND THEY TOLD ME YOU WERE AT SCHOOL.
IT WAS A DREAM.
I CALLED THE SANATORIUM. WE SHOULD GO AS SOON AS POSSIBLE.
DR. OIKAWA ...
FSSH FSSH

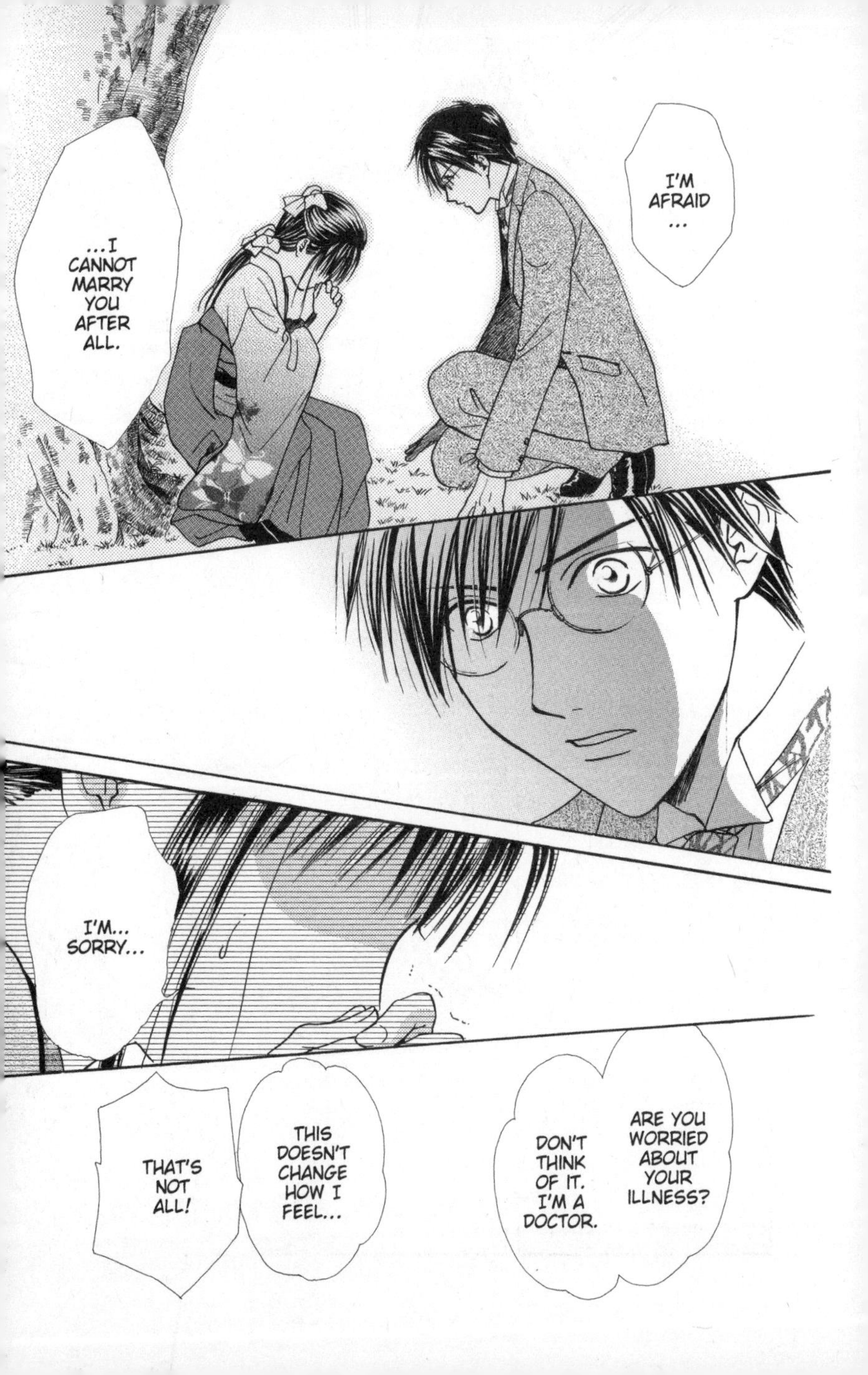
I'M AFRAID ...
...I CANNOT MARRY YOU AFTER ALL.
I'M... SORRY...
ARE YOU WORRIED ABOUT YOUR ILLNESS?
DON'T THINK OF IT. I'M A DOCTOR.
THIS DOESN'T CHANGE HOW I FEEL...
THAT'S NOT ALL!

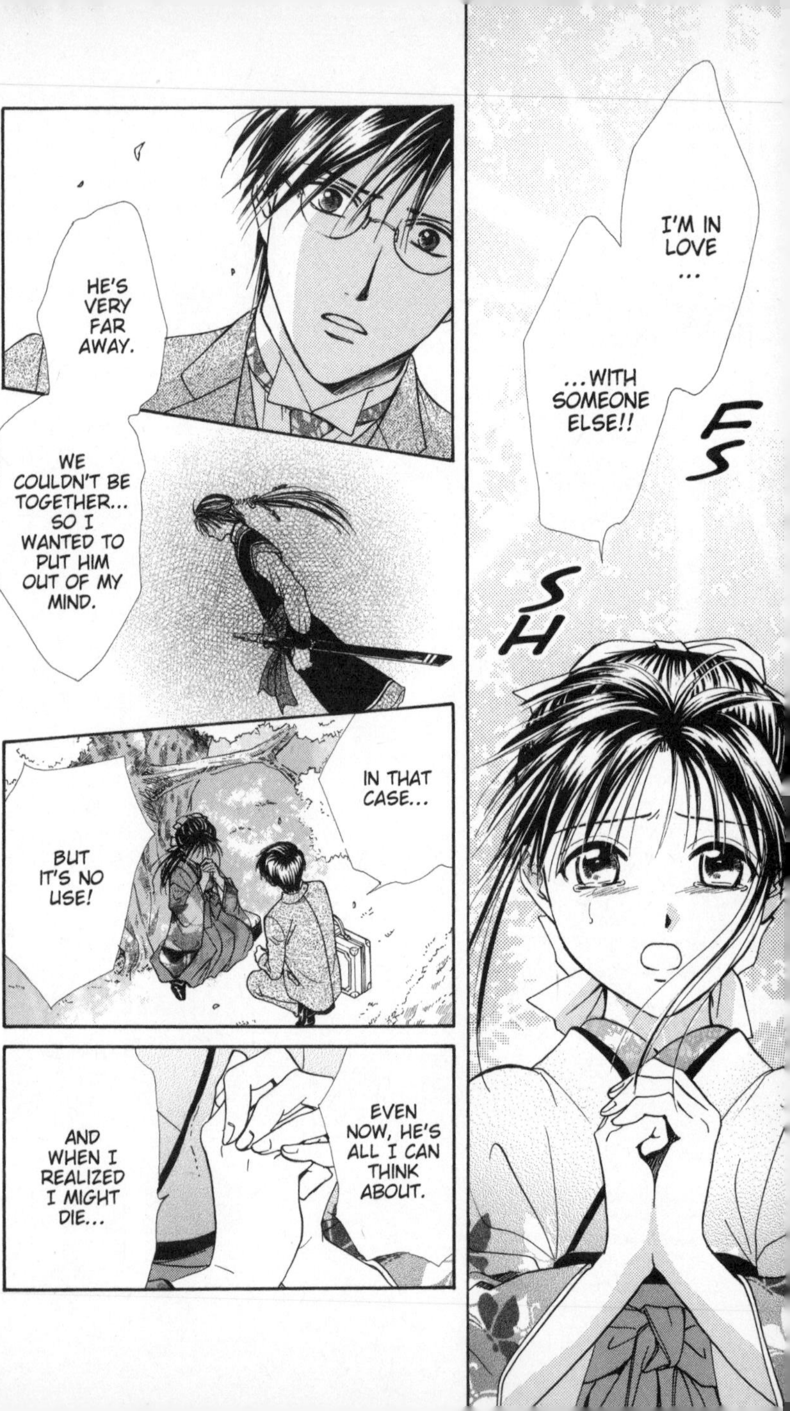
I'M IN LOVE ...
...WITH SOMEONE ELSE!!
FS
SH
HE'S VERY FAR AWAY.
WE COULDN'T BE TOGETHER... SO I WANTED TO PUT HIM OUT OF MY MIND.
IN THAT CASE...
BUT IT'S NO USE!
EVEN NOW, HE'S ALL I CAN THINK ABOUT.
AND WHEN I REALIZED I MIGHT DIE...

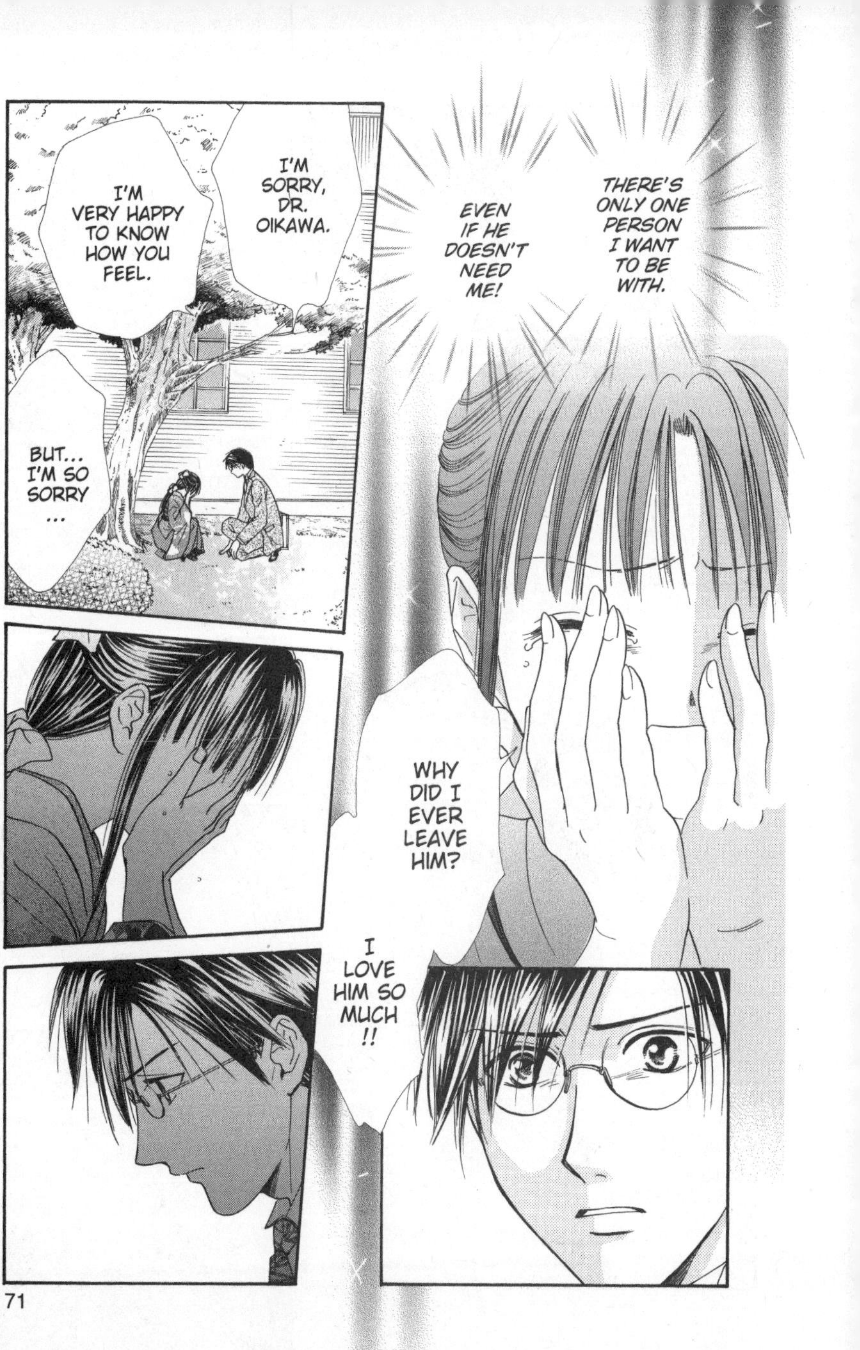
THERE'S ONLY ONE PERSON I WANT TO BE WITH.
EVEN IF HE DOESN'T NEED ME!
WHY DID I EVER LEAVE HIM?
I LOVE HIM SO MUCH !!
I'M SORRY, DR. OIKAWA.
I'M VERY HAPPY TO KNOW HOW YOU FEEL.
BUT... I'M SO SORRY ...

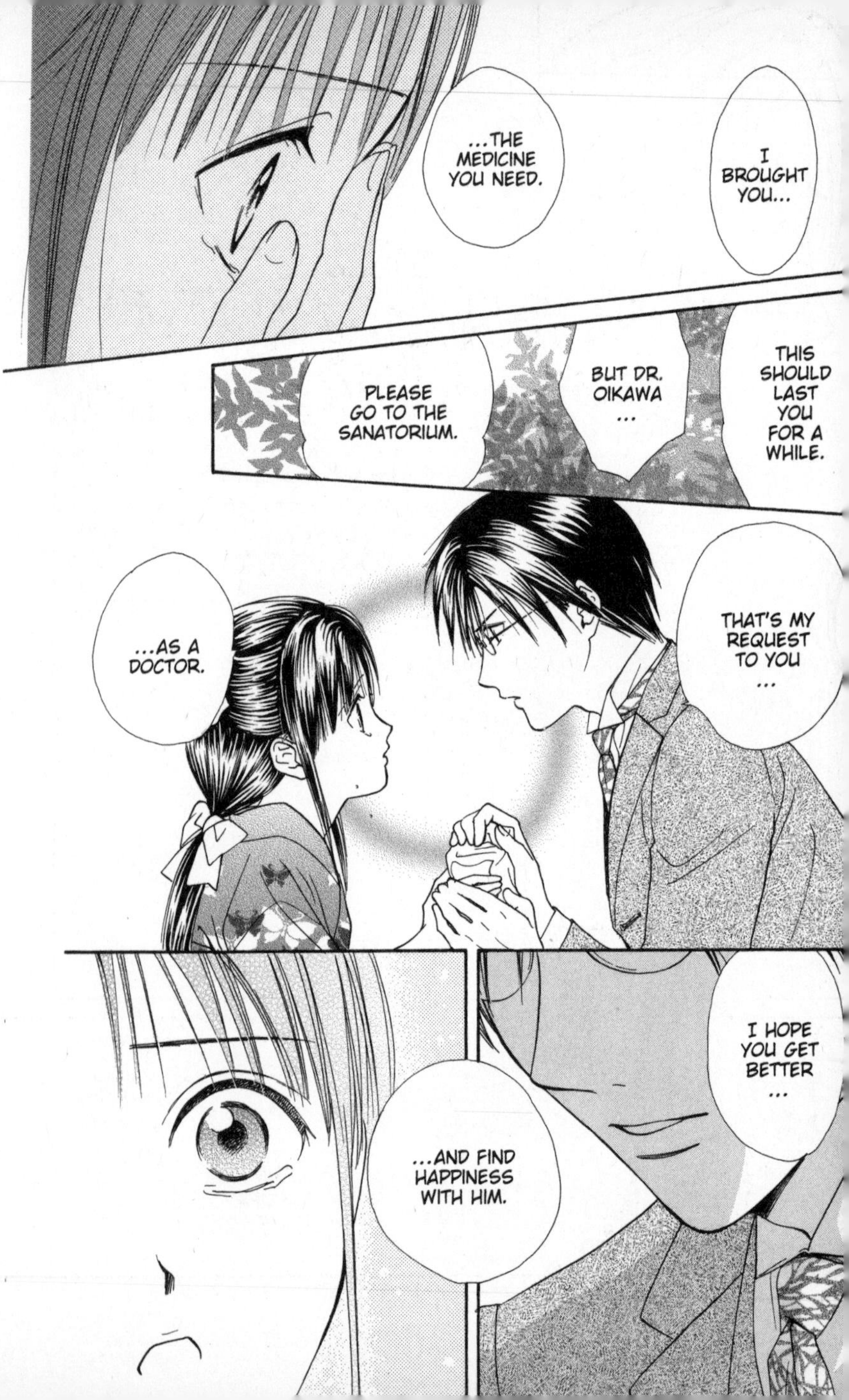
I BROUGHT YOU...
...THE MEDICINE YOU NEED.
THIS SHOULD LAST YOU FOR A WHILE.
BUT DR. OIKAWA ...
PLEASE GO TO THE SANATORIUM.
THAT'S MY REQUEST TO YOU ...
...AS A DOCTOR.
I HOPE YOU GET BETTER ...
...AND FIND HAPPINESS WITH HIM.

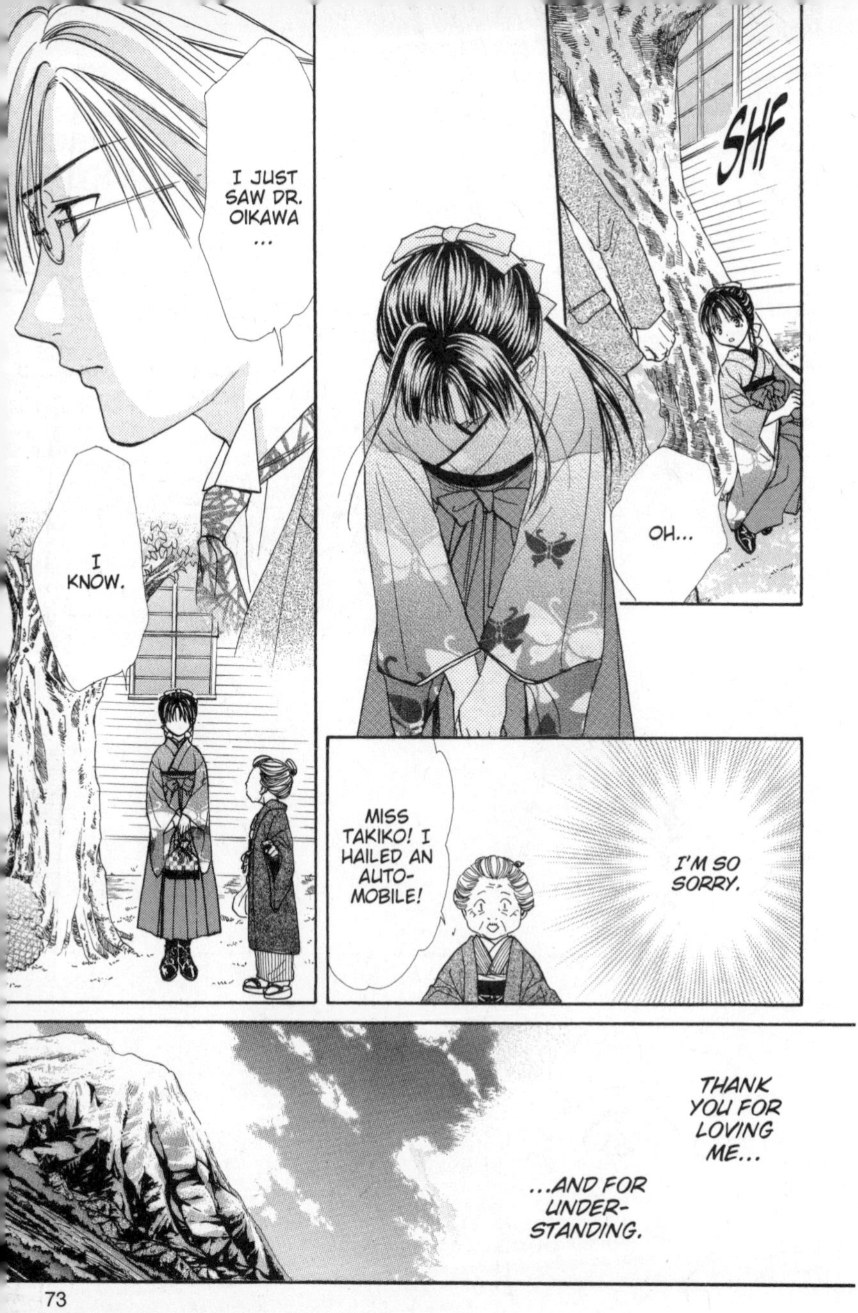
SHF
OH...
I'M SO SORRY.
MISS TAKIKO! I HAILED AN AUTO-MOBILE!
I JUST SAW DR. OIKAWA ...
I KNOW.
THANK YOU FOR LOVING ME...
...AND FOR UNDER-STANDING.

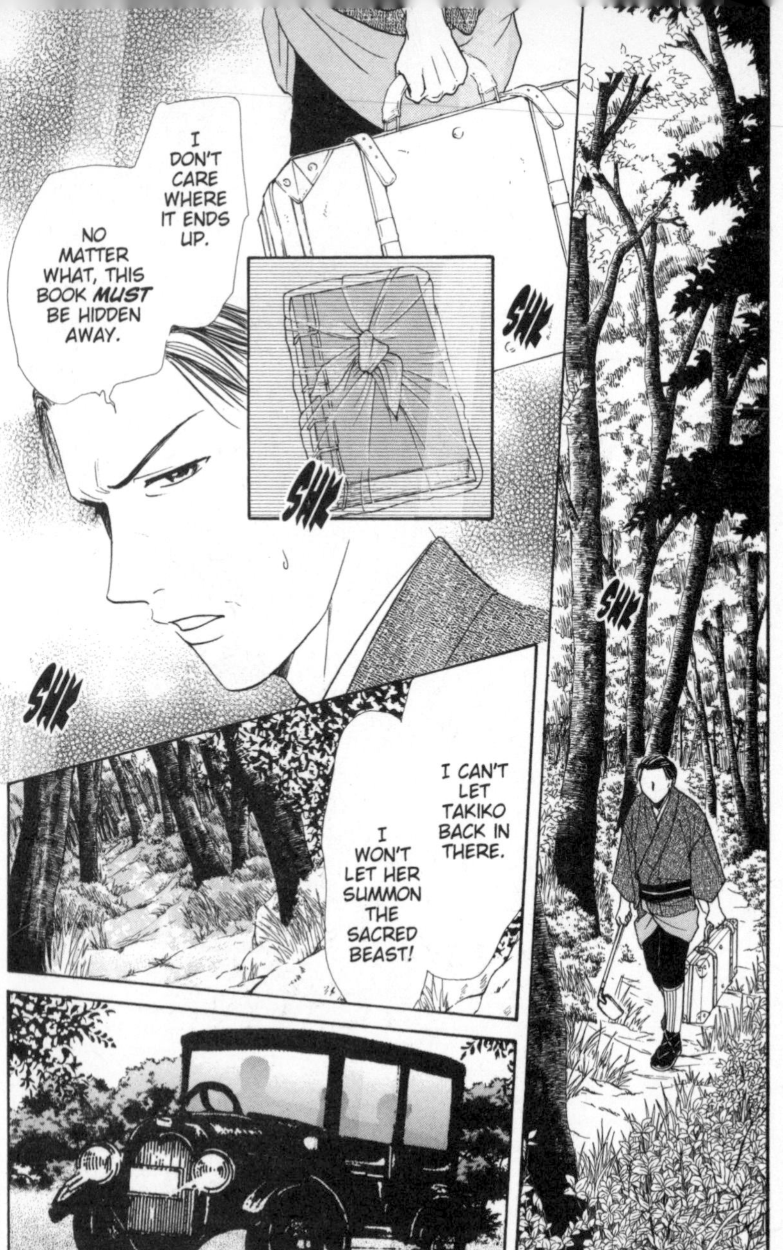
SHK
I DON'T CARE WHERE IT ENDS UP.
NO MATTER WHAT, THIS BOOK *MUST* BE HIDDEN AWAY.
SHK
SHK
SHK
I CAN'T LET TAKIKO BACK IN THERE.
I WON'T LET HER SUMMON THE SACRED BEAST!

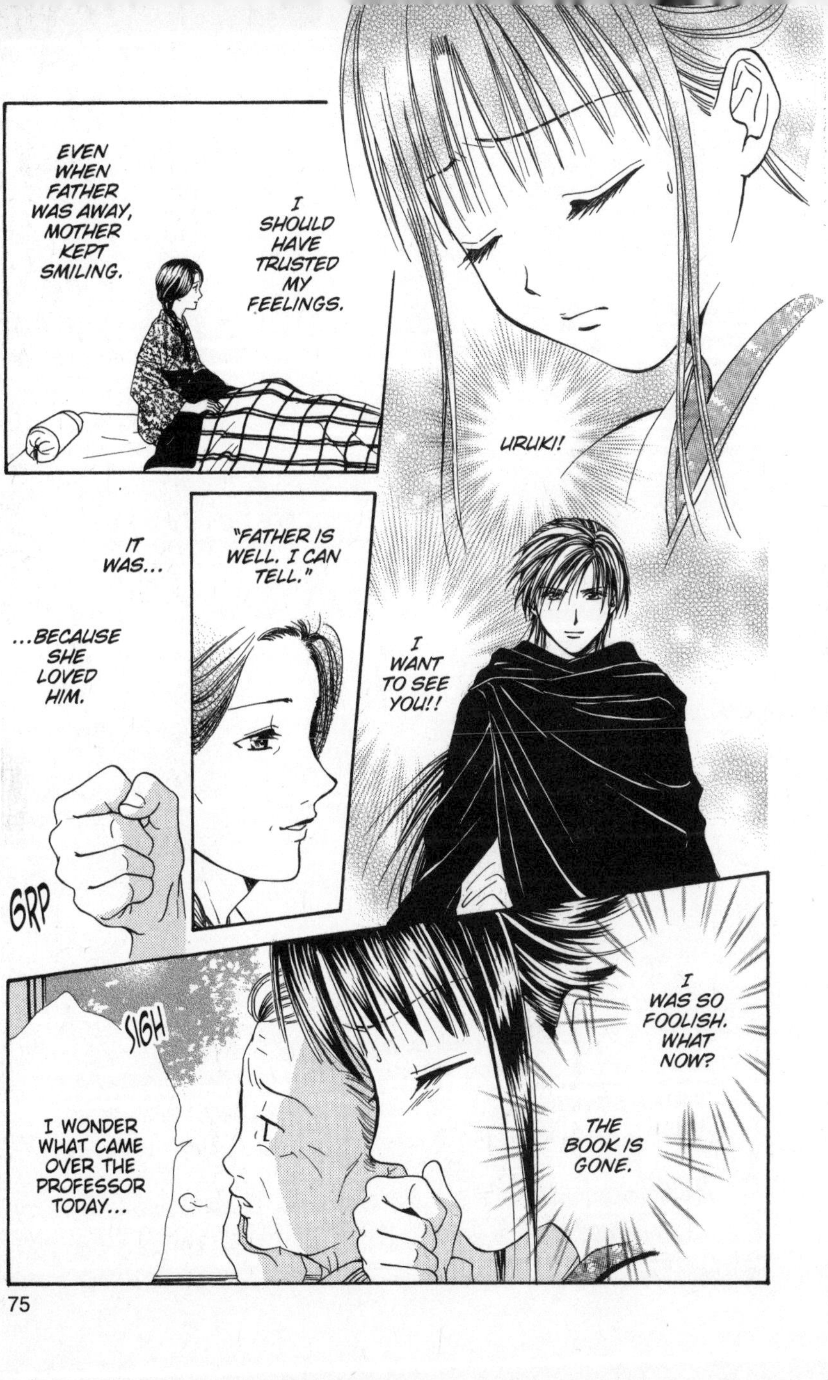
I SHOULD HAVE TRUSTED MY FEELINGS.
URUKI!
I WANT TO SEE YOU!!
EVEN WHEN FATHER WAS AWAY, MOTHER KEPT SMILING.
"FATHER IS WELL. I CAN TELL."
IT WAS...
...BECAUSE SHE LOVED HIM.
GRP
I WAS SO FOOLISH. WHAT NOW?
THE BOOK IS GONE.
SIGH
I WONDER WHAT CAME OVER THE PROFESSOR TODAY...

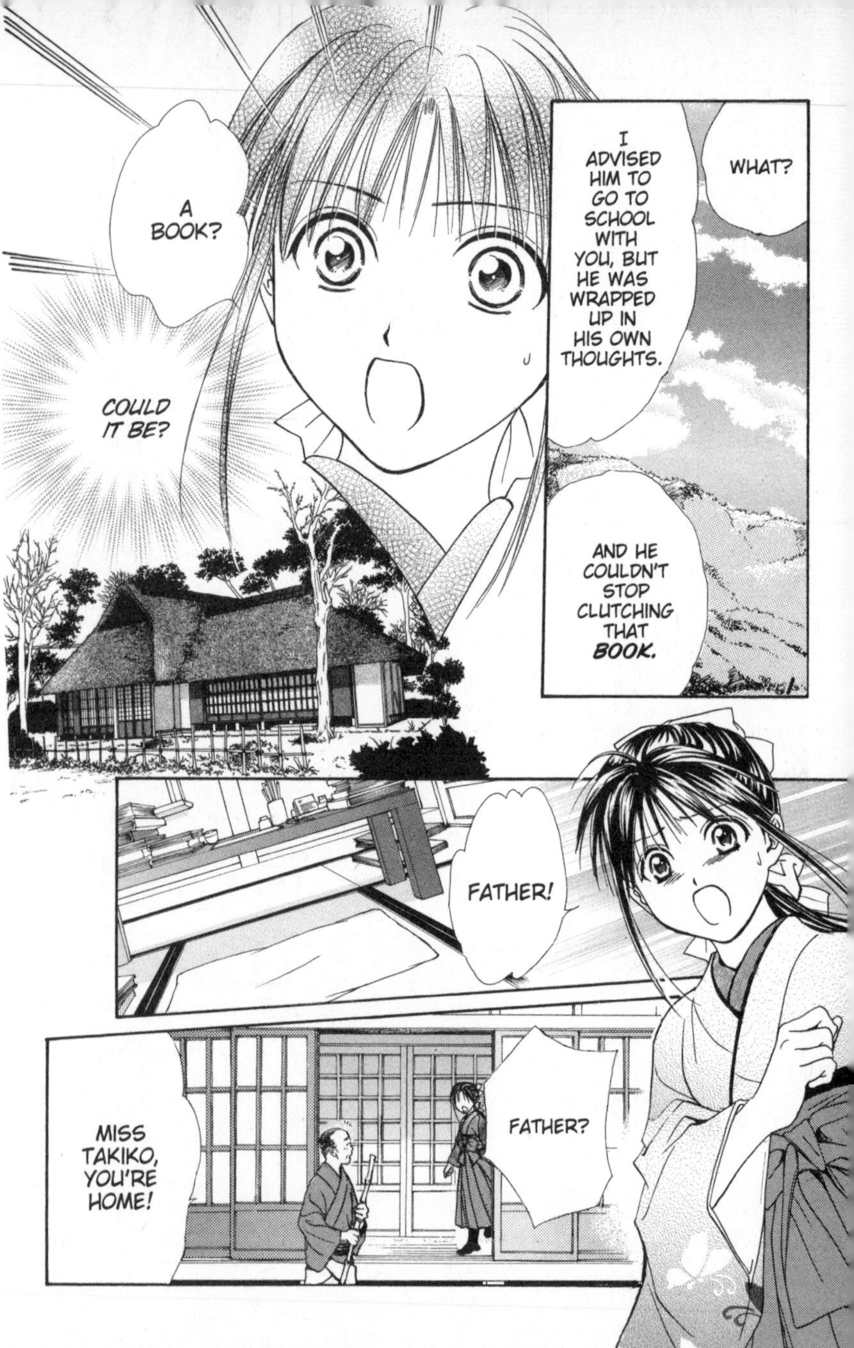
WHAT?
I ADVISED HIM TO GO TO SCHOOL WITH YOU, BUT HE WAS WRAPPED UP IN HIS OWN THOUGHTS.
AND HE COULDN'T STOP CLUTCHING THAT BOOK.
A BOOK?
COULD IT BE?
FATHER!
FATHER?
MISS TAKIKO, YOU'RE HOME!

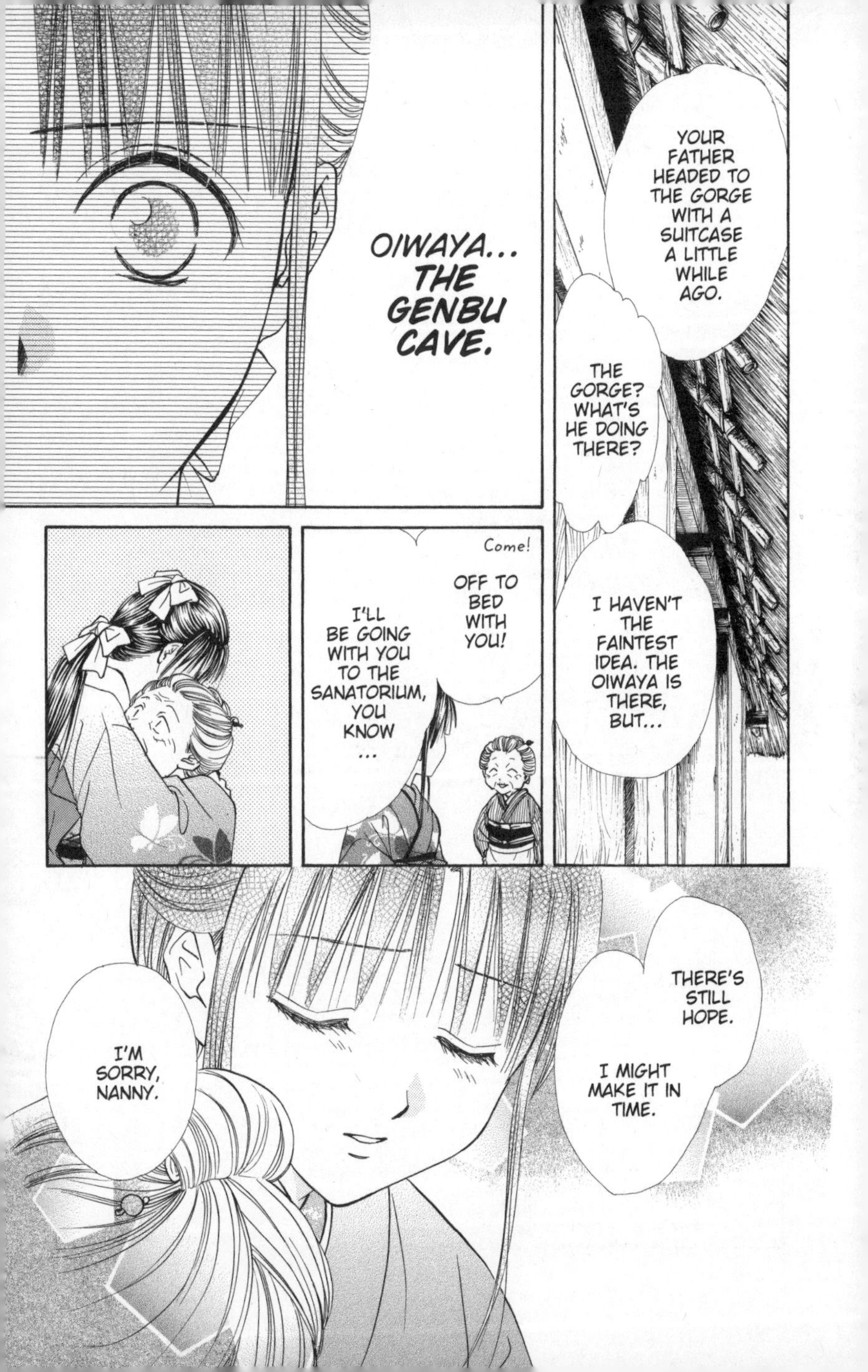
YOUR FATHER HEADED TO THE GORGE WITH A SUITCASE A LITTLE WHILE AGO.
THE GORGE? WHAT'S HE DOING THERE?
I HAVEN'T THE FAINTEST IDEA. THE OIWAYA IS THERE, BUT...
OIWAYA... THE GENBU CAVE.
Come!
OFF TO BED WITH YOU!
I'LL BE GOING WITH YOU TO THE SANATORIUM, YOU KNOW ...
THERE'S STILL HOPE.
I MIGHT MAKE IT IN TIME.
I'M SORRY, NANNY.

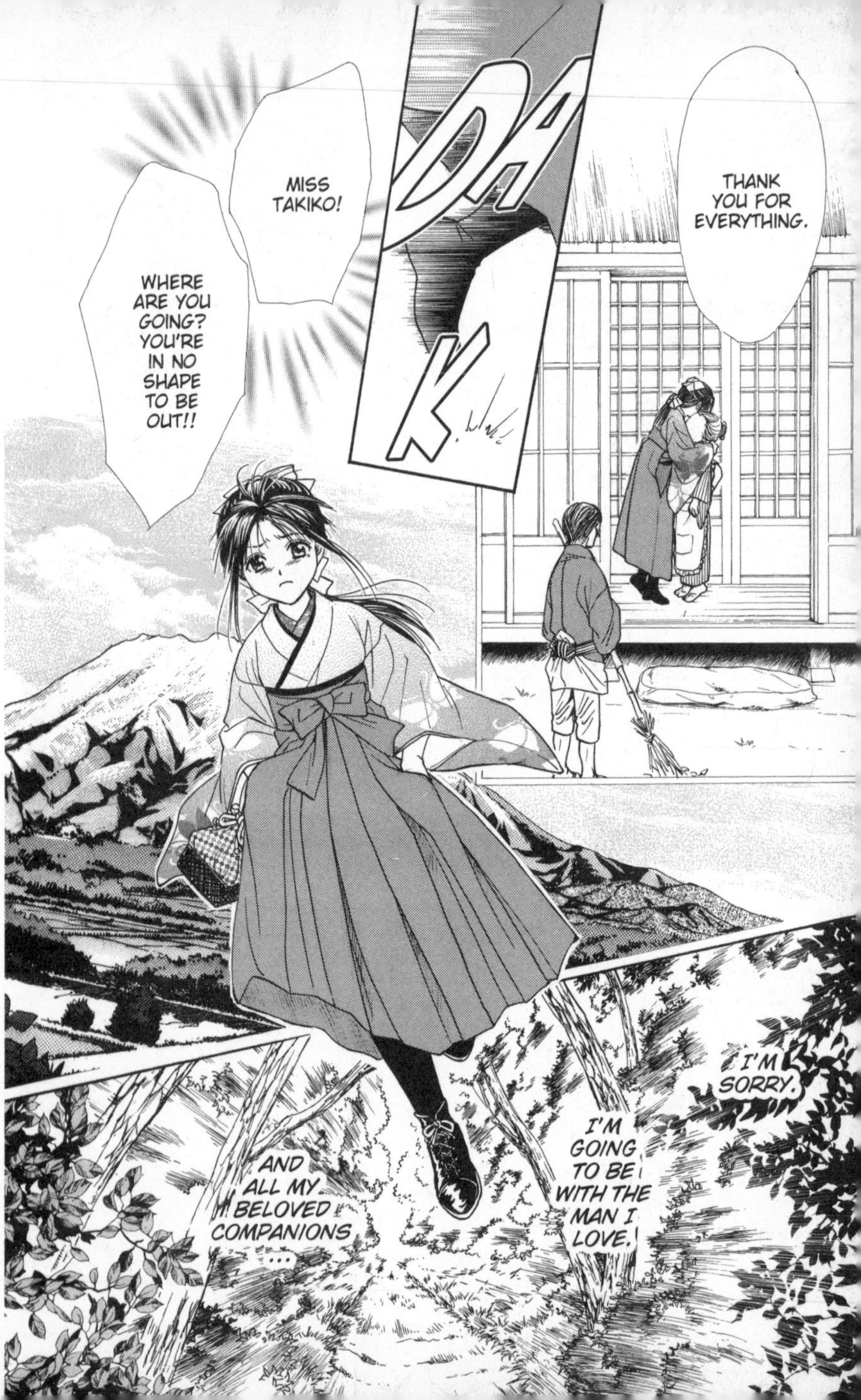
THANK YOU FOR EVERYTHING.
DAK
MISS TAKIKO!
WHERE ARE YOU GOING? YOU'RE IN NO SHAPE TO BE OUT!!
I'M SORRY.
I'M GOING TO BE WITH THE MAN I LOVE.
AND ALL MY BELOVED COMPANIONS ...

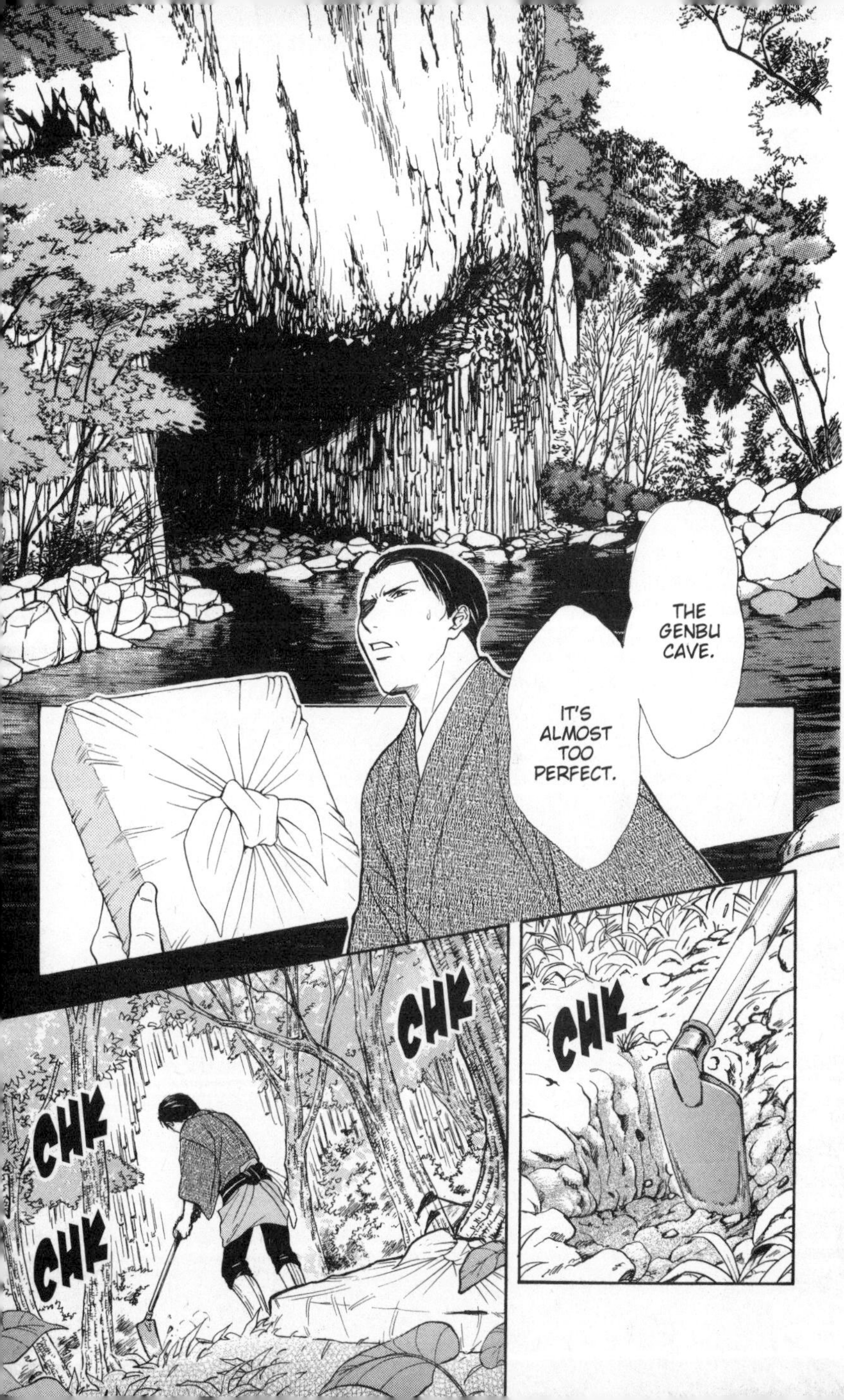
THE GENBU CAVE.
IT'S ALMOST TOO PERFECT.
CHK
CHK
CHK
CHK

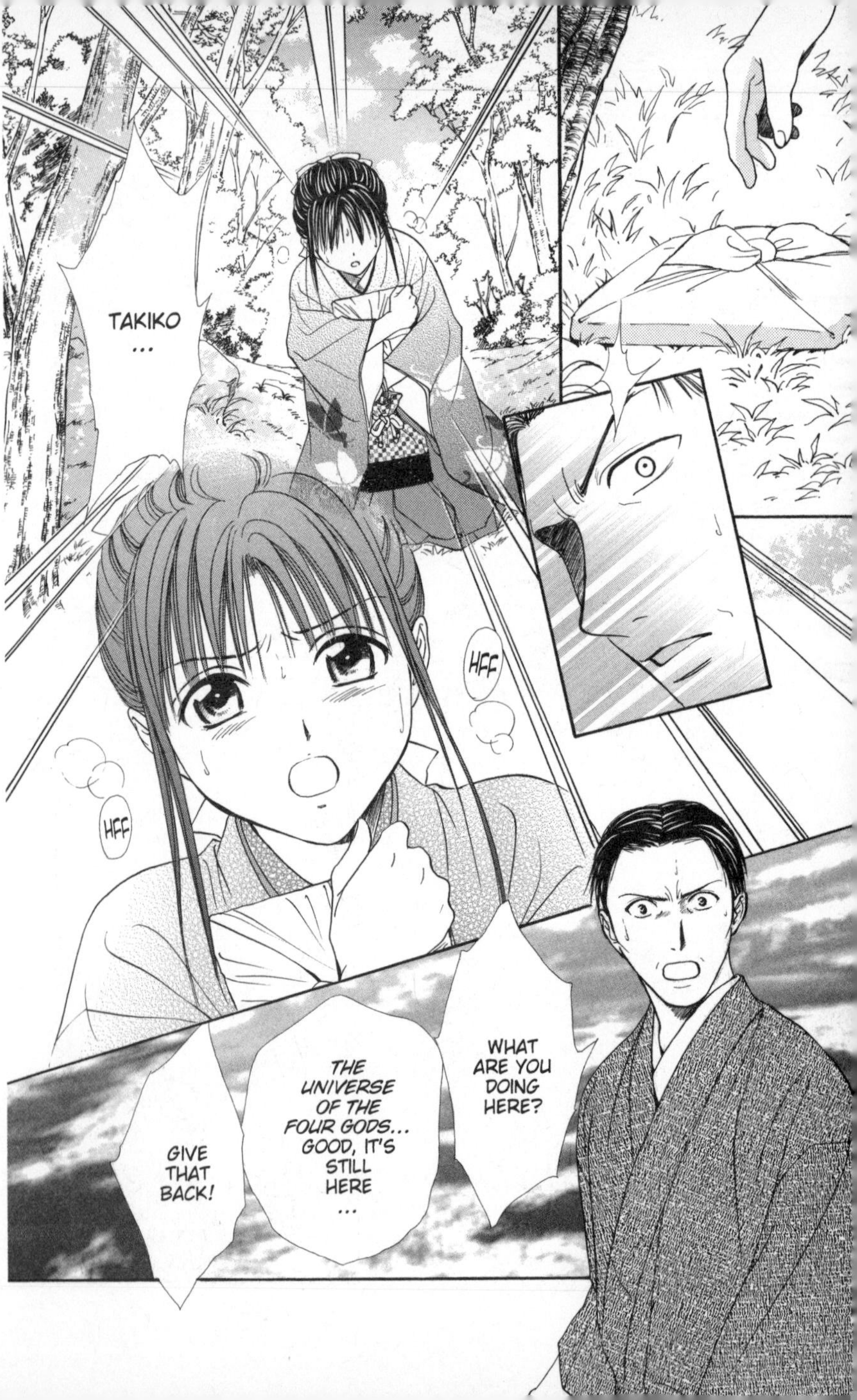
TAKIKO ...
HFF
HFF
WHAT ARE YOU DOING HERE?
THE UNIVERSE OF THE FOUR GODS... GOOD, IT'S STILL HERE ...
GIVE THAT BACK!

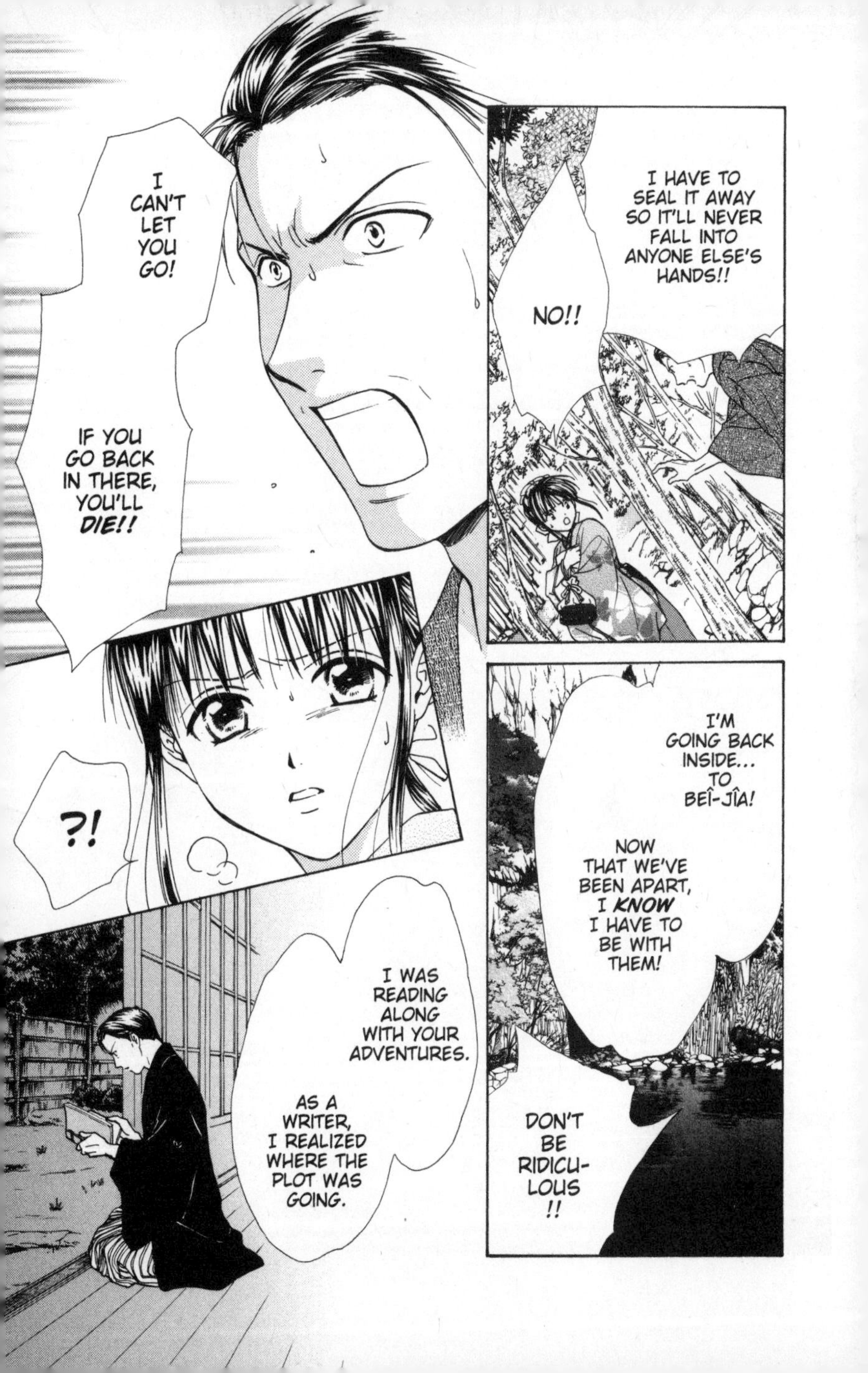
I HAVE TO SEAL IT AWAY SO IT'LL NEVER FALL INTO ANYONE ELSE'S HANDS!!
NO!!
I'M GOING BACK INSIDE... TO BEÎ-JÎA!
NOW THAT WE'VE BEEN APART, I *KNOW* I HAVE TO BE WITH THEM!
DON'T BE RIDICU-LOUS !!
I CAN'T LET YOU GO!
IF YOU GO BACK IN THERE, YOU'LL *DIE!!*
?!
I WAS READING ALONG WITH YOUR ADVENTURES.
AS A WRITER, I REALIZED WHERE THE PLOT WAS GOING.

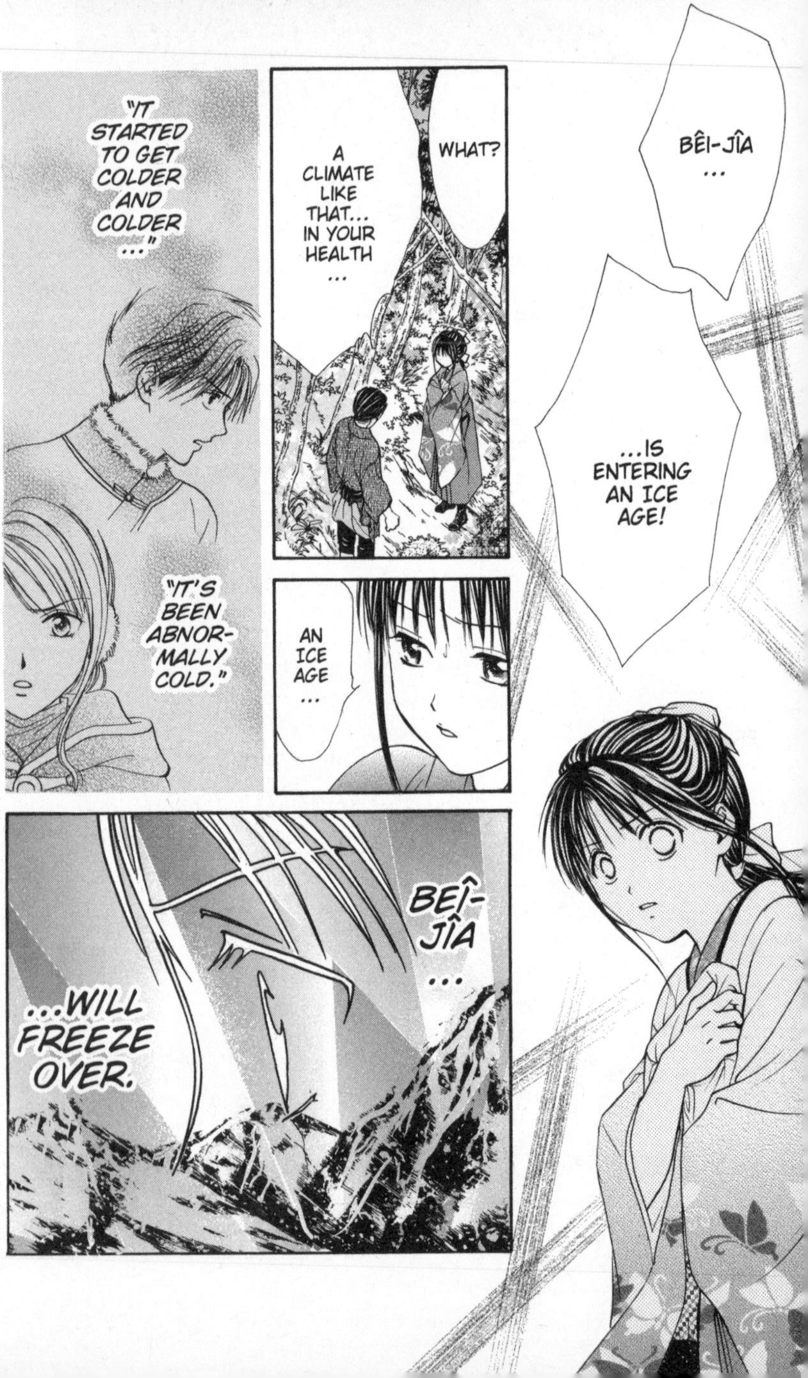
BÊI-JÎA ...
...IS ENTERING AN ICE AGE!
WHAT?
A CLIMATE LIKE THAT... IN YOUR HEALTH ...
"IT STARTED TO GET COLDER AND COLDER ..."
"IT'S BEEN ABNORMALLY COLD."
AN ICE AGE ...
BEÎ-JÎA ...
...WILL FREEZE OVER.

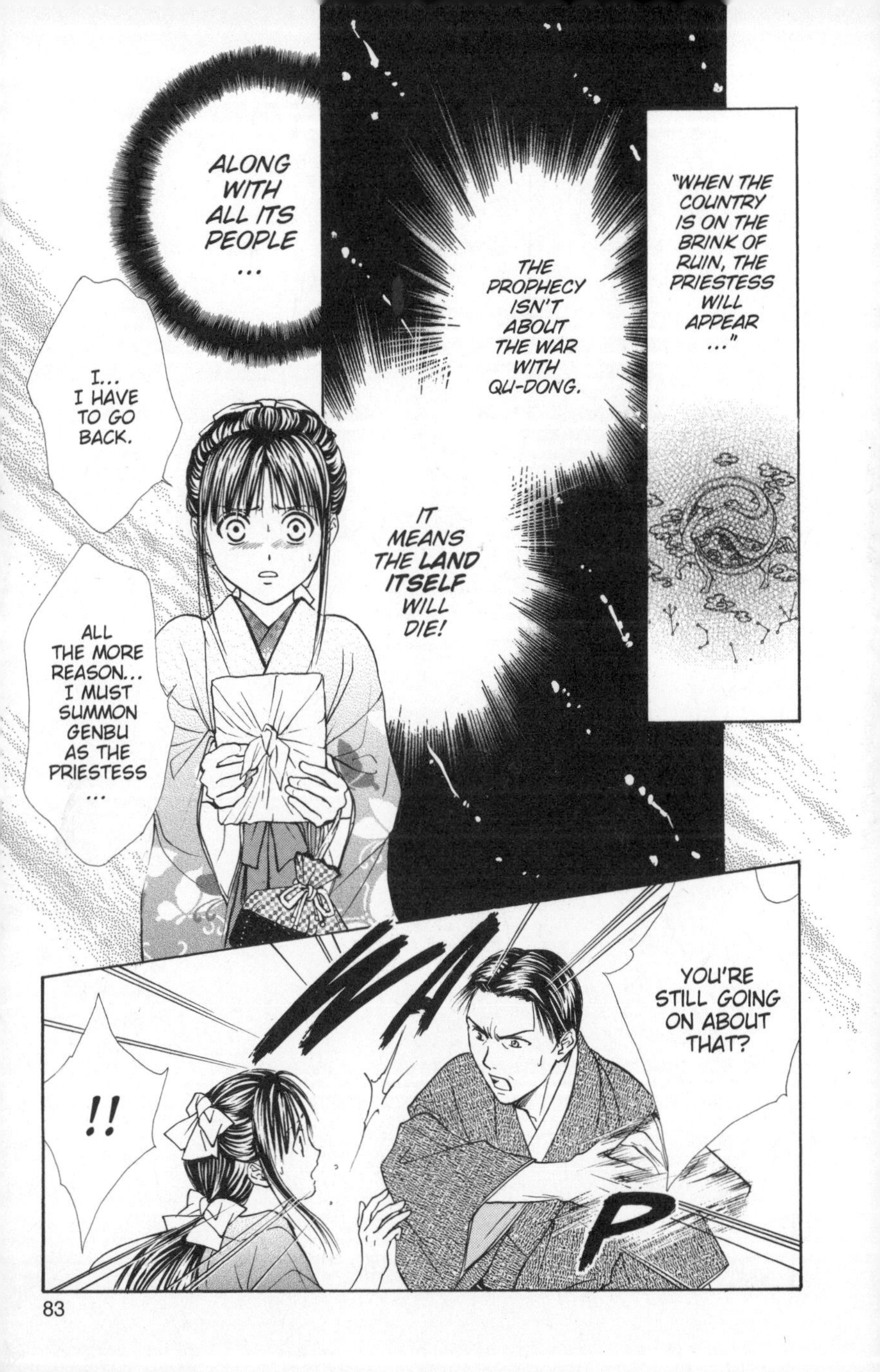
"WHEN THE COUNTRY IS ON THE BRINK OF RUIN, THE PRIESTESS WILL APPEAR..."
THE PROPHECY ISN'T ABOUT THE WAR WITH QU-DONG.
IT MEANS THE LAND ITSELF WILL DIE!
ALONG WITH ALL ITS PEOPLE...
I... I HAVE TO GO BACK.
ALL THE MORE REASON... I MUST SUMMON GENBU AS THE PRIESTESS...
YOU'RE STILL GOING ON ABOUT THAT?
WA
P
!!

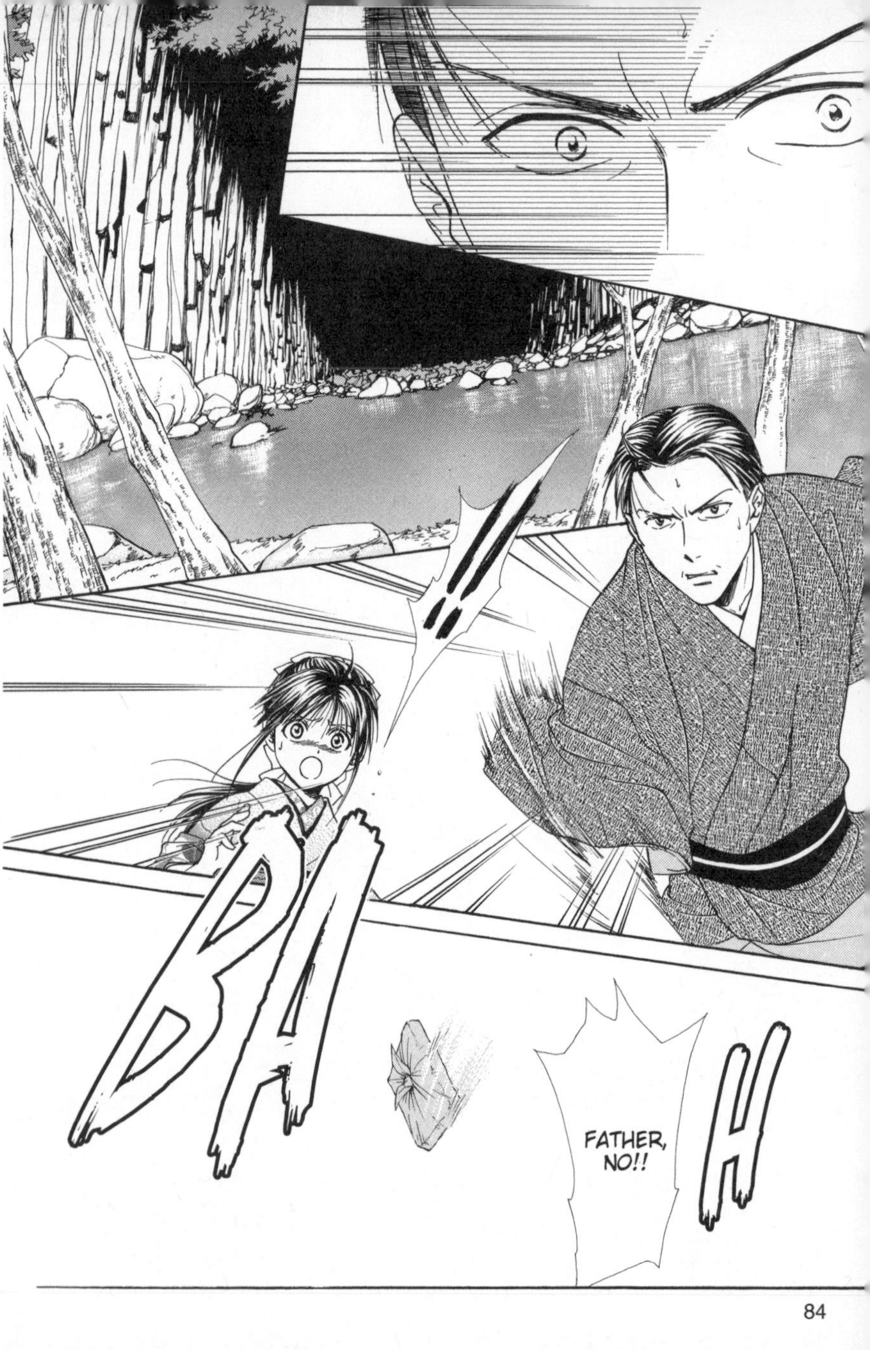
BAM
FATHER, NO!!
H

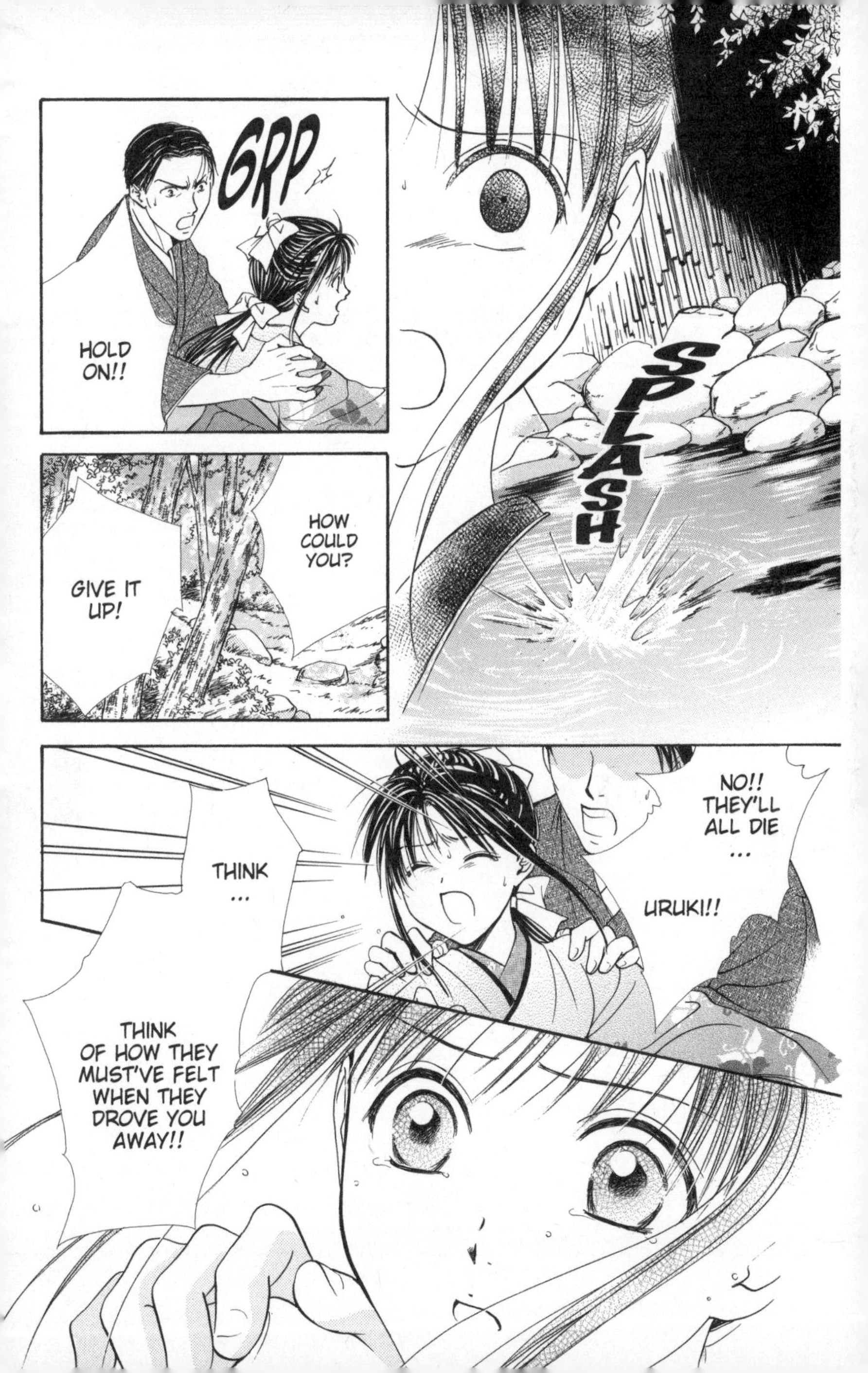
SPLASH
GRP
HOLD ON!!
HOW COULD YOU?
GIVE IT UP!
NO!! THEY'LL ALL DIE ...
URUKI!!
THINK ...
THINK OF HOW THEY MUST'VE FELT WHEN THEY DROVE YOU AWAY!!

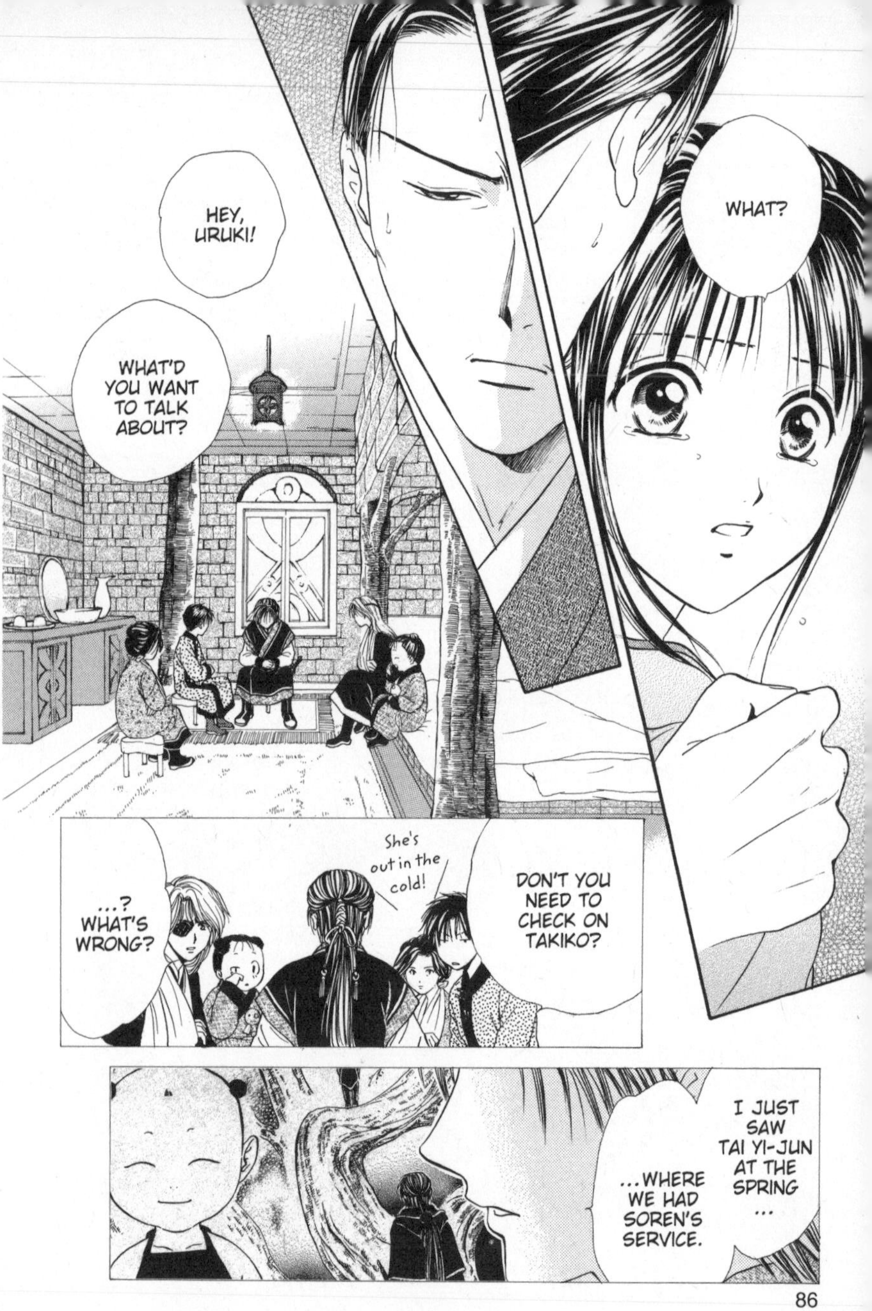
WHAT?
HEY, URUKI!
WHAT'D YOU WANT TO TALK ABOUT?
DON'T YOU NEED TO CHECK ON TAKIKO?
She's out in the cold!
...? WHAT'S WRONG?
I JUST SAW TAI YI-JUN AT THE SPRING ...
...WHERE WE HAD SOREN'S SERVICE.

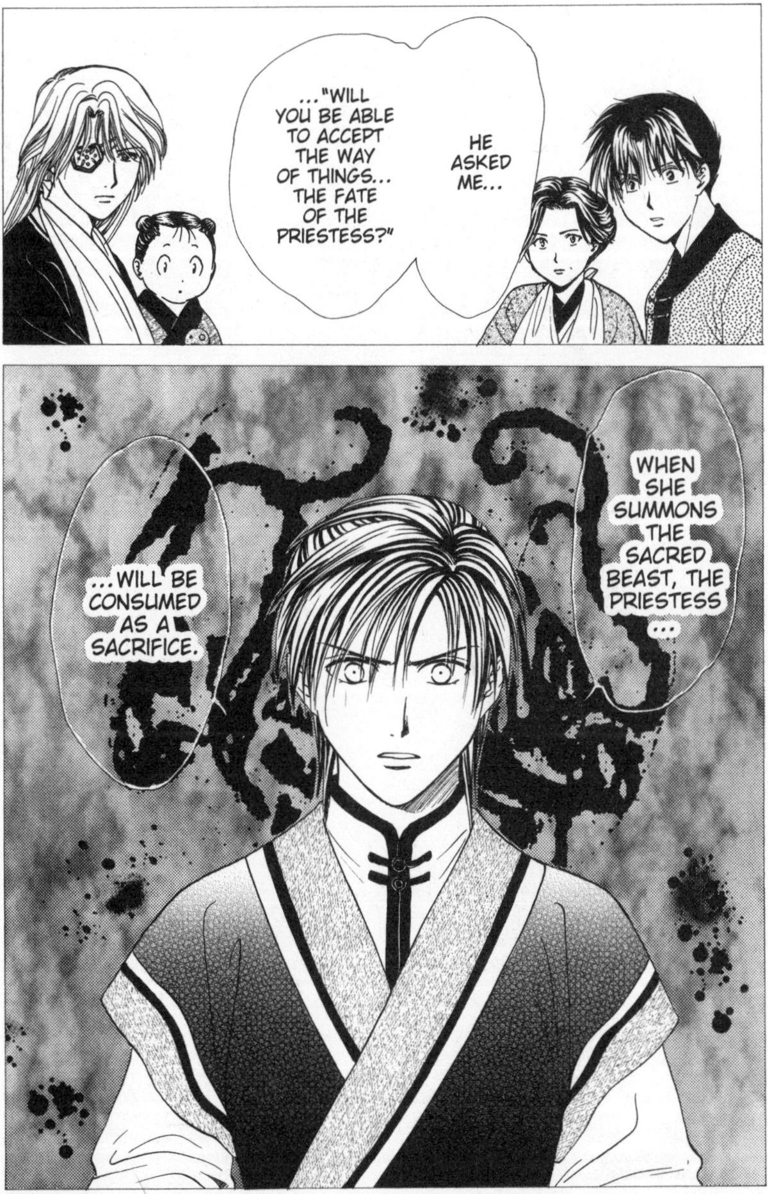
HE ASKED ME...
..."WILL YOU BE ABLE TO ACCEPT THE WAY OF THINGS... THE FATE OF THE PRIESTESS?"
WHEN SHE SUMMONS THE SACRED BEAST, THE PRIESTESS ...
...WILL BE CONSUMED AS A SACRIFICE.

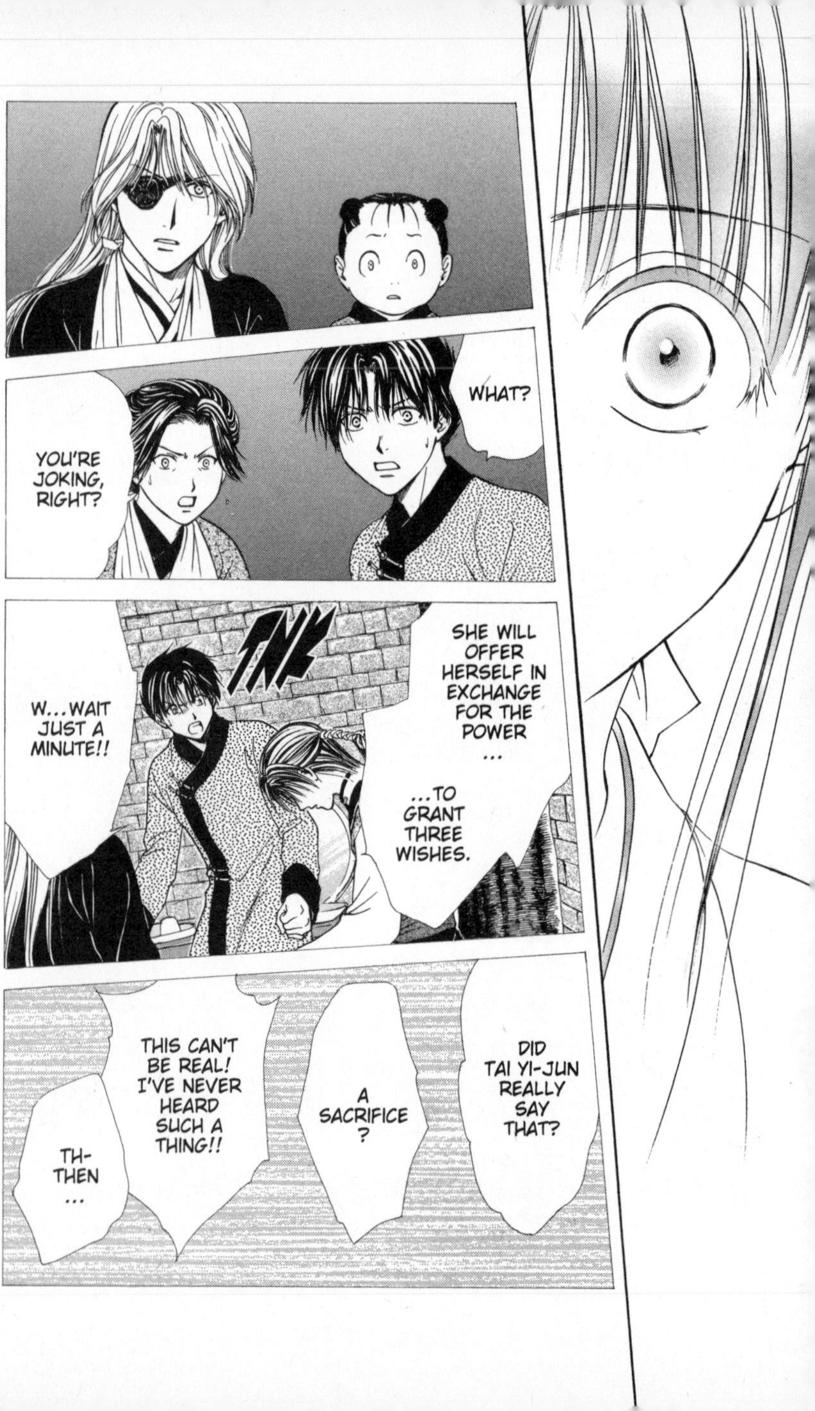
WHAT?
YOU'RE JOKING, RIGHT?
SHE WILL OFFER HERSELF IN EXCHANGE FOR THE POWER ...
TNK
...TO GRANT THREE WISHES.
W...WAIT JUST A MINUTE!!
DID TAI YI-JUN REALLY SAY THAT?
A SACRIFICE?
THIS CAN'T BE REAL! I'VE NEVER HEARD SUCH A THING!!
TH-THEN ...

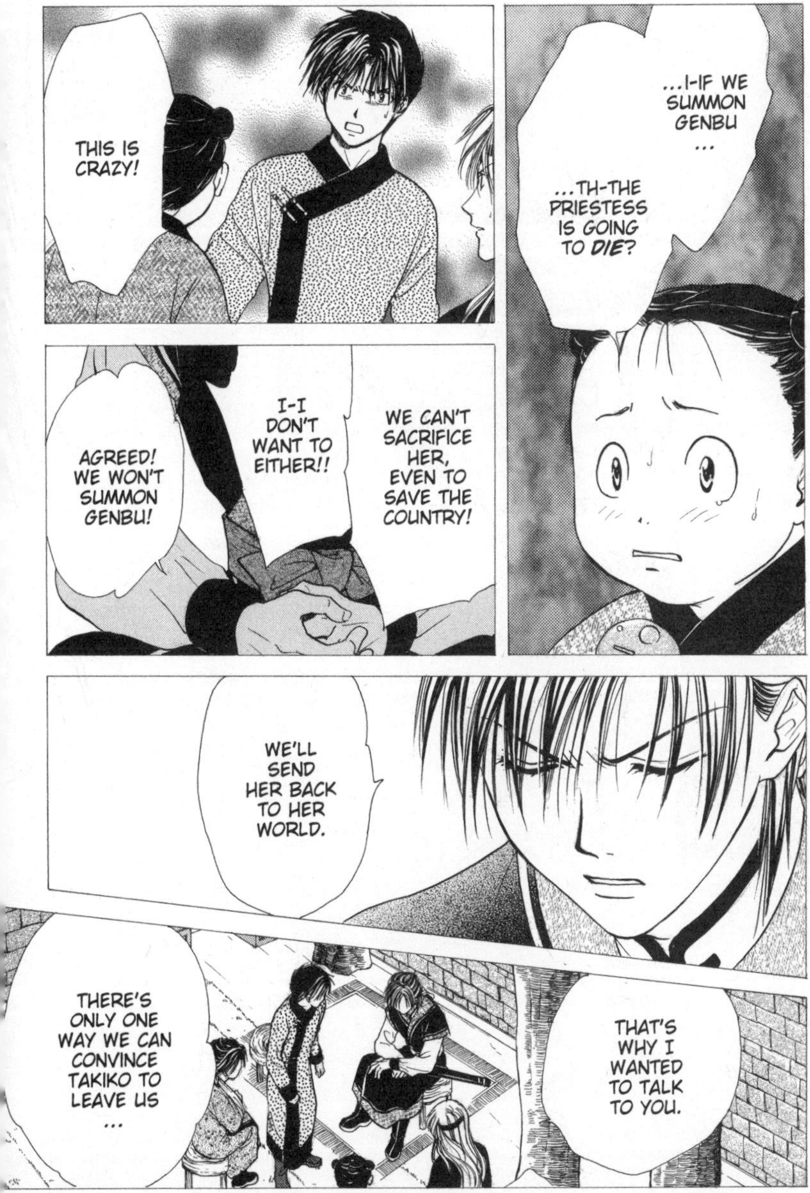

...I-IF WE SUMMON GENBU ...
...TH-THE PRIESTESS IS GOING TO *DIE*?
THIS IS CRAZY!
WE CAN'T SACRIFICE HER, EVEN TO SAVE THE COUNTRY!
I-I DON'T WANT TO EITHER!!
AGREED! WE WON'T SUMMON GENBU!
WE'LL SEND HER BACK TO HER WORLD.
THAT'S WHY I WANTED TO TALK TO YOU.
THERE'S ONLY ONE WAY WE CAN CONVINCE TAKIKO TO LEAVE US ...

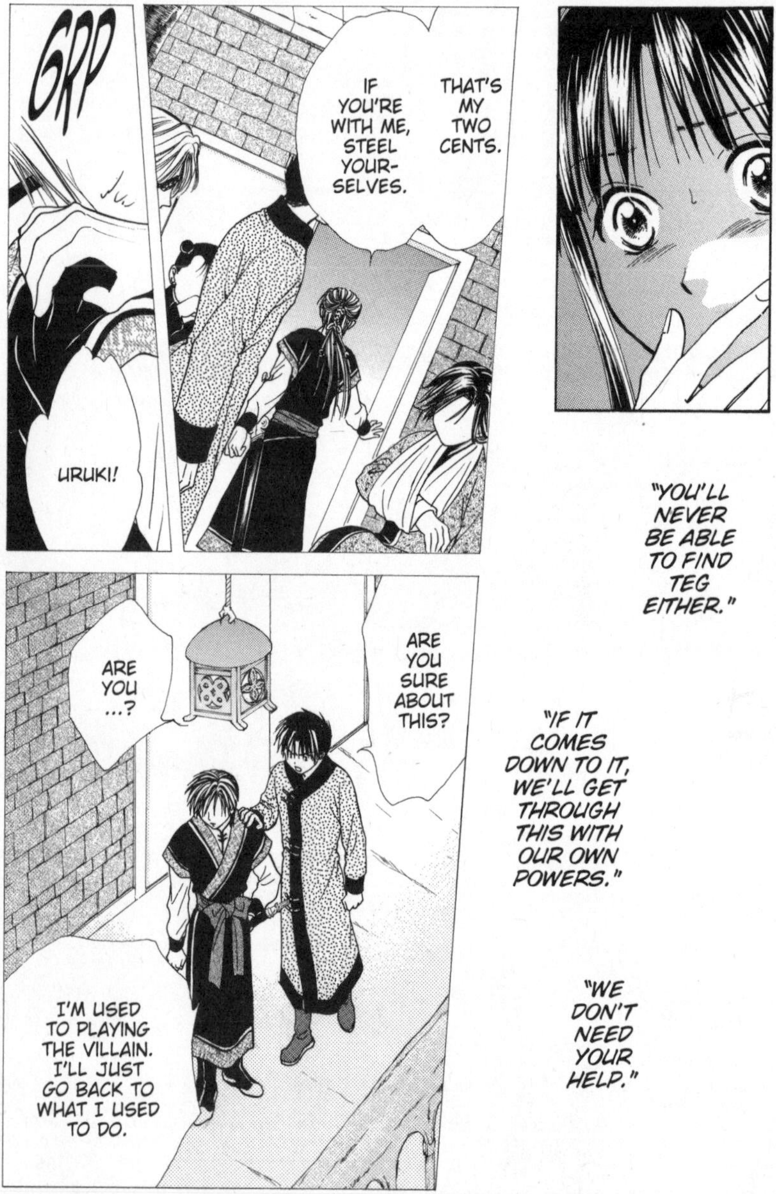
IF YOU'RE WITH ME, STEEL YOUR-SELVES.
THAT'S MY TWO CENTS.
GRP
URUKI!
"YOU'LL NEVER BE ABLE TO FIND TEG EITHER."
"IF IT COMES DOWN TO IT, WE'LL GET THROUGH THIS WITH OUR OWN POWERS."
"WE DON'T NEED YOUR HELP."
ARE YOU SURE ABOUT THIS?
ARE YOU ...?
I'M USED TO PLAYING THE VILLAIN. I'LL JUST GO BACK TO WHAT I USED TO DO.

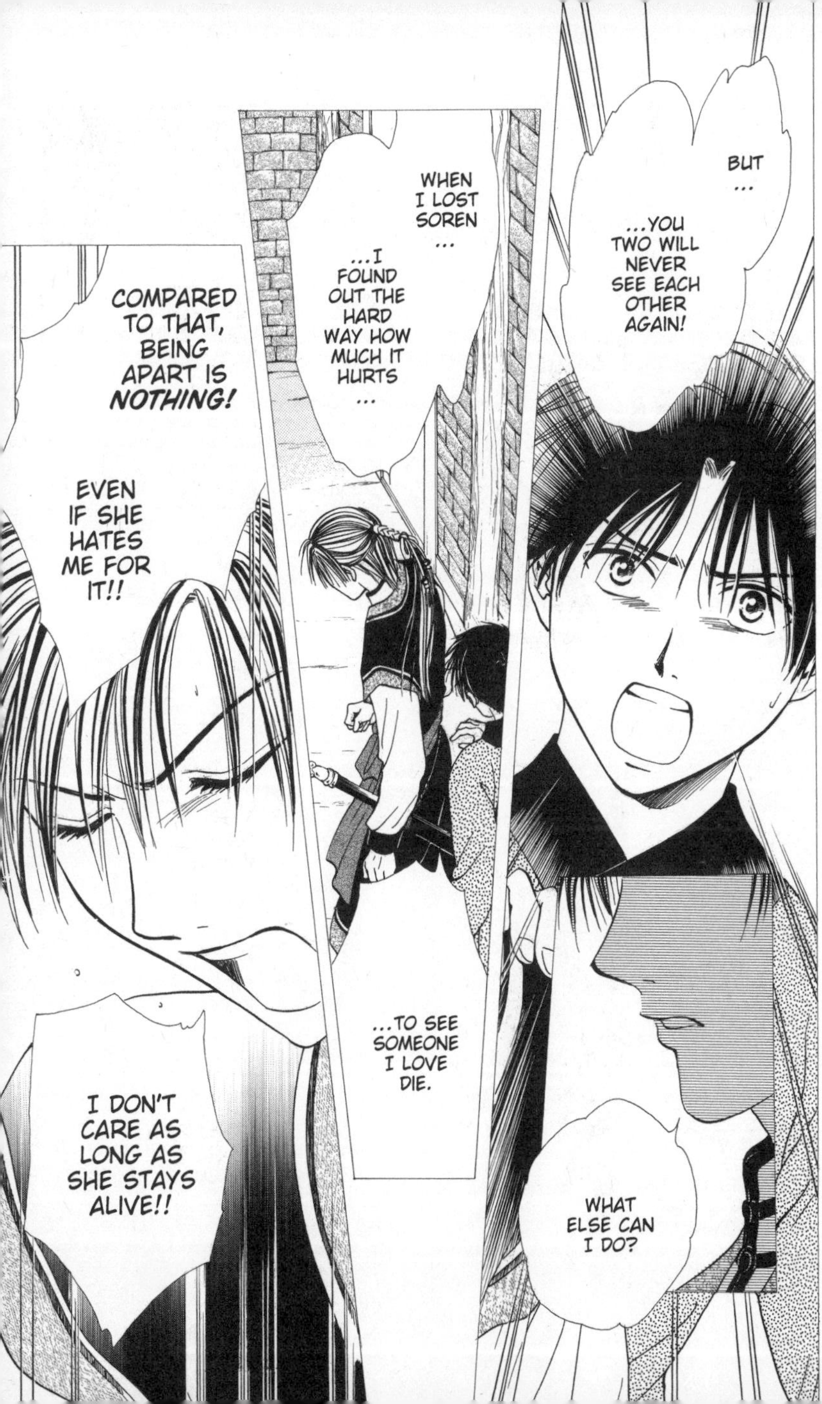
BUT ...
...YOU TWO WILL NEVER SEE EACH OTHER AGAIN!
WHAT ELSE CAN I DO?
WHEN I LOST SOREN ...
...I FOUND OUT THE HARD WAY HOW MUCH IT HURTS ...
...TO SEE SOMEONE I LOVE DIE.
COMPARED TO THAT, BEING APART IS *NOTHING!*
EVEN IF SHE HATES ME FOR IT!!
I DON'T CARE AS LONG AS SHE STAYS ALIVE!!

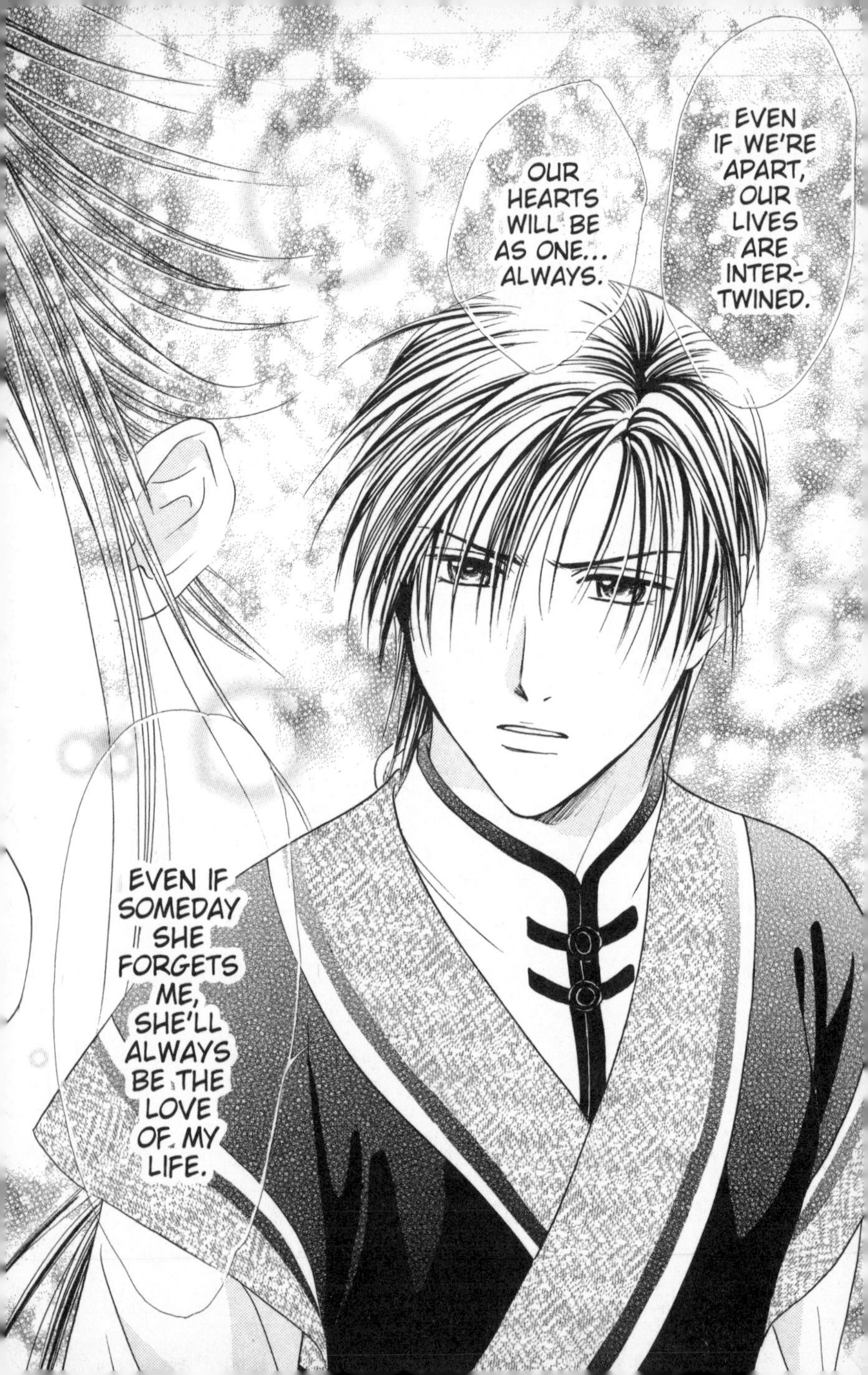
EVEN IF WE'RE APART, OUR LIVES ARE INTER-TWINED.
OUR HEARTS WILL BE AS ONE... ALWAYS.
EVEN IF SOMEDAY SHE FORGETS ME, SHE'LL ALWAYS BE THE LOVE OF MY LIFE.

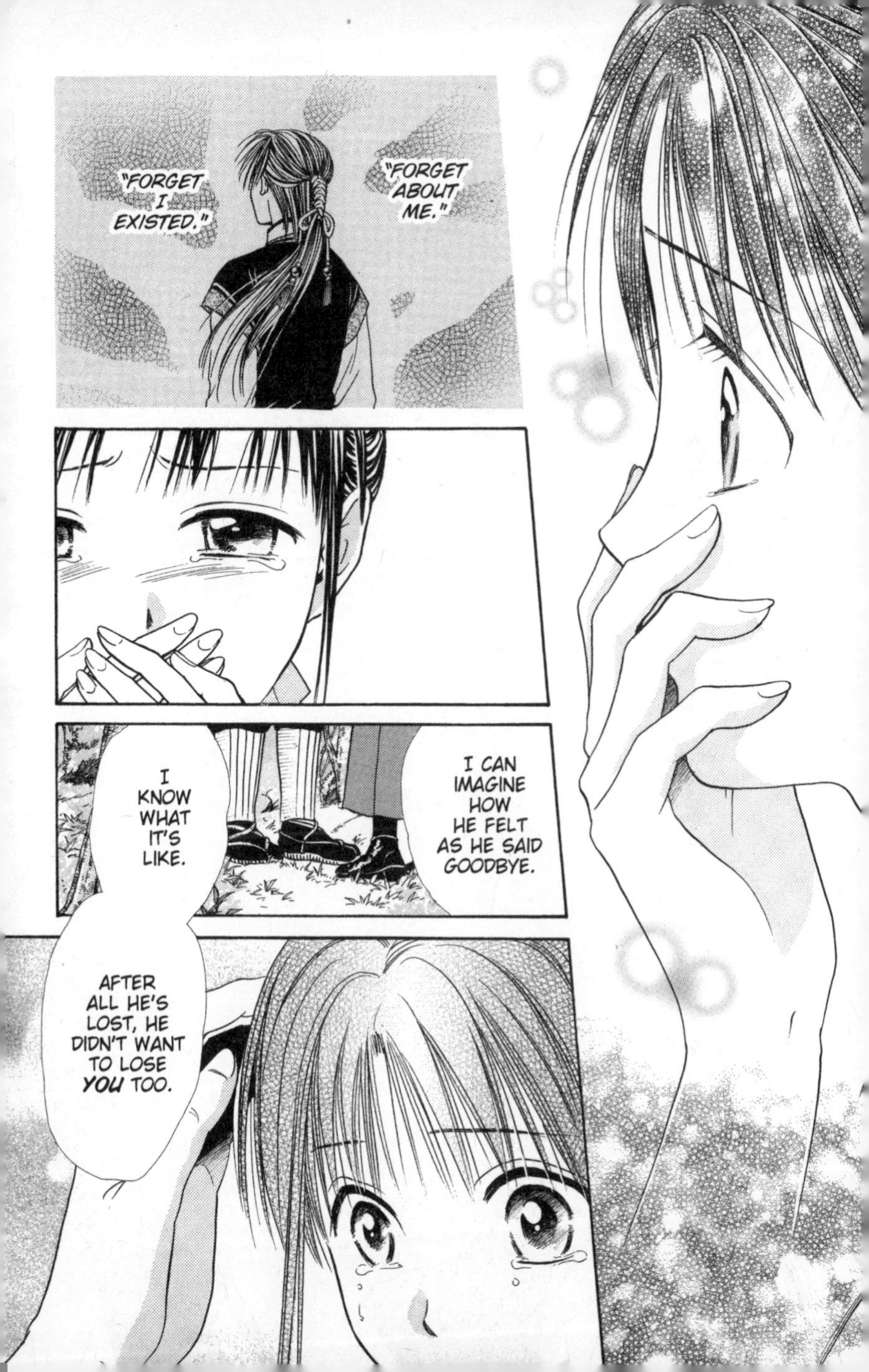
"FORGET ABOUT ME."
"FORGET I EXISTED."
I CAN IMAGINE HOW HE FELT AS HE SAID GOODBYE.
I KNOW WHAT IT'S LIKE.
AFTER ALL HE'S LOST, HE DIDN'T WANT TO LOSE ***YOU*** TOO.

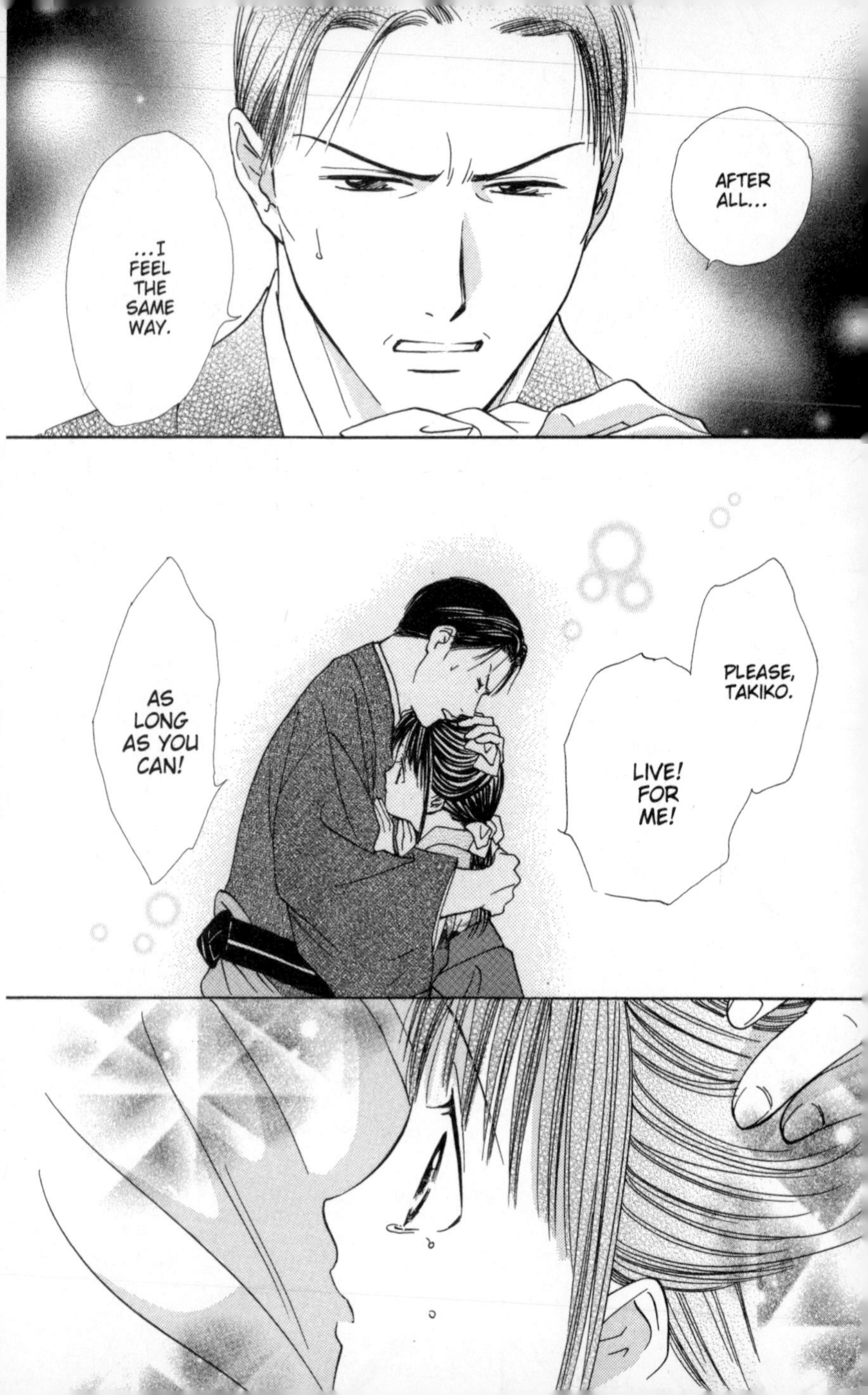
AFTER ALL...
...I FEEL THE SAME WAY.
PLEASE, TAKIKO.
LIVE! FOR ME!
AS LONG AS YOU CAN!

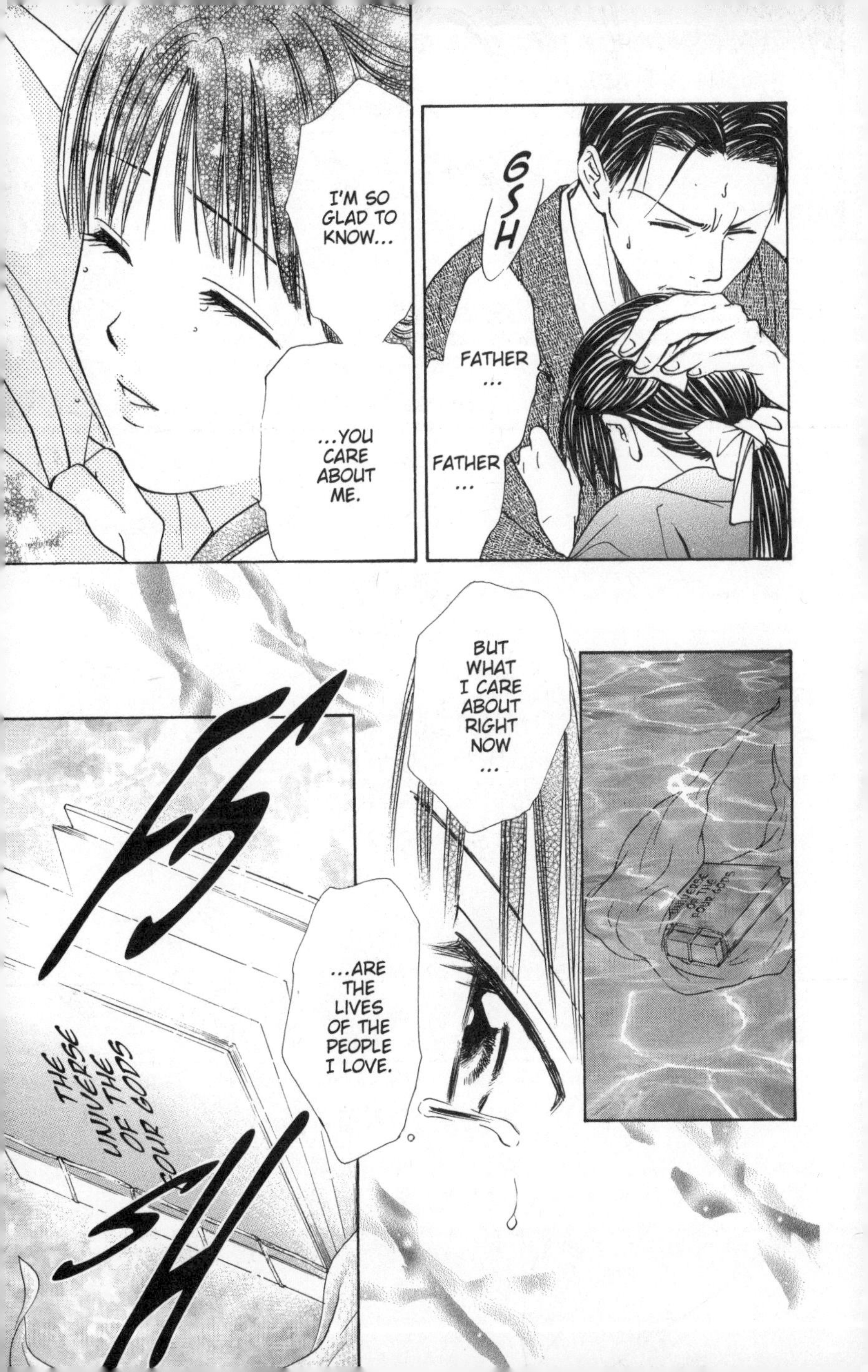
GSH
FATHER ...
FATHER ...
I'M SO GLAD TO KNOW...
...YOU CARE ABOUT ME.
BUT WHAT I CARE ABOUT RIGHT NOW ...
...ARE THE LIVES OF THE PEOPLE I LOVE.
FS
SH
THE UNIVERSE OF THE FOUR GODS

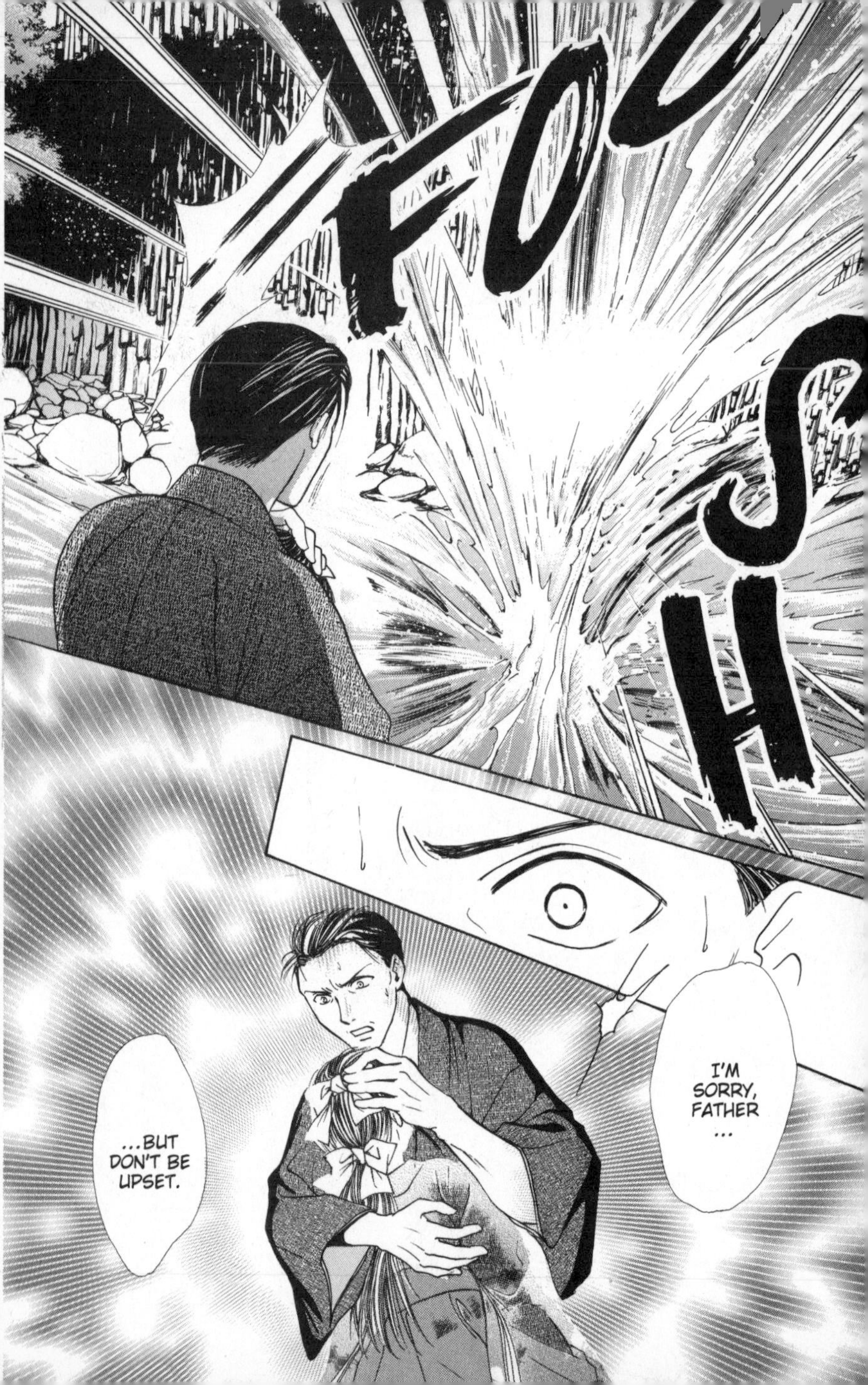
FOOSH
I'M SORRY, FATHER ...
...BUT DON'T BE UPSET.

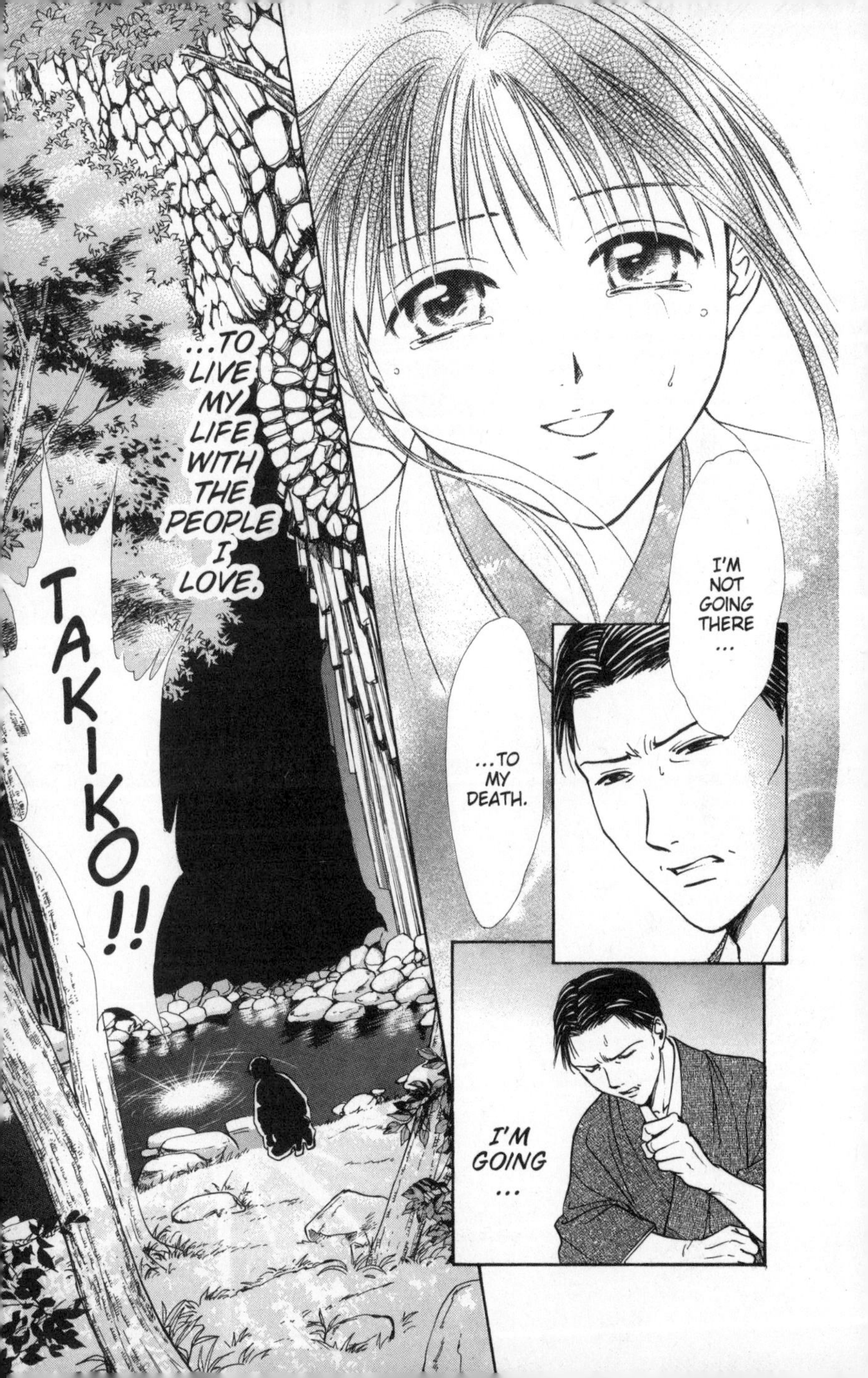
I'M NOT GOING THERE ...
...TO MY DEATH.
...TO LIVE MY LIFE WITH THE PEOPLE I LOVE.
I'M GOING ...
TAKIKO!!

FUSHIGI YÛGI:
GENBU KAIDEN

TO YOUR SIDE

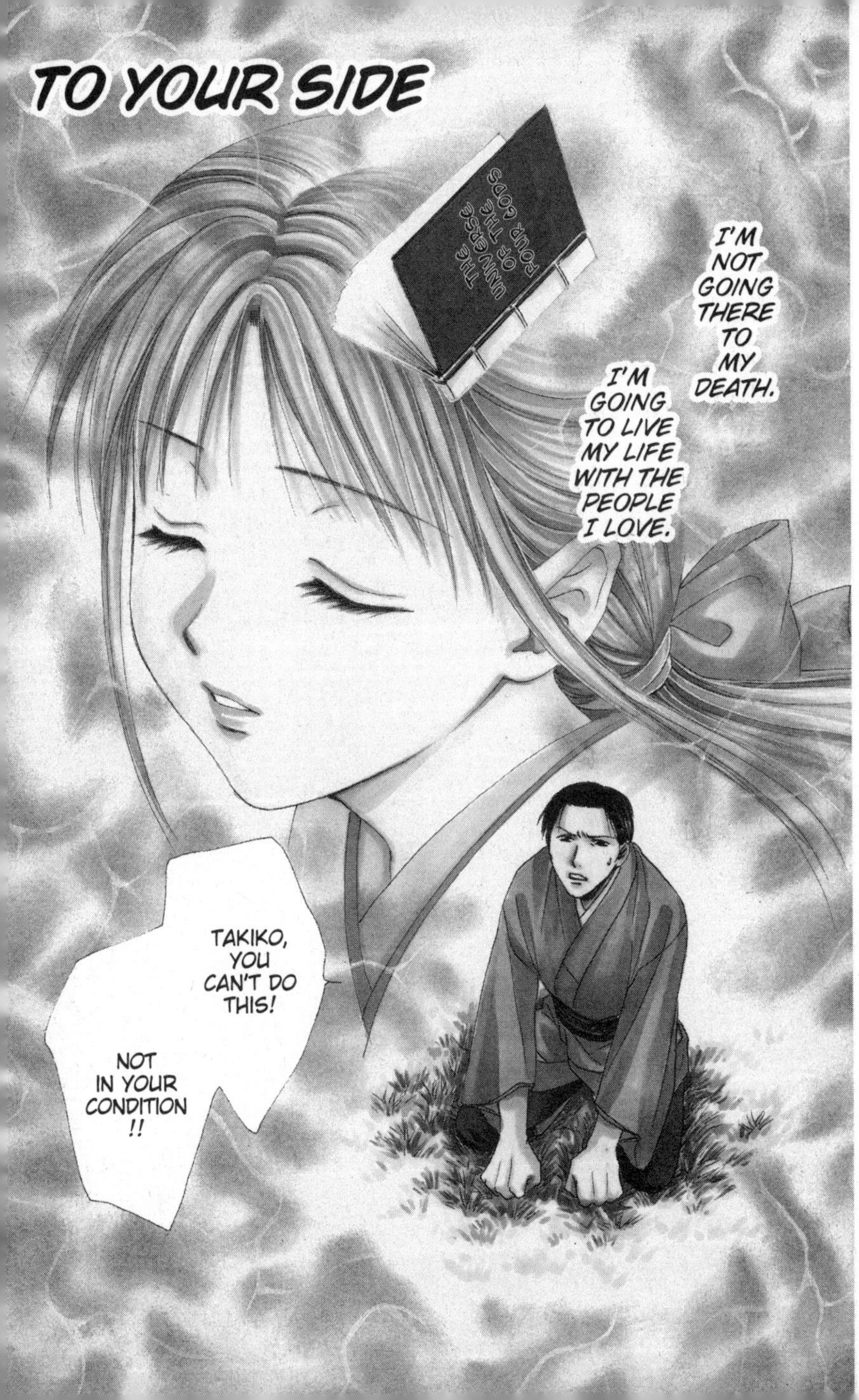
THE UNIVERSE OF THE FOUR GODS
I'M NOT GOING THERE TO MY DEATH.
I'M GOING TO LIVE MY LIFE WITH THE PEOPLE I LOVE.
TAKIKO, YOU CAN'T DO THIS!
NOT IN YOUR CONDITION !!

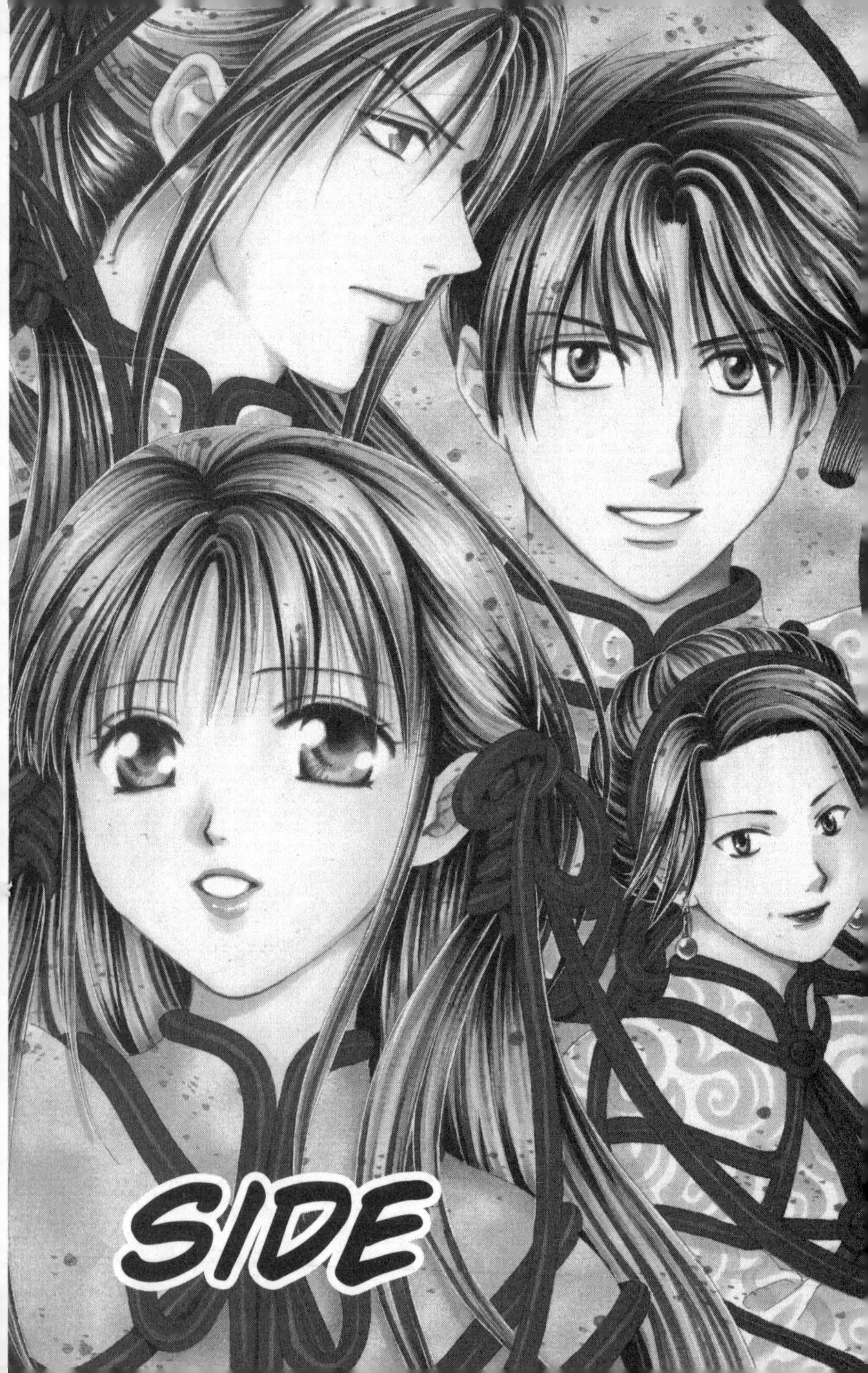
SIDE

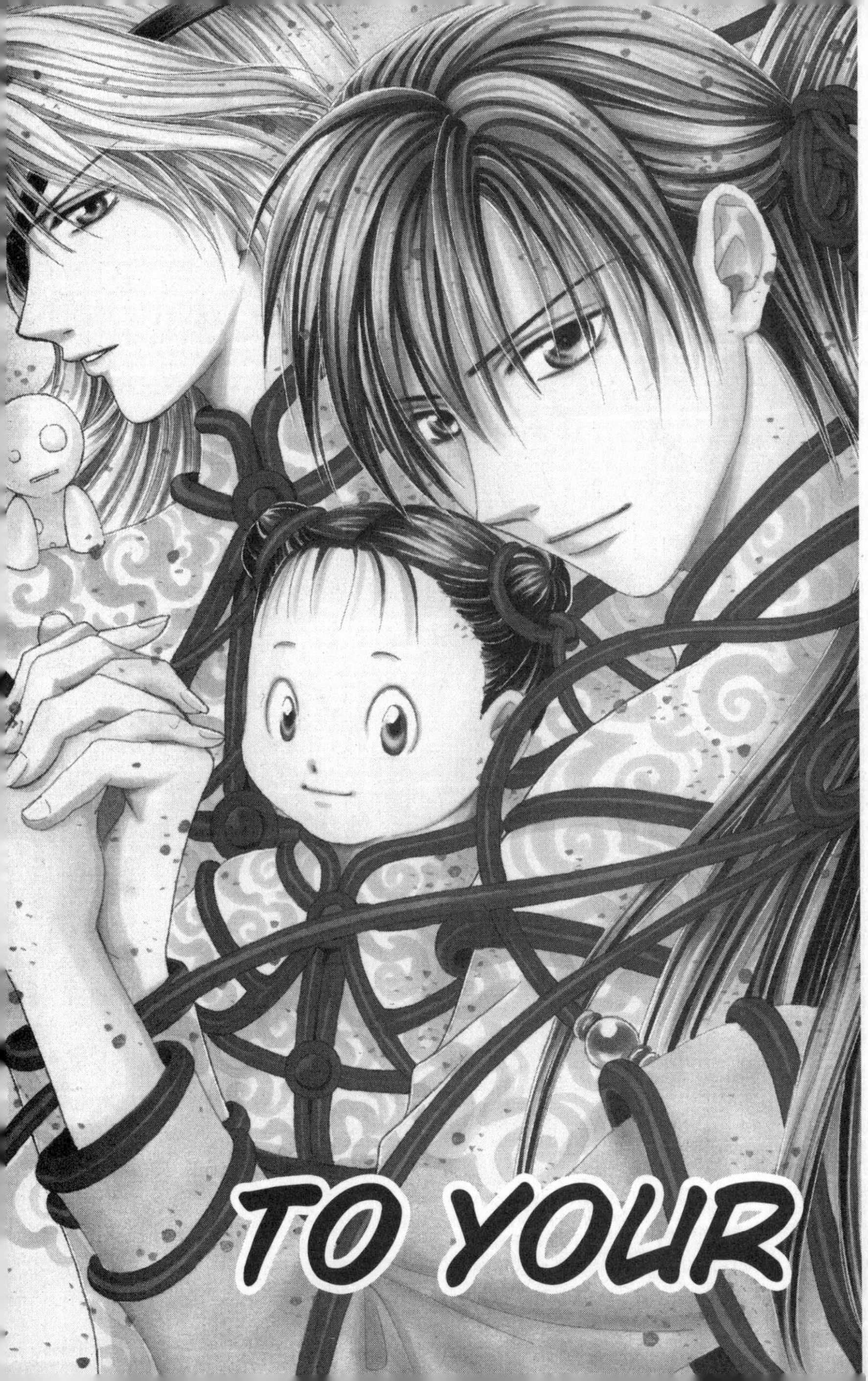
TO YOUR

3

Even though they share a title, *Genbu* is a completely different entity from the previous *Fushigi Yugi*. I'm sure the readers who have come this far have been enjoying it for different reasons. The common elements are the book *The Universe of the Four Gods* and the Celestial Warriors—the basics of the world. Now I think I should've gone with a different title, with "Fushigi Yugi" as the subtitle. If I ever write the *Byakko* story arc, I'm sure it'll be a totally different story as well. Creators are always changing their point of view, and we don't want to do the same thing over and over. Also, I want people to be able to enjoy *Genbu* even if they've never read *Fushigi Yugi*.

So from now on *Genbu* will be running in the monthly magazine *Flowers*... though that doesn't mean it'll run every month. (The magazine doesn't have space for it every month anyway.) My other current series, *Sakura-gari*, will continue to run in *Rinka*, the supplement to *Flowers*. The two series will sort of take turns appearing. I hope you'll be patient... I mean, the story is just about to get really exciting, and I'm planning a lot of major events!! So I'm feeling pretty ← right now.

Gotta be patient myself...

So if *Genbu* has me on pins and needles, why aren't I drawing it any faster? Because I'm starting a new series that will run ***weekly***!! (That's the biggest reason!) Imagine: a weekly magazine! I planned to do this a couple of years ago, but then I had to take a hiatus due to health issues, and after I got back to work I had to slowly acclimate myself to a faster schedule. That's why it took so long.

The next installment of *Fushigi Yugi: Genbu Kaiden* is scheduled to appear in the monthly manga magazine *Flowers*.

4

Okay. So...***my new manga will start in Shonen Sunday issue 44.*** Yes, I'm branching out into boys' manga—although I did a one-shot for *Shonen Sunday* once before. Yes, ***I'll be doing three series at once.*** Eek! Working out the schedules has been so hard... You must be wondering why I don't end a manga before starting a new one. Many people have asked me that! No matter how I try to explain, I don't think anyone can understand unless they're creators themselves. Sometimes there's a right (and only) time in your life to create a particular work. And stories have to be written down before they start to go stale. That's getting a bit metaphorical, but I think there's always a right time for these things. I can't go without any of my three titles right now!

I do kind of wish they didn't have to be all at once...

Anyway, *Genbu* and the *FY* universe are pretty established at this point. I figured this series was timeless and I could work on it as a long-term project, so it was okay if it came out more slowly. It's my life's work. I agonized over the decision though. Hmm... maybe this is kind of confusing to readers. I hope I can express what I'm feeling through my manga! I'm rarin' to draw. And of course I'll put my best efforts into all three series. I'll never cut any corners. Obviously! But there's only one of me... I wish I had a clone. I'm so sorry that the readers of *Genbu* will have to wait!! Volume 10 won't come out for another year. *Sakura-gari* and the new *Shonen Sunday* comic will be running, though, so please check them out!! I'll keep trying my hardest to create interesting manga! n(--)n°

Aug. '08

Thank you for all the fan mail! It fires me up!

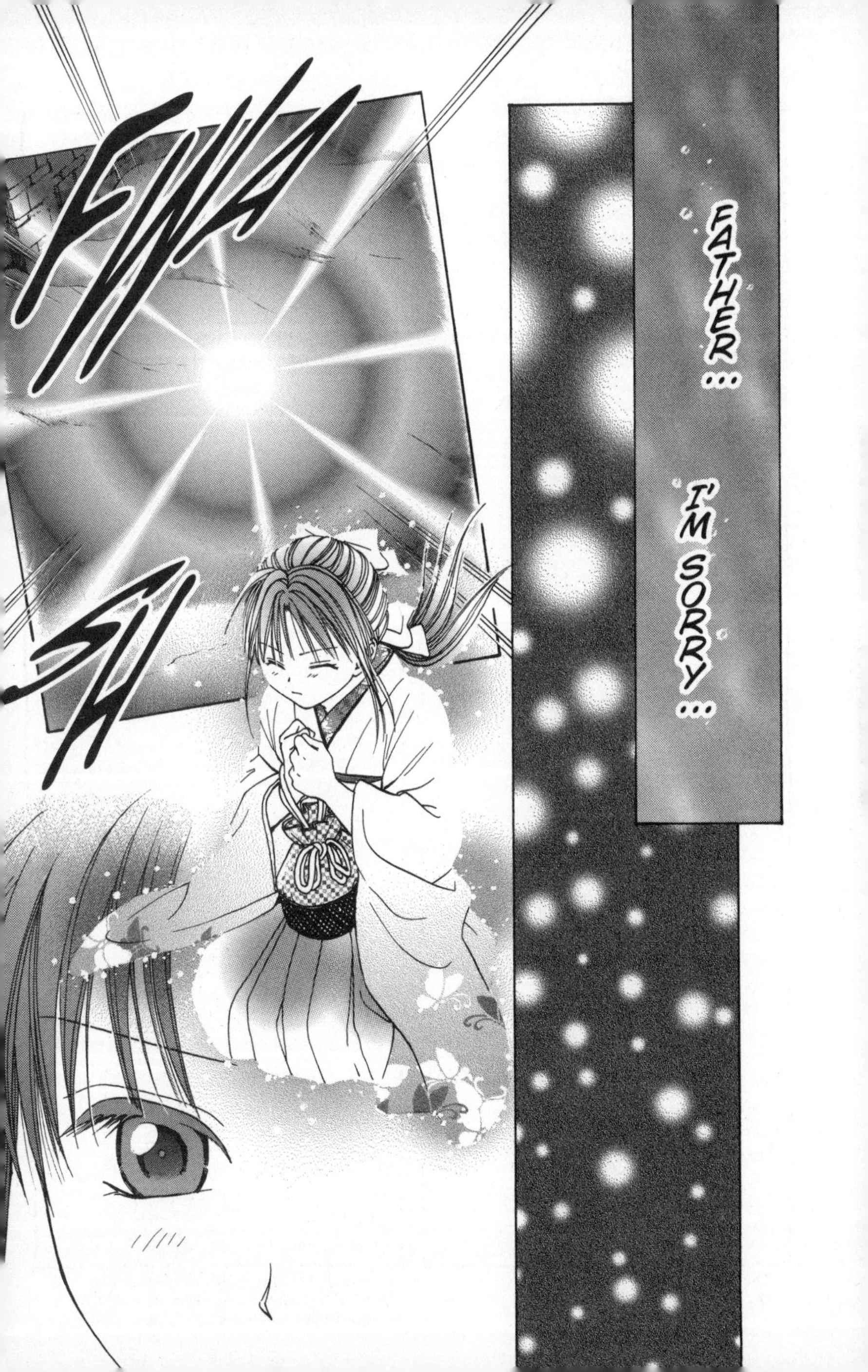
FATHER...
I'M SORRY...

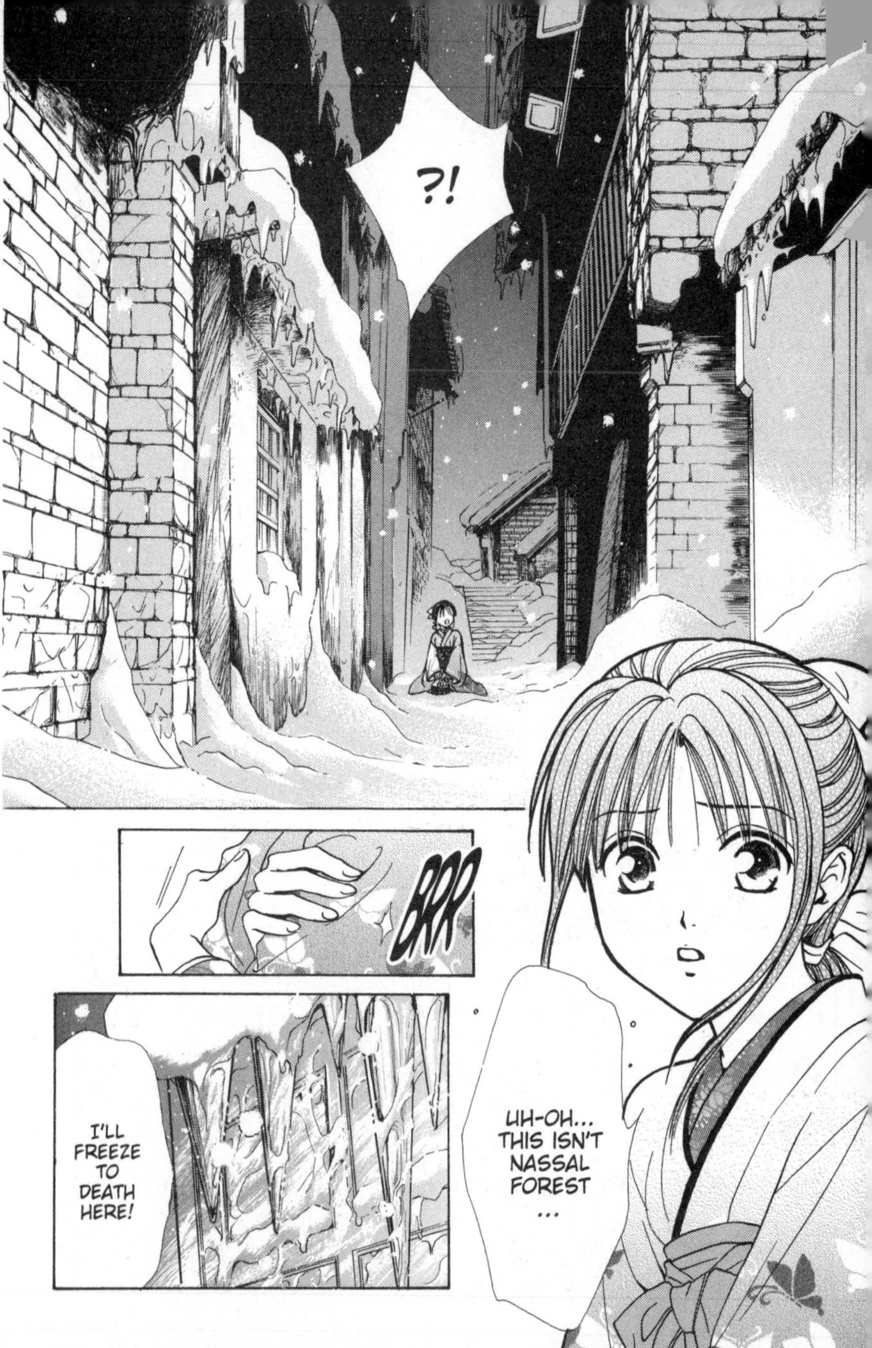
?!
UH-OH... THIS ISN'T NASSAL FOREST ...
BRR
I'LL FREEZE TO DEATH HERE!

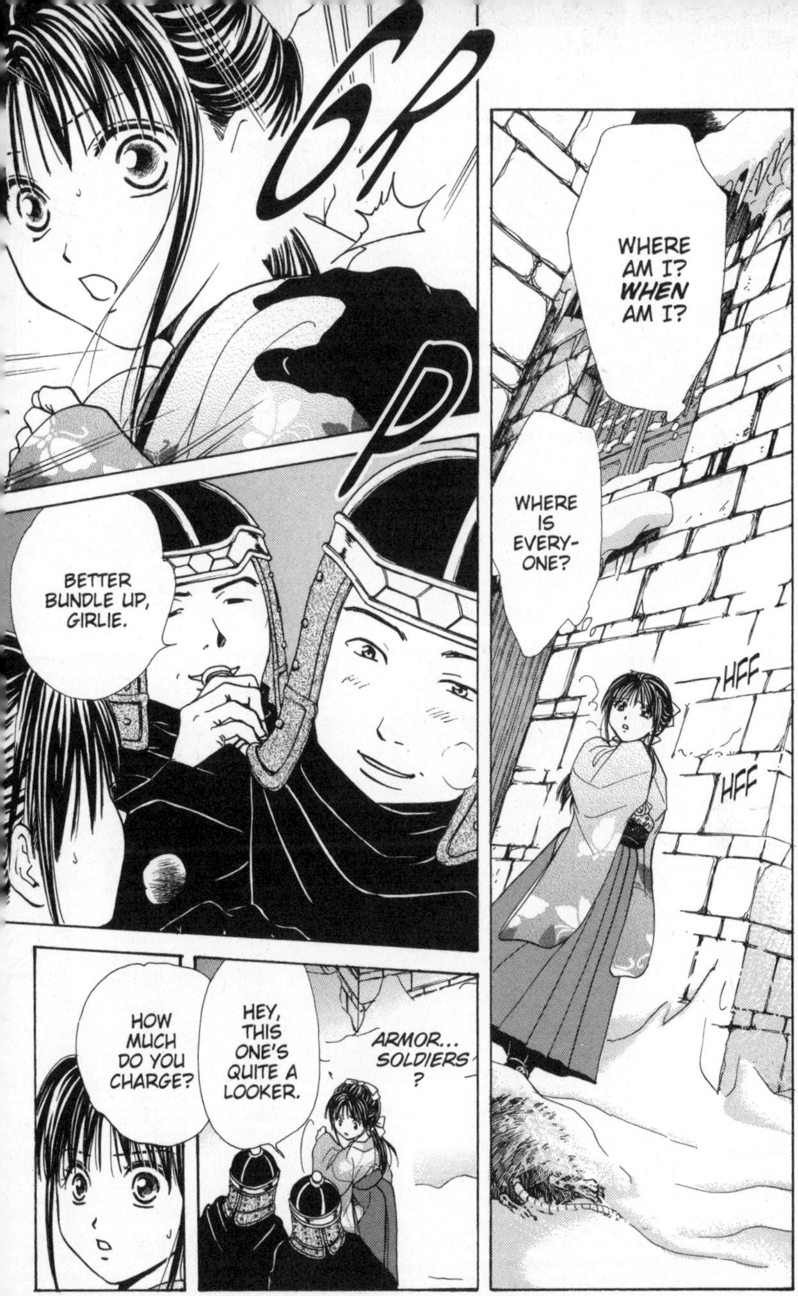
WHERE AM I? *WHEN* AM I?
WHERE IS EVERY-ONE?
HFF
HFF
GR
P
BETTER BUNDLE UP, GIRLIE.
ARMOR... SOLDIERS ?
HEY, THIS ONE'S QUITE A LOOKER.
HOW MUCH DO YOU CHARGE?

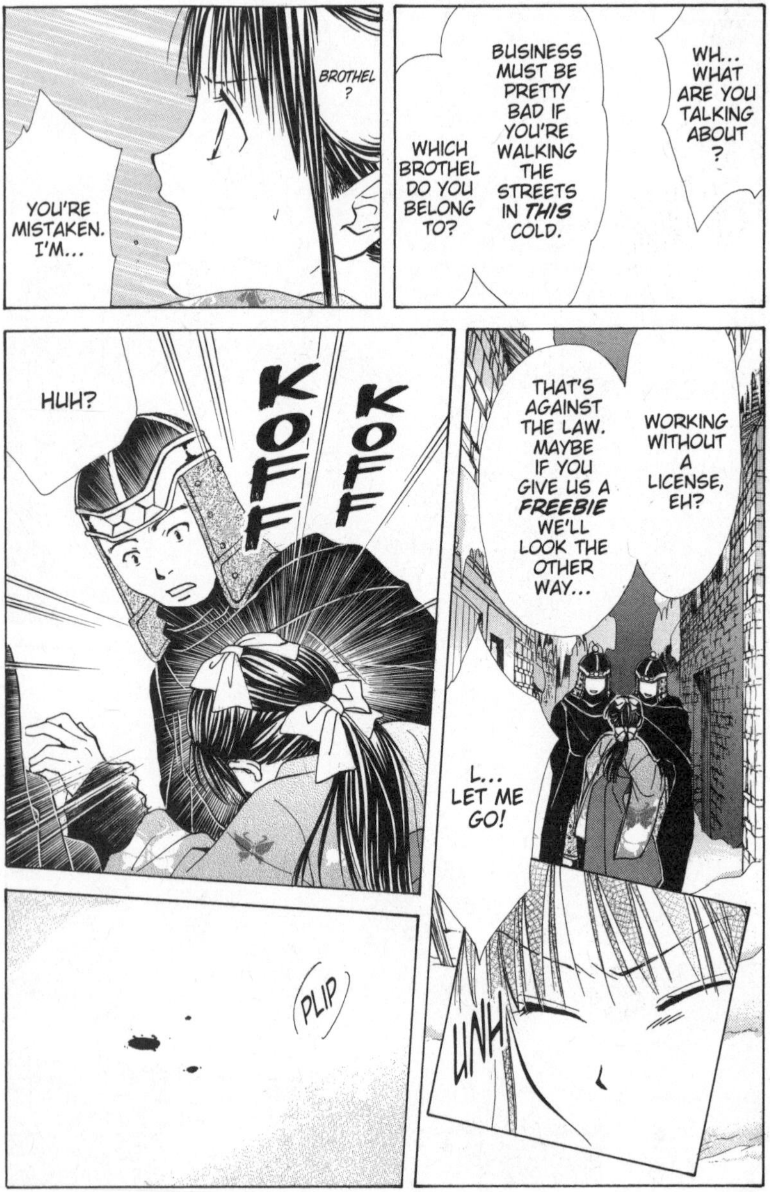
WH... WHAT ARE YOU TALKING ABOUT?
BUSINESS MUST BE PRETTY BAD IF YOU'RE WALKING THE STREETS IN *THIS* COLD.
WHICH BROTHEL DO YOU BELONG TO?
BROTHEL?
YOU'RE MISTAKEN. I'M...
WORKING WITHOUT A LICENSE, EH?
THAT'S AGAINST THE LAW. MAYBE IF YOU GIVE US A *FREEBIE* WE'LL LOOK THE OTHER WAY...
L... LET ME GO!
KOFF KOFF
HUH?
UNH
PLIP

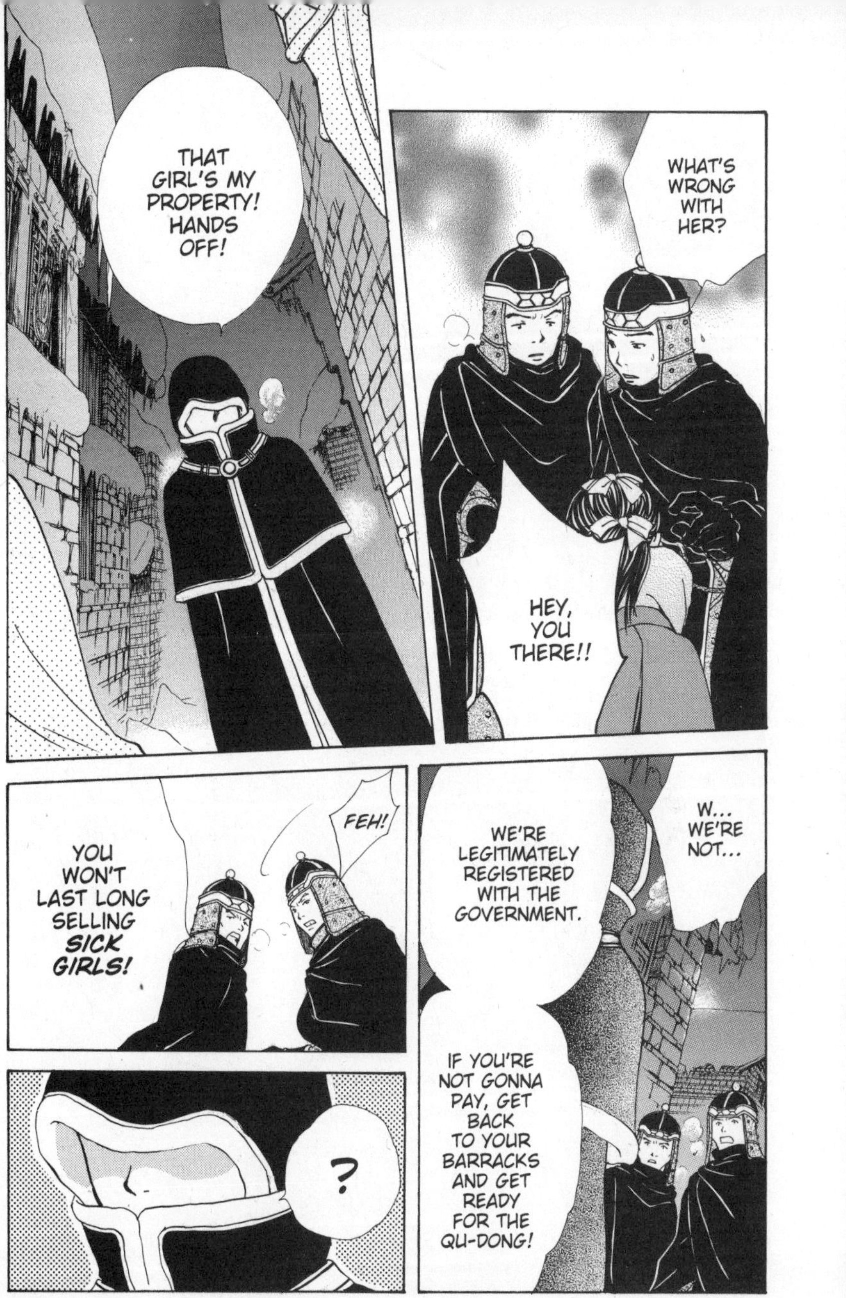
WHAT'S WRONG WITH HER?
HEY, YOU THERE!!
THAT GIRL'S MY PROPERTY! HANDS OFF!
W... WE'RE NOT...
WE'RE LEGITIMATELY REGISTERED WITH THE GOVERNMENT.
IF YOU'RE NOT GONNA PAY, GET BACK TO YOUR BARRACKS AND GET READY FOR THE QU-DONG!
FEH!
YOU WON'T LAST LONG SELLING SICK GIRLS!
?

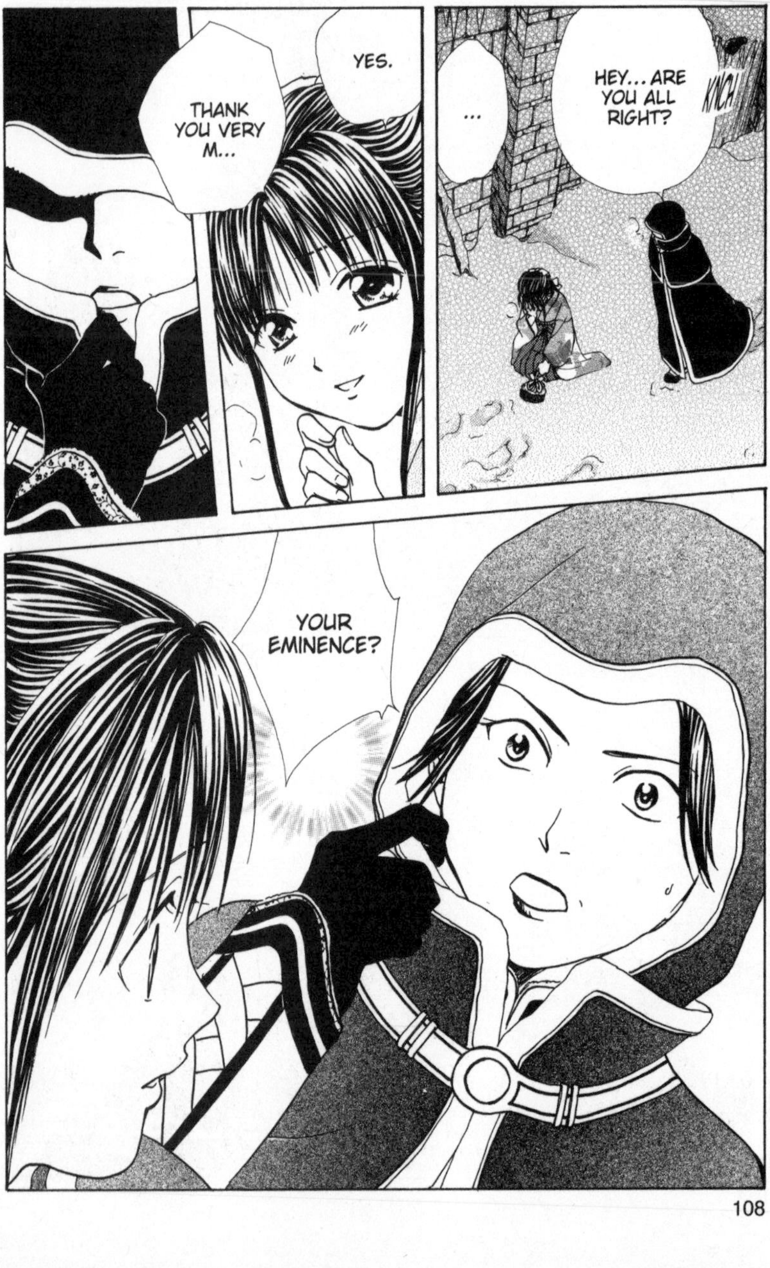
KNCH
HEY... ARE YOU ALL RIGHT?
...
YES.
THANK YOU VERY M...
YOUR EMINENCE?

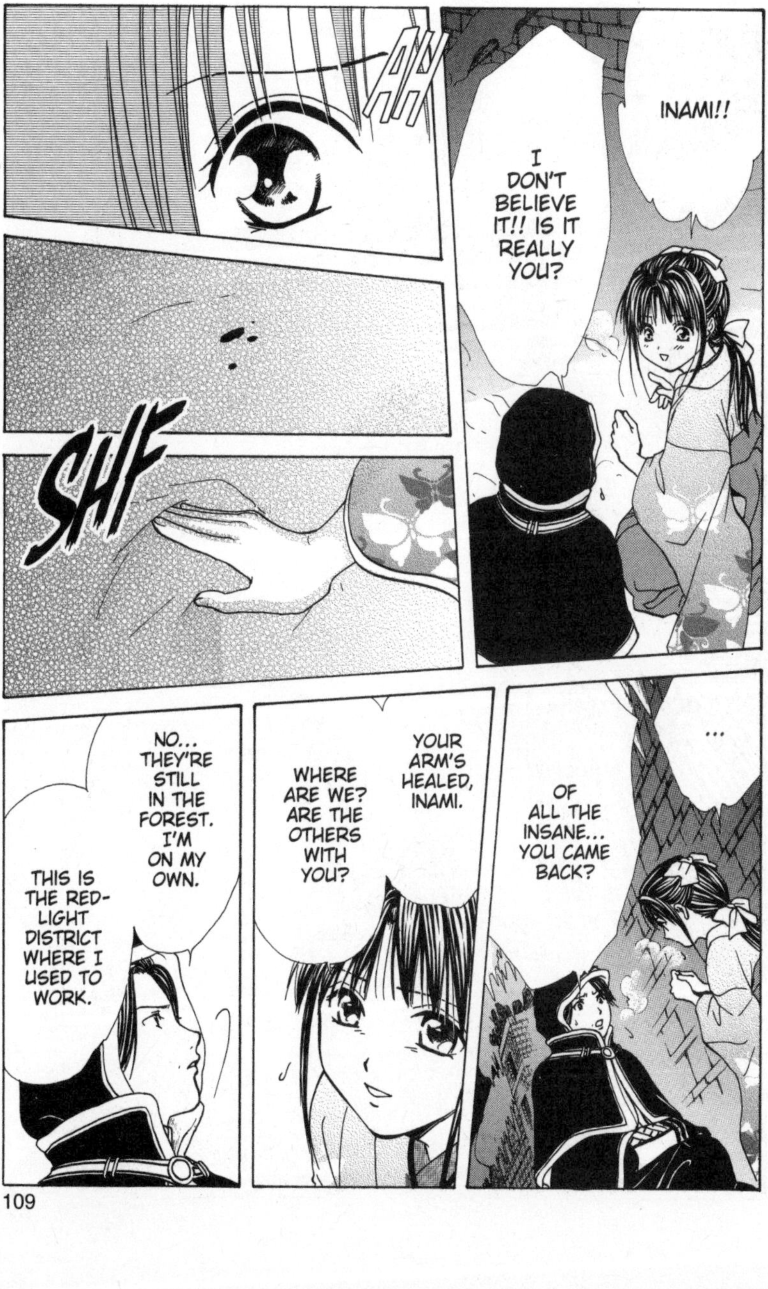
INAMI!!
I DON'T BELIEVE IT!! IS IT REALLY YOU?
AH
SHF
...
OF ALL THE INSANE... YOU CAME BACK?
YOUR ARM'S HEALED, INAMI.
WHERE ARE WE? ARE THE OTHERS WITH YOU?
NO... THEY'RE STILL IN THE FOREST. I'M ON MY OWN.
THIS IS THE RED-LIGHT DISTRICT WHERE I USED TO WORK.

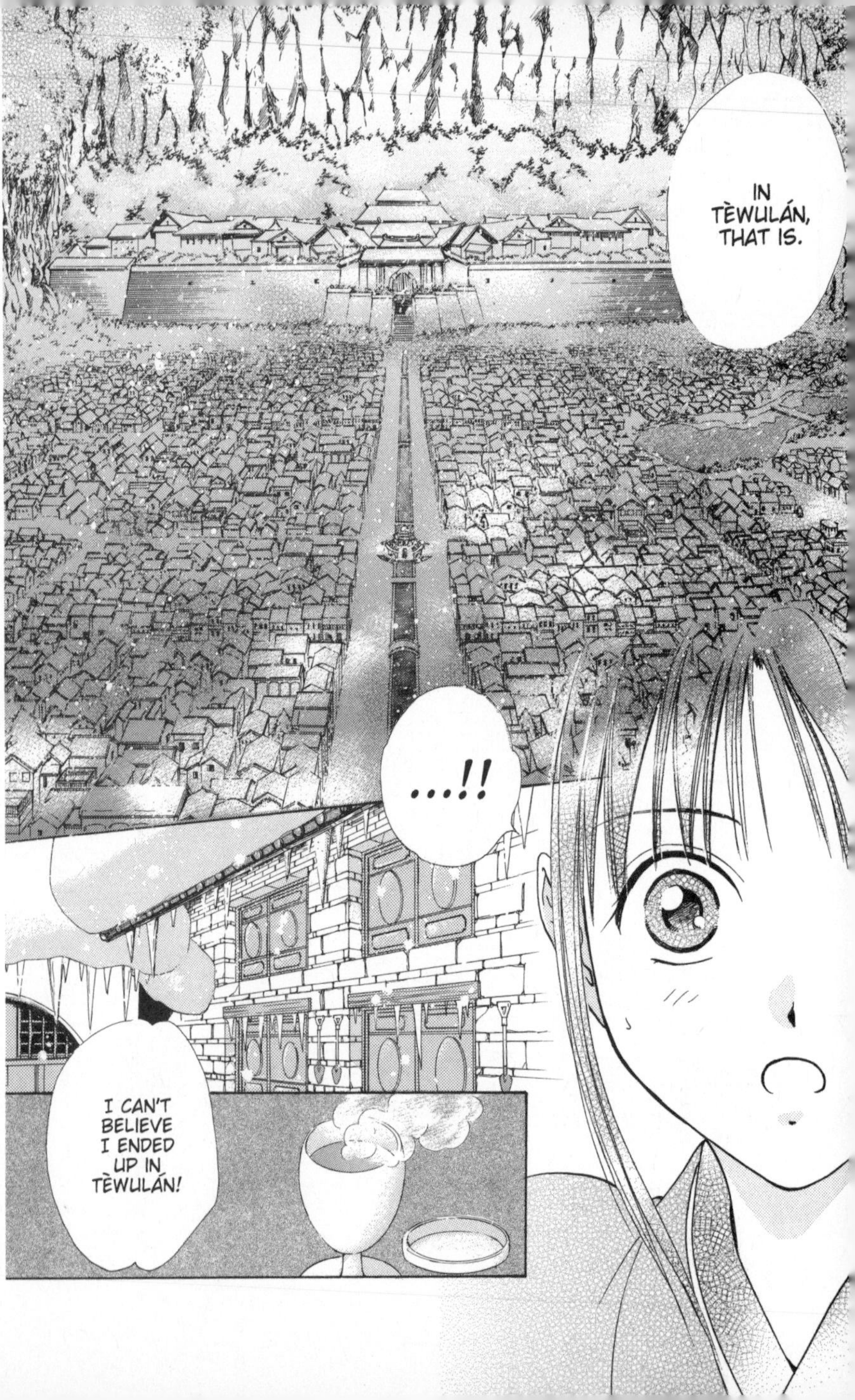
IN TÈWULÁN, THAT IS.
...!!
I CAN'T BELIEVE I ENDED UP IN TÈWULÁN!

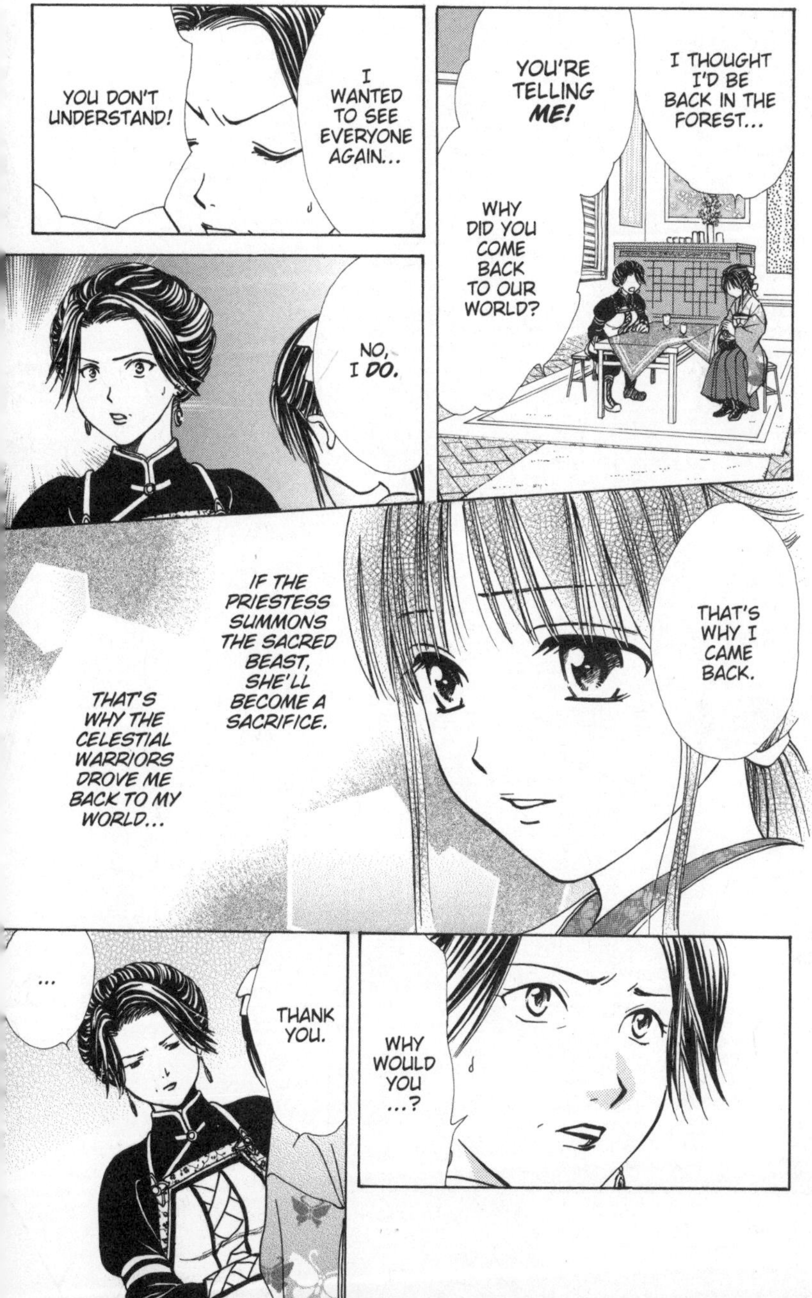

I THOUGHT I'D BE BACK IN THE FOREST...
YOU'RE TELLING *ME!*
WHY DID YOU COME BACK TO OUR WORLD?
I WANTED TO SEE EVERYONE AGAIN...
YOU DON'T UNDERSTAND!
NO, I *DO.*
THAT'S WHY I CAME BACK.
IF THE PRIESTESS SUMMONS THE SACRED BEAST, SHE'LL BECOME A SACRIFICE.
THAT'S WHY THE CELESTIAL WARRIORS DROVE ME BACK TO MY WORLD...
WHY WOULD YOU ...?
THANK YOU.
...

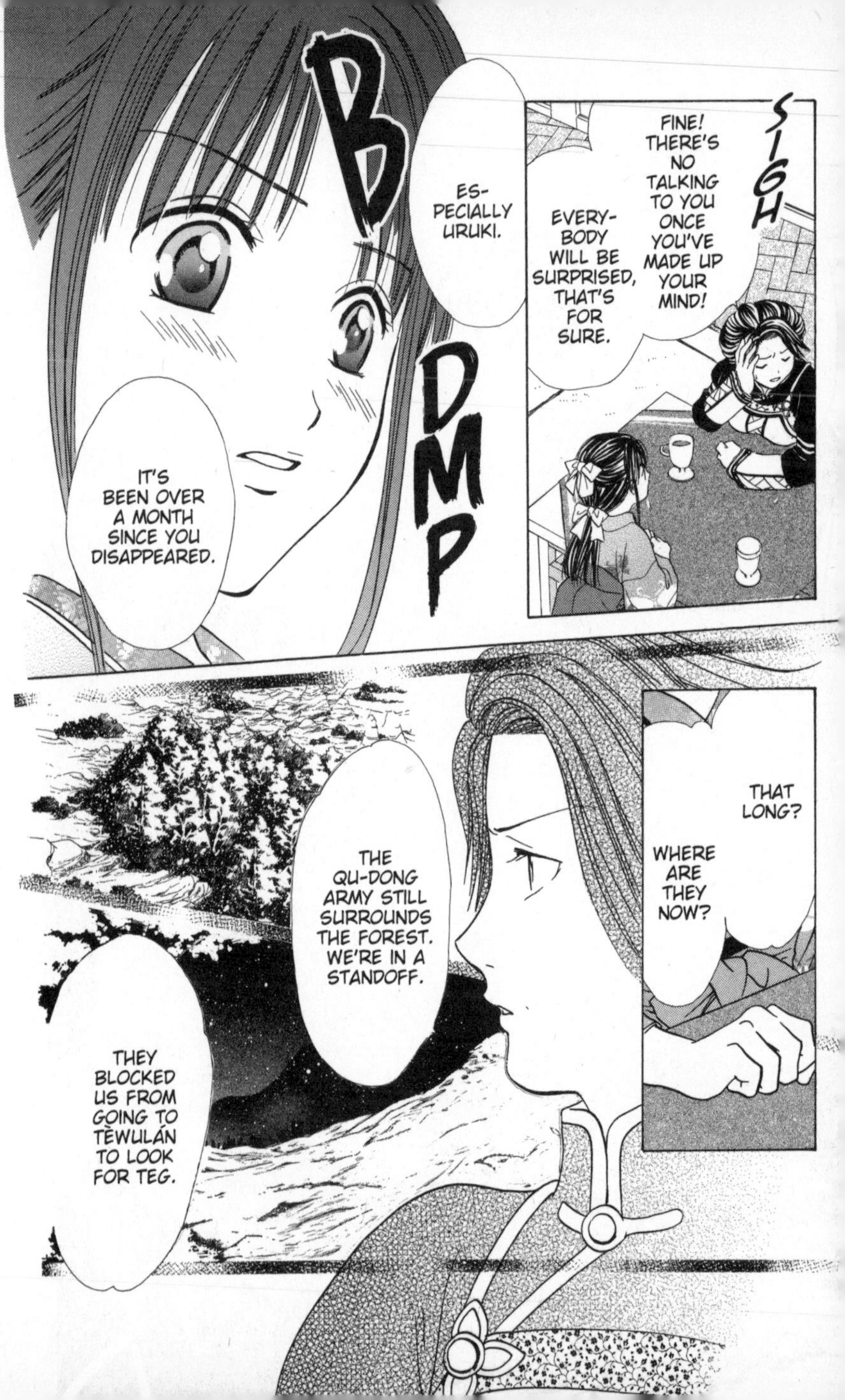
SIGH
FINE! THERE'S NO TALKING TO YOU ONCE YOU'VE MADE UP YOUR MIND!
EVERY-BODY WILL BE SURPRISED, THAT'S FOR SURE.
ES-PECIALLY URUKI.
BDMP
IT'S BEEN OVER A MONTH SINCE YOU DISAPPEARED.
THAT LONG?
WHERE ARE THEY NOW?
THE QU-DONG ARMY STILL SURROUNDS THE FOREST. WE'RE IN A STANDOFF.
THEY BLOCKED US FROM GOING TO TÈWULÁN TO LOOK FOR TEG.

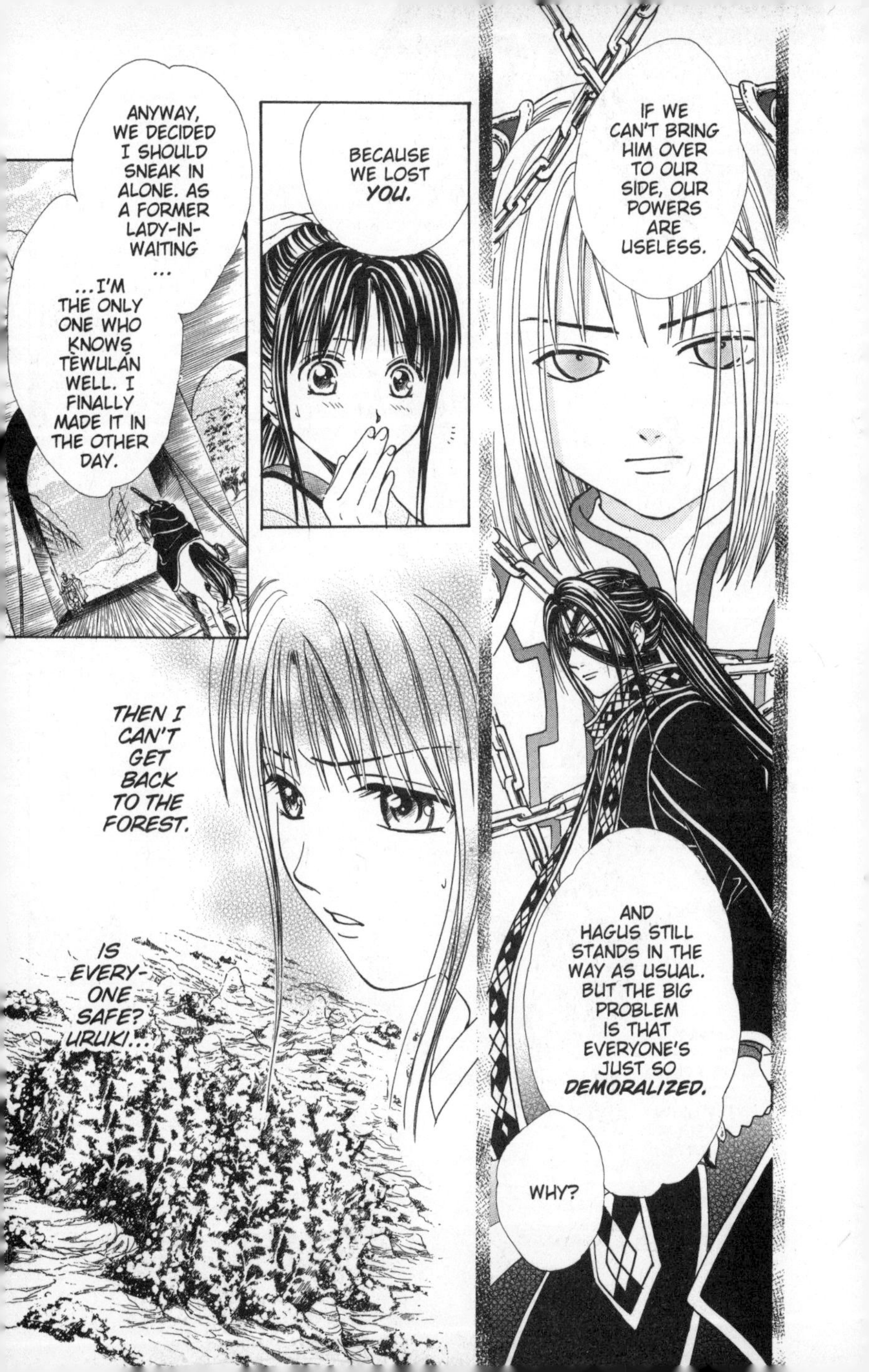
IF WE CAN'T BRING HIM OVER TO OUR SIDE, OUR POWERS ARE USELESS.
AND HAGUS STILL STANDS IN THE WAY AS USUAL. BUT THE BIG PROBLEM IS THAT EVERYONE'S JUST SO **DEMORALIZED.**
WHY?
BECAUSE WE LOST ***YOU.***
ANYWAY, WE DECIDED I SHOULD SNEAK IN ALONE. AS A FORMER LADY-IN-WAITING ...
...I'M THE ONLY ONE WHO KNOWS TÈWULÁN WELL. I FINALLY MADE IT IN THE OTHER DAY.
THEN I CAN'T GET BACK TO THE FOREST.
IS EVERYONE SAFE? URUKI...

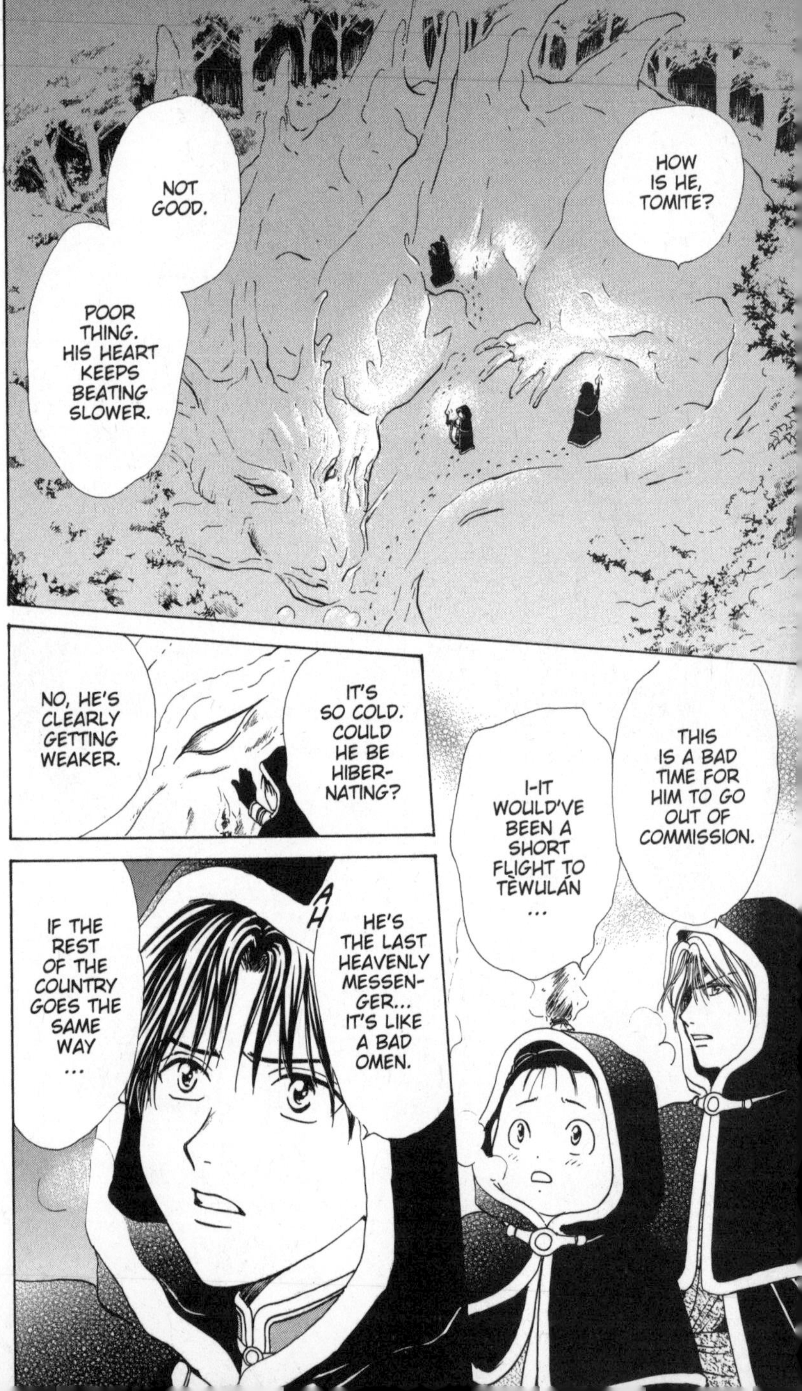
HOW IS HE, TOMITE?
NOT GOOD.
POOR THING. HIS HEART KEEPS BEATING SLOWER.
IT'S SO COLD. COULD HE BE HIBER-NATING?
NO, HE'S CLEARLY GETTING WEAKER.
THIS IS A BAD TIME FOR HIM TO GO OUT OF COMMISSION.
I-IT WOULD'VE BEEN A SHORT FLIGHT TO TÈWULÁN ...
AH
HE'S THE LAST HEAVENLY MESSEN-GER... IT'S LIKE A BAD OMEN.
IF THE REST OF THE COUNTRY GOES THE SAME WAY ...

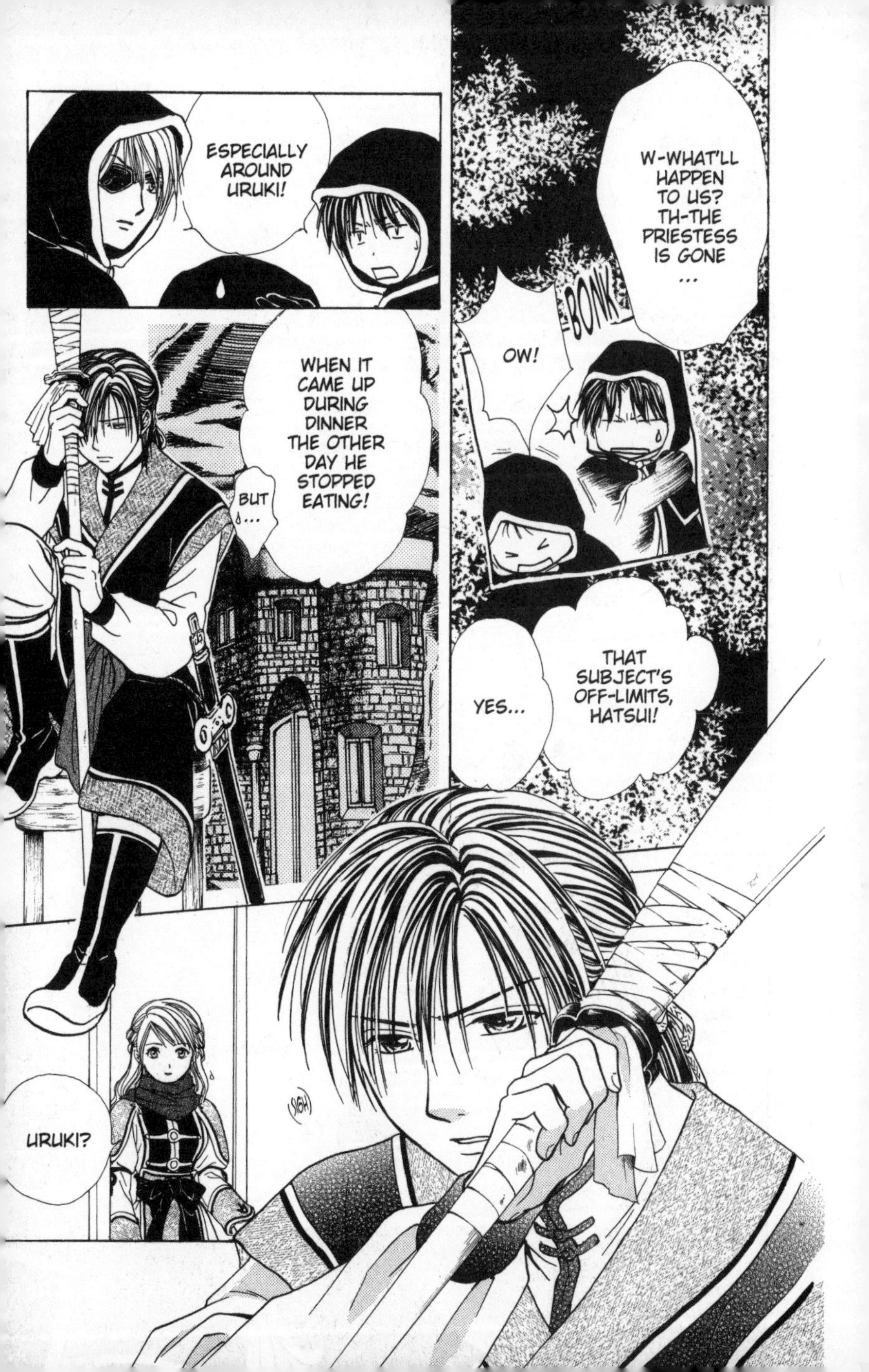
W-WHAT'LL HAPPEN TO US? TH-THE PRIESTESS IS GONE ...
BONK
OW!
THAT SUBJECT'S OFF-LIMITS, HATSUI!
YES...
ESPECIALLY AROUND URUKI!
WHEN IT CAME UP DURING DINNER THE OTHER DAY HE STOPPED EATING!
BUT...
(SIGH)
URUKI?

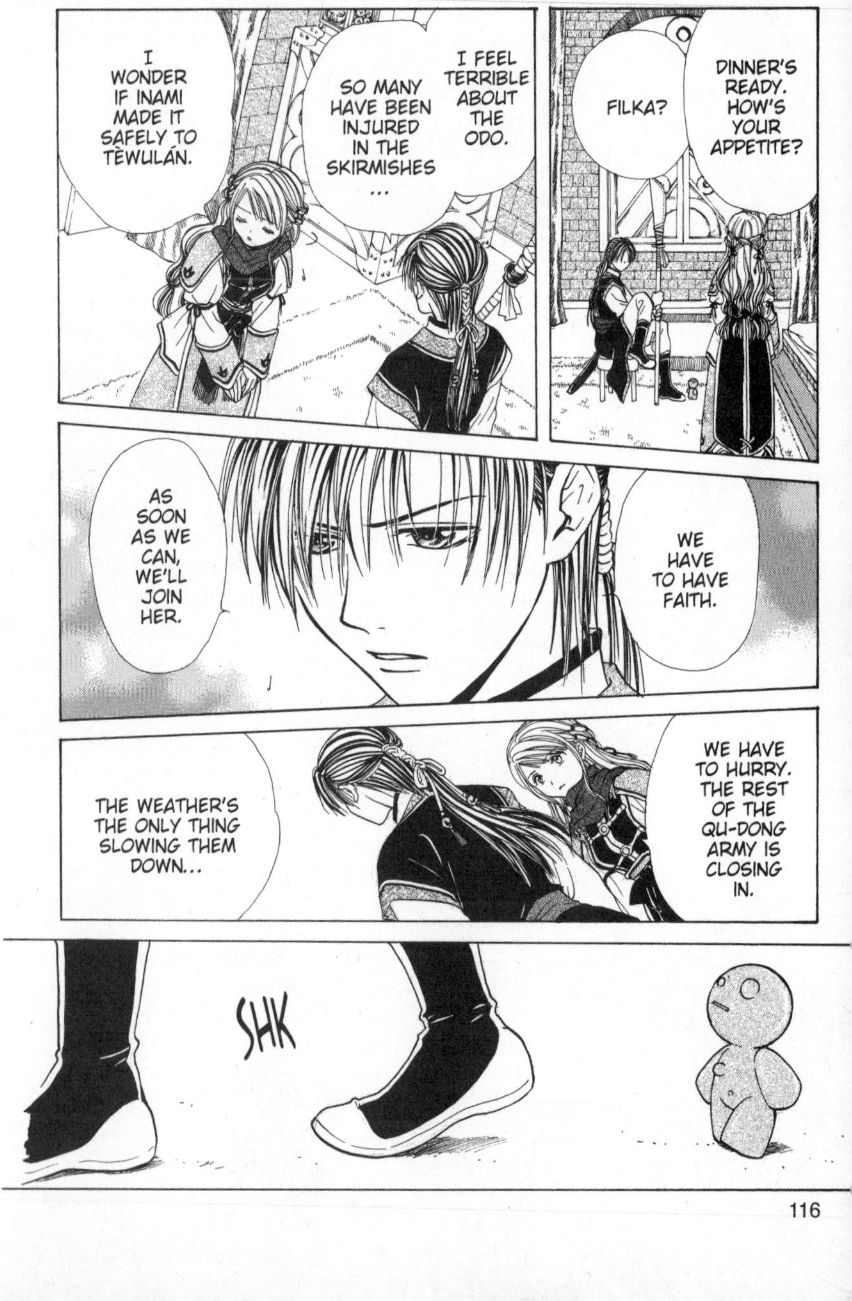
DINNER'S READY. HOW'S YOUR APPETITE?
FILKA?
I FEEL TERRIBLE ABOUT THE ODO.
SO MANY HAVE BEEN INJURED IN THE SKIRMISHES ...
I WONDER IF INAMI MADE IT SAFELY TO TÈWULÁN.
WE HAVE TO HAVE FAITH.
AS SOON AS WE CAN, WE'LL JOIN HER.
WE HAVE TO HURRY. THE REST OF THE QU-DONG ARMY IS CLOSING IN.
THE WEATHER'S THE ONLY THING SLOWING THEM DOWN...
SHK

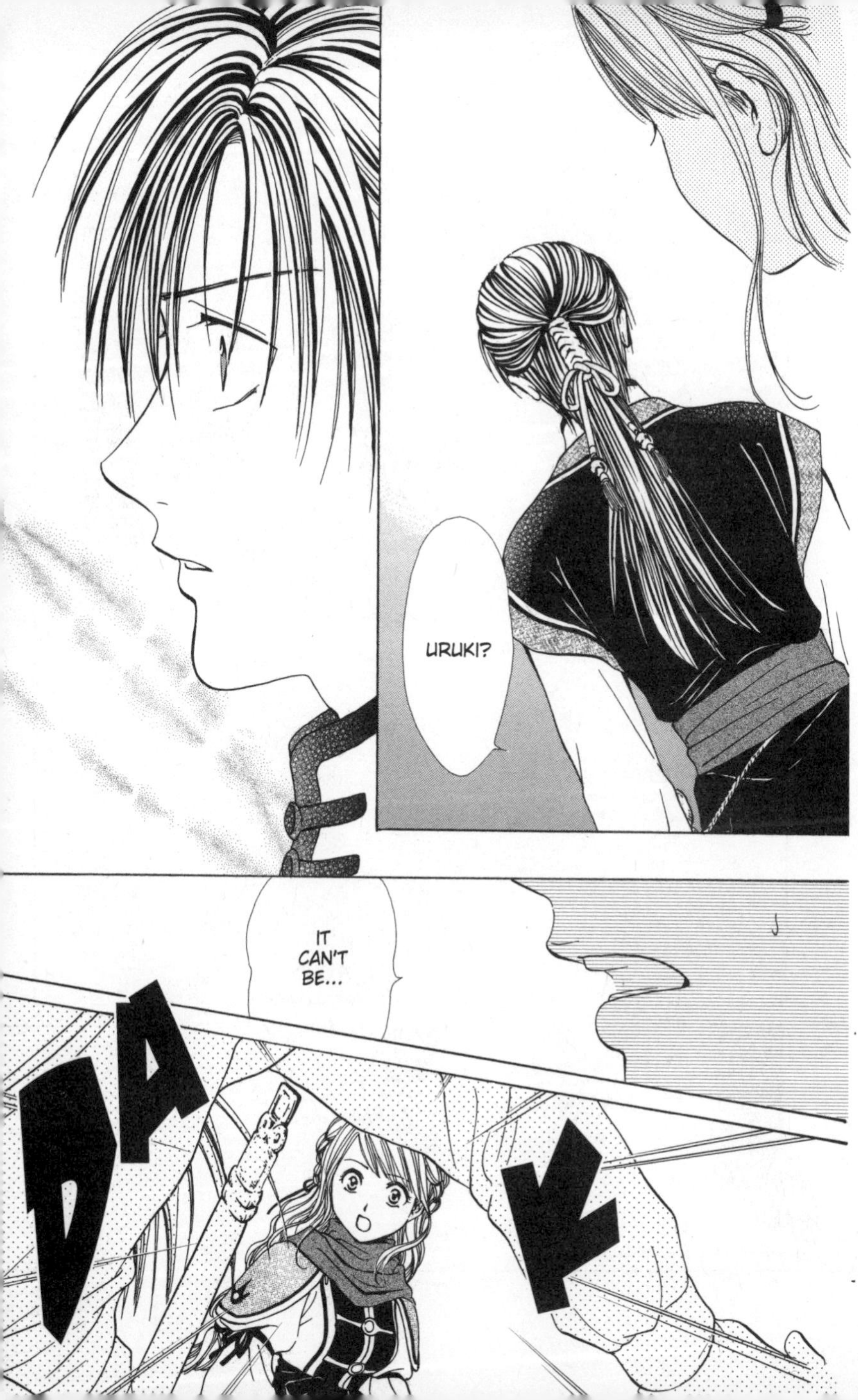
URUKI?
IT CAN'T BE...
DAK

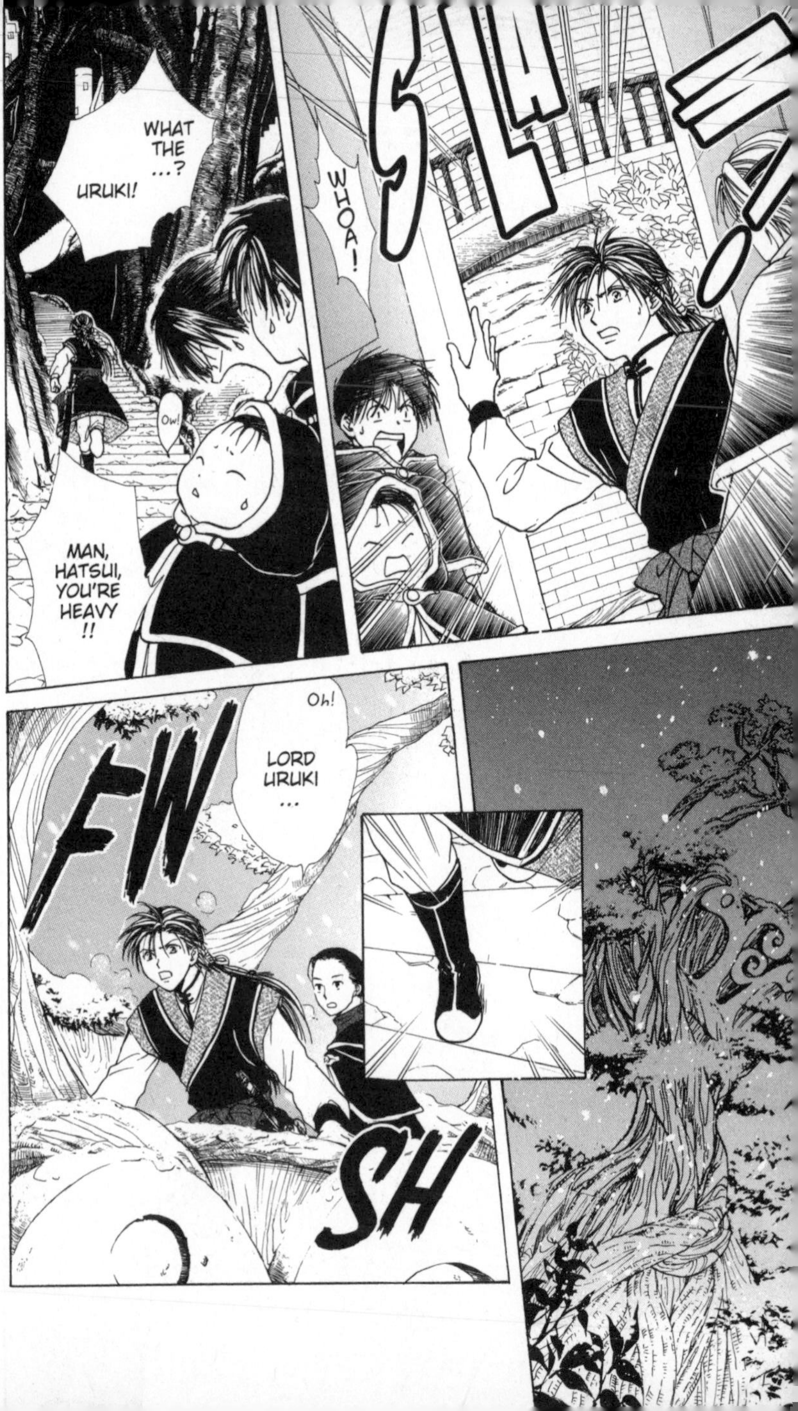
SLAM
WHOA!
WHAT THE ...?
URUKI!
Ow!
MAN, HATSUI, YOU'RE HEAVY!!
Oh!
LORD URUKI ...
FW
SH

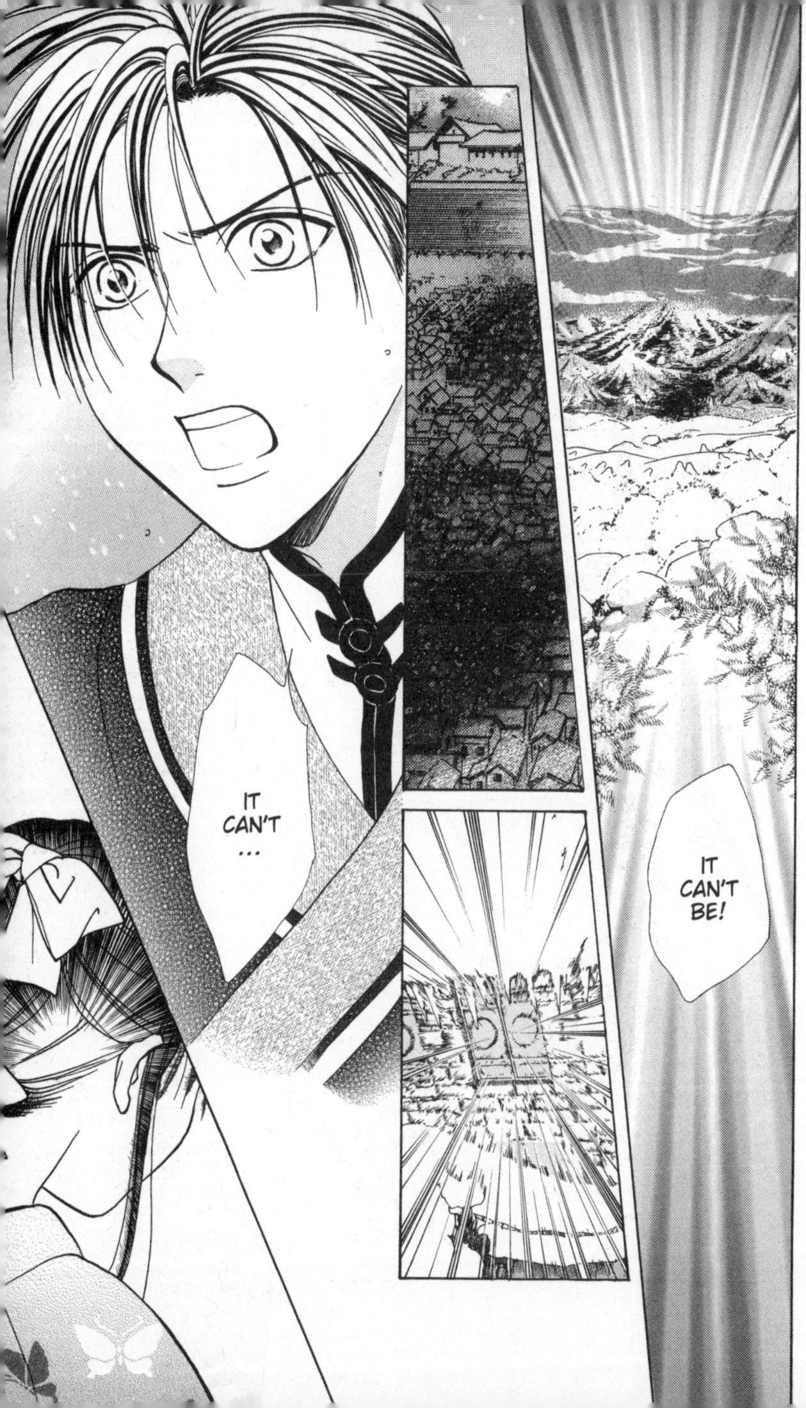
IT CAN'T BE!
IT CAN'T ...

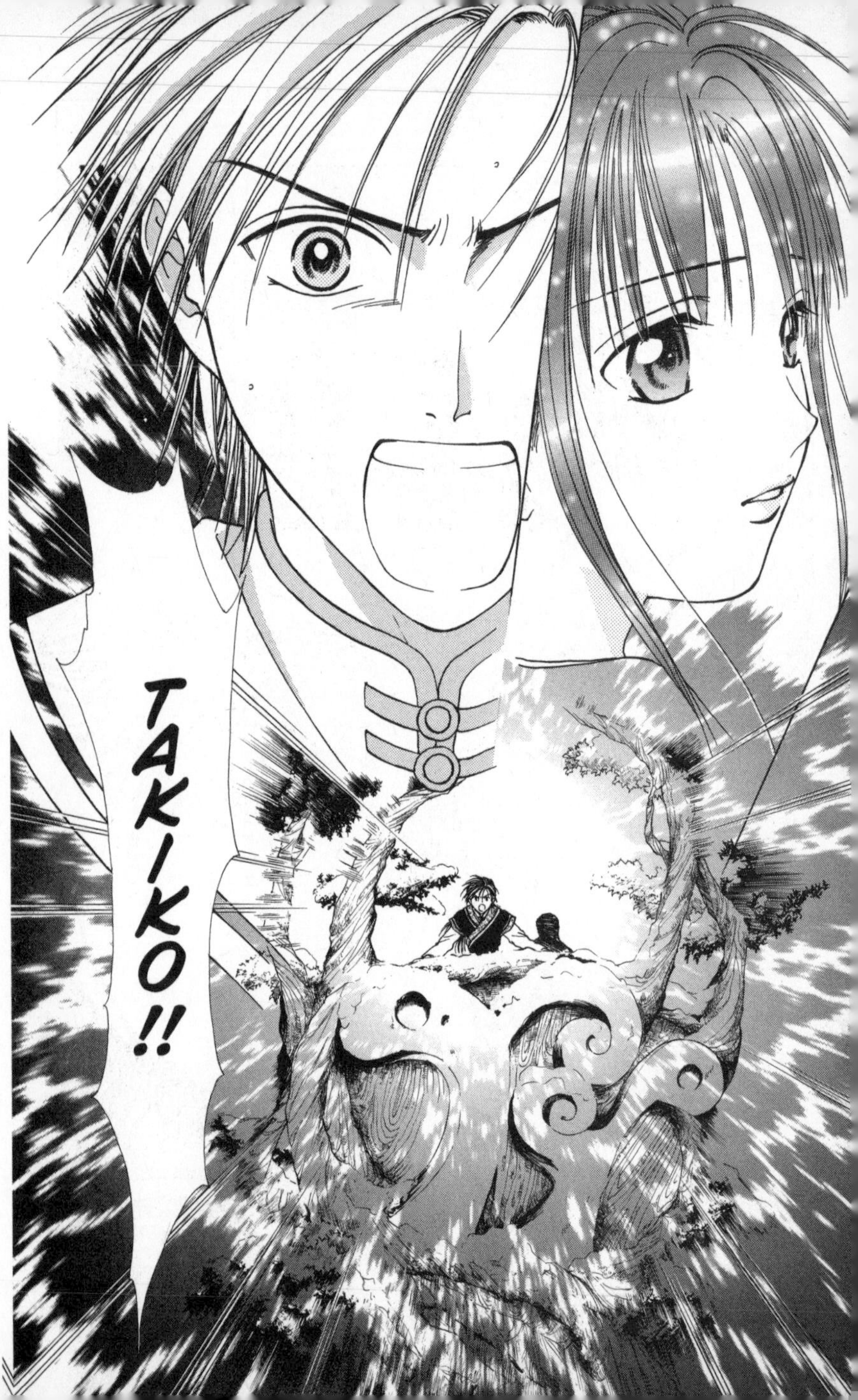
TAKIKO!!

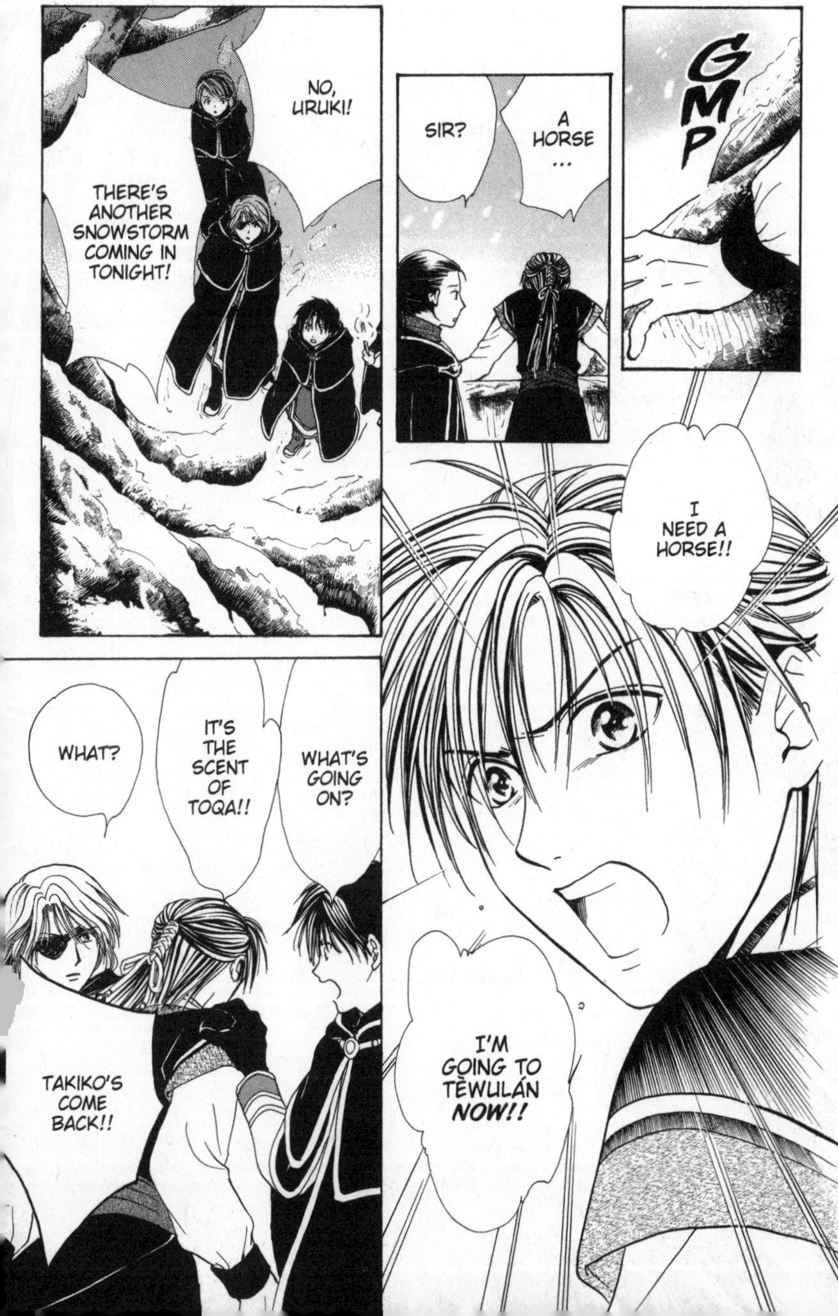
GMP
A HORSE ...
SIR?
I NEED A HORSE!!
NO, URUKI!
THERE'S ANOTHER SNOWSTORM COMING IN TONIGHT!
I'M GOING TO TÈWULÁN NOW!!
WHAT'S GOING ON?
IT'S THE SCENT OF TOQA!!
WHAT?
TAKIKO'S COME BACK!!

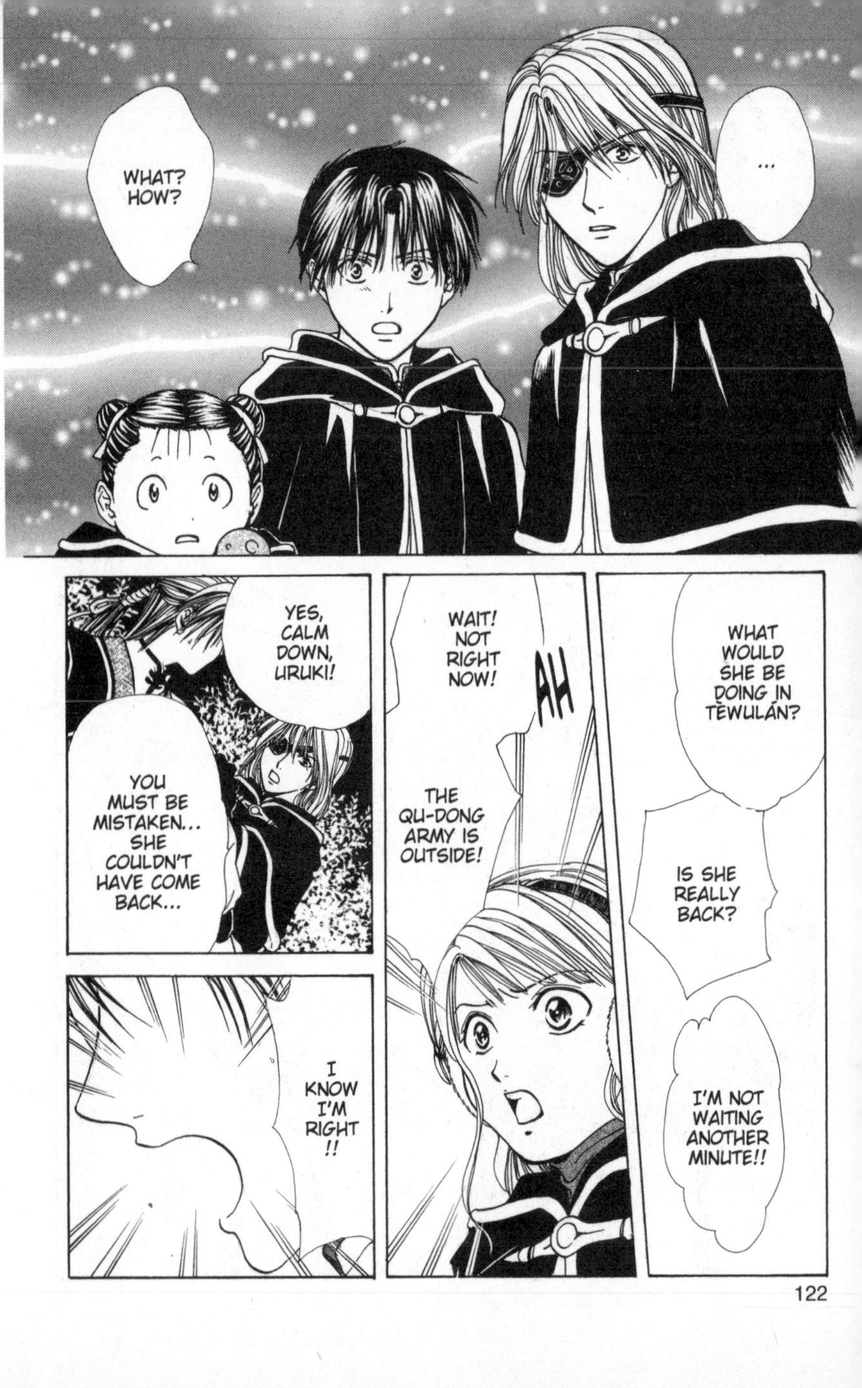
...
WHAT? HOW?
WHAT WOULD SHE BE DOING IN TÈWULÁN?
IS SHE REALLY BACK?
I'M NOT WAITING ANOTHER MINUTE!!
WAIT! NOT RIGHT NOW!
AH
THE QU-DONG ARMY IS OUTSIDE!
YES, CALM DOWN, URUKI!
YOU MUST BE MISTAKEN... SHE COULDN'T HAVE COME BACK...
I KNOW I'M RIGHT!!

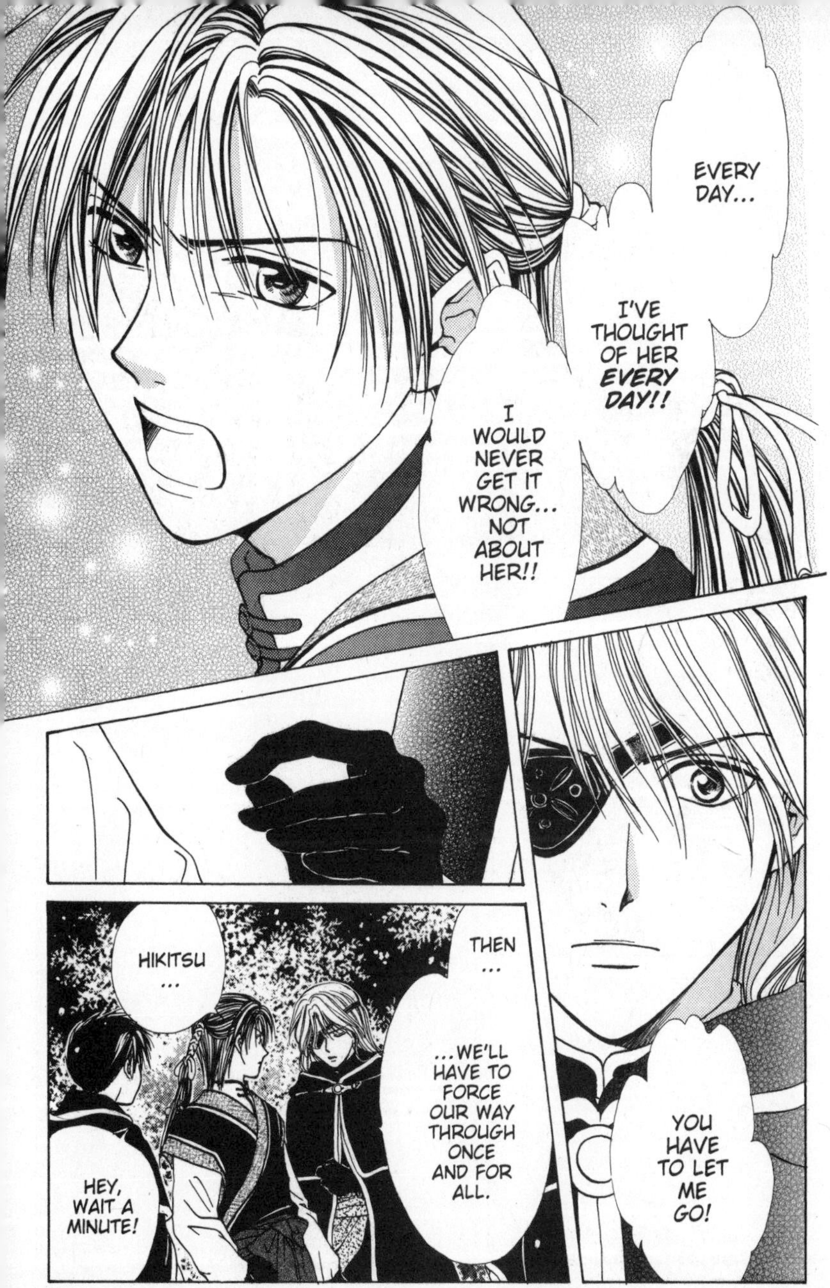
EVERY DAY...
I'VE THOUGHT OF HER ***EVERY DAY!!***
I WOULD NEVER GET IT WRONG... NOT ABOUT HER!!
YOU HAVE TO LET ME GO!
THEN ...
...WE'LL HAVE TO FORCE OUR WAY THROUGH ONCE AND FOR ALL.
HIKITSU ...
HEY, WAIT A MINUTE!

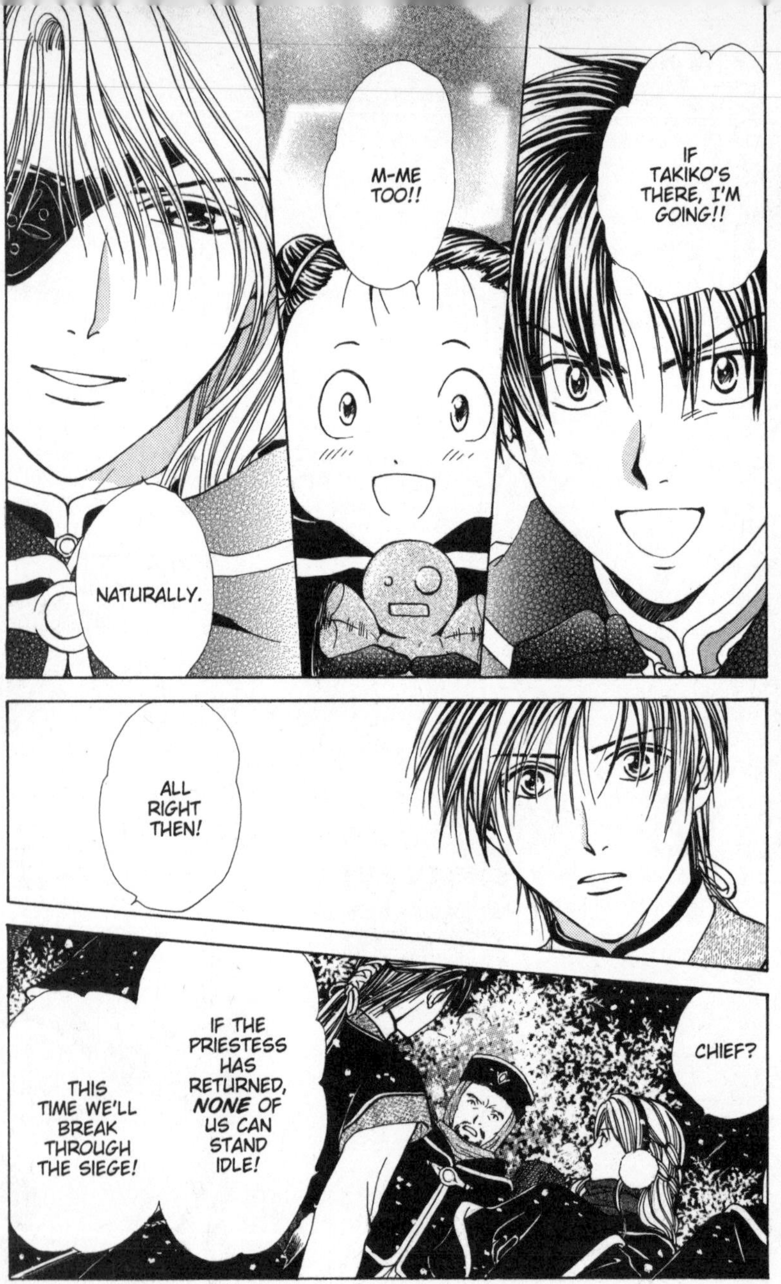
IF TAKIKO'S THERE, I'M GOING!!
M-ME TOO!!
NATURALLY.
ALL RIGHT THEN!
CHIEF?
IF THE PRIESTESS HAS RETURNED, *NONE* OF US CAN STAND IDLE!
THIS TIME WE'LL BREAK THROUGH THE SIEGE!

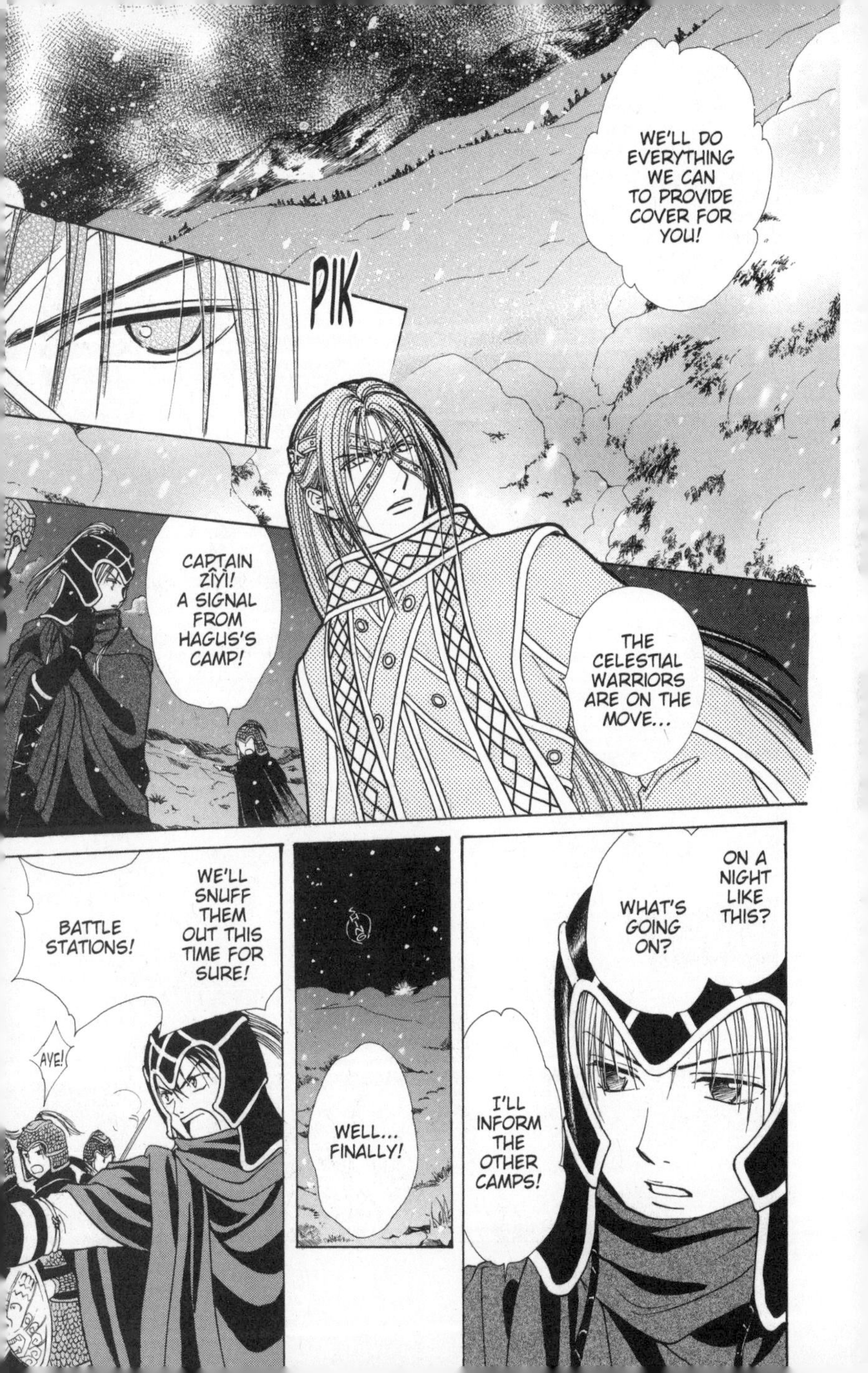
WE'LL DO EVERYTHING WE CAN TO PROVIDE COVER FOR YOU!
PIK
CAPTAIN ZÎYÎ! A SIGNAL FROM HAGUS'S CAMP!
THE CELESTIAL WARRIORS ARE ON THE MOVE...
ON A NIGHT LIKE THIS?
WHAT'S GOING ON?
I'LL INFORM THE OTHER CAMPS!
SHINE
WELL... FINALLY!
WE'LL SNUFF THEM OUT THIS TIME FOR SURE!
BATTLE STATIONS!
AYE!

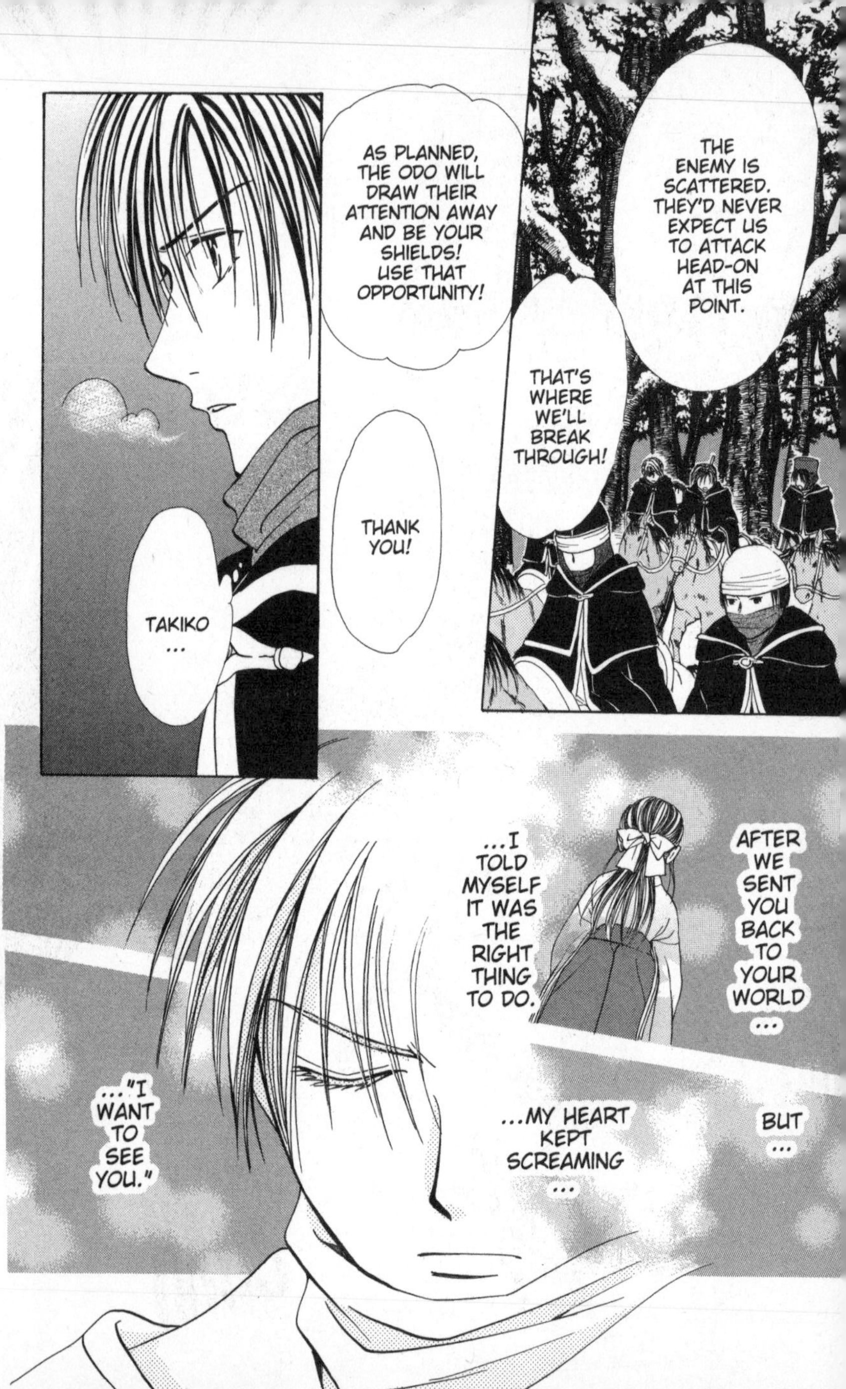
THE ENEMY IS SCATTERED. THEY'D NEVER EXPECT US TO ATTACK HEAD-ON AT THIS POINT.
THAT'S WHERE WE'LL BREAK THROUGH!
AS PLANNED, THE ODO WILL DRAW THEIR ATTENTION AWAY AND BE YOUR SHIELDS! USE THAT OPPORTUNITY!
THANK YOU!
TAKIKO ...
AFTER WE SENT YOU BACK TO YOUR WORLD ...
...I TOLD MYSELF IT WAS THE RIGHT THING TO DO.
BUT ...
...MY HEART KEPT SCREAMING ...
..."I WANT TO SEE YOU."

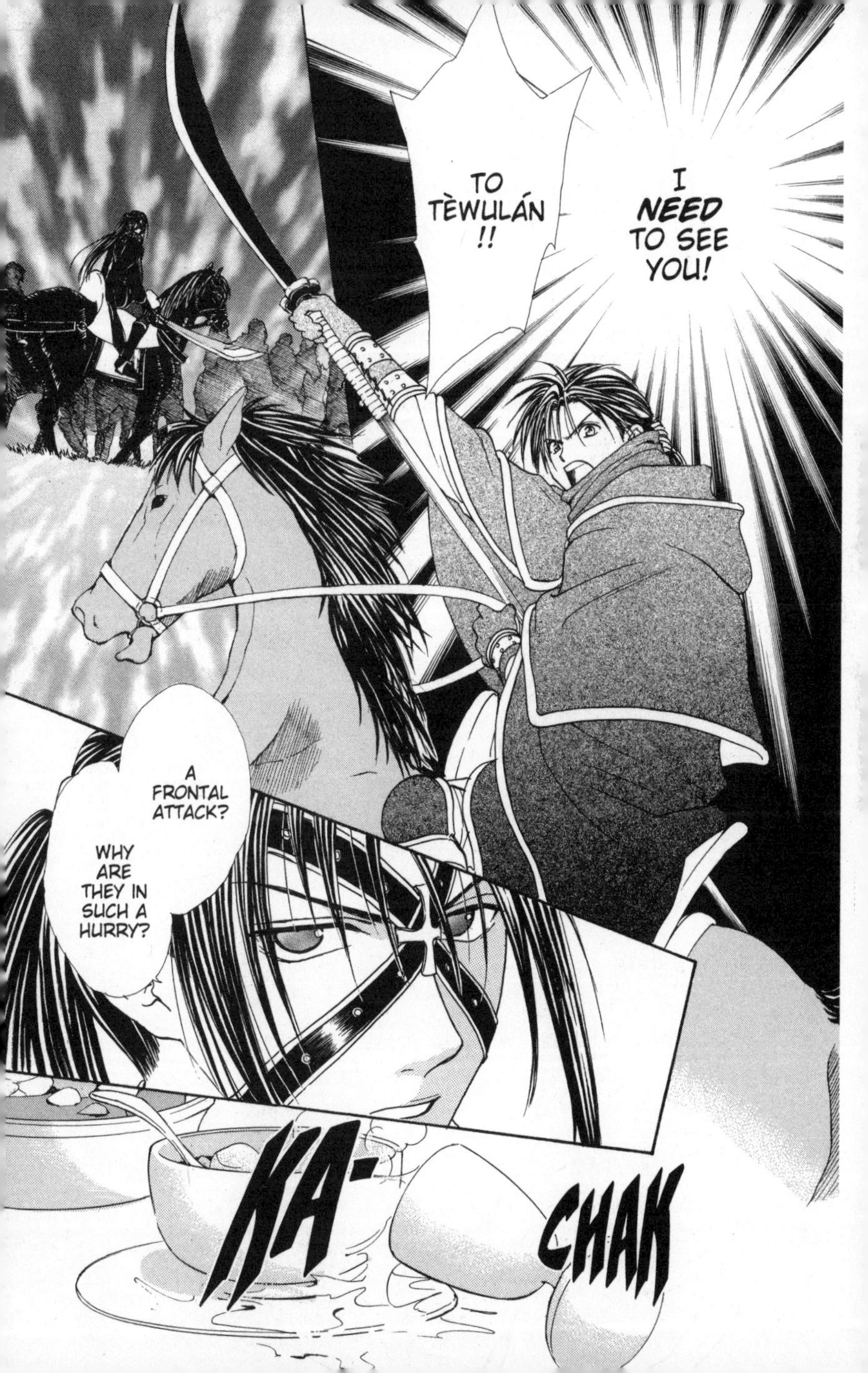
I ***NEED*** TO SEE YOU!
TO TÈWULÁN !!
A FRONTAL ATTACK?
WHY ARE THEY IN SUCH A HURRY?
KA-CHAK

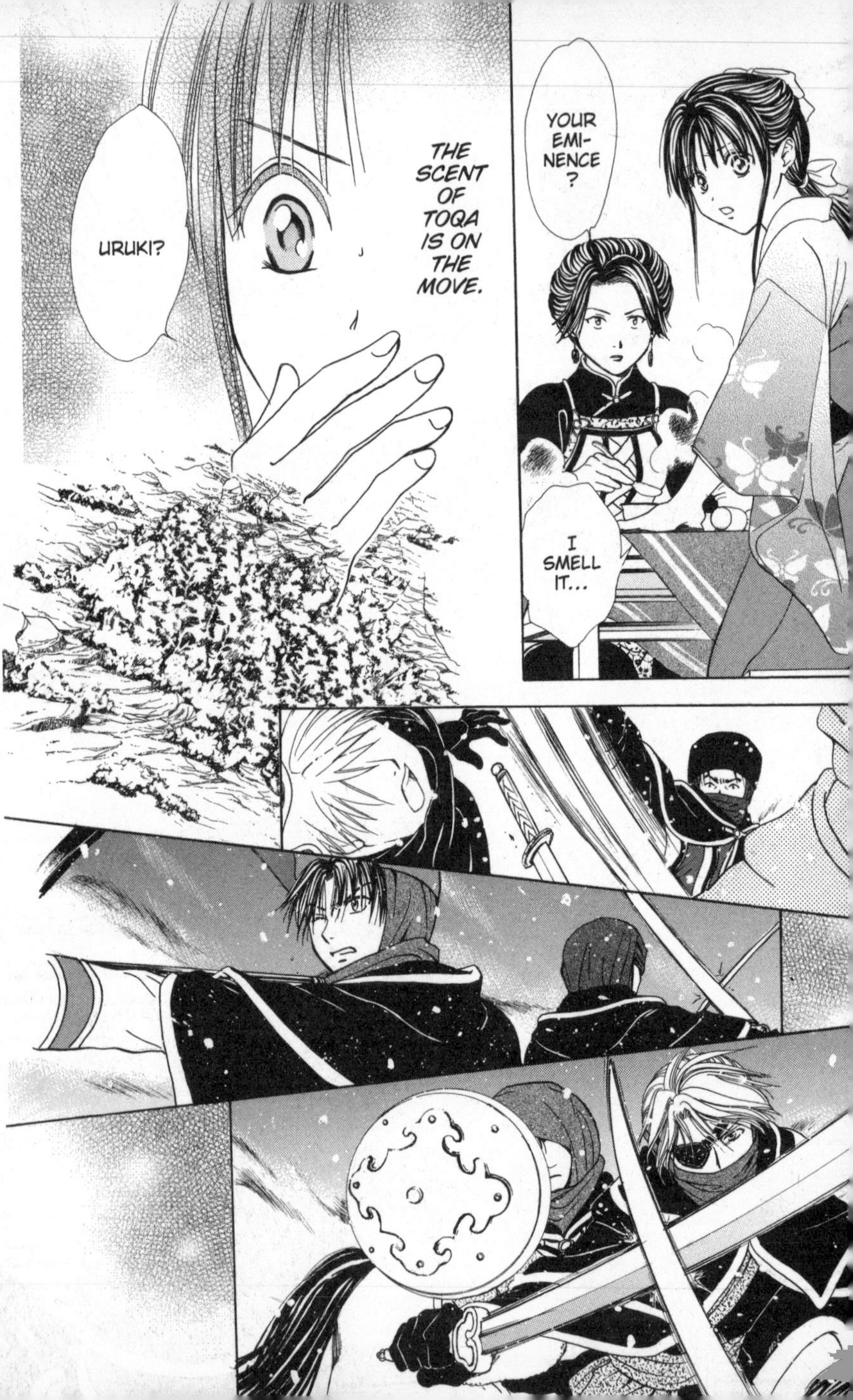
YOUR EMINENCE?
I SMELL IT...
THE SCENT OF TOQA IS ON THE MOVE.
URUKI?

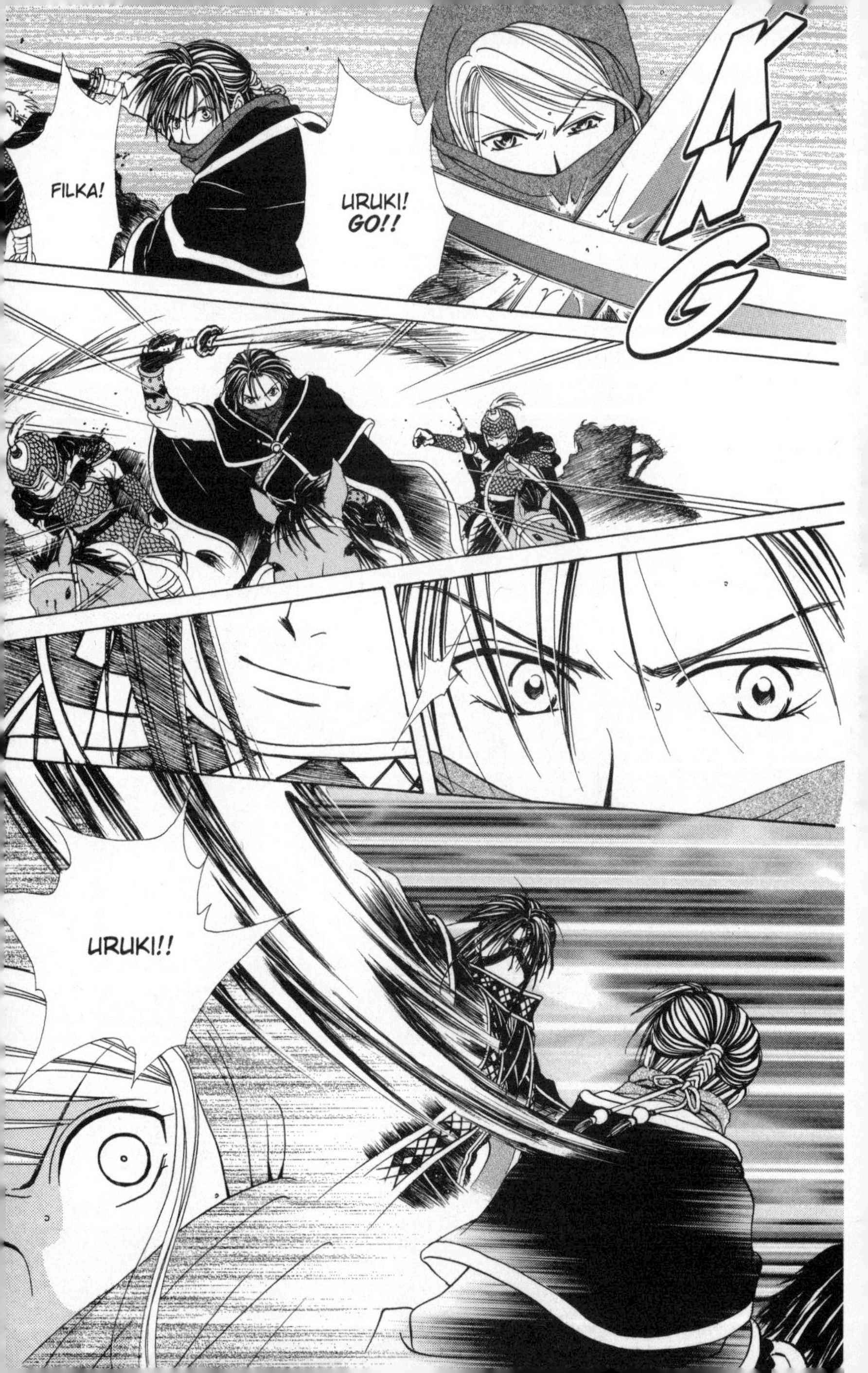
KANG
URUKI! GO!!
FILKA!
URUKI!!

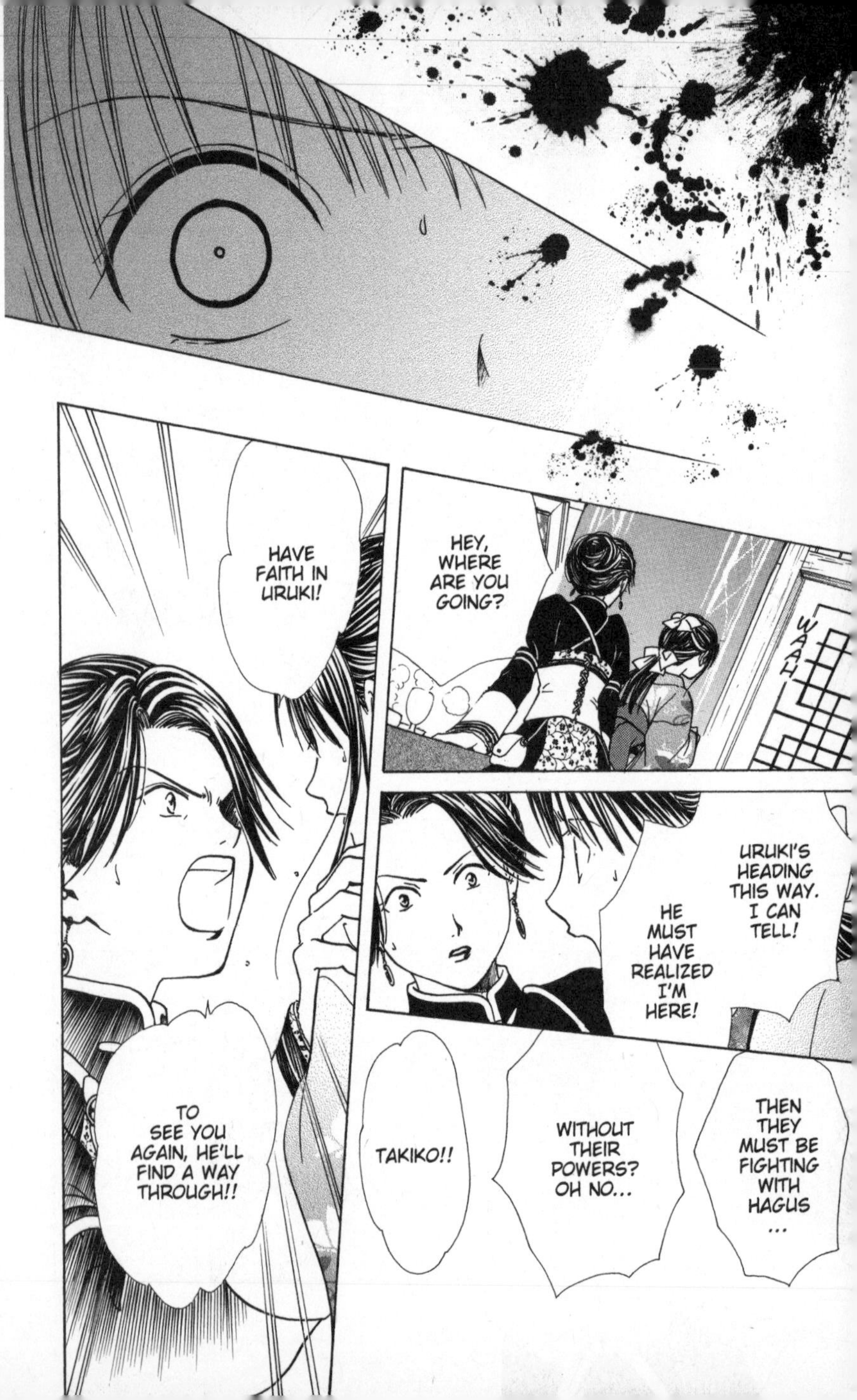
HEY, WHERE ARE YOU GOING?
WAAH
URUKI'S HEADING THIS WAY. I CAN TELL!
HE MUST HAVE REALIZED I'M HERE!
THEN THEY MUST BE FIGHTING WITH HAGUS...
WITHOUT THEIR POWERS? OH NO...
TAKIKO!!
HAVE FAITH IN URUKI!
TO SEE YOU AGAIN, HE'LL FIND A WAY THROUGH!!

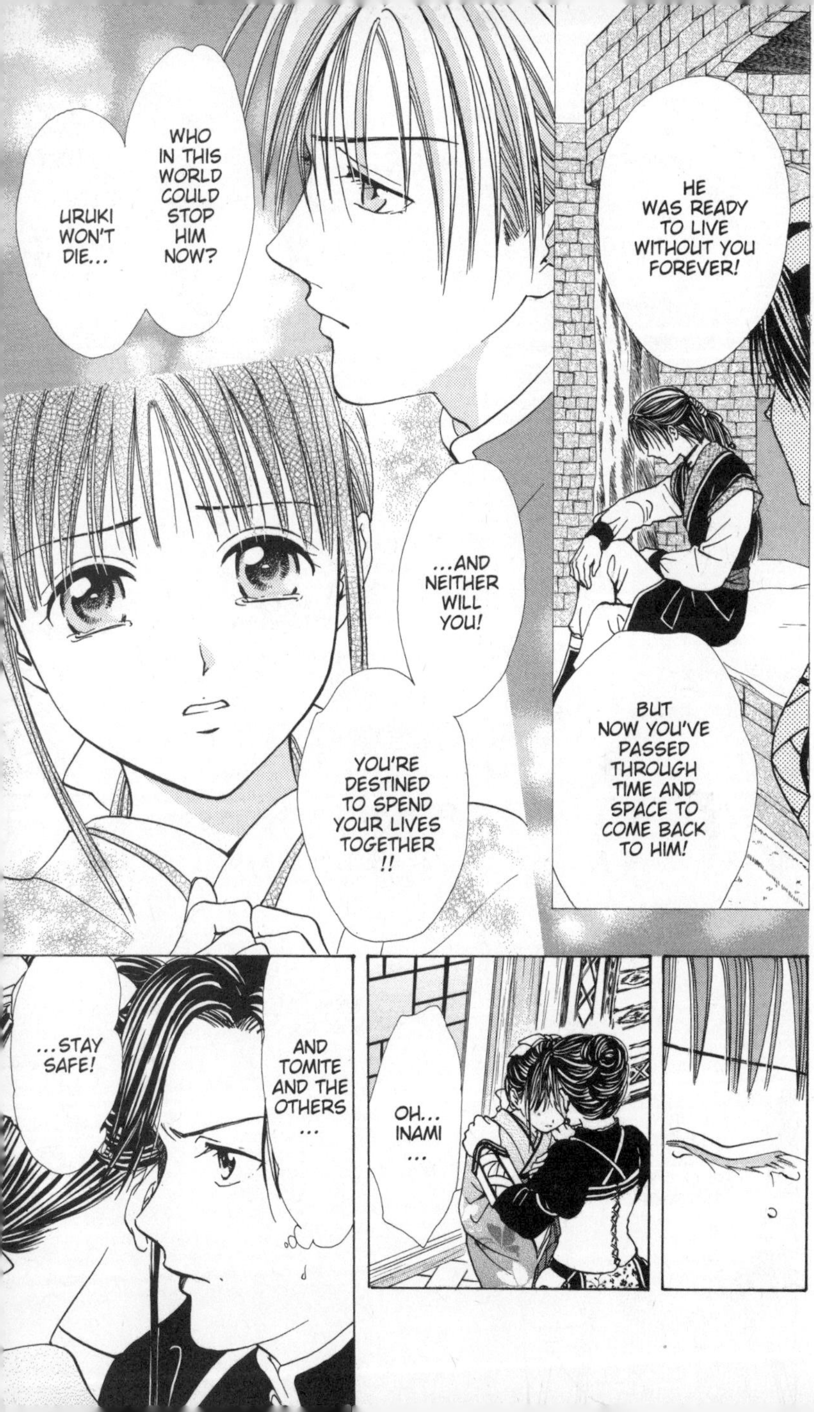
HE WAS READY TO LIVE WITHOUT YOU FOREVER!
BUT NOW YOU'VE PASSED THROUGH TIME AND SPACE TO COME BACK TO HIM!
WHO IN THIS WORLD COULD STOP HIM NOW?
URUKI WON'T DIE...
...AND NEITHER WILL YOU!
YOU'RE DESTINED TO SPEND YOUR LIVES TOGETHER !!
OH... INAMI ...
AND TOMITE AND THE OTHERS ...
...STAY SAFE!

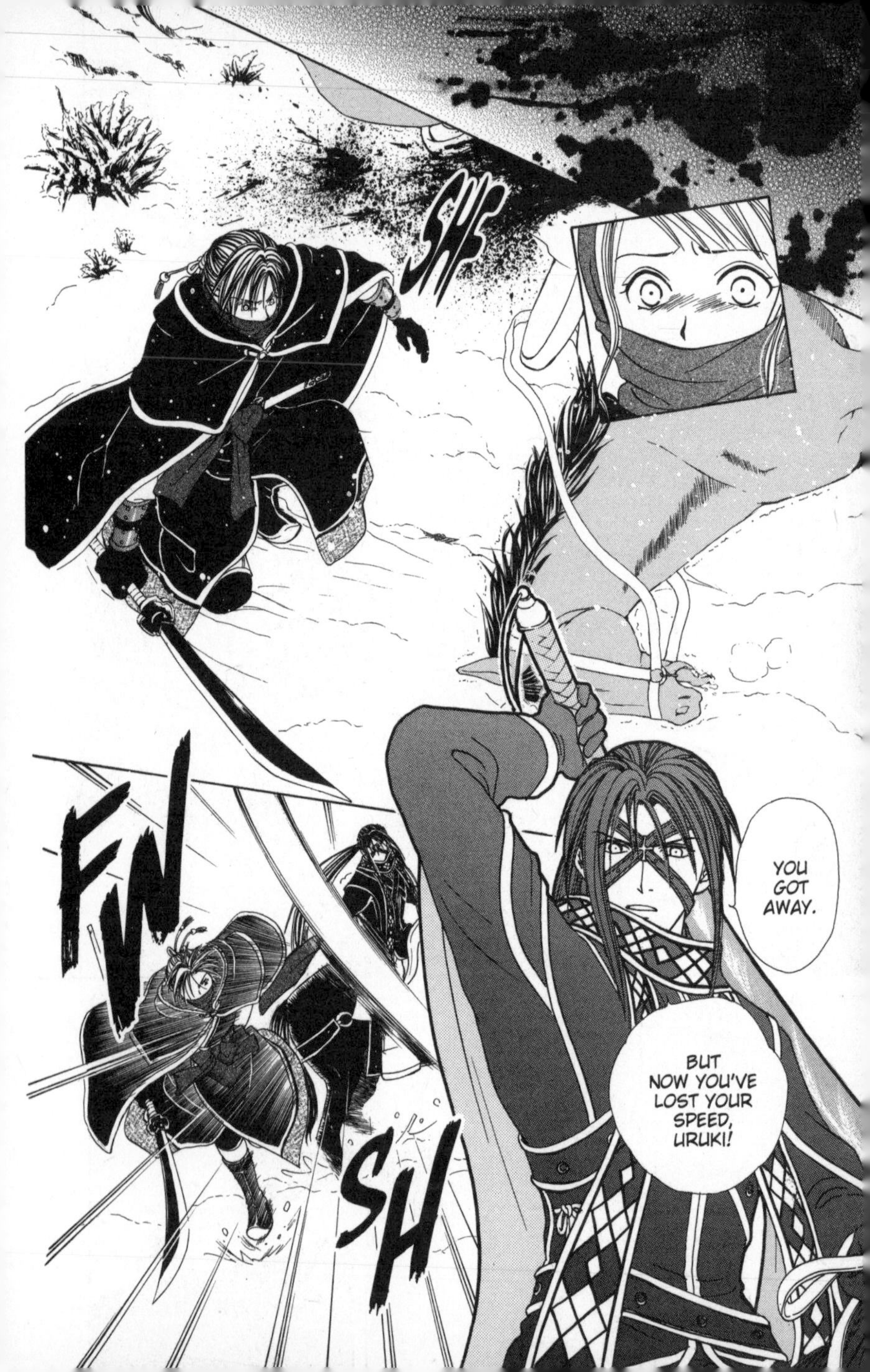
SHF
YOU GOT AWAY.
BUT NOW YOU'VE LOST YOUR SPEED, URUKI!
SH
FW

KRii

FFF

HAGUS!

REMEMBER ME?

iiS

UNH!

H

DAMN! THEY'RE CATCHING UP!

RMMM

WHH

WP

POP

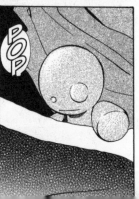

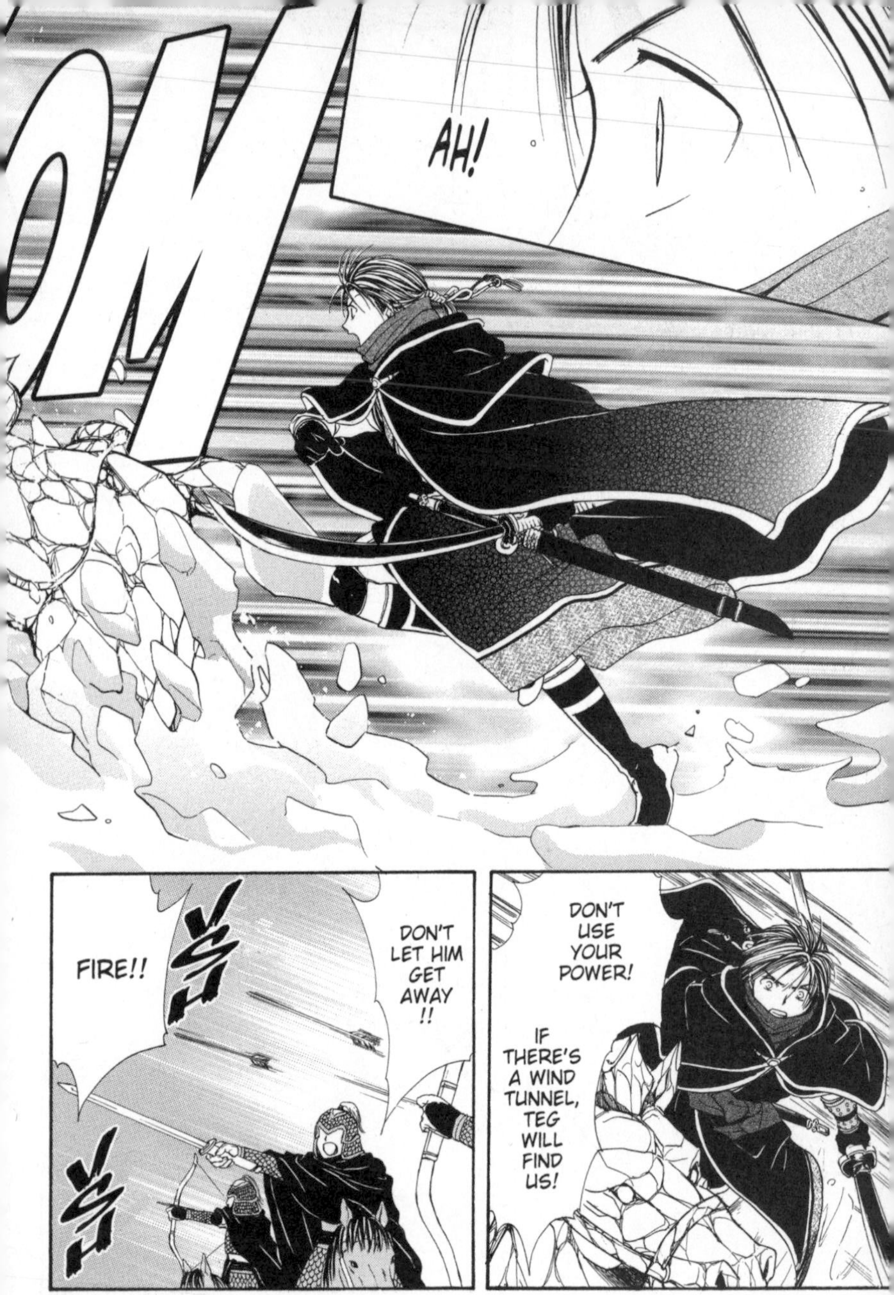
AH!
DON'T USE YOUR POWER!
IF THERE'S A WIND TUNNEL, TEG WILL FIND US!
DON'T LET HIM GET AWAY !!
FIRE!!

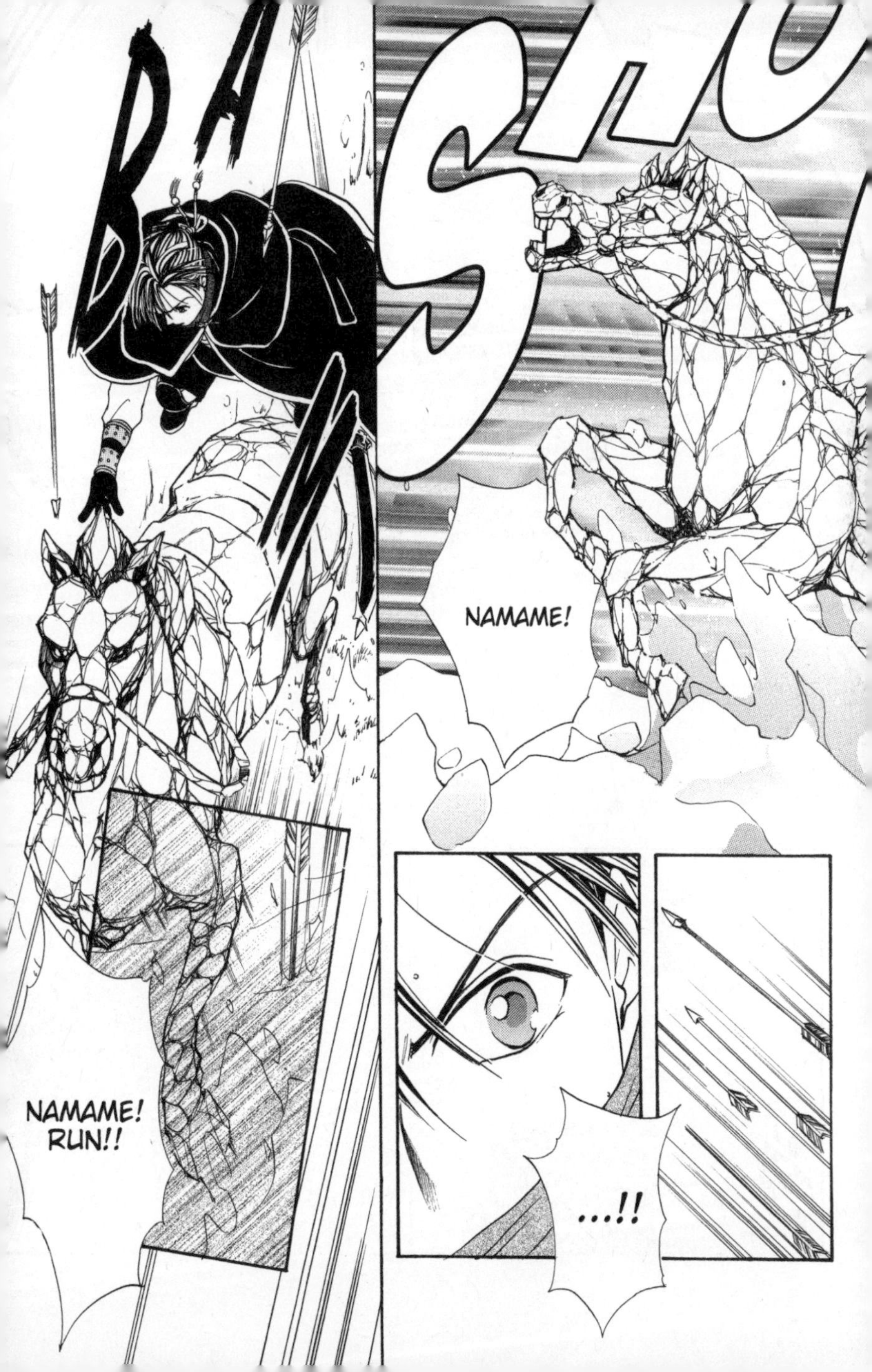
NAMAME!
...!!
NAMAME! RUN!!

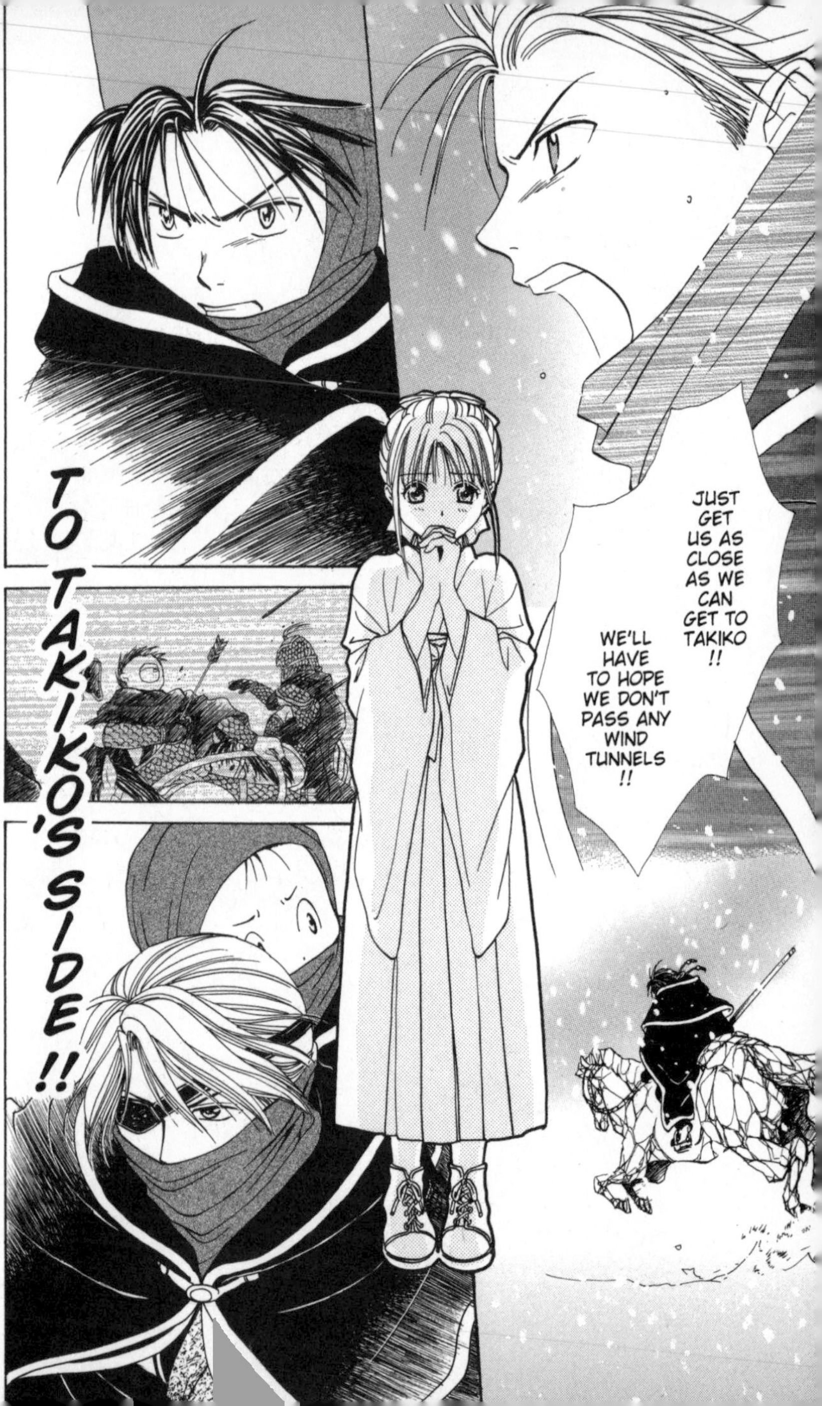
JUST GET US AS CLOSE AS WE CAN GET TO TAKIKO !!
WE'LL HAVE TO HOPE WE DON'T PASS ANY WIND TUNNELS !!
TO TAKIKO'S SIDE!!

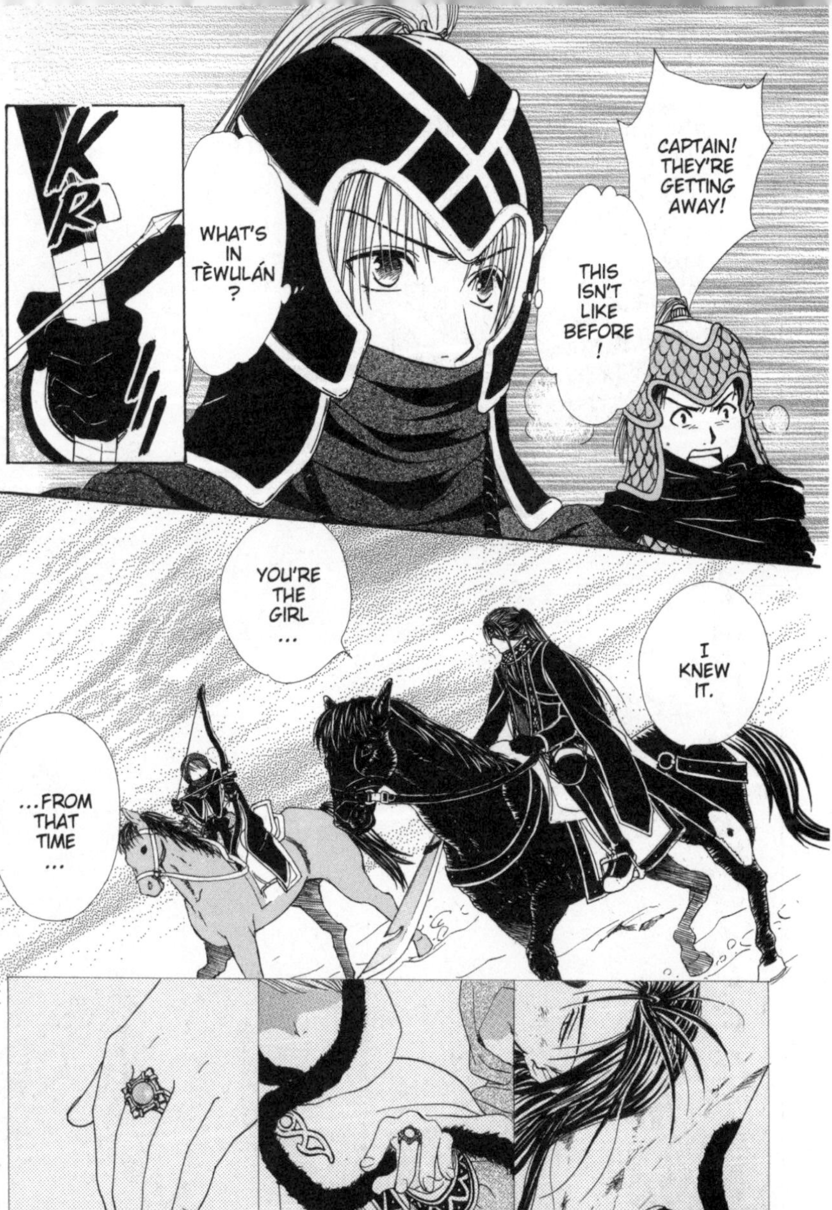
CAPTAIN! THEY'RE GETTING AWAY!
THIS ISN'T LIKE BEFORE!
WHAT'S IN TÈWULÁN?
KR
I KNEW IT.
YOU'RE THE GIRL...
...FROM THAT TIME...

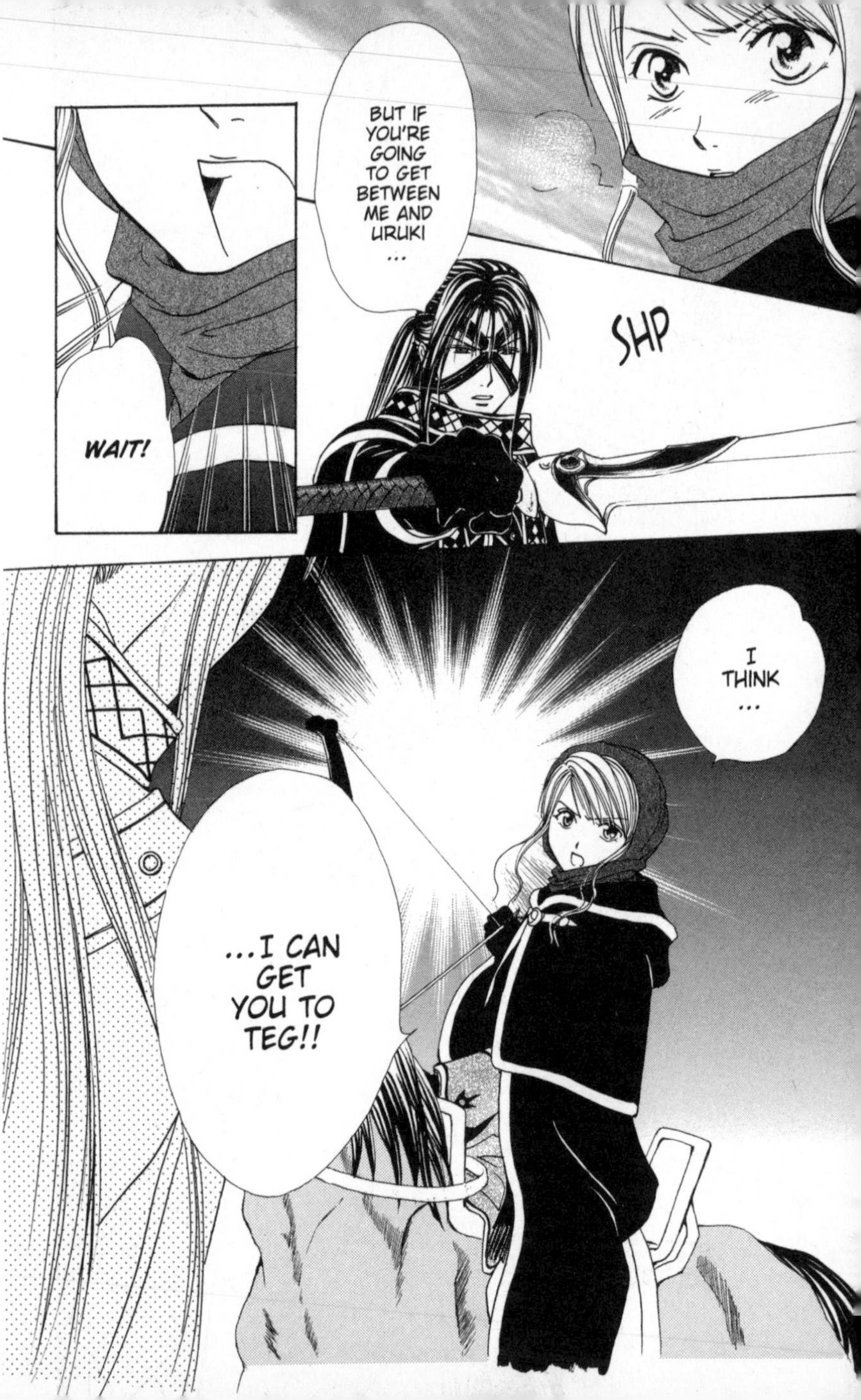
BUT IF YOU'RE GOING TO GET BETWEEN ME AND URUKI ...
SHP
WAIT!
I THINK ...
...I CAN GET YOU TO TEG!!

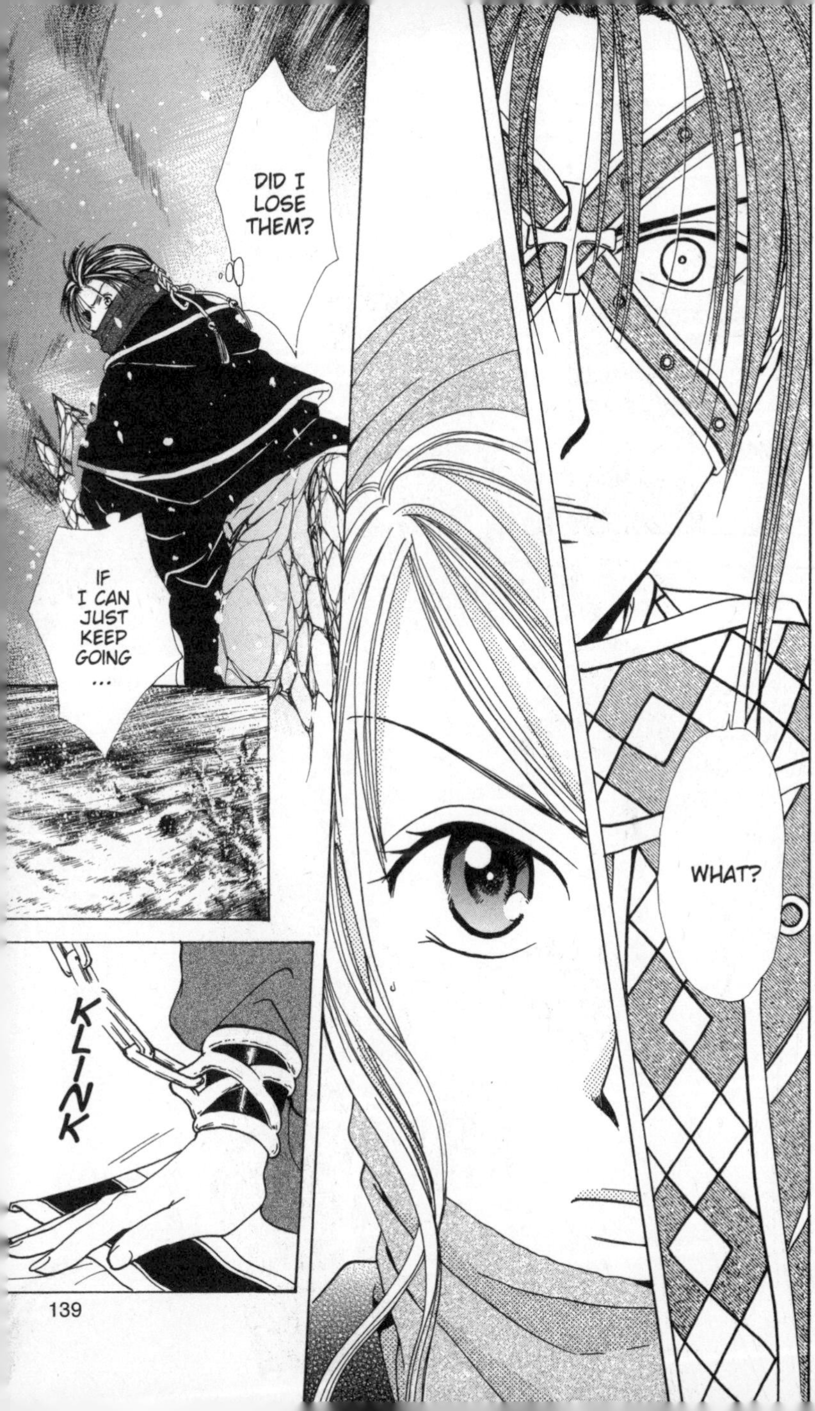
WHAT?
DID I LOSE THEM?
IF I CAN JUST KEEP GOING ...
KLINK

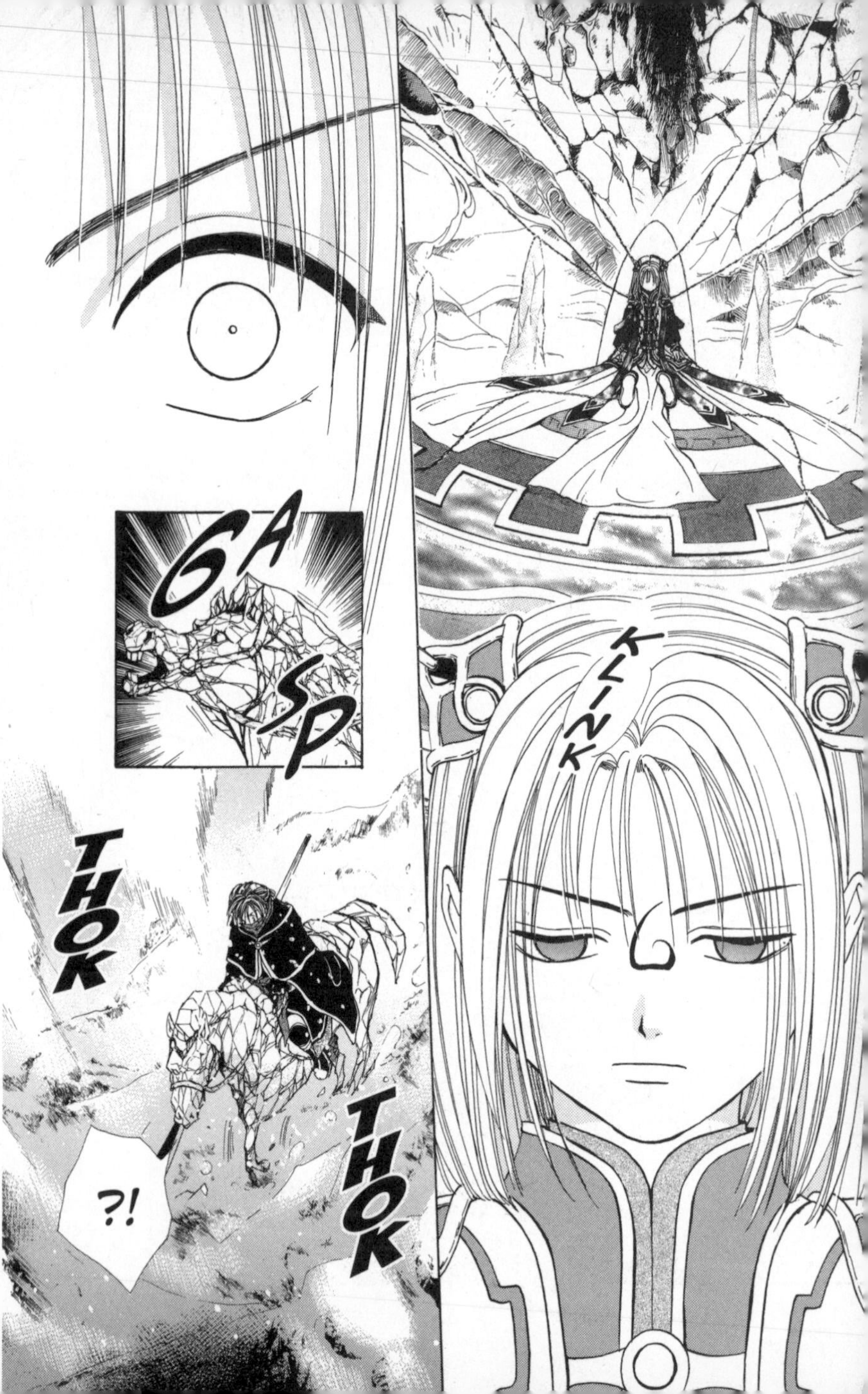
KLINK
GASP
THOK
THOK
?!

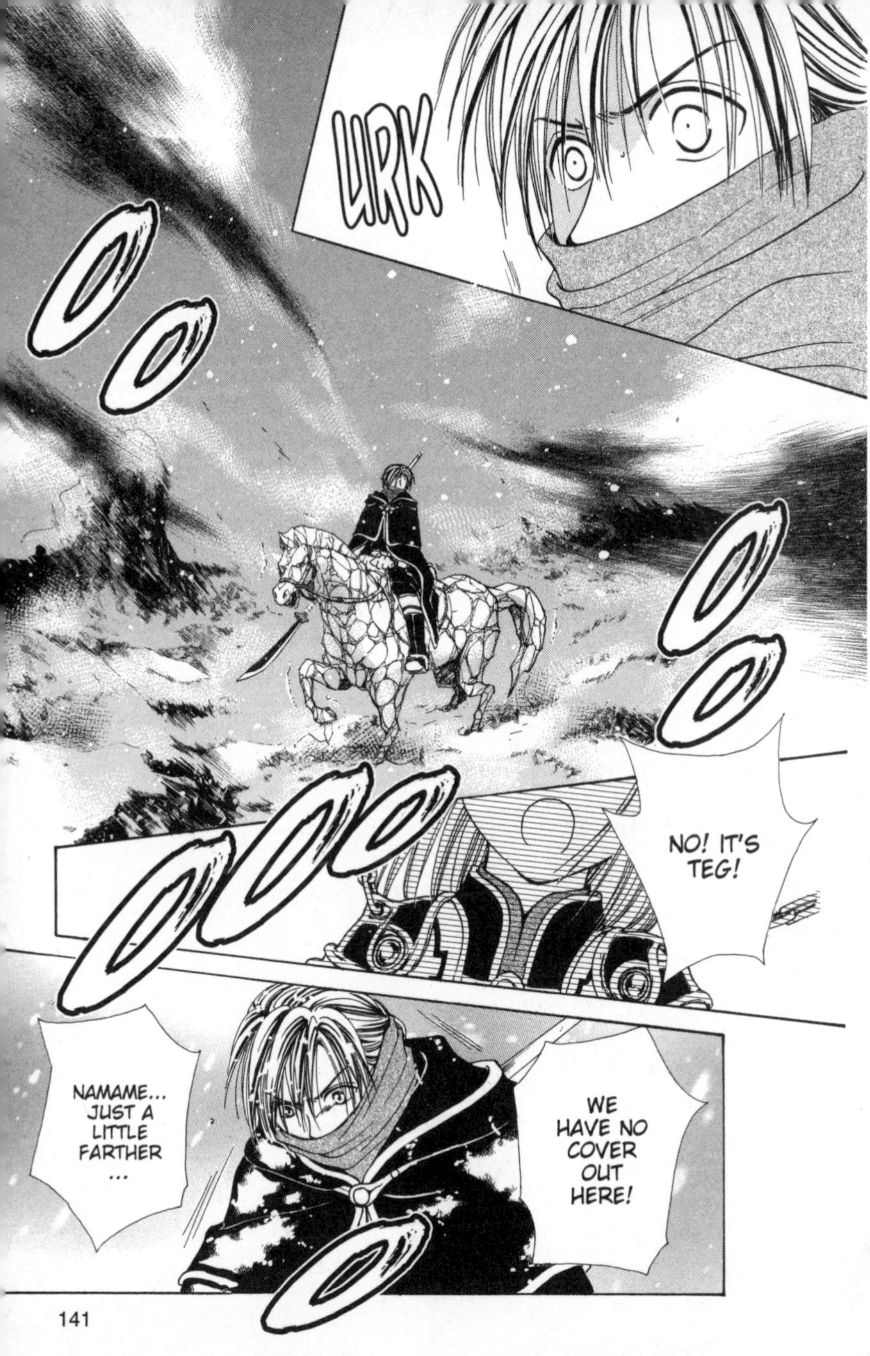
URK
OOO
OOO
OOOO
NO! IT'S TEG!
WE HAVE NO COVER OUT HERE!
NAMAME... JUST A LITTLE FARTHER ...
O

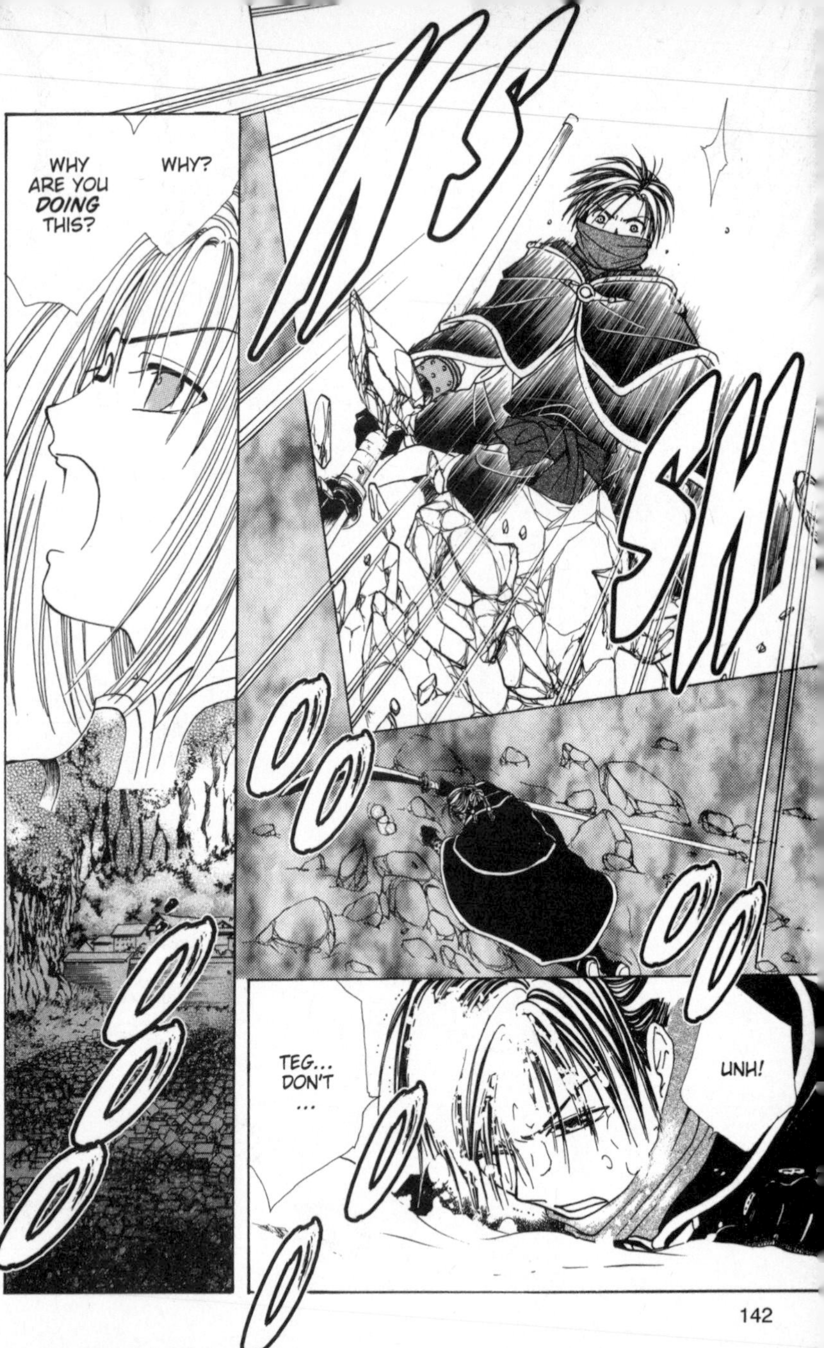
UNH!
TEG... DON'T ...
WHY?
WHY ARE YOU *DOING* THIS?

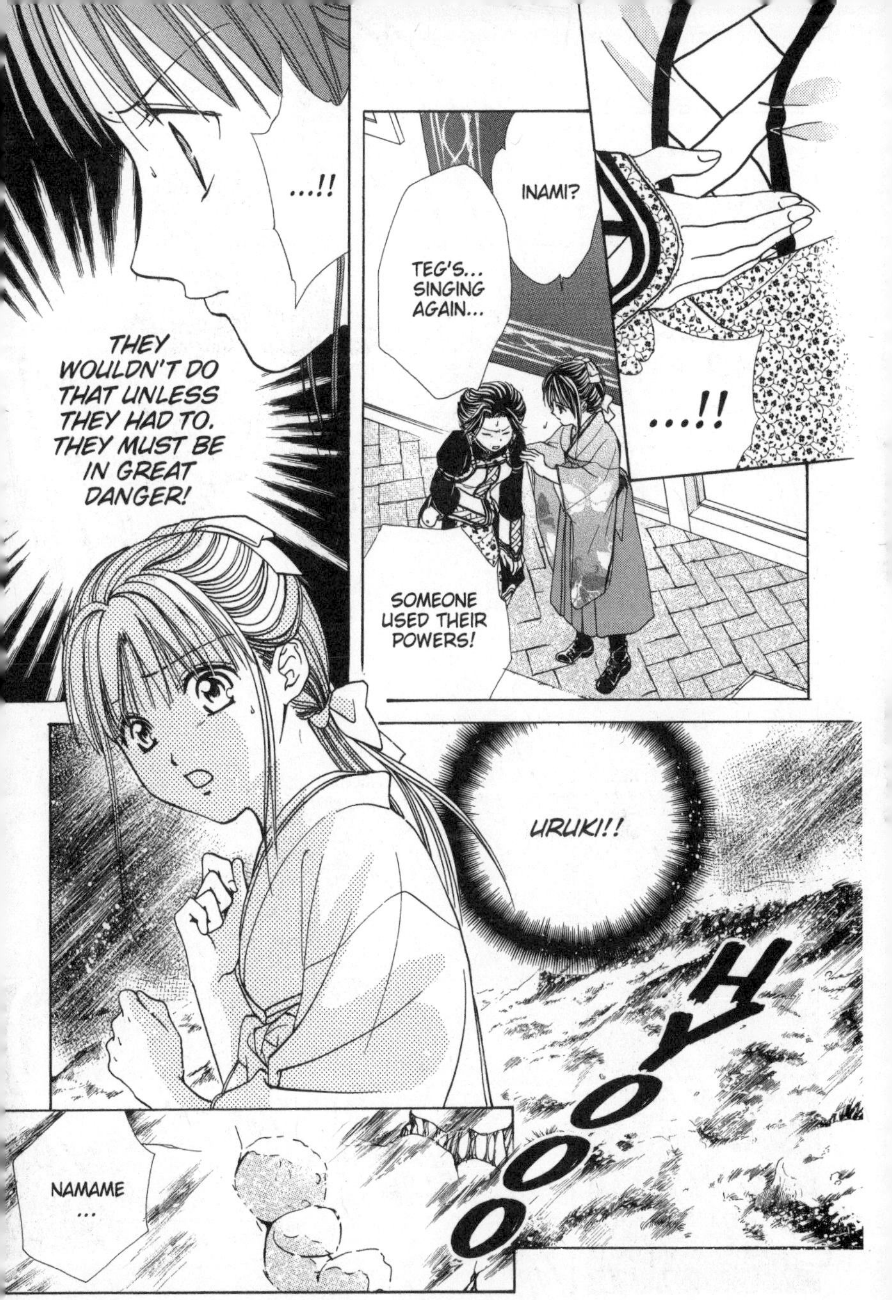
...!!
INAMI?
TEG'S... SINGING AGAIN...
SOMEONE USED THEIR POWERS!
...!!
THEY WOULDN'T DO THAT UNLESS THEY HAD TO. THEY MUST BE IN GREAT DANGER!
URUKI!!
HYOOOOO
NAMAME ...

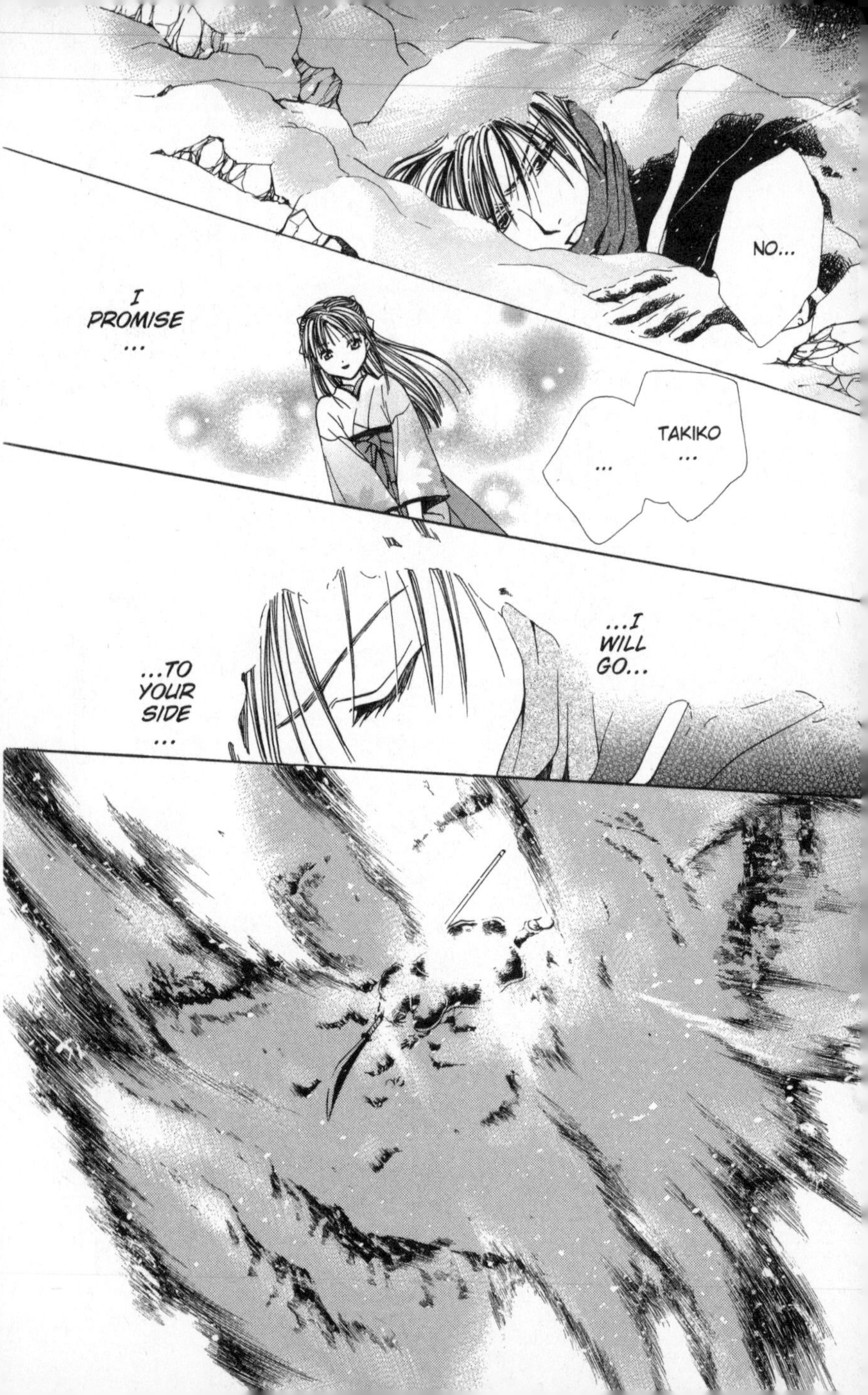
NO...
TAKIKO ... ...
I PROMISE ...
...I WILL GO...
...TO YOUR SIDE ...

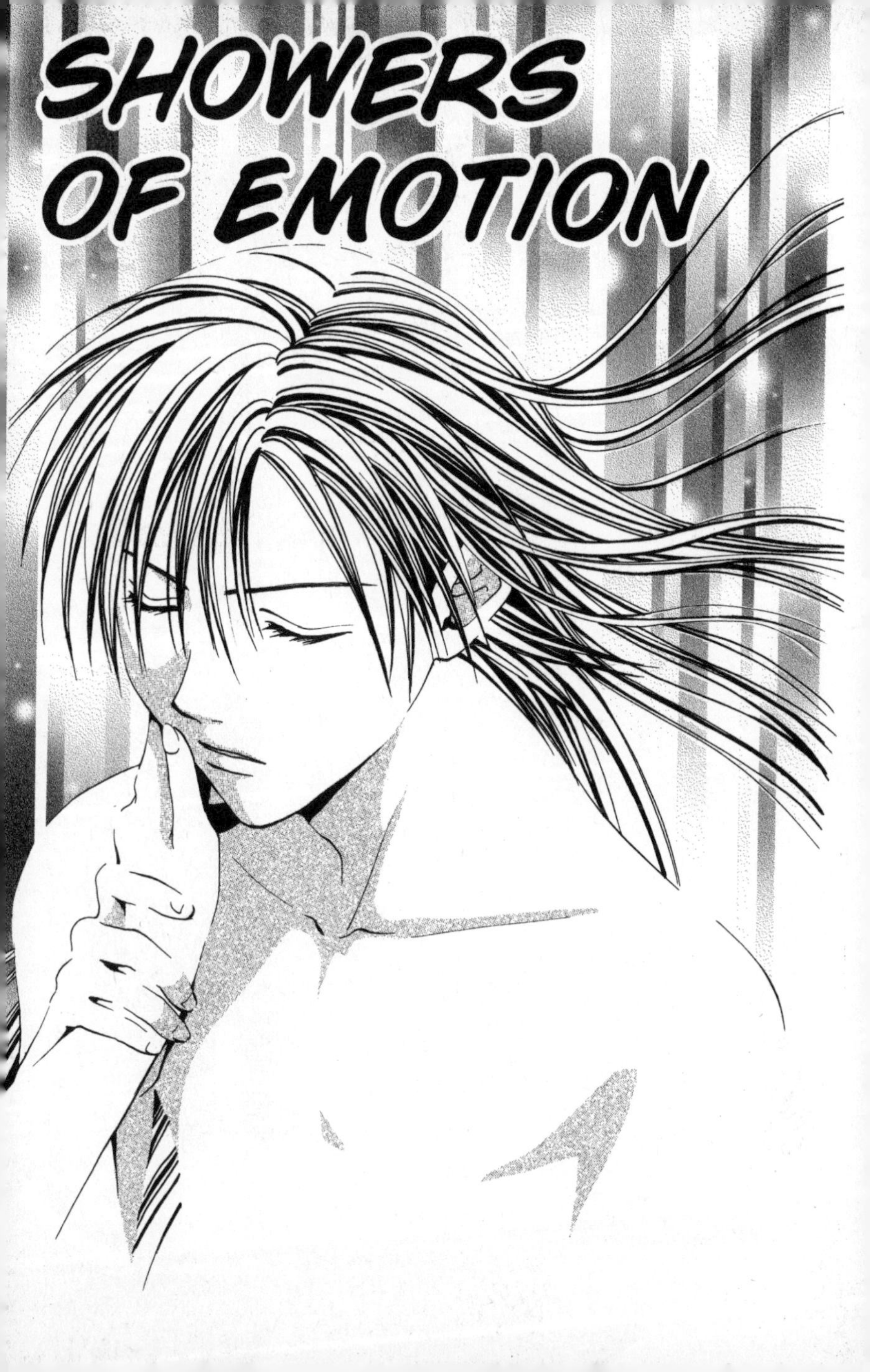
SHOWERS OF EMOTION

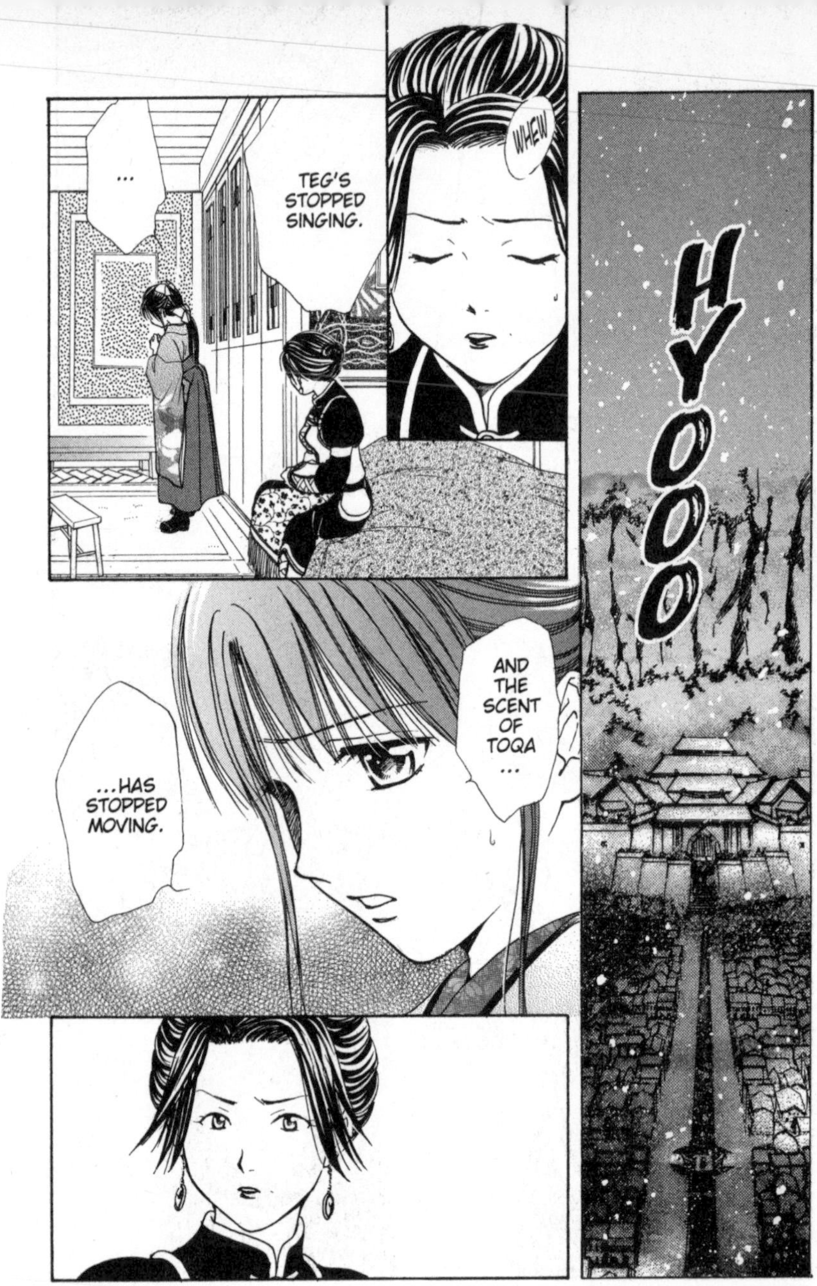
HYOOO
WHEW
TEG'S STOPPED SINGING.
...
AND THE SCENT OF TOQA ...
...HAS STOPPED MOVING.

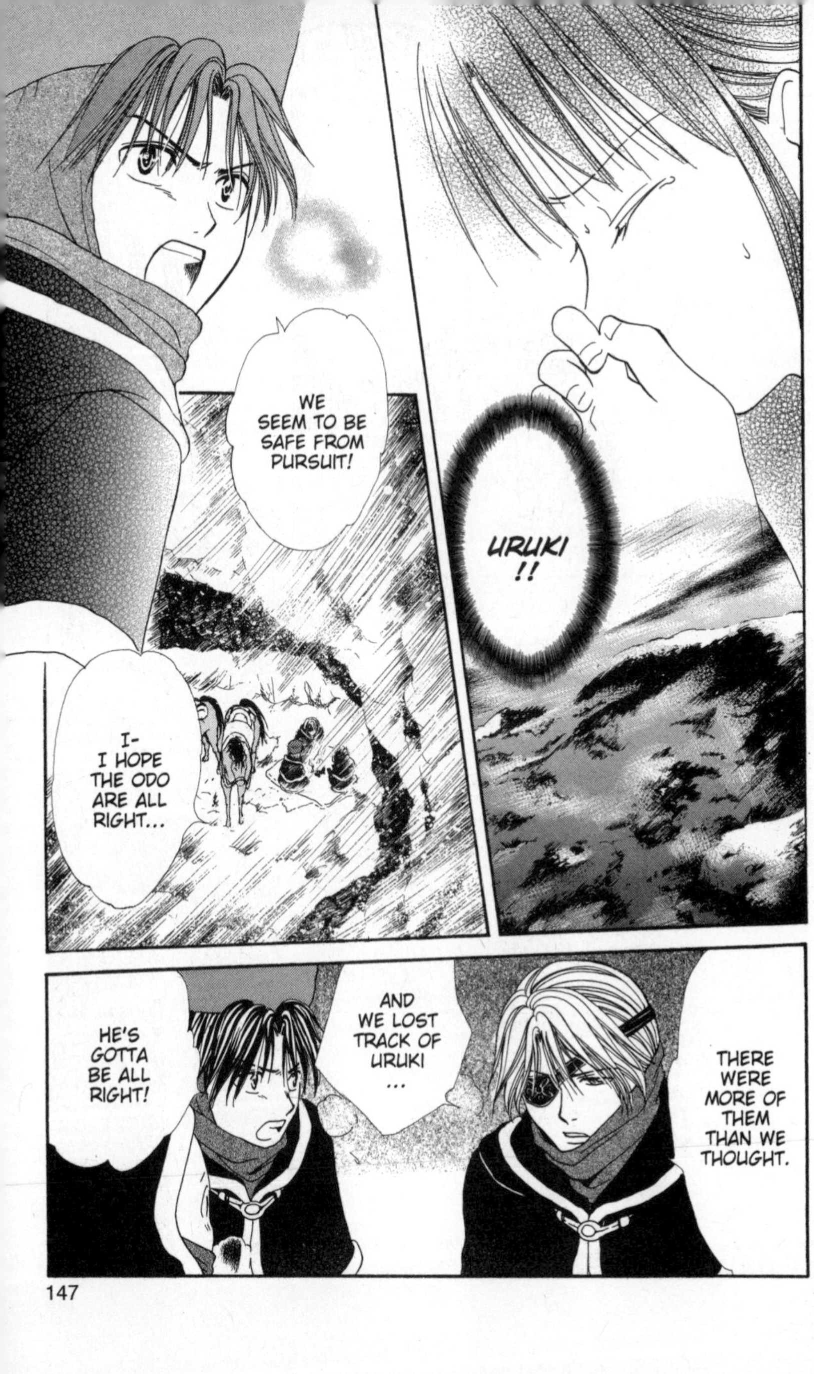
URUKI !!
WE SEEM TO BE SAFE FROM PURSUIT!
I- I HOPE THE ODO ARE ALL RIGHT...
THERE WERE MORE OF THEM THAN WE THOUGHT.
AND WE LOST TRACK OF URUKI ...
HE'S GOTTA BE ALL RIGHT!

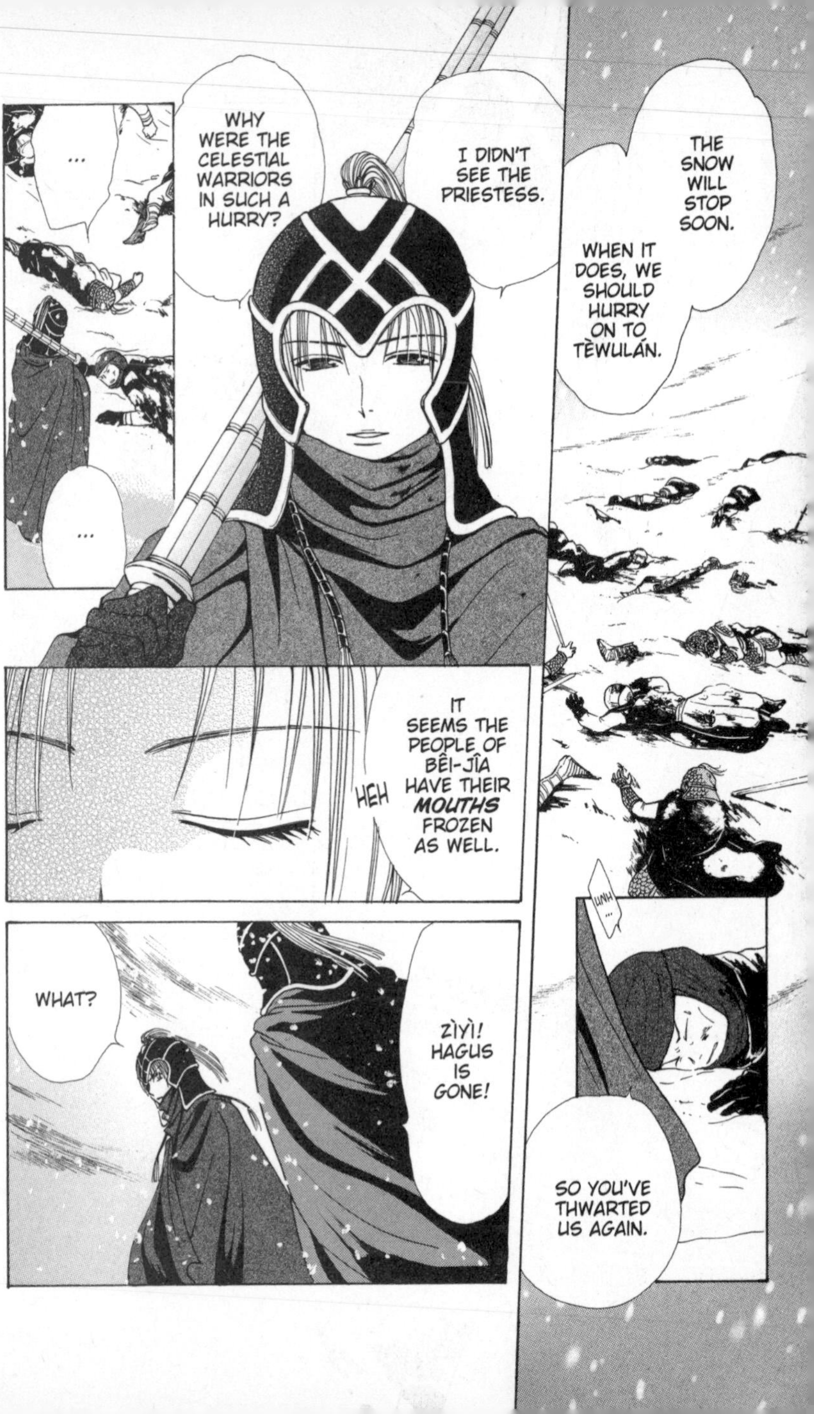
THE SNOW WILL STOP SOON.
WHEN IT DOES, WE SHOULD HURRY ON TO TÈWULÁN.
UNH...
SO YOU'VE THWARTED US AGAIN.
I DIDN'T SEE THE PRIESTESS.
WHY WERE THE CELESTIAL WARRIORS IN SUCH A HURRY?
...
...
IT SEEMS THE PEOPLE OF BÊI-JÎA HAVE THEIR *MOUTHS* FROZEN AS WELL.
HEH
ZÌYÌ! HAGUS IS GONE!
WHAT?

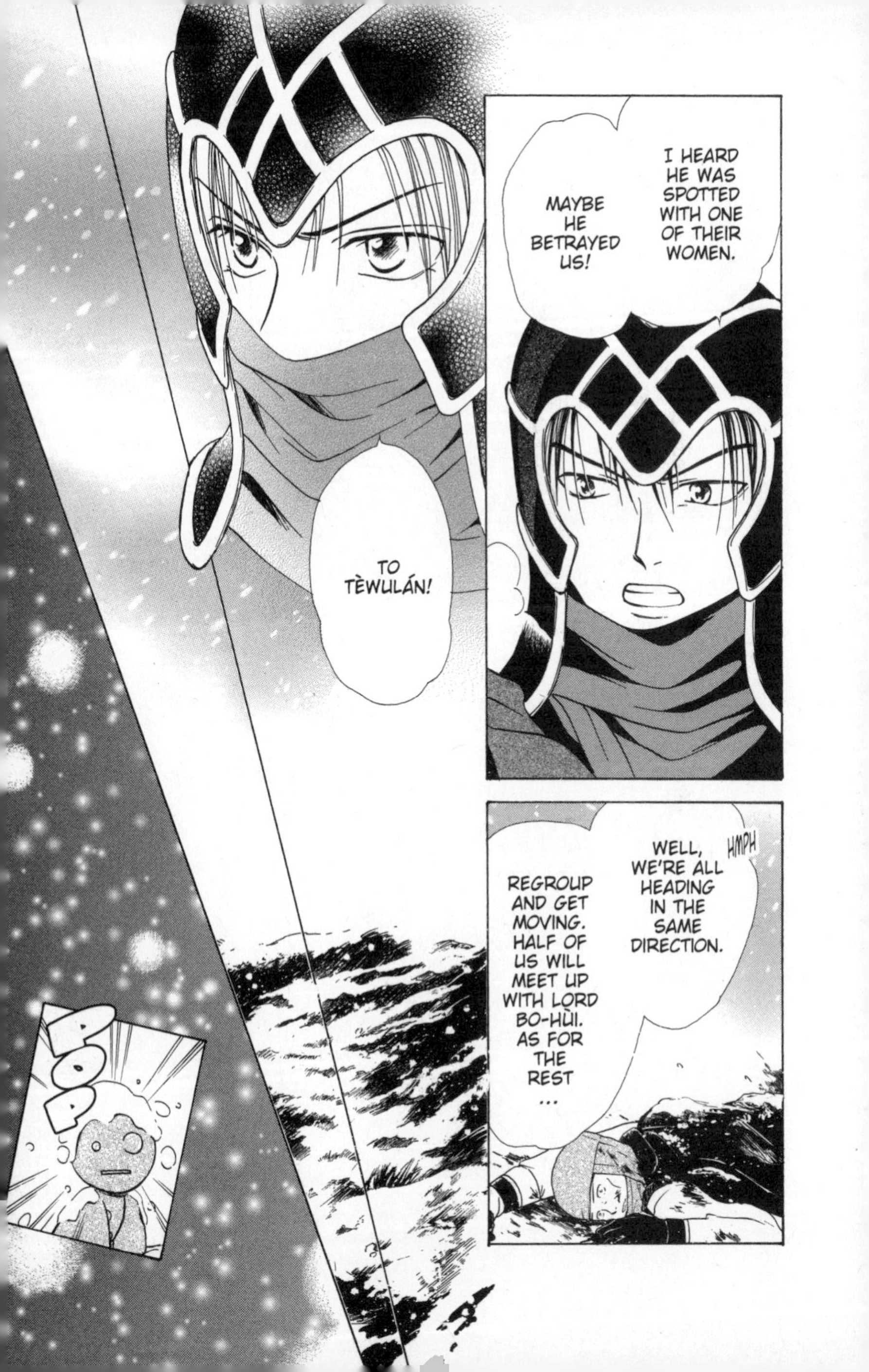
I HEARD HE WAS SPOTTED WITH ONE OF THEIR WOMEN.
MAYBE HE BETRAYED US!
WELL, WE'RE ALL HEADING IN THE SAME DIRECTION.
HMPH
REGROUP AND GET MOVING. HALF OF US WILL MEET UP WITH LORD BO-HÙI. AS FOR THE REST ...
TO TÈWULÁN!
POP

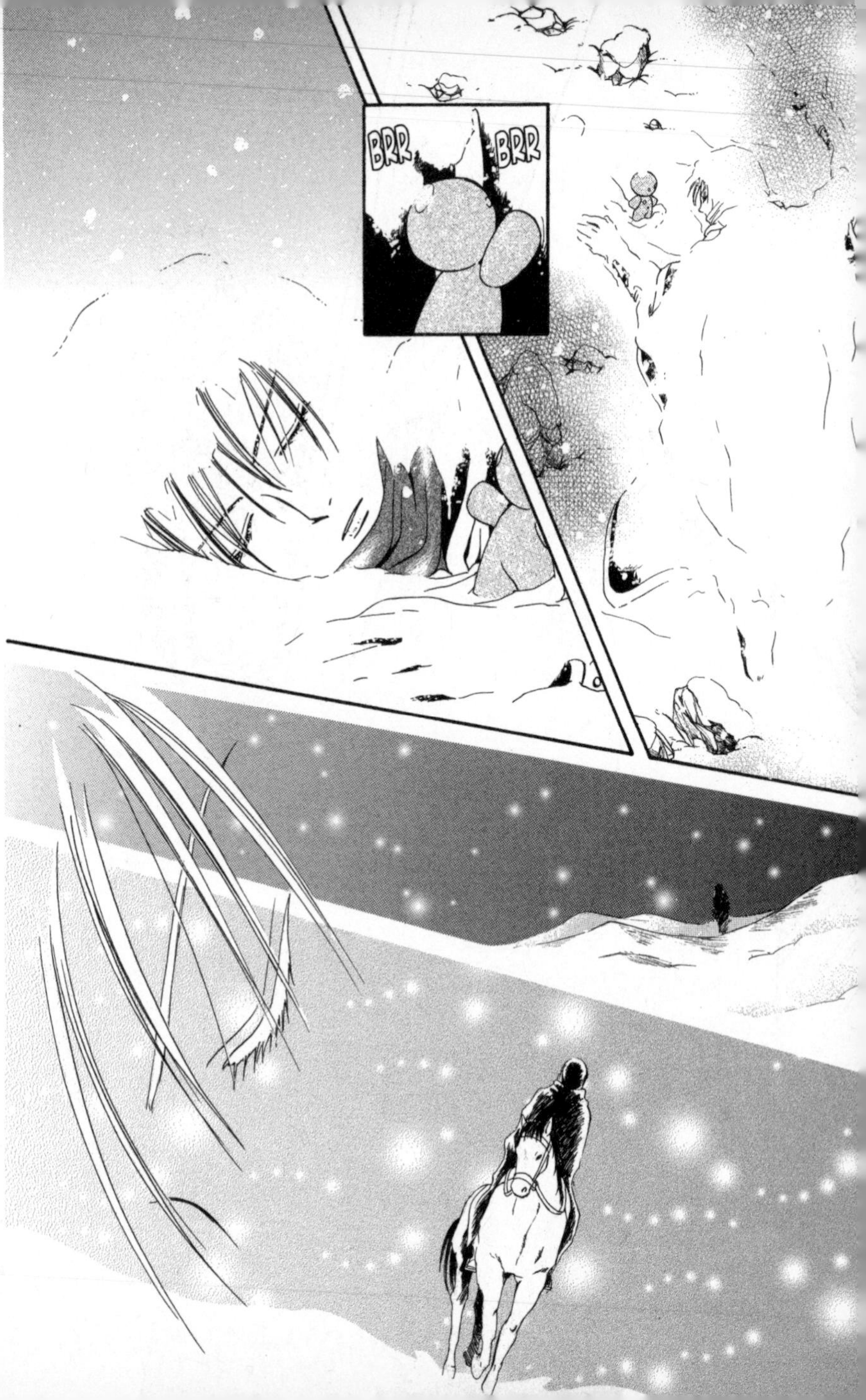
BRR
BRR

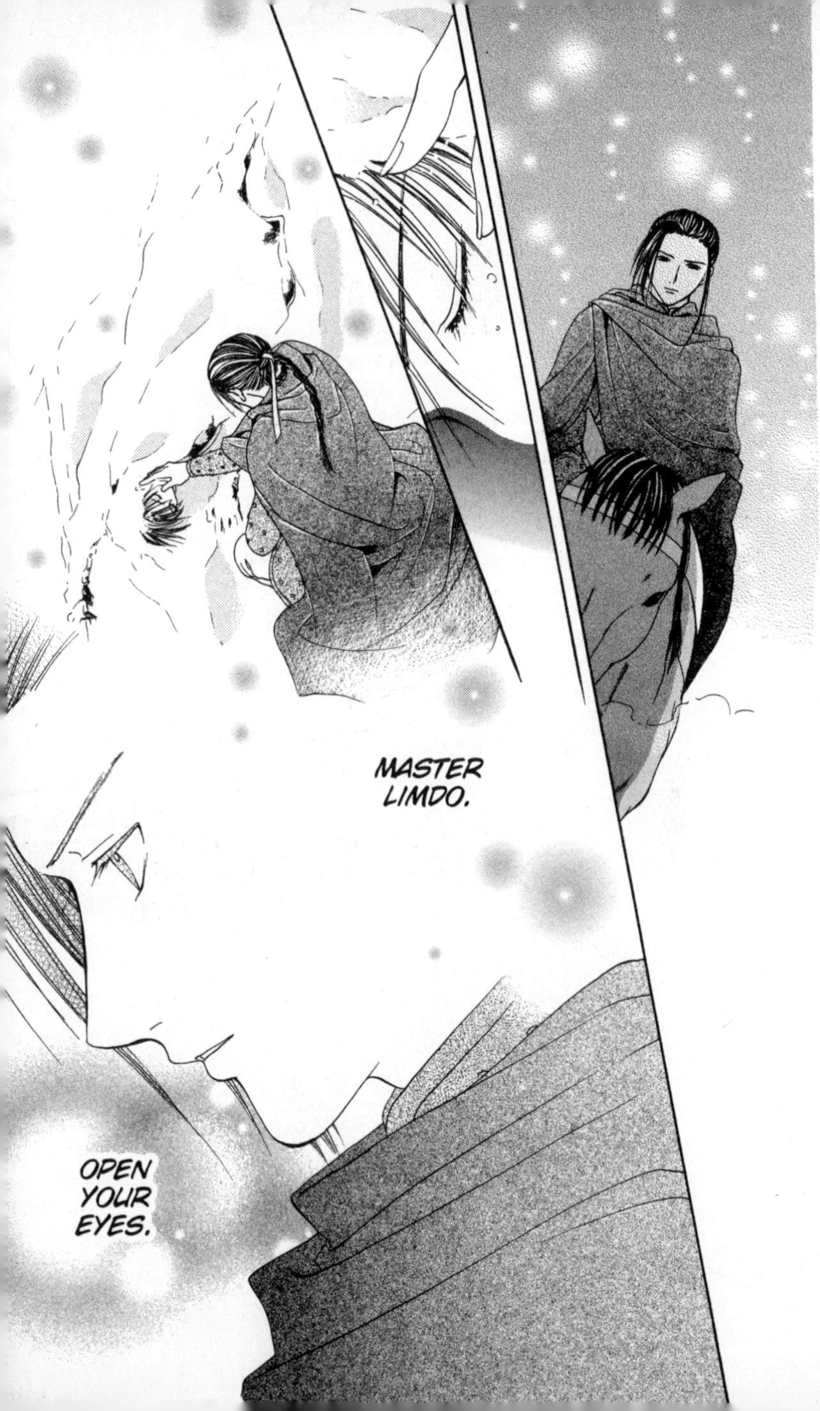
MASTER LIMDO.
OPEN YOUR EYES.

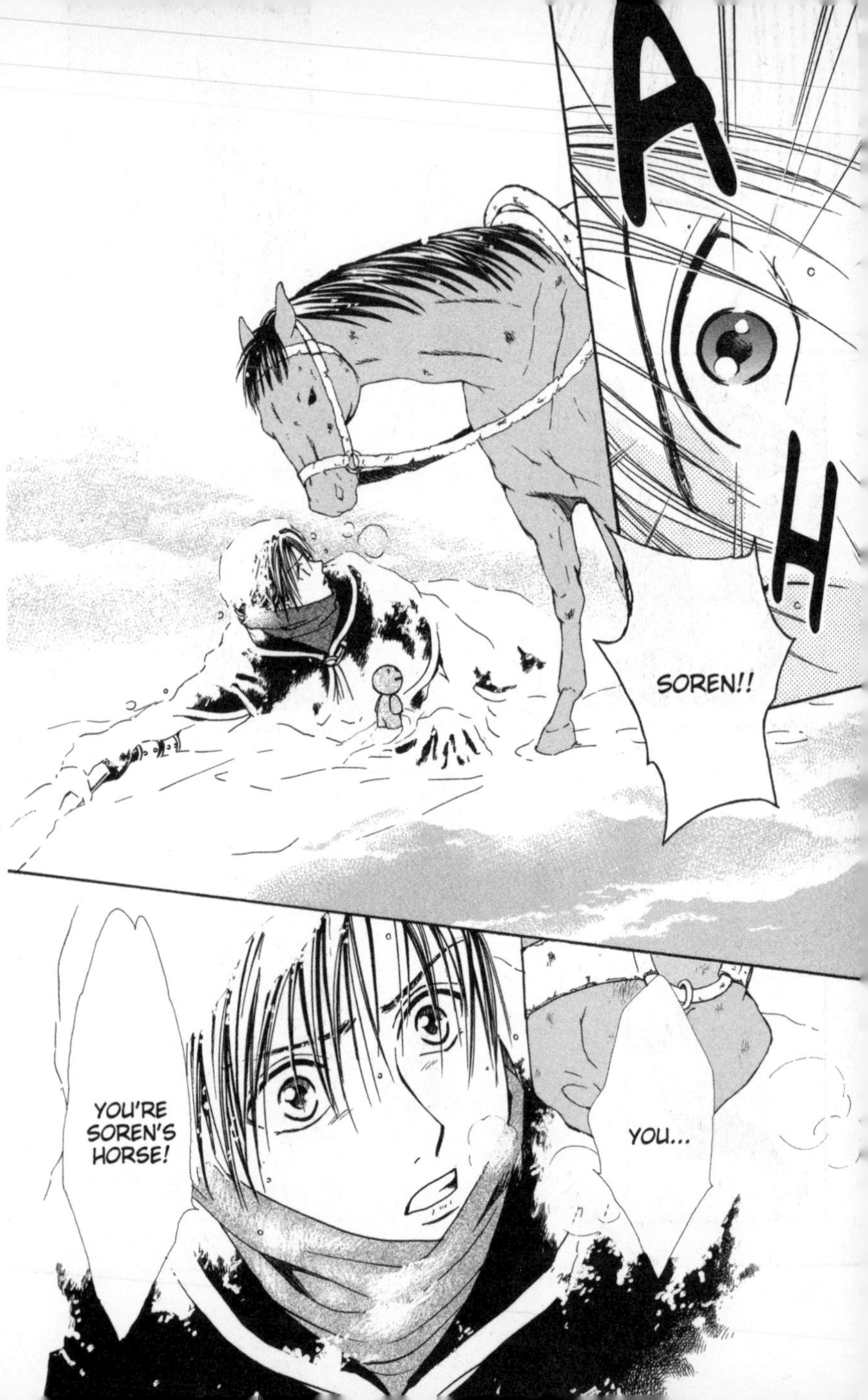
AH
SOREN!!
YOU...
YOU'RE SOREN'S HORSE!

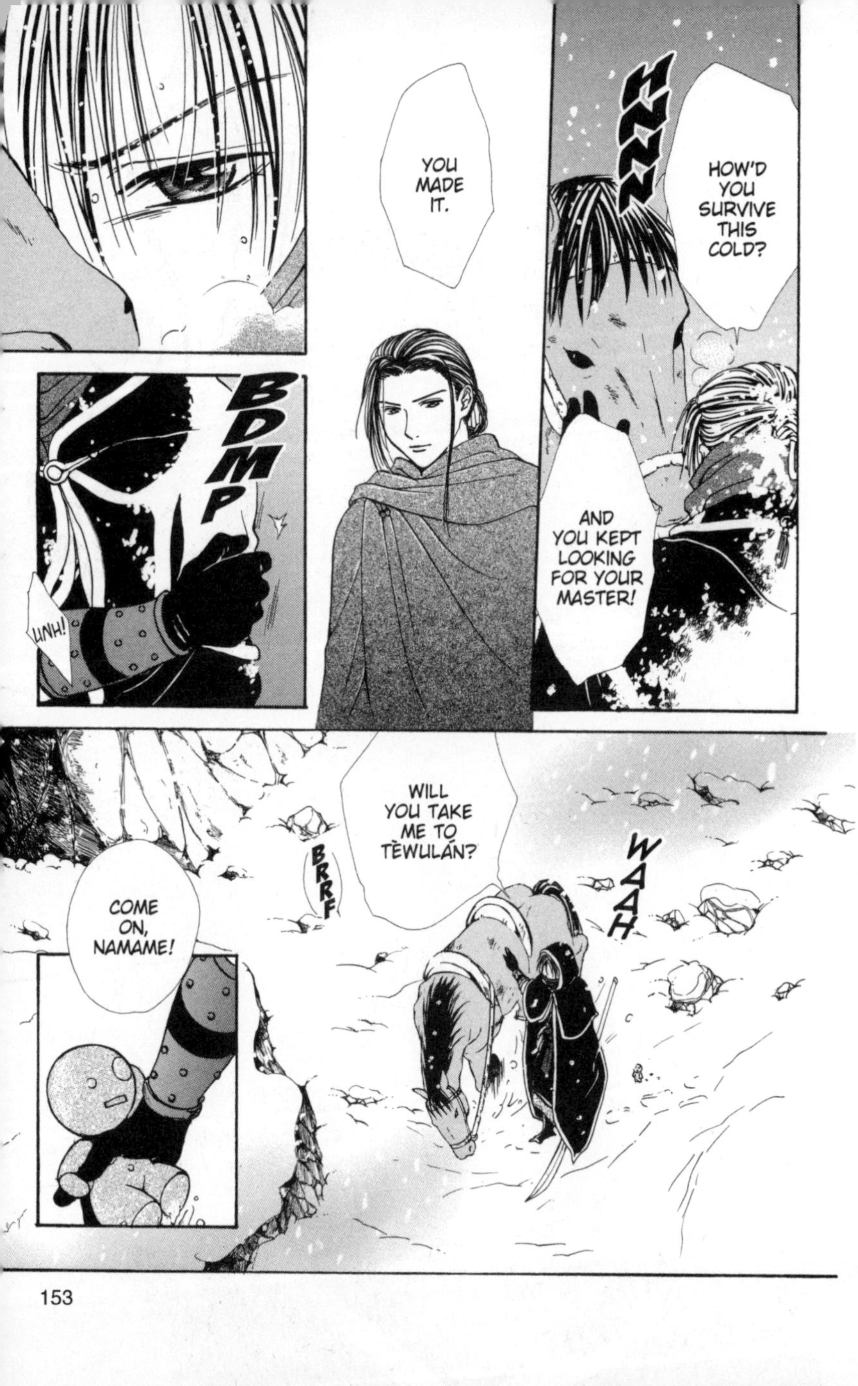
HNNN
HOW'D YOU SURVIVE THIS COLD?
AND YOU KEPT LOOKING FOR YOUR MASTER!
YOU MADE IT.
BDMP
UNH!
WILL YOU TAKE ME TO TÈWULÁN?
WAAH
BRRF
COME ON, NAMAME!

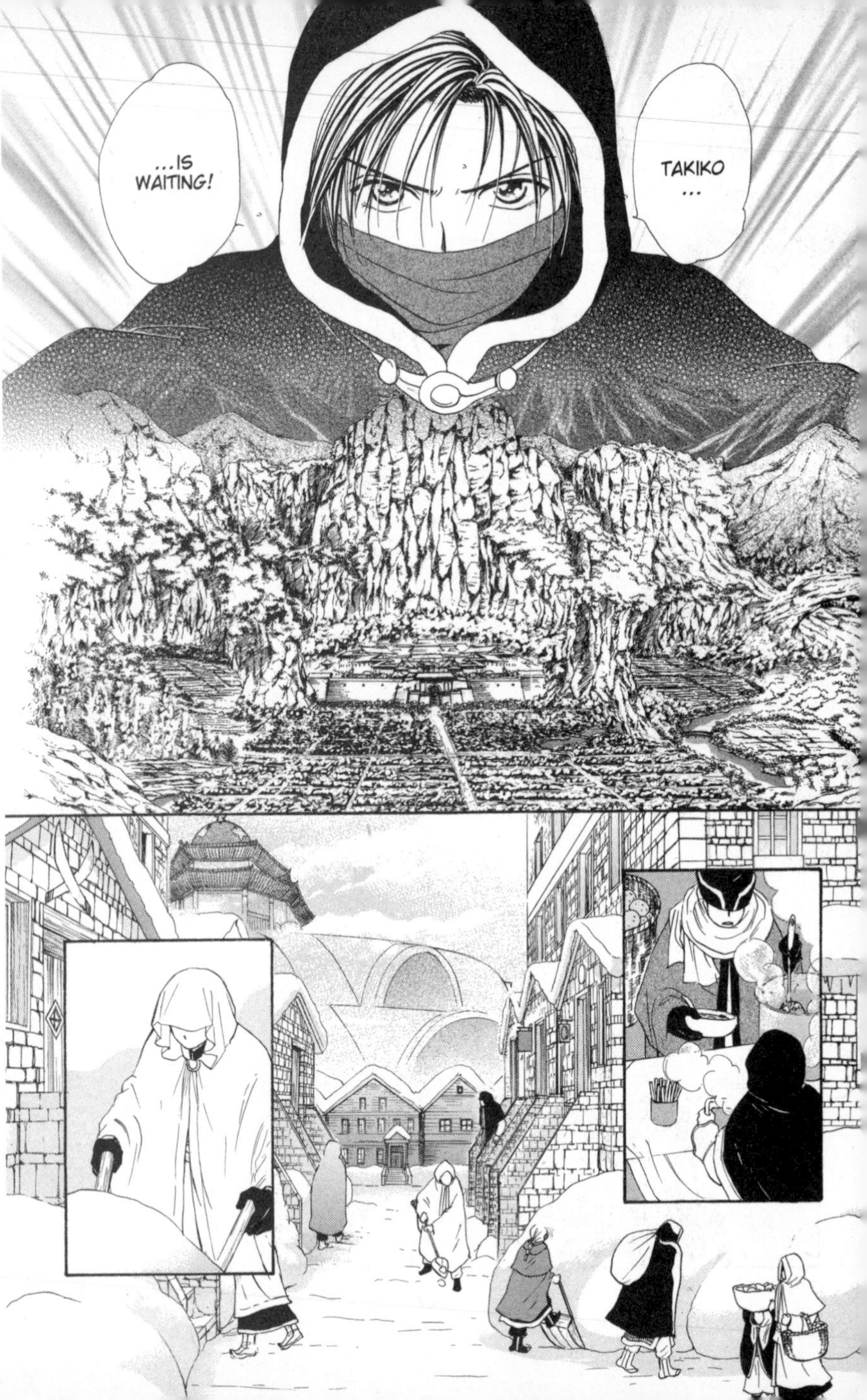
TAKIKO
...
...IS
WAITING!

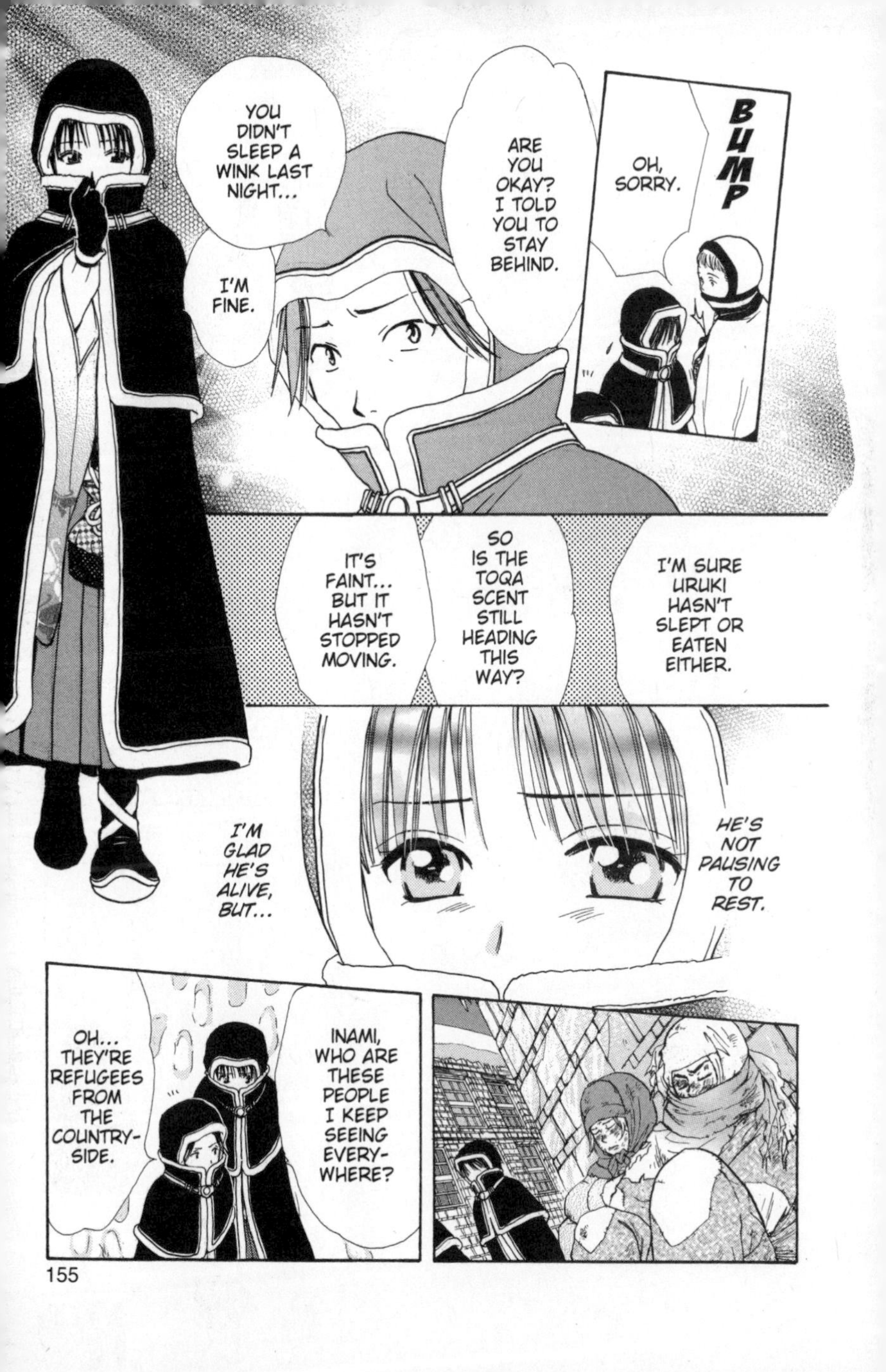
BUMP
OH, SORRY.
ARE YOU OKAY? I TOLD YOU TO STAY BEHIND.
YOU DIDN'T SLEEP A WINK LAST NIGHT...
I'M FINE.
I'M SURE URUKI HASN'T SLEPT OR EATEN EITHER.
SO IS THE TOQA SCENT STILL HEADING THIS WAY?
IT'S FAINT... BUT IT HASN'T STOPPED MOVING.
HE'S NOT PAUSING TO REST.
I'M GLAD HE'S ALIVE, BUT...
INAMI, WHO ARE THESE PEOPLE I KEEP SEEING EVERY-WHERE?
OH... THEY'RE REFUGEES FROM THE COUNTRY-SIDE.

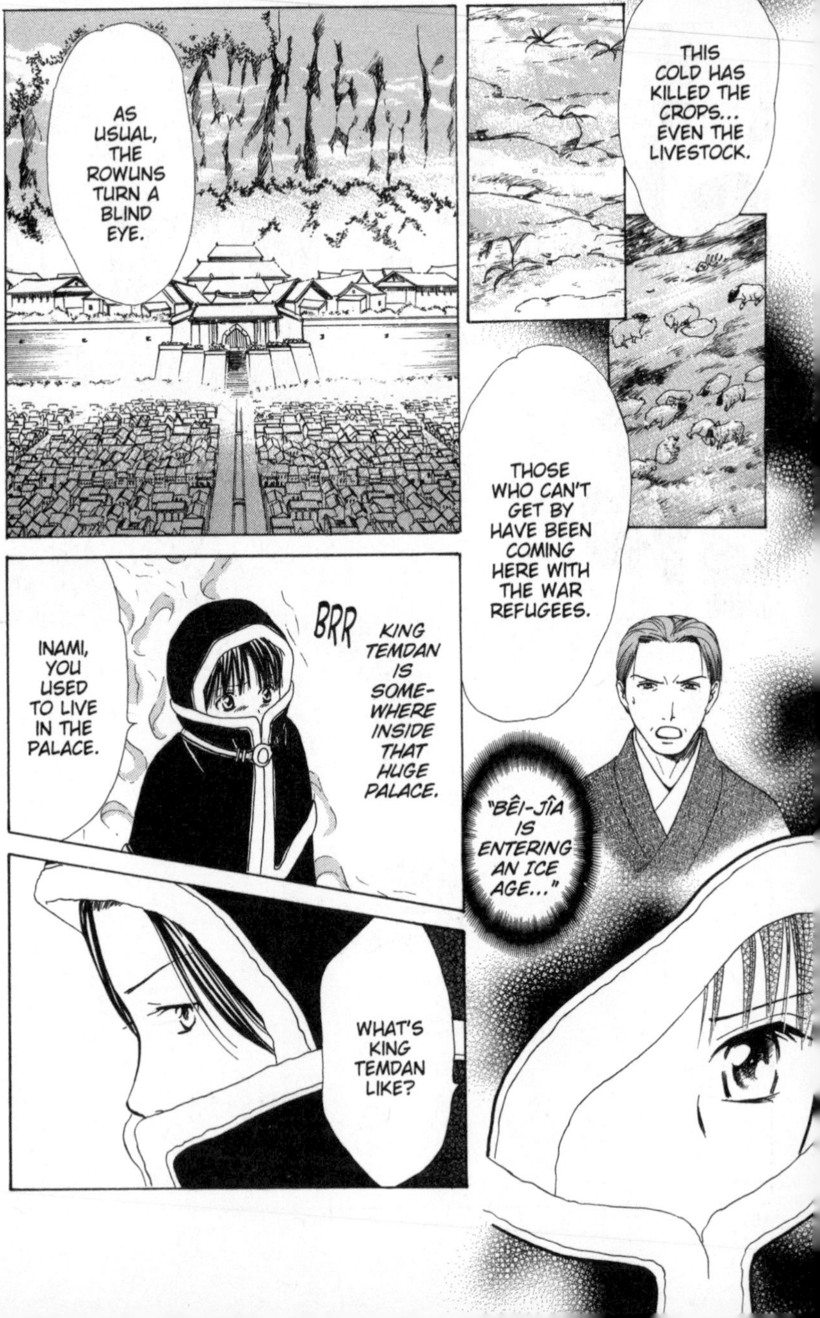
THIS COLD HAS KILLED THE CROPS... EVEN THE LIVESTOCK.
THOSE WHO CAN'T GET BY HAVE BEEN COMING HERE WITH THE WAR REFUGEES.
AS USUAL, THE ROWUNS TURN A BLIND EYE.
"BÊI-JÎA IS ENTERING AN ICE AGE..."
BRR
KING TEMDAN IS SOME-WHERE INSIDE THAT HUGE PALACE.
INAMI, YOU USED TO LIVE IN THE PALACE.
WHAT'S KING TEMDAN LIKE?

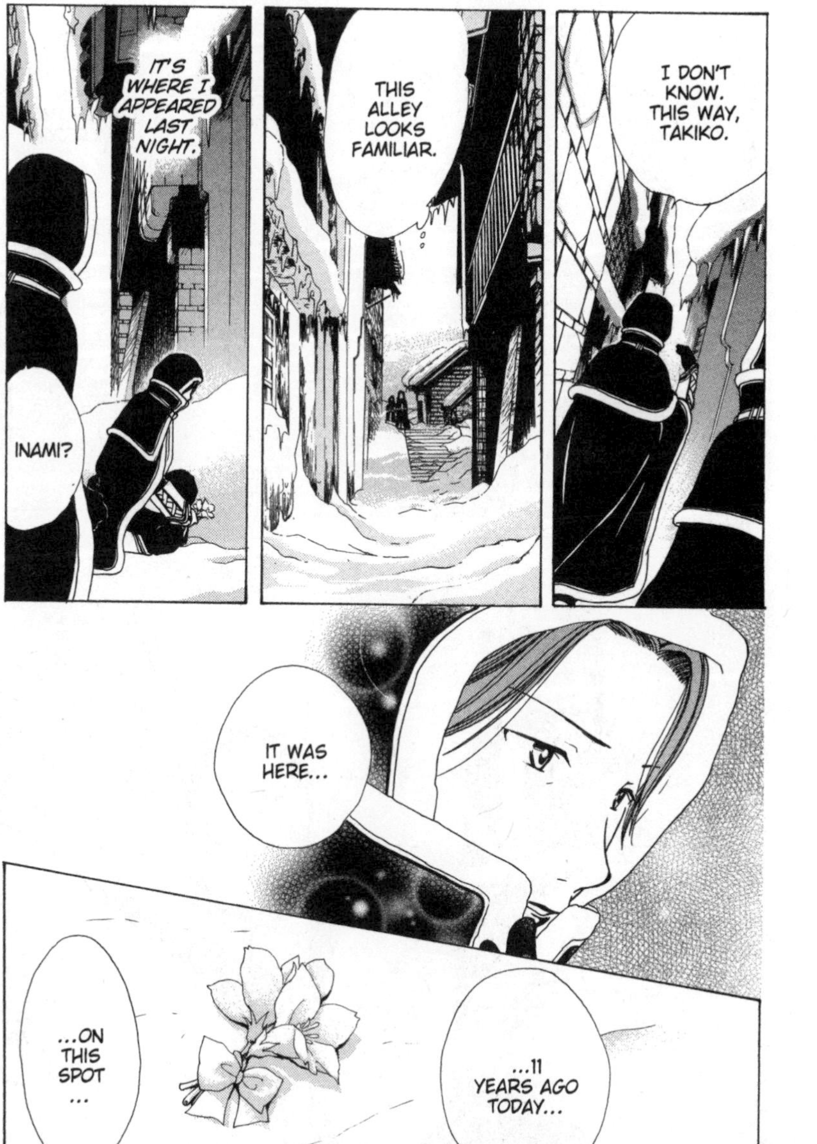
I DON'T KNOW. THIS WAY, TAKIKO.
THIS ALLEY LOOKS FAMILIAR.
IT'S WHERE I APPEARED LAST NIGHT.
INAMI?
IT WAS HERE...
...11 YEARS AGO TODAY...
...ON THIS SPOT...

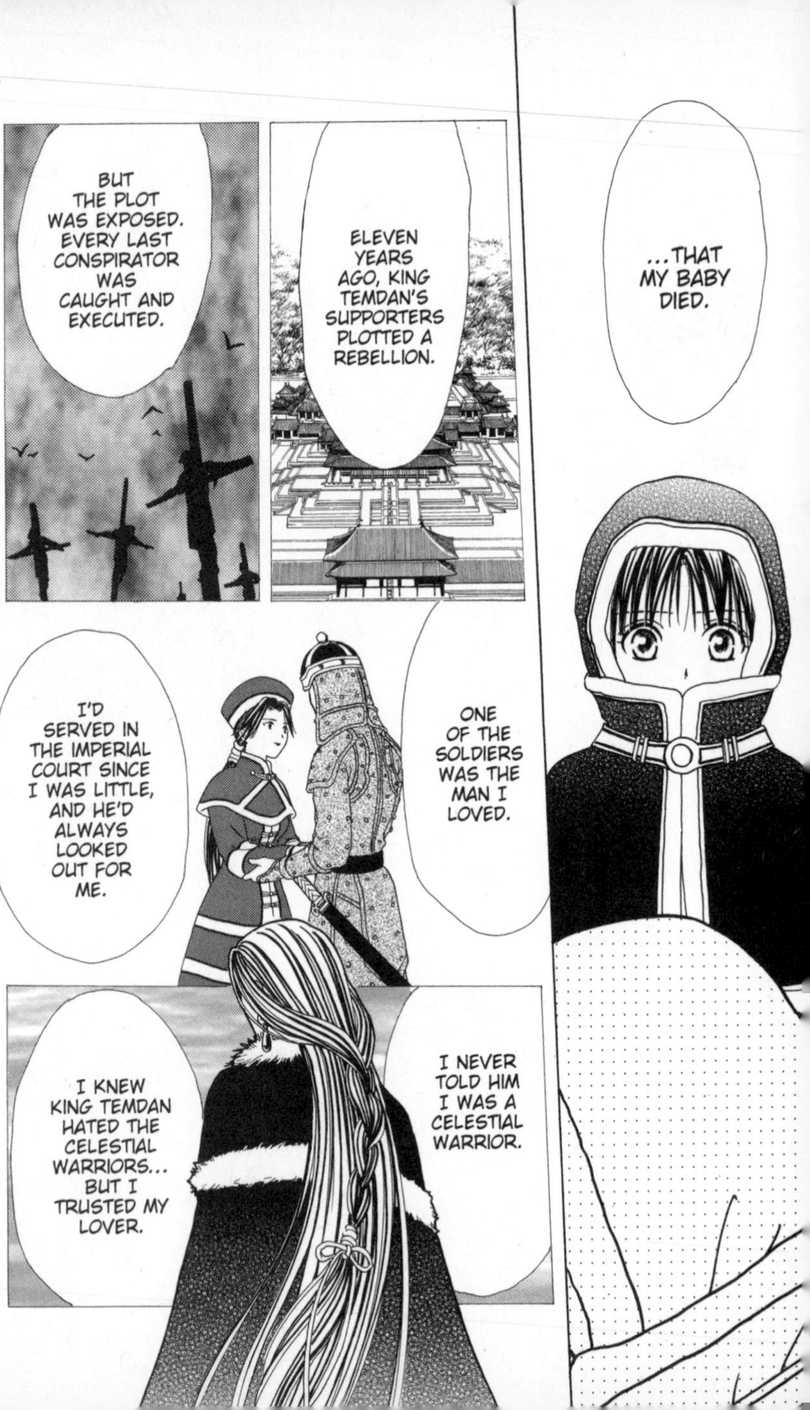
...THAT MY BABY DIED.
ELEVEN YEARS AGO, KING TEMDAN'S SUPPORTERS PLOTTED A REBELLION.
BUT THE PLOT WAS EXPOSED. EVERY LAST CONSPIRATOR WAS CAUGHT AND EXECUTED.
ONE OF THE SOLDIERS WAS THE MAN I LOVED.
I'D SERVED IN THE IMPERIAL COURT SINCE I WAS LITTLE, AND HE'D ALWAYS LOOKED OUT FOR ME.
I NEVER TOLD HIM I WAS A CELESTIAL WARRIOR.
I KNEW KING TEMDAN HATED THE CELESTIAL WARRIORS... BUT I TRUSTED MY LOVER.

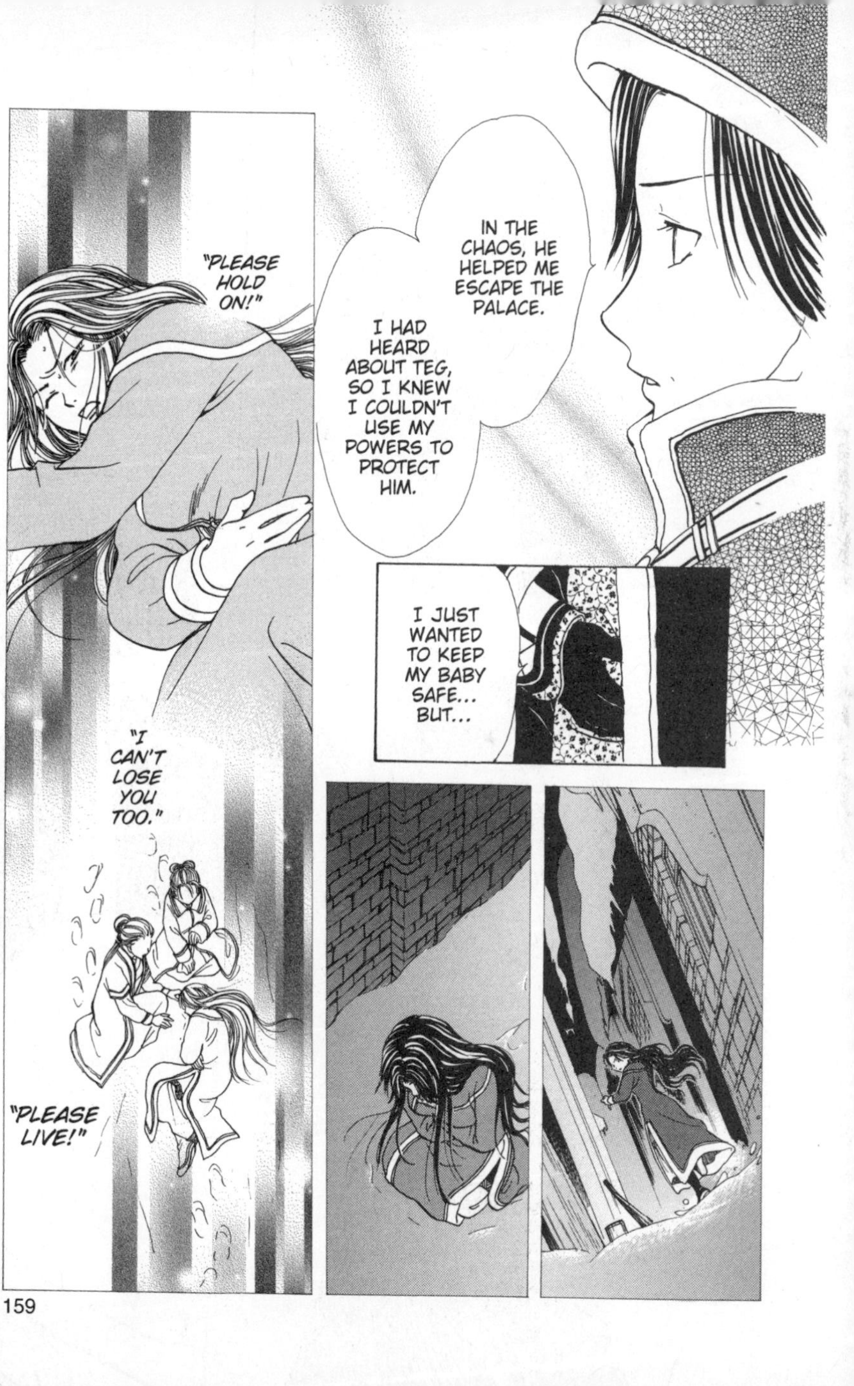
IN THE CHAOS, HE HELPED ME ESCAPE THE PALACE.
I HAD HEARD ABOUT TEG, SO I KNEW I COULDN'T USE MY POWERS TO PROTECT HIM.
I JUST WANTED TO KEEP MY BABY SAFE... BUT...
"PLEASE HOLD ON!"
"I CAN'T LOSE YOU TOO."
"PLEASE LIVE!"

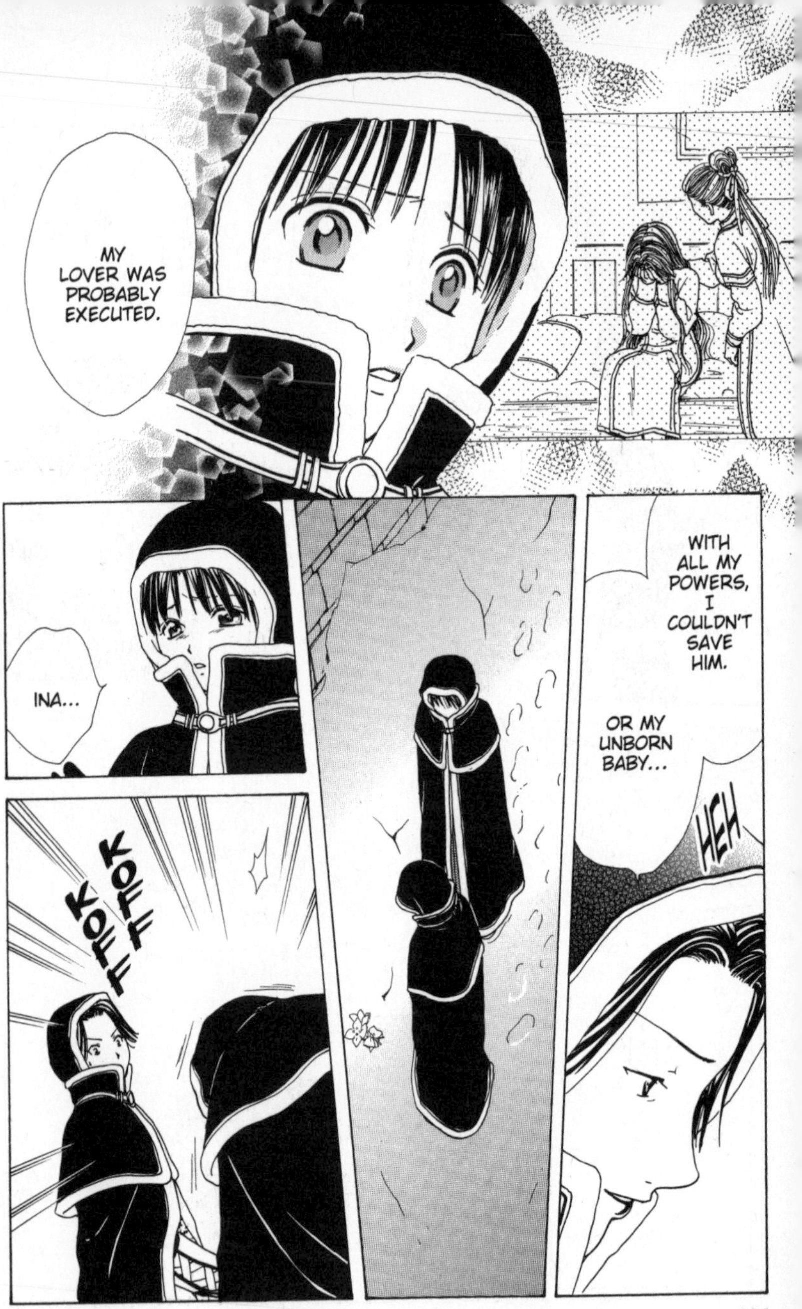
MY LOVER WAS PROBABLY EXECUTED.
WITH ALL MY POWERS, I COULDN'T SAVE HIM.
OR MY UNBORN BABY...
HEH
INA...
KOFF KOFF

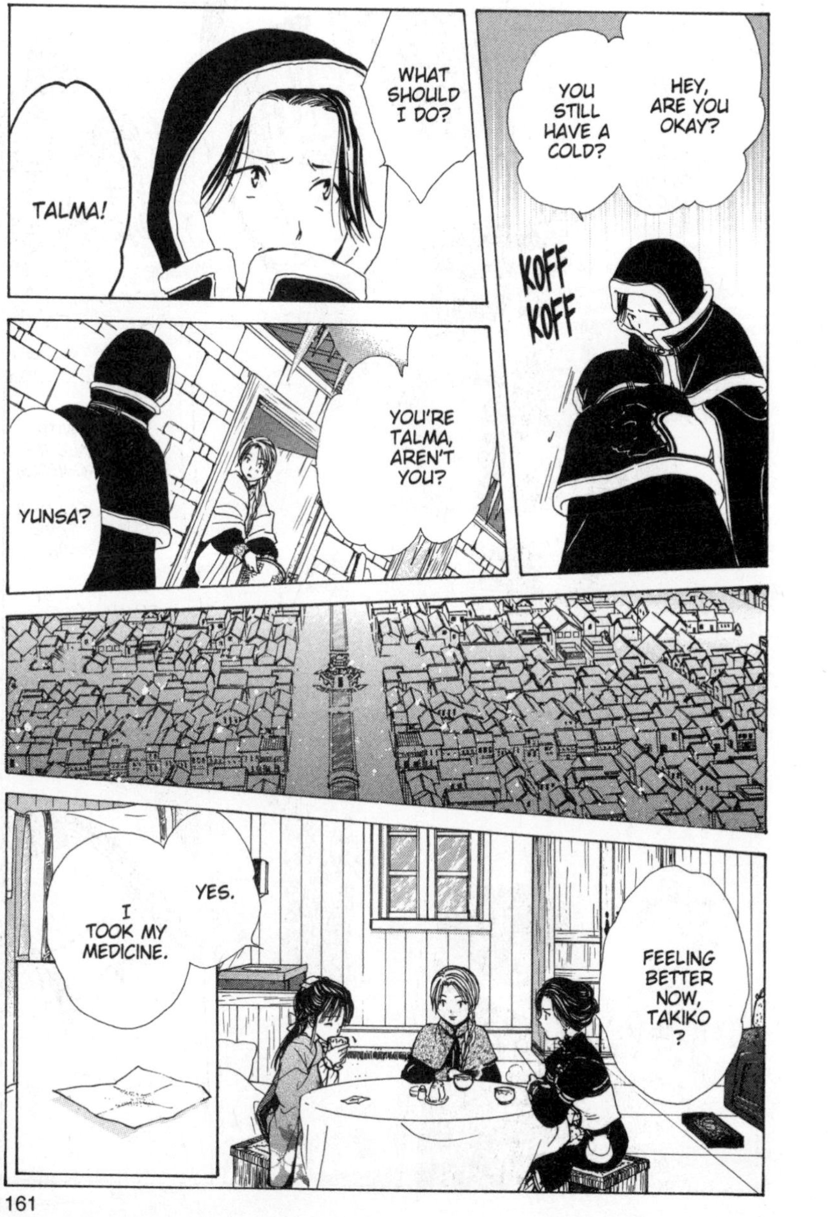
HEY, ARE YOU OKAY?
YOU STILL HAVE A COLD?
KOFF KOFF
WHAT SHOULD I DO?
TALMA!
YOU'RE TALMA, AREN'T YOU?
YUNSA?
FEELING BETTER NOW, TAKIKO ?
YES.
I TOOK MY MEDICINE.

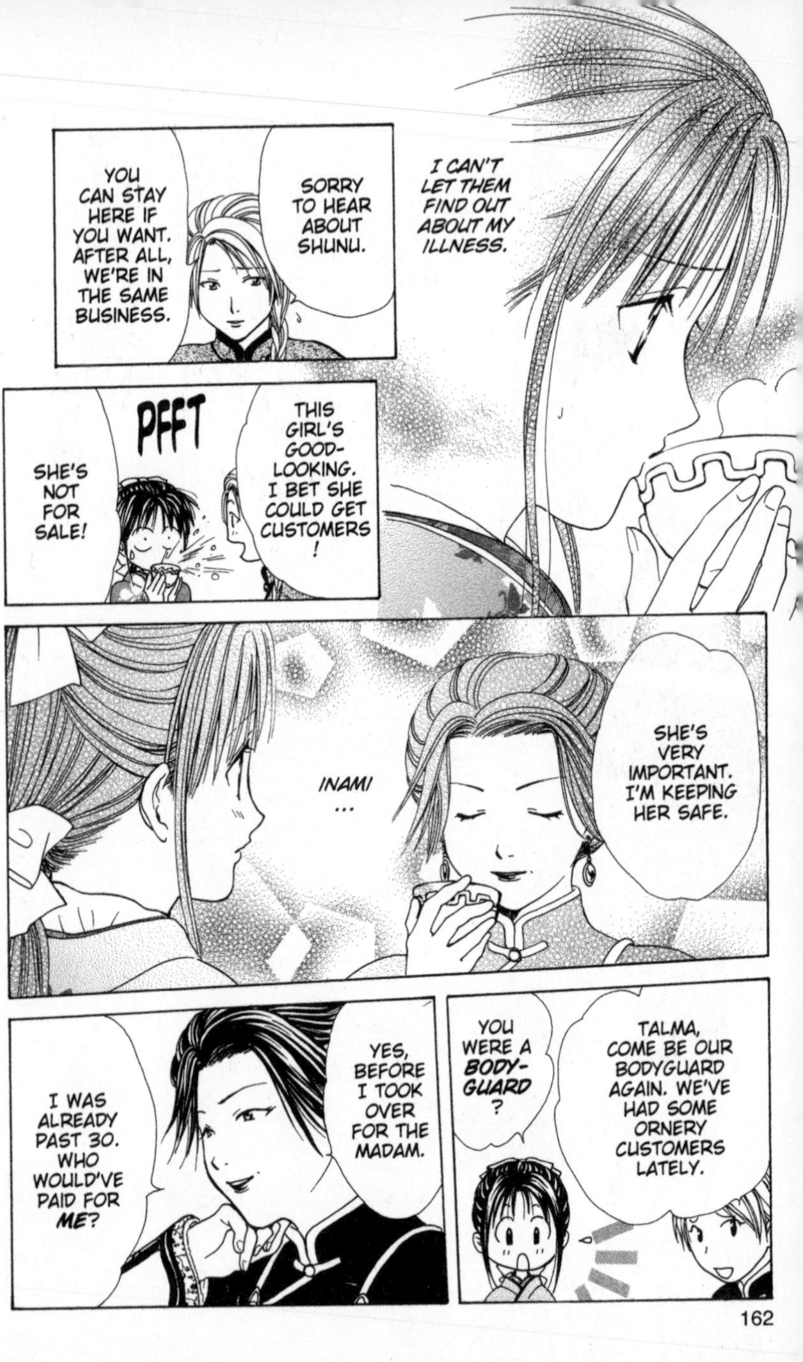

I CAN'T LET THEM FIND OUT ABOUT MY ILLNESS.
SORRY TO HEAR ABOUT SHUNU.
YOU CAN STAY HERE IF YOU WANT. AFTER ALL, WE'RE IN THE SAME BUSINESS.
THIS GIRL'S GOOD-LOOKING. I BET SHE COULD GET CUSTOMERS!
PFFT
SHE'S NOT FOR SALE!
SHE'S VERY IMPORTANT. I'M KEEPING HER SAFE.
INAMI ...
TALMA, COME BE OUR BODYGUARD AGAIN. WE'VE HAD SOME ORNERY CUSTOMERS LATELY.
YOU WERE A *BODYGUARD*?
YES, BEFORE I TOOK OVER FOR THE MADAM.
I WAS ALREADY PAST 30. WHO WOULD'VE PAID FOR *ME*?

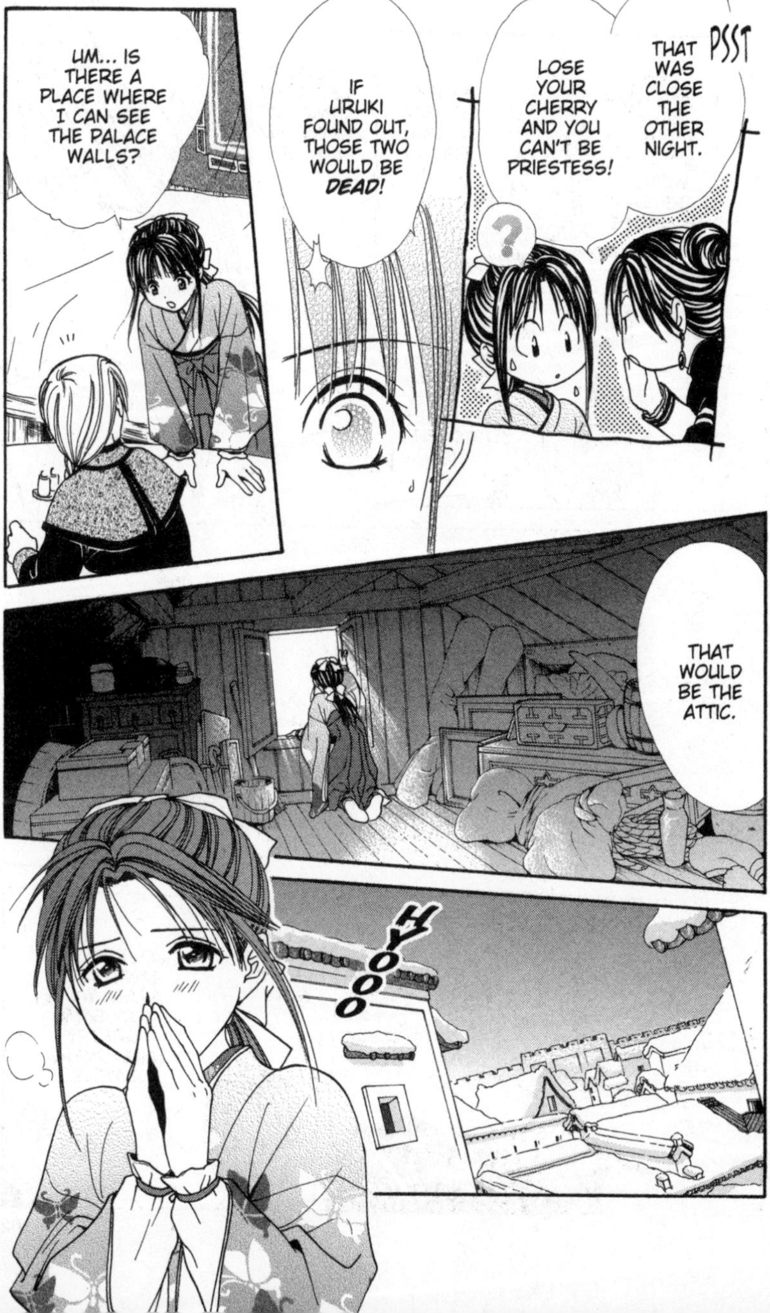
PSST
THAT WAS CLOSE THE OTHER NIGHT.
LOSE YOUR CHERRY AND YOU CAN'T BE PRIESTESS!
?
IF URUKI FOUND OUT, THOSE TWO WOULD BE *DEAD*!
UM... IS THERE A PLACE WHERE I CAN SEE THE PALACE WALLS?
THAT WOULD BE THE ATTIC.
HYOOOO

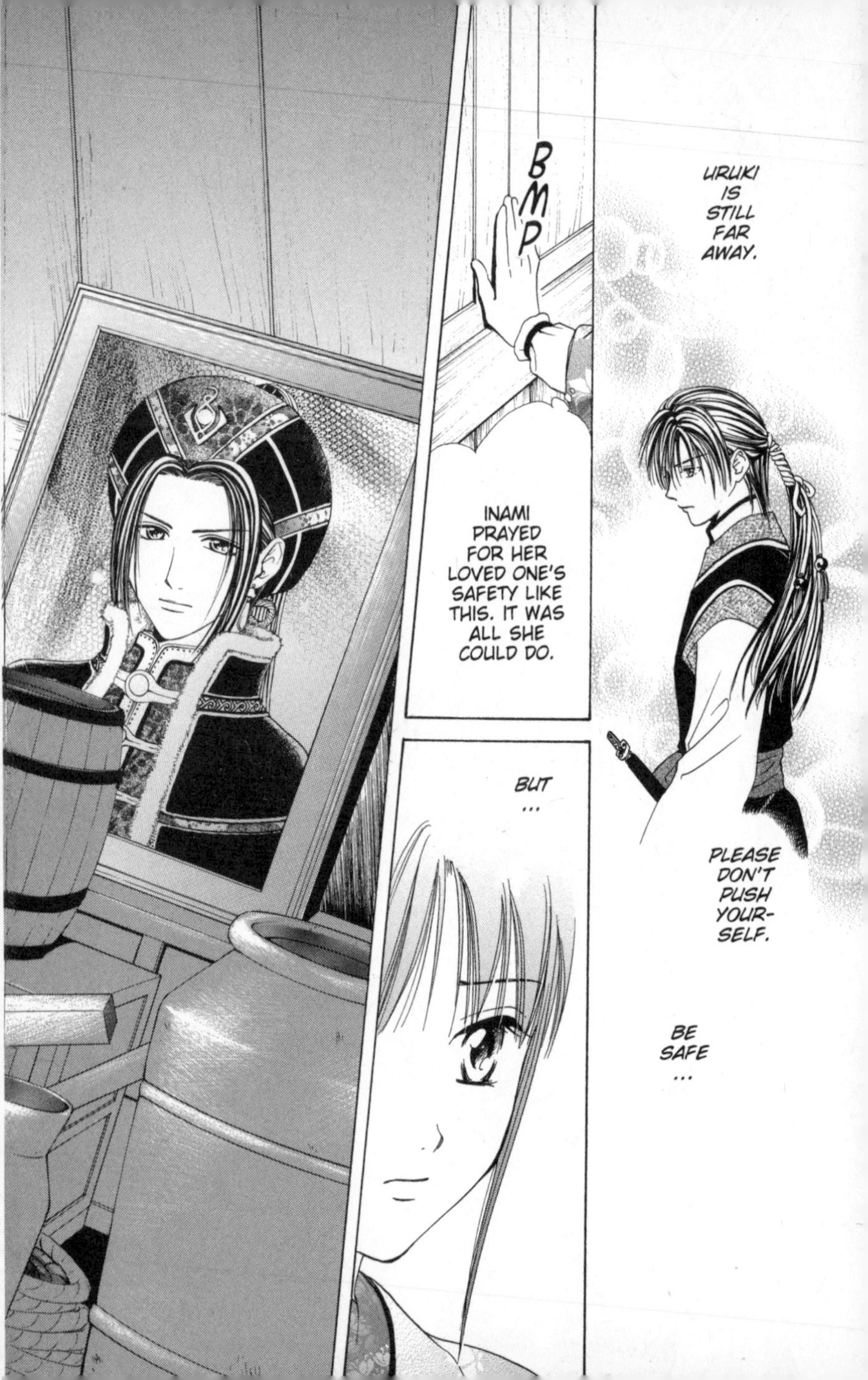
URUKI IS STILL FAR AWAY.
PLEASE DON'T PUSH YOURSELF.
BE SAFE ...
BMP
INAMI PRAYED FOR HER LOVED ONE'S SAFETY LIKE THIS. IT WAS ALL SHE COULD DO.
BUT ...

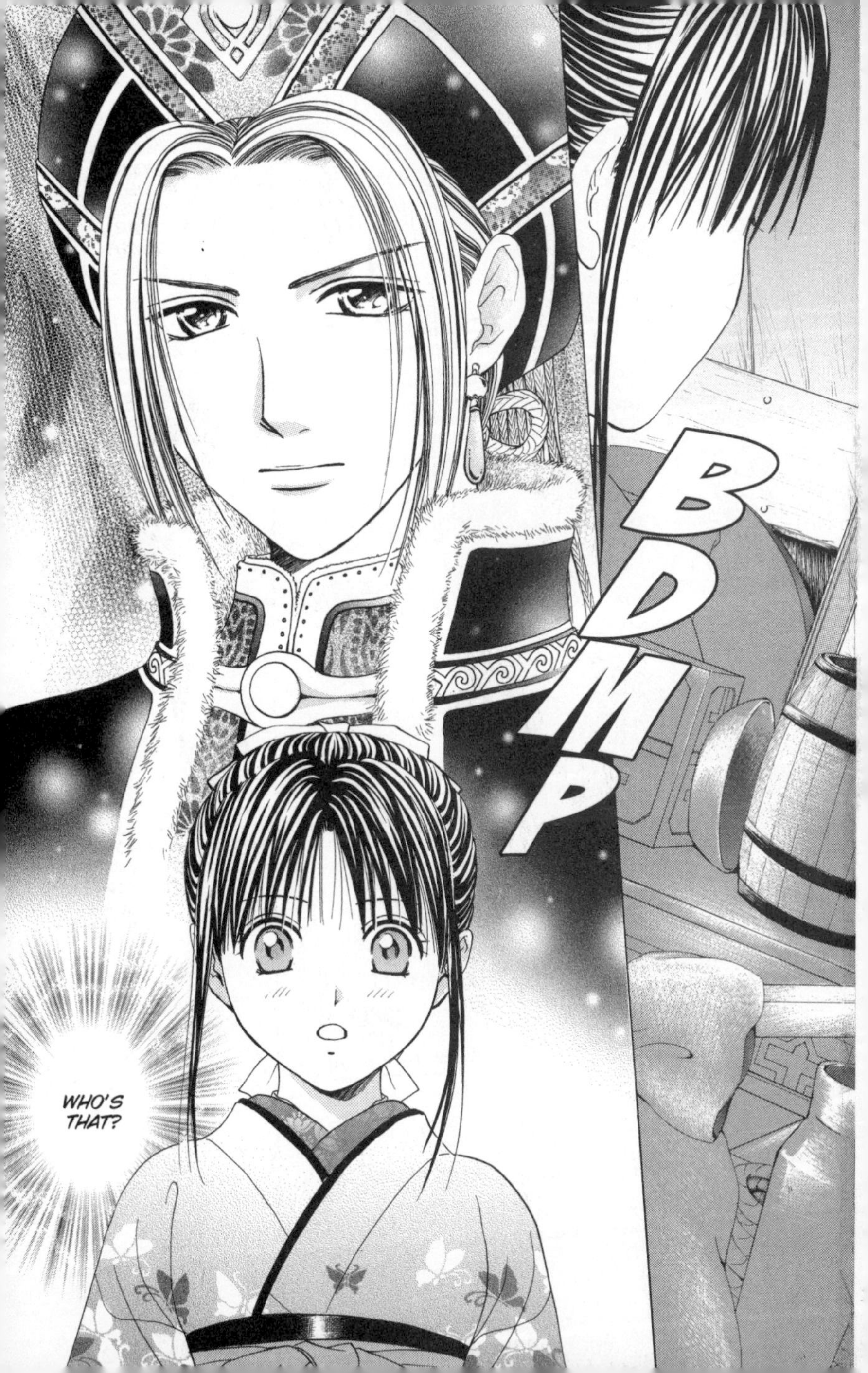
BDMP
WHO'S THAT?

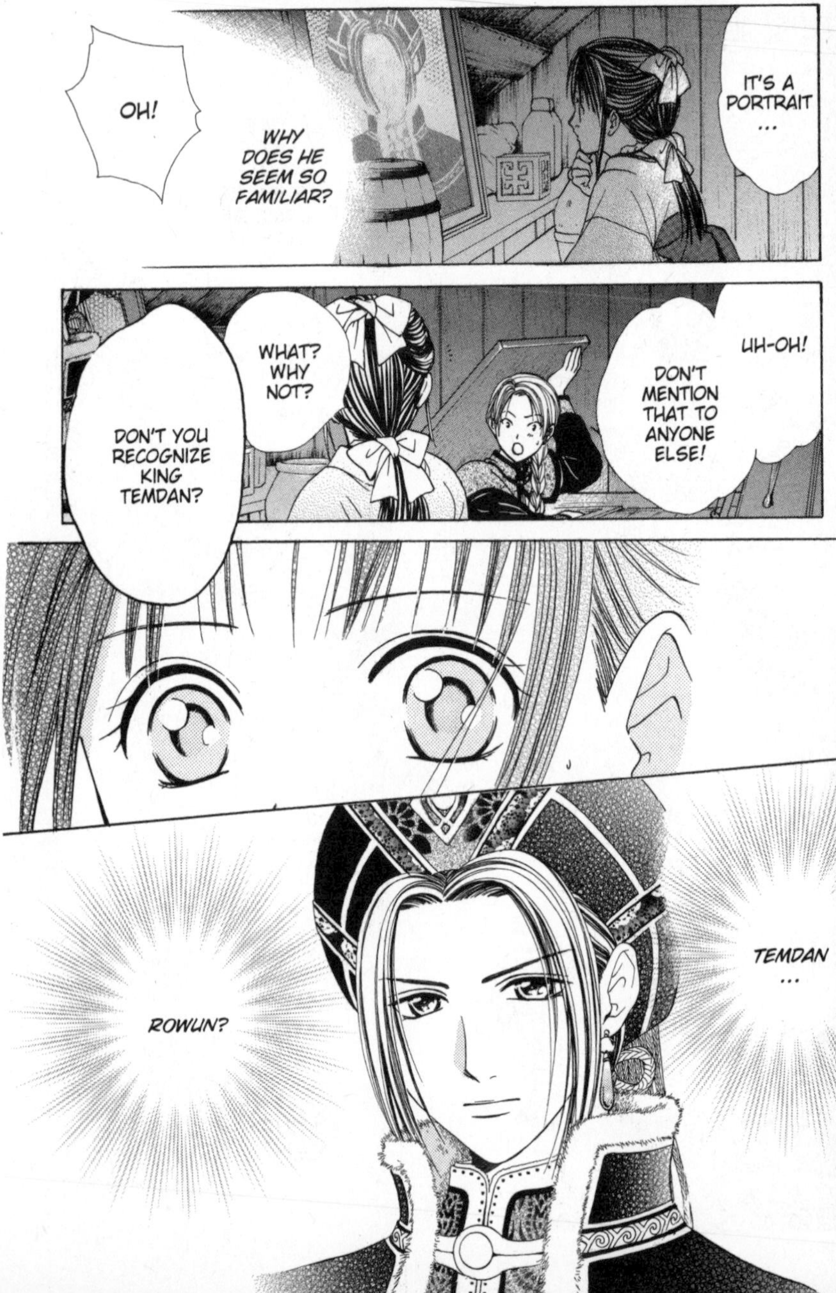
IT'S A PORTRAIT ...
WHY DOES HE SEEM SO FAMILIAR?
OH!
UH-OH!
DON'T MENTION THAT TO ANYONE ELSE!
WHAT? WHY NOT?
DON'T YOU RECOGNIZE KING TEMDAN?
TEMDAN ...
ROWUN?

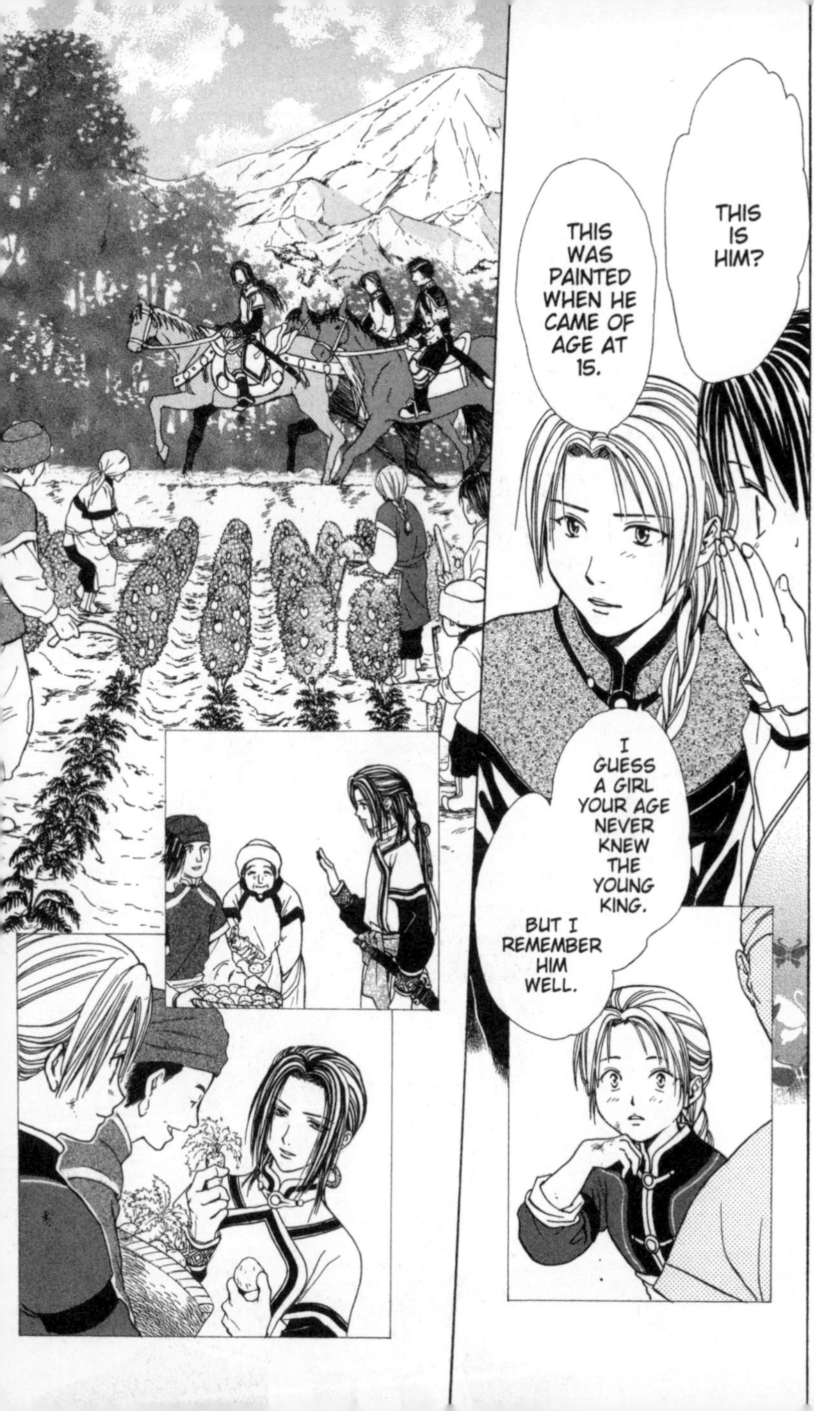
THIS IS HIM?
THIS WAS PAINTED WHEN HE CAME OF AGE AT 15.
I GUESS A GIRL YOUR AGE NEVER KNEW THE YOUNG KING.
BUT I REMEMBER HIM WELL.

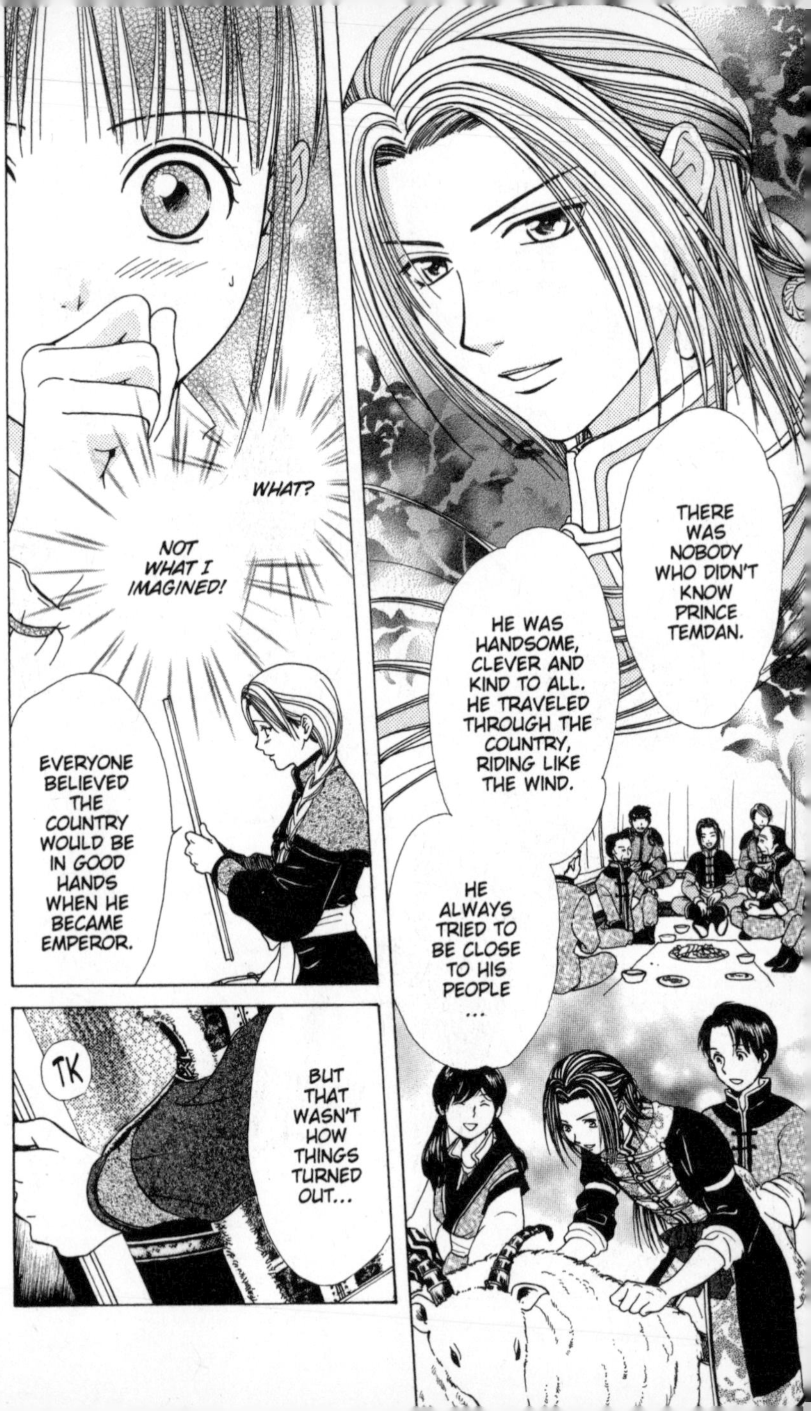
THERE WAS NOBODY WHO DIDN'T KNOW PRINCE TEMDAN.
HE WAS HANDSOME, CLEVER AND KIND TO ALL. HE TRAVELED THROUGH THE COUNTRY, RIDING LIKE THE WIND.
HE ALWAYS TRIED TO BE CLOSE TO HIS PEOPLE...
WHAT?
NOT WHAT I IMAGINED!
EVERYONE BELIEVED THE COUNTRY WOULD BE IN GOOD HANDS WHEN HE BECAME EMPEROR.
TK
BUT THAT WASN'T HOW THINGS TURNED OUT...

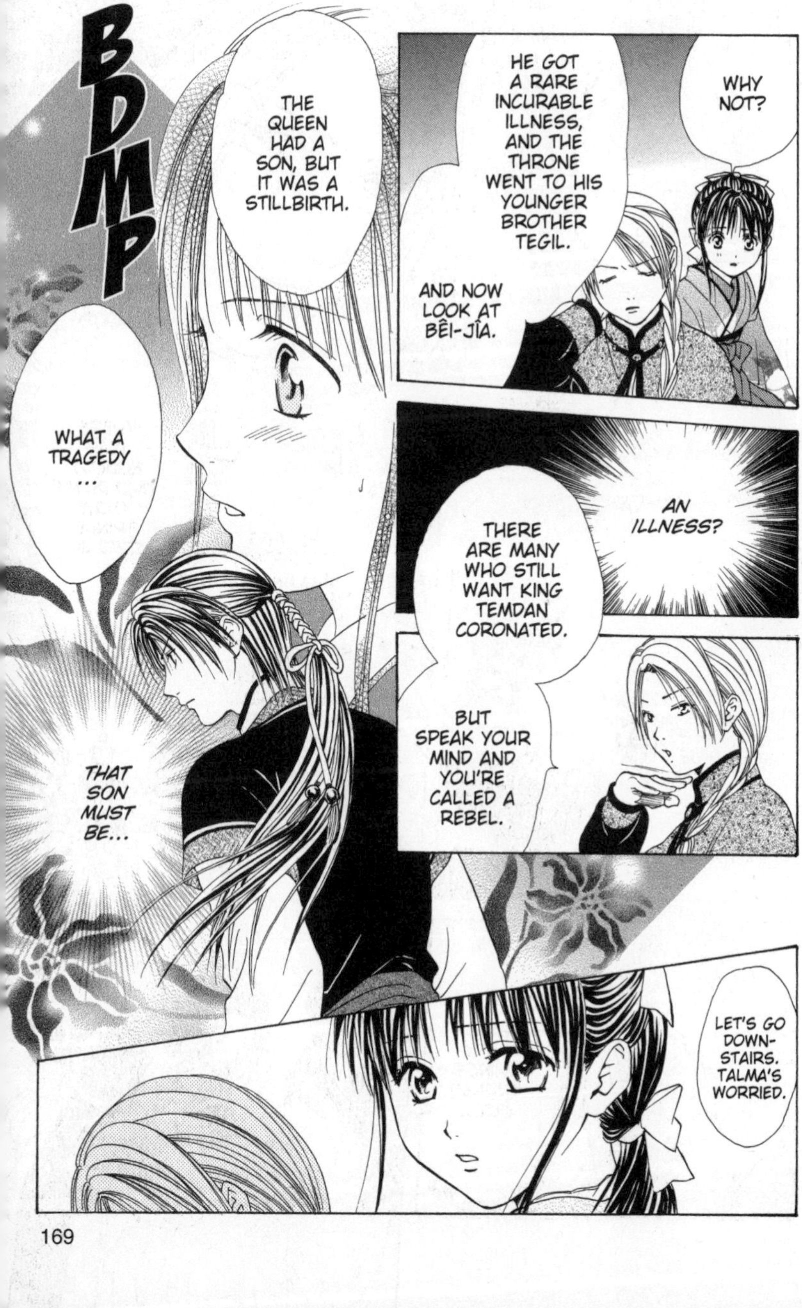
WHY NOT?
HE GOT A RARE INCURABLE ILLNESS, AND THE THRONE WENT TO HIS YOUNGER BROTHER TEGIL.
AND NOW LOOK AT BÊI-JÎA.
AN ILLNESS?
THERE ARE MANY WHO STILL WANT KING TEMDAN CORONATED.
BUT SPEAK YOUR MIND AND YOU'RE CALLED A REBEL.
THE QUEEN HAD A SON, BUT IT WAS A STILLBIRTH.
BDMP
WHAT A TRAGEDY ...
THAT SON MUST BE...
LET'S GO DOWN-STAIRS. TALMA'S WORRIED.

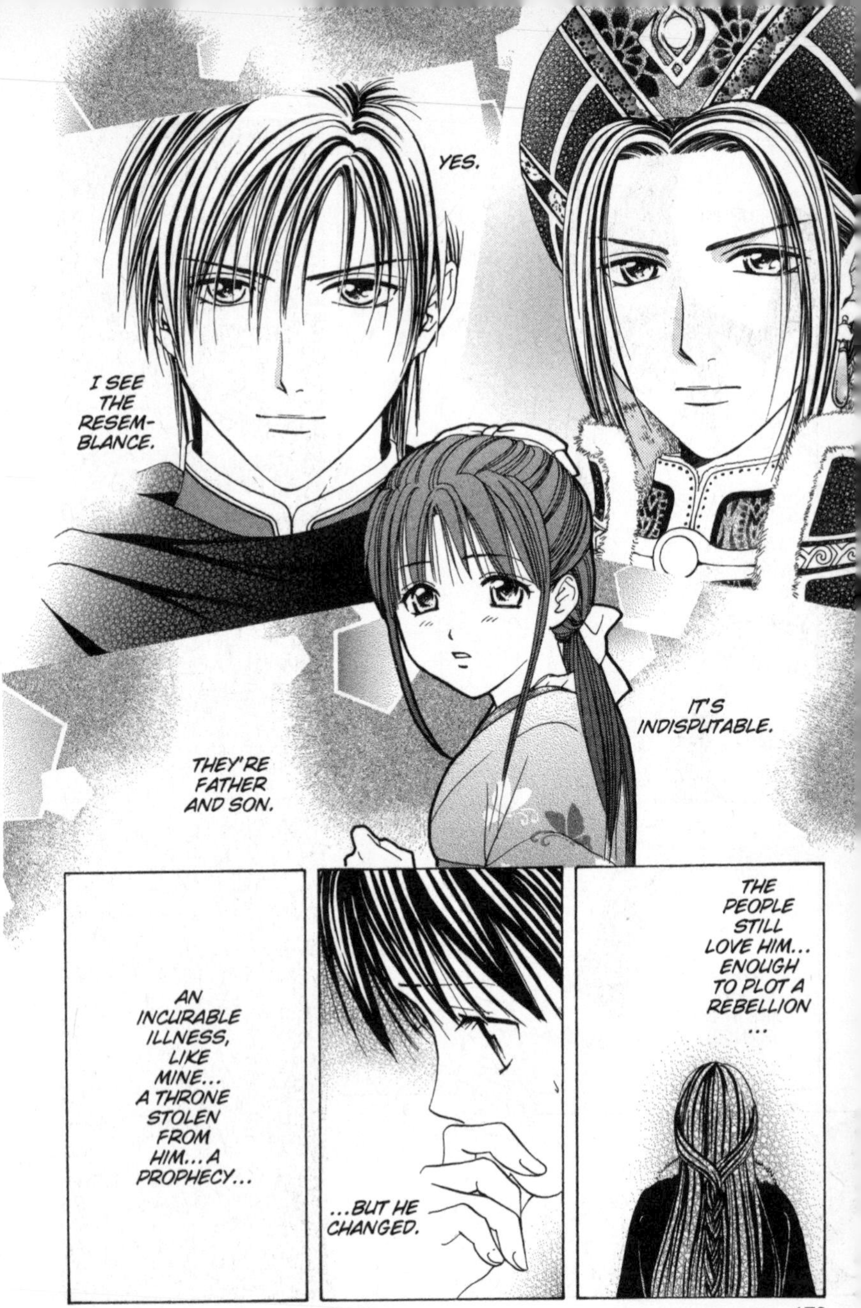
YES.
I SEE THE RESEM-BLANCE.
IT'S INDISPUTABLE.
THEY'RE FATHER AND SON.
THE PEOPLE STILL LOVE HIM... ENOUGH TO PLOT A REBELLION...
...BUT HE CHANGED.
AN INCURABLE ILLNESS, LIKE MINE... A THRONE STOLEN FROM HIM... A PROPHECY...

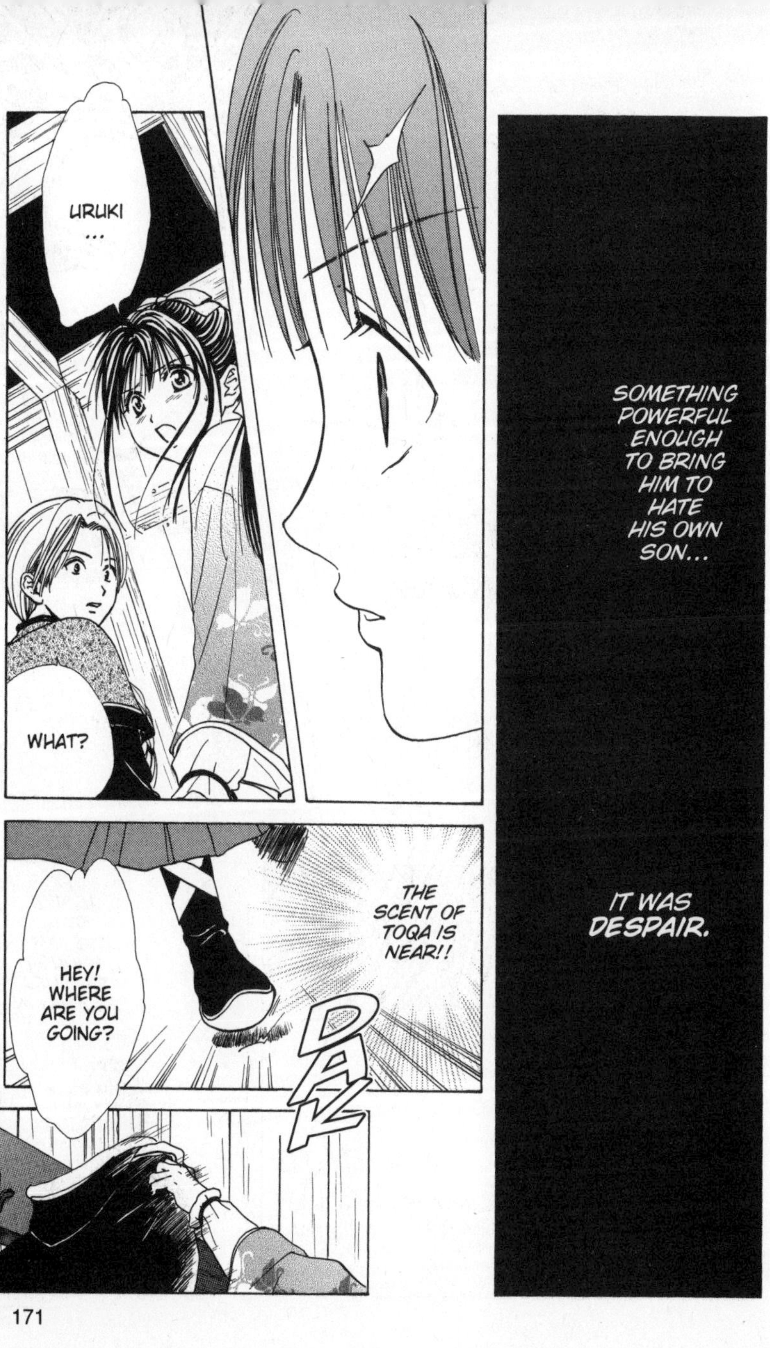
SOMETHING POWERFUL ENOUGH TO BRING HIM TO HATE HIS OWN SON...
IT WAS DESPAIR.
URUKI ...
WHAT?
THE SCENT OF TOQA IS NEAR!!
HEY! WHERE ARE YOU GOING?
DAH

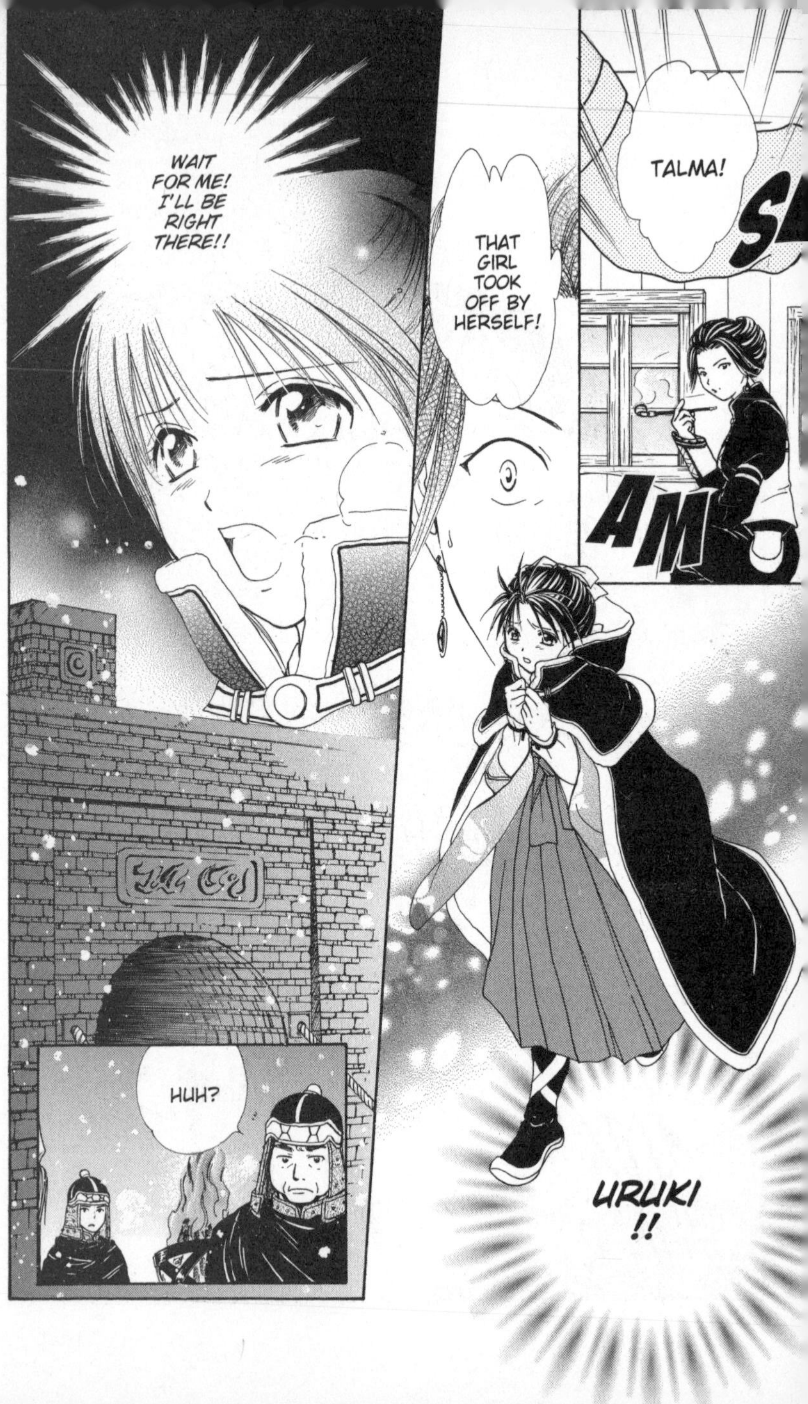
TALMA!
SL
AM
THAT GIRL TOOK OFF BY HERSELF!
URUKI !!
WAIT FOR ME! I'LL BE RIGHT THERE!!
HUH?

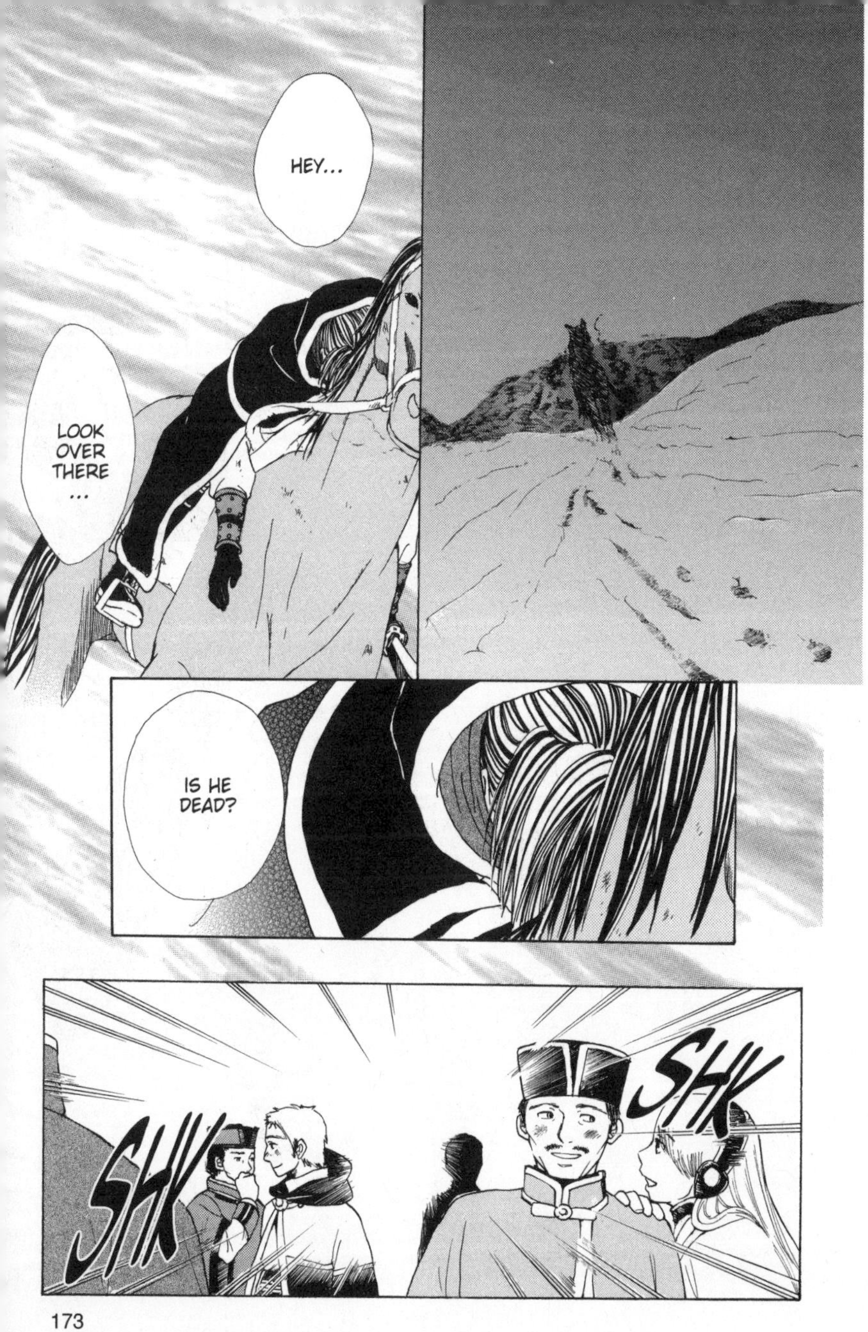
HEY...
LOOK OVER THERE ...
IS HE DEAD?
SHK
SHK

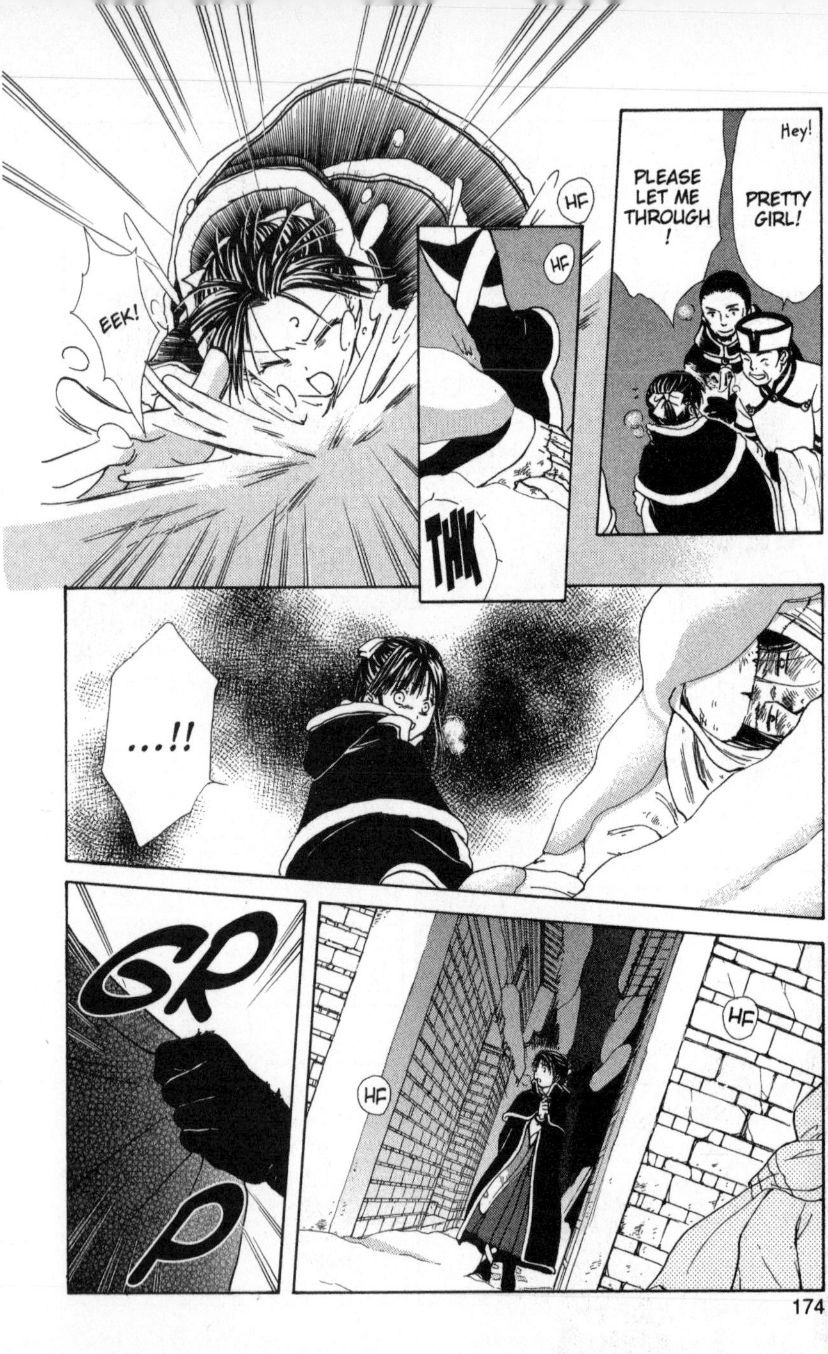
Hey!
PRETTY GIRL!
PLEASE LET ME THROUGH!
HF
HF
THK
EEK!
...!!
HF
HF
GRP

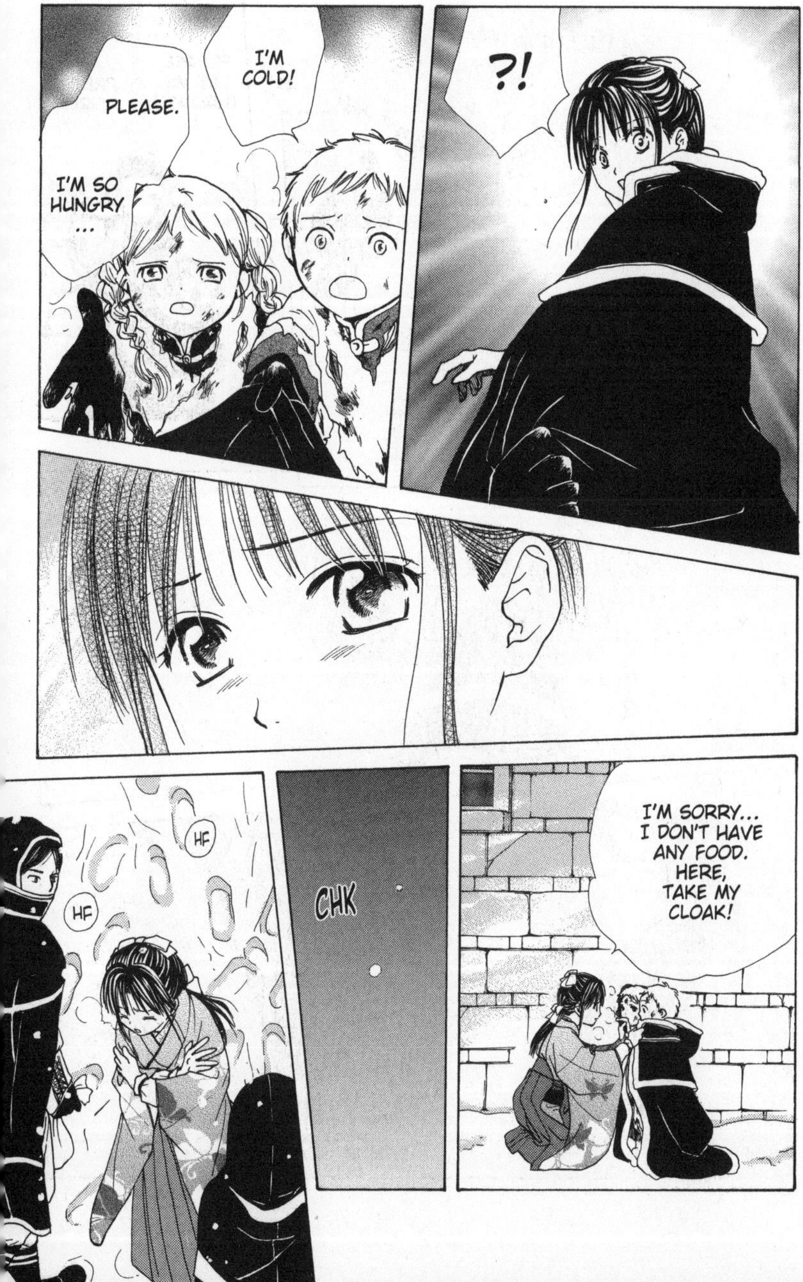
?!
I'M COLD!
PLEASE.
I'M SO HUNGRY ...
I'M SORRY... I DON'T HAVE ANY FOOD. HERE, TAKE MY CLOAK!
CHK
HF
HF

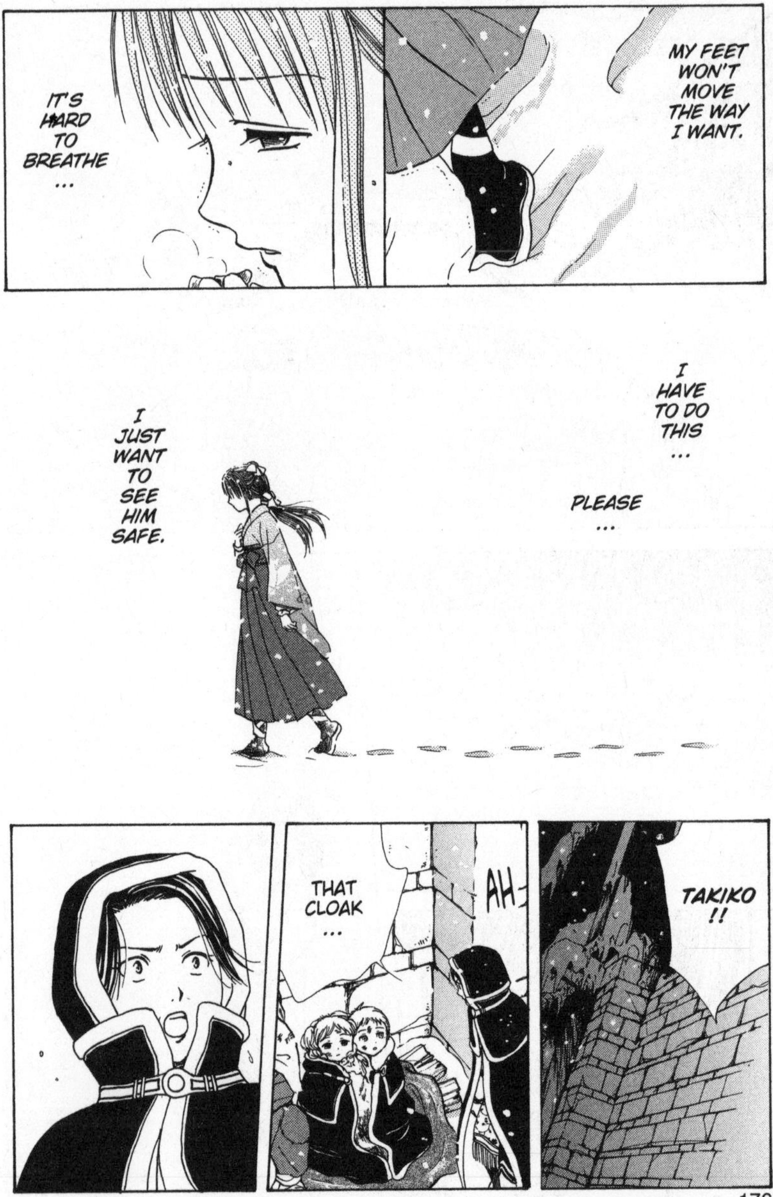
MY FEET WON'T MOVE THE WAY I WANT.
IT'S HARD TO BREATHE ...
I HAVE TO DO THIS ...
PLEASE ...
I JUST WANT TO SEE HIM SAFE.
TAKIKO !!
AH
THAT CLOAK ...

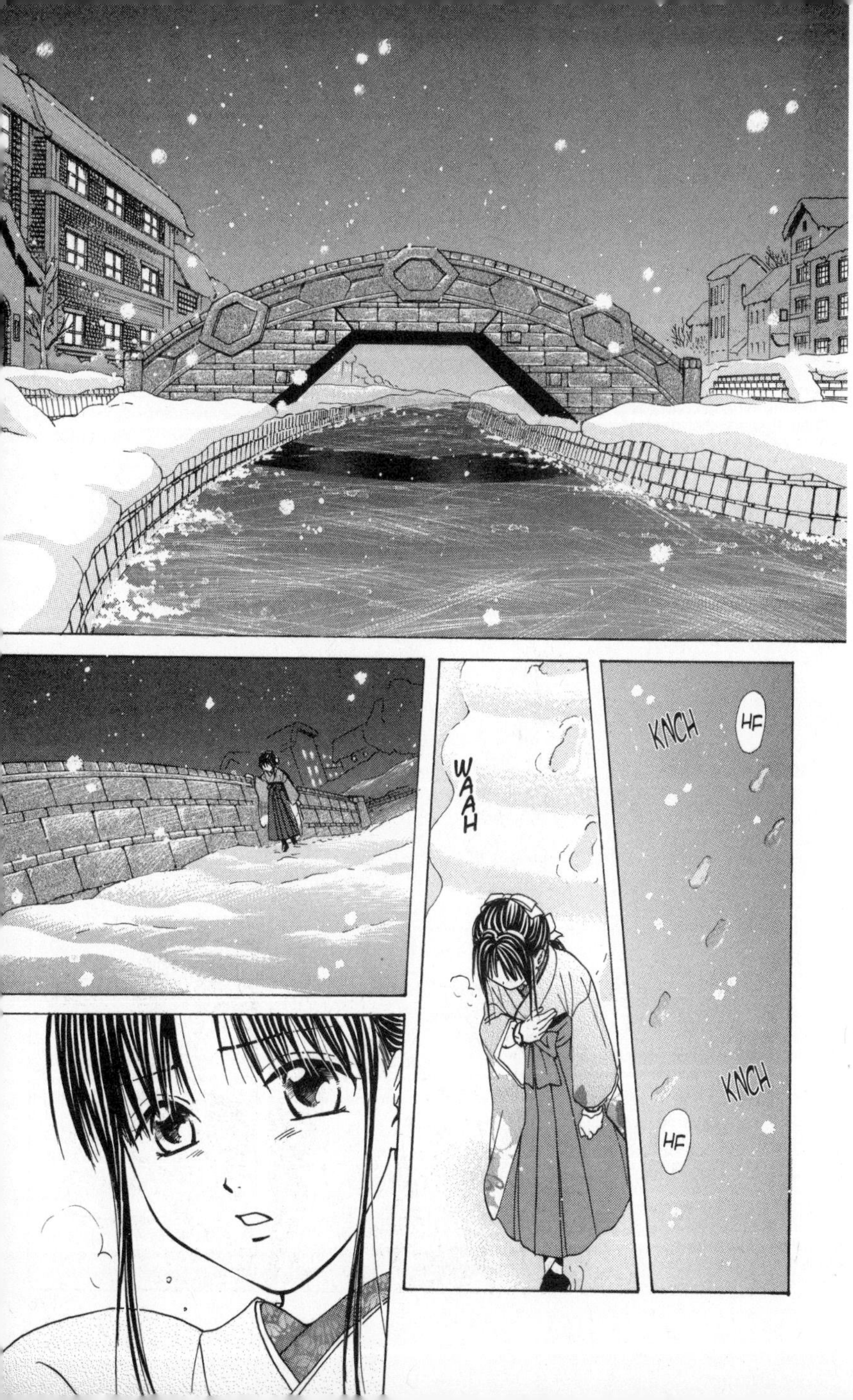
HF
KNCH
KNCH
HF
WAAH

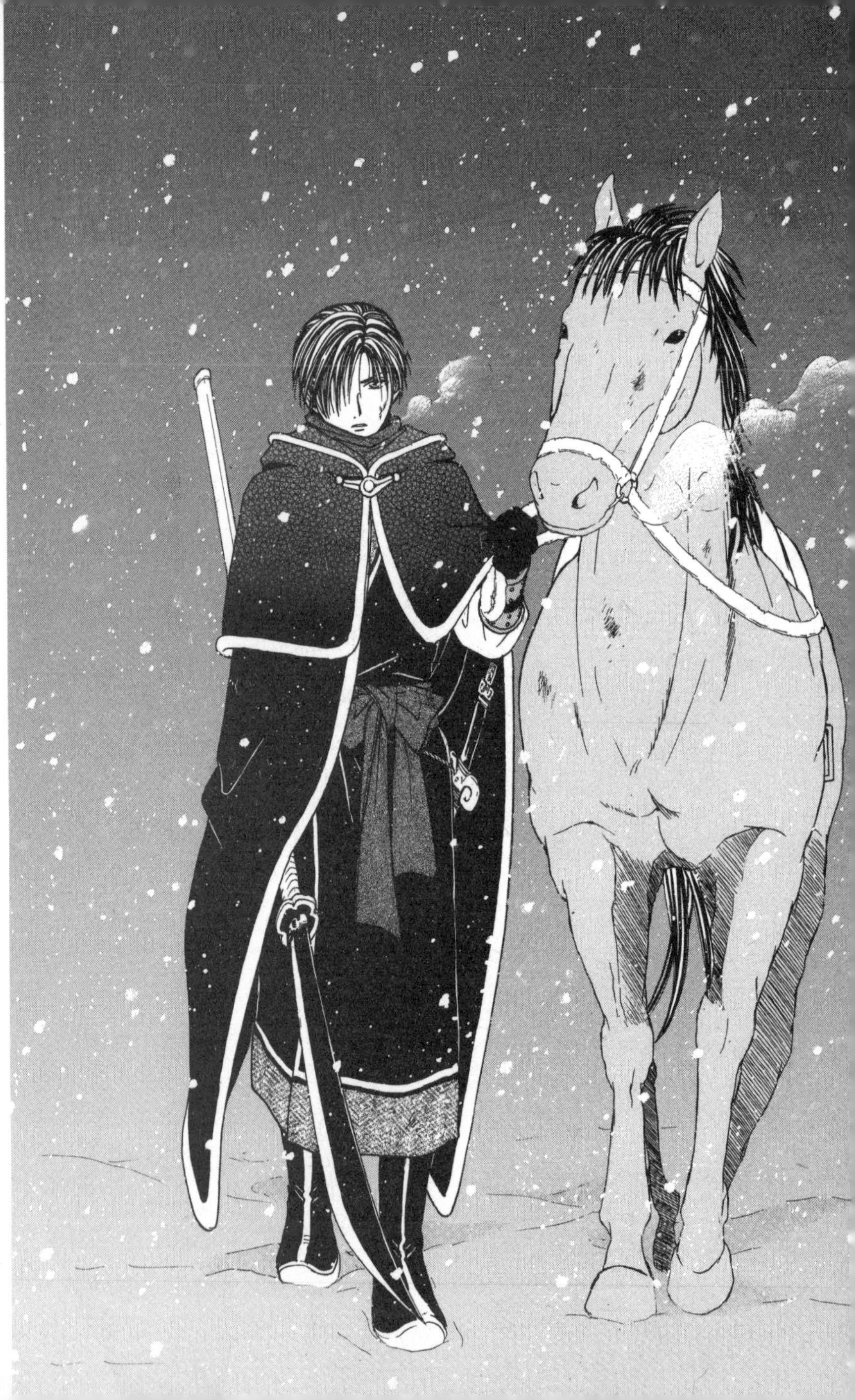

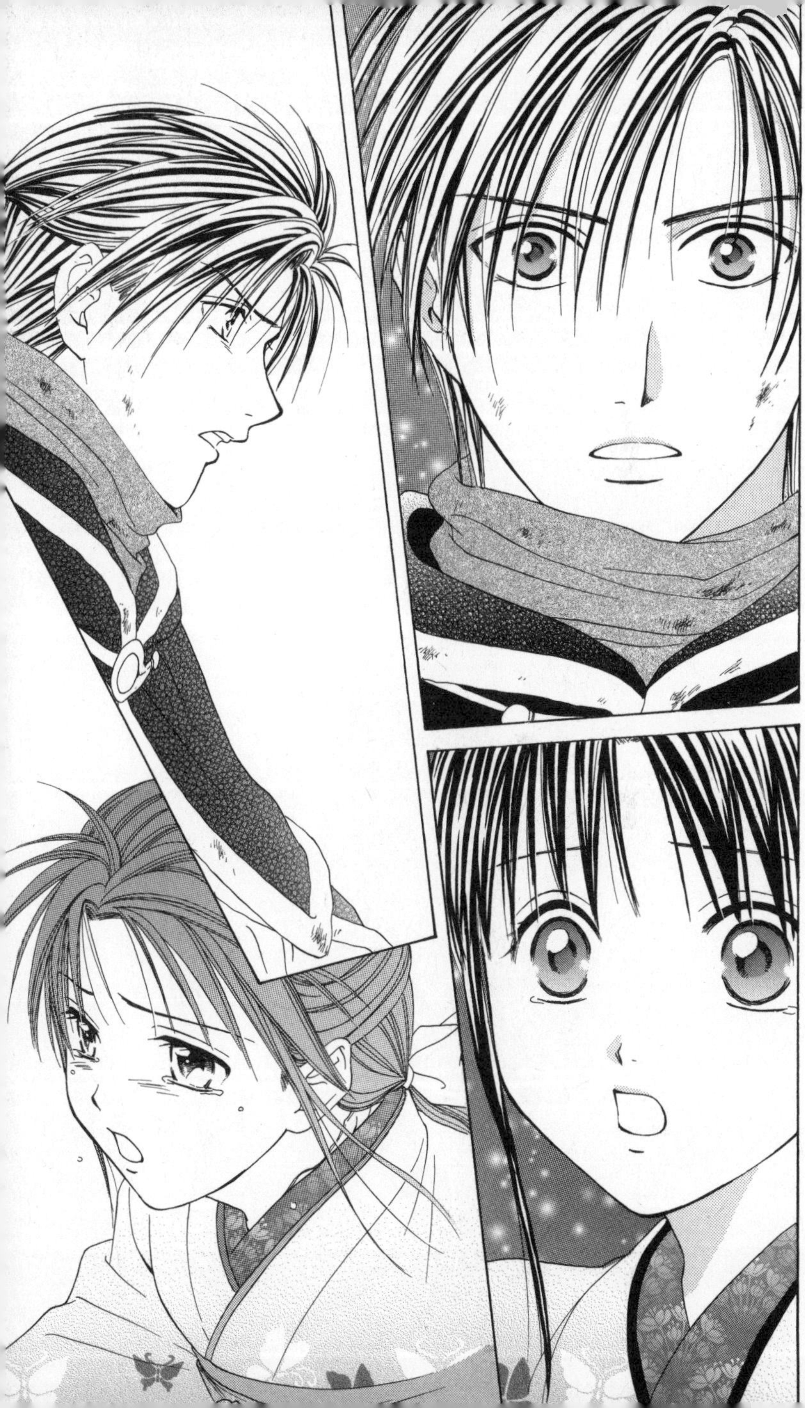

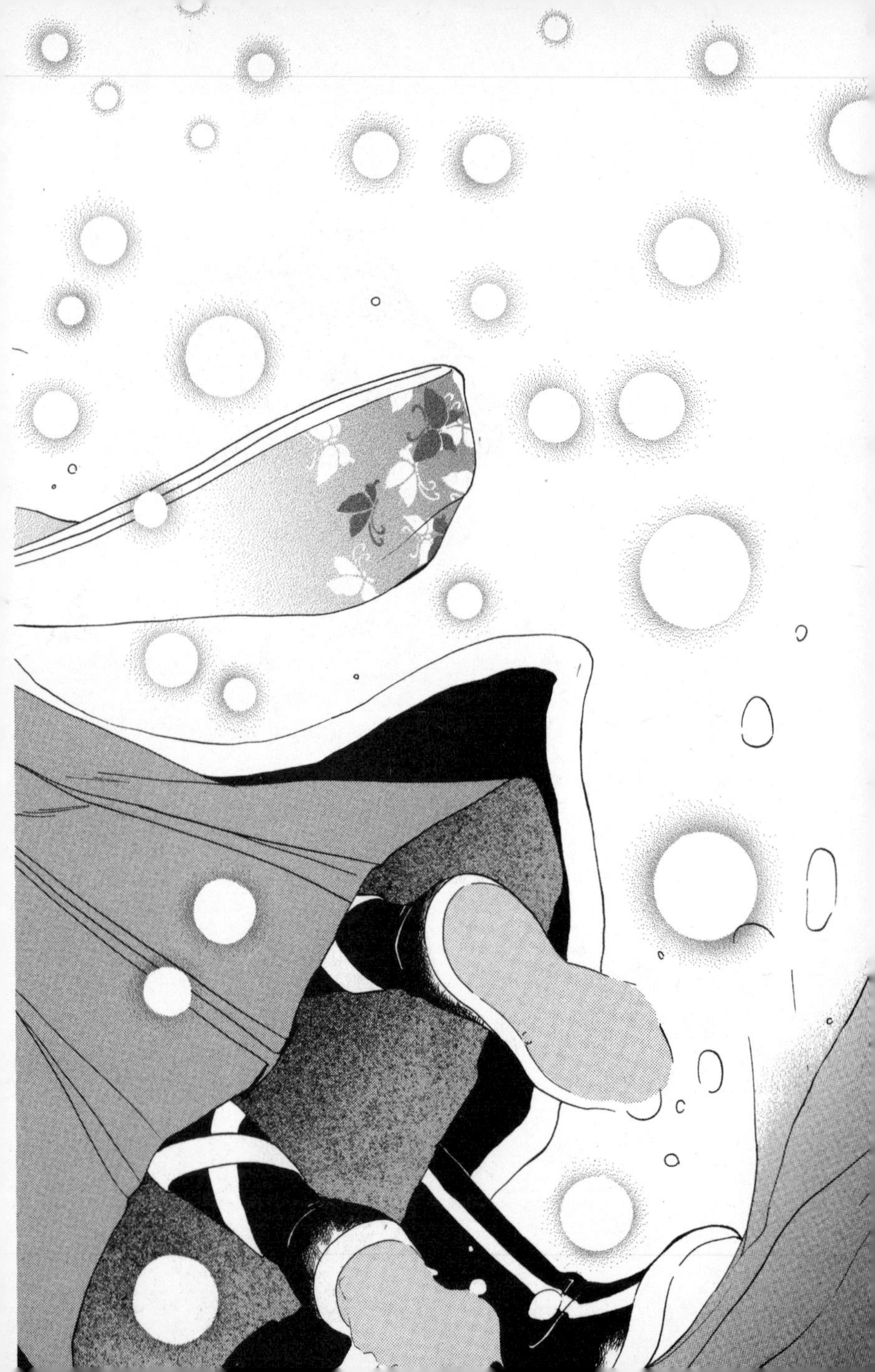

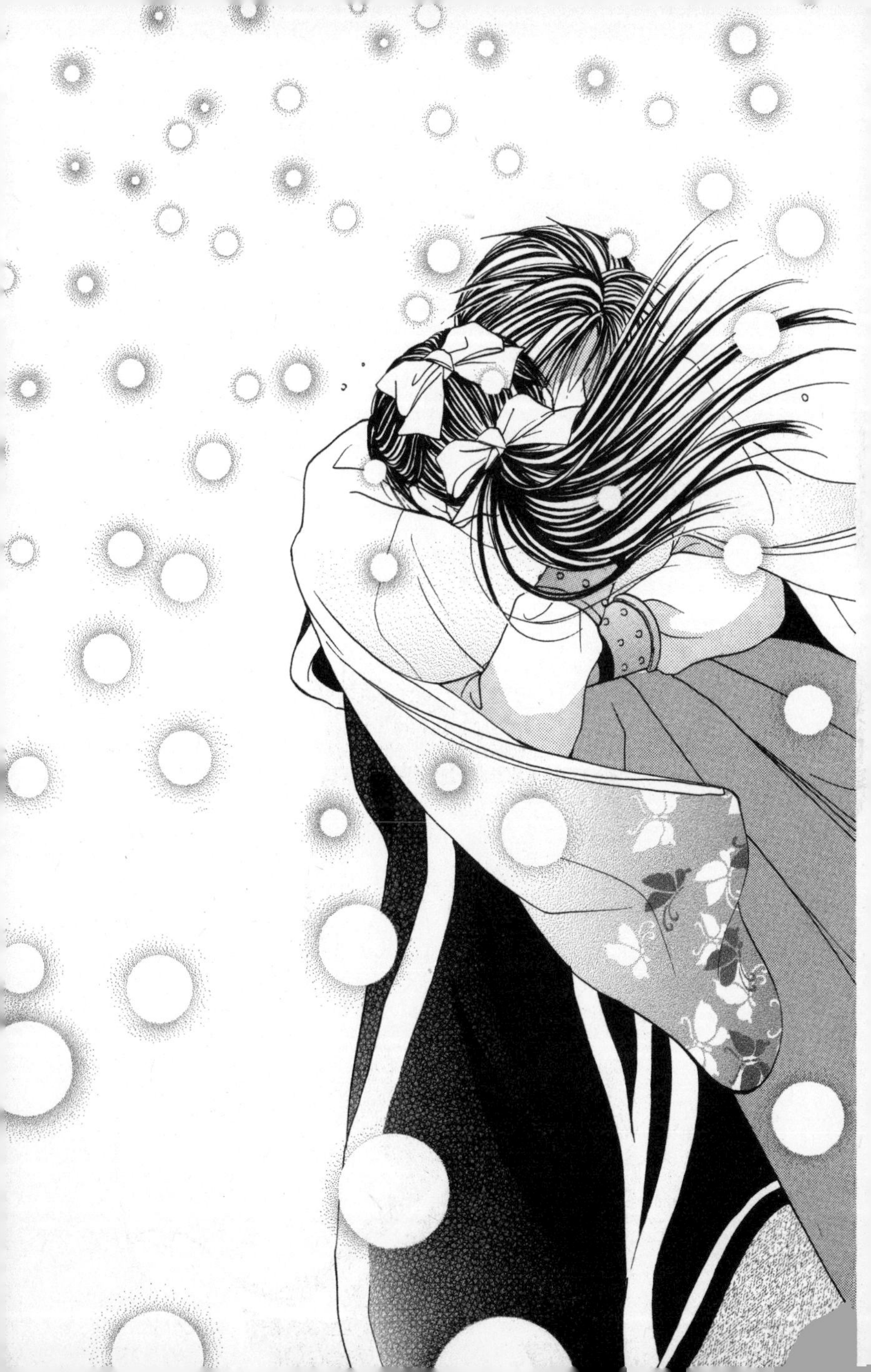

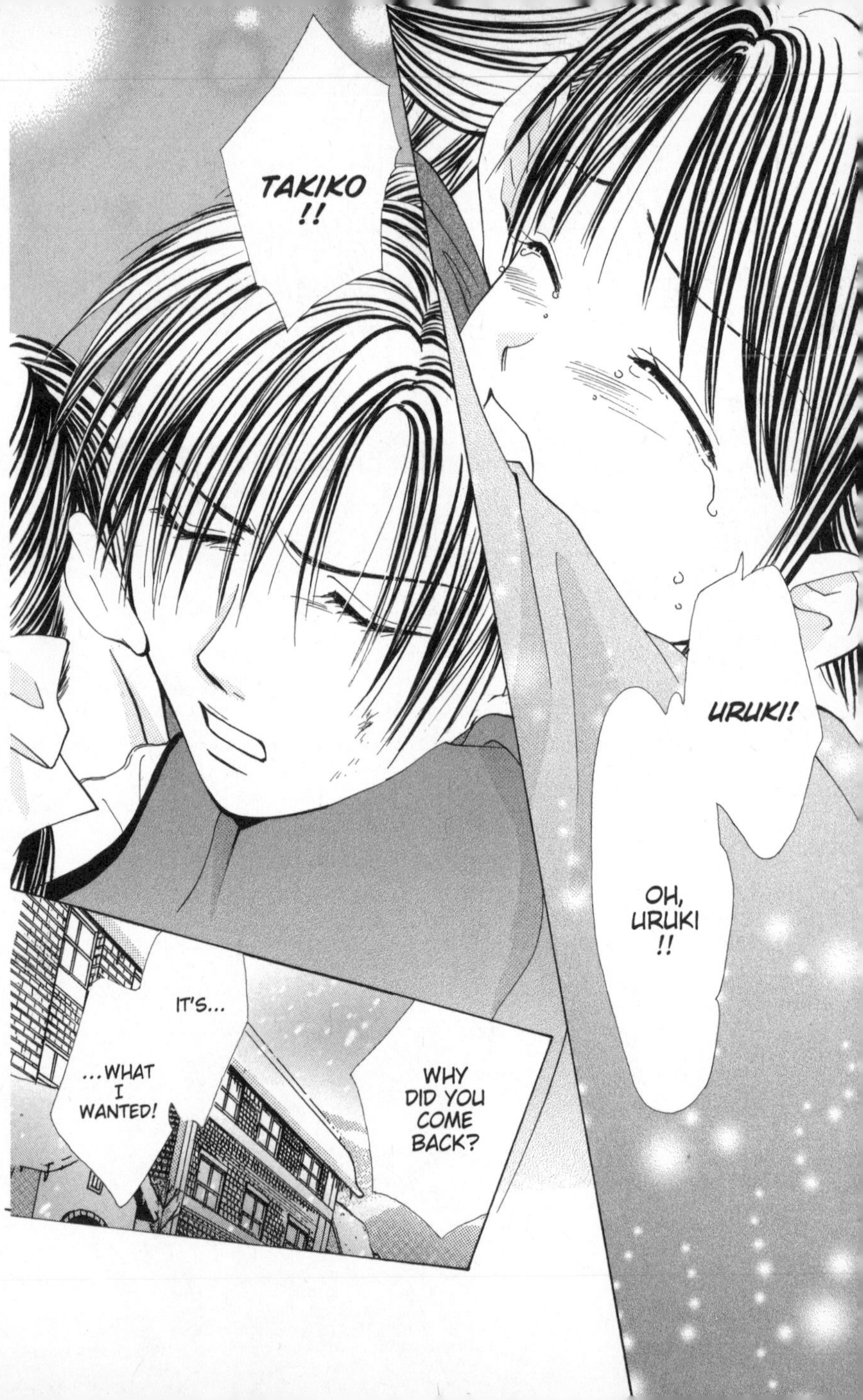
TAKIKO !!
URUKI!
OH, URUKI !!
WHY DID YOU COME BACK?
IT'S...
...WHAT I WANTED!

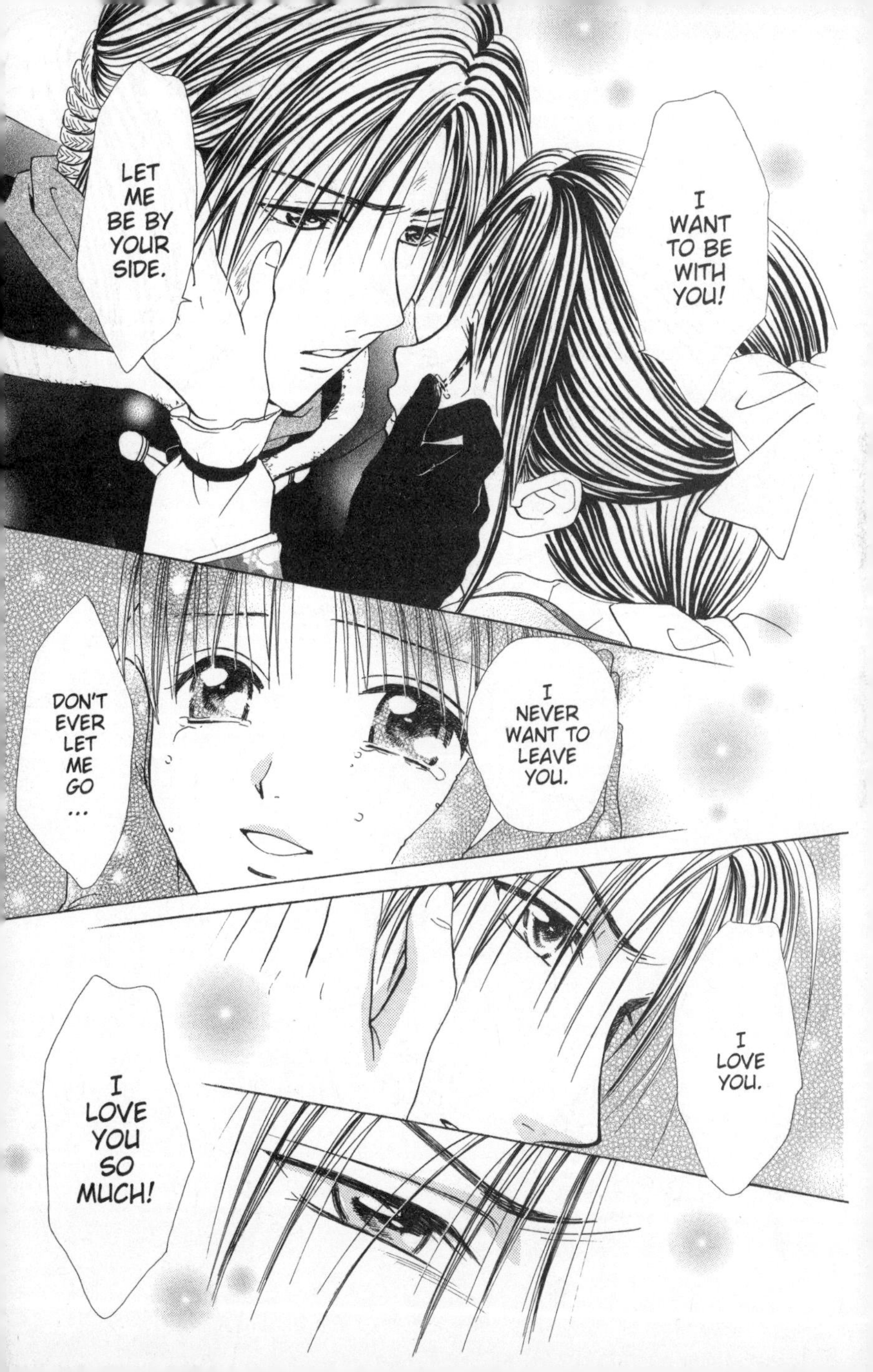
I WANT TO BE WITH YOU!
LET ME BE BY YOUR SIDE.
I NEVER WANT TO LEAVE YOU.
DON'T EVER LET ME GO...
I LOVE YOU.
I LOVE YOU SO MUCH!

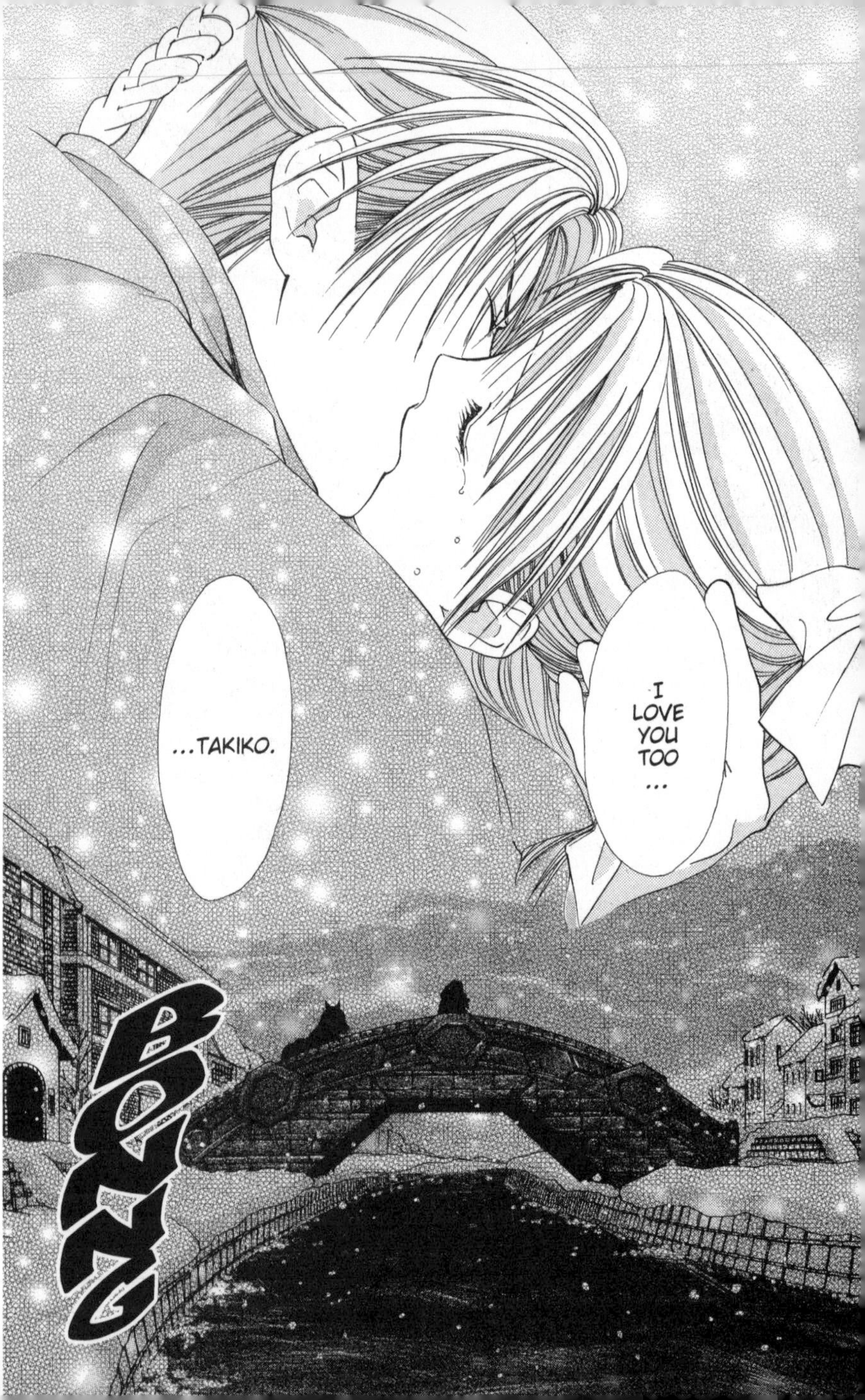
I LOVE YOU TOO ...
...TAKIKO.
BONG

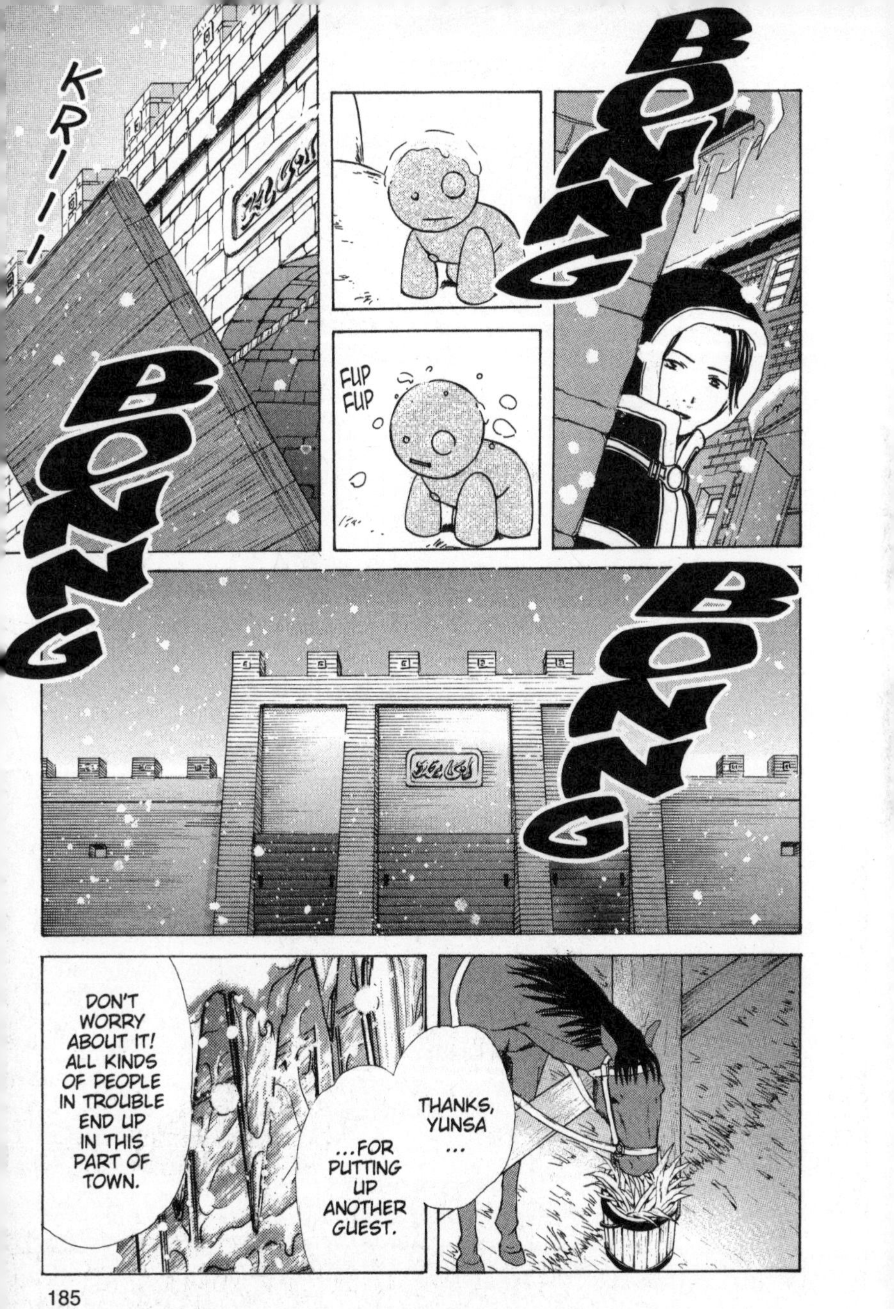
BONG
FUP FUP
KRIIII
BONG
BONG
THANKS, YUNSA ...
...FOR PUTTING UP ANOTHER GUEST.
DON'T WORRY ABOUT IT! ALL KINDS OF PEOPLE IN TROUBLE END UP IN THIS PART OF TOWN.

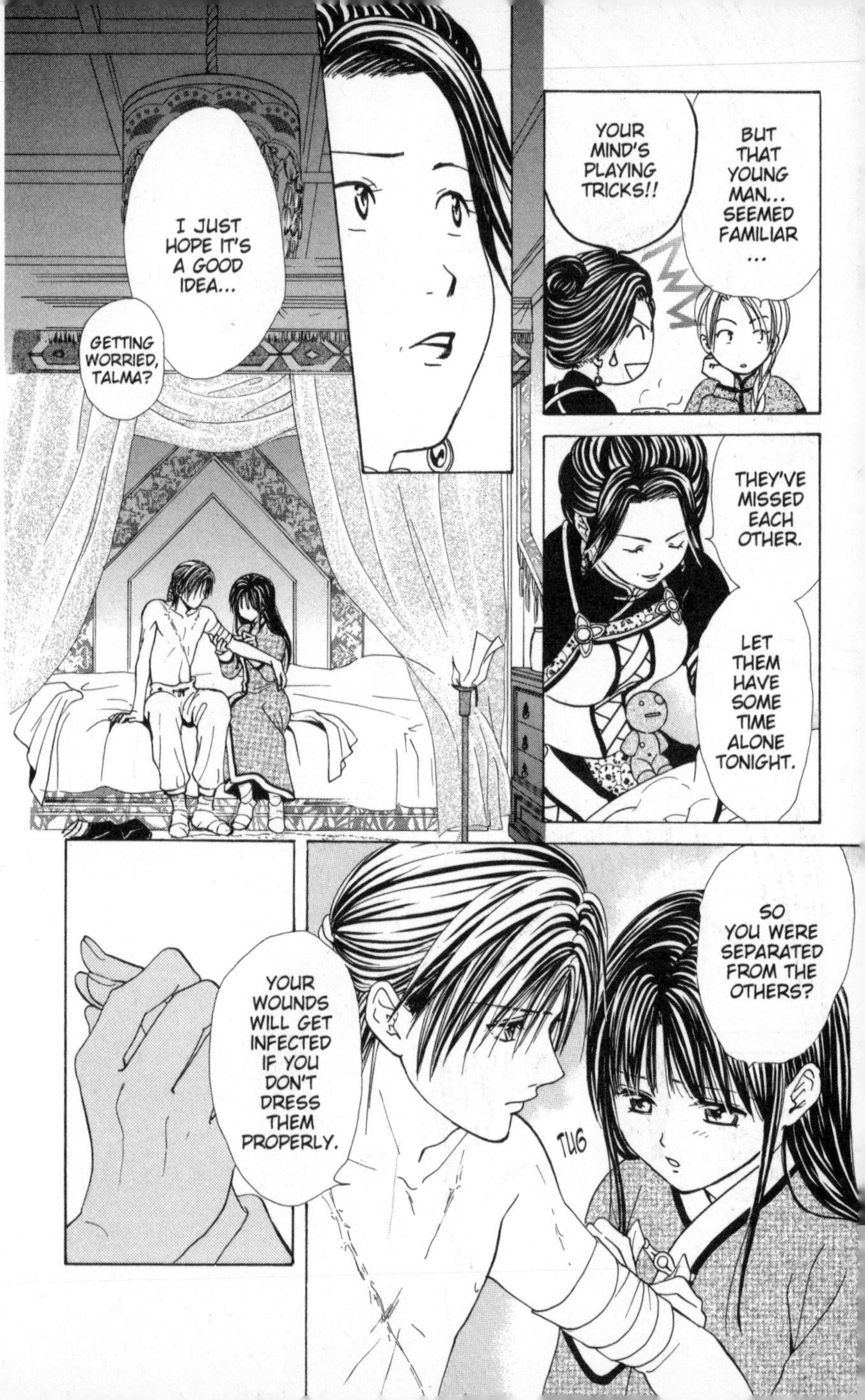
BUT THAT YOUNG MAN... SEEMED FAMILIAR ...
YOUR MIND'S PLAYING TRICKS!!
THEY'VE MISSED EACH OTHER.
LET THEM HAVE SOME TIME ALONE TONIGHT.
I JUST HOPE IT'S A GOOD IDEA...
GETTING WORRIED, TALMA?
SO YOU WERE SEPARATED FROM THE OTHERS?
TUG
YOUR WOUNDS WILL GET INFECTED IF YOU DON'T DRESS THEM PROPERLY.

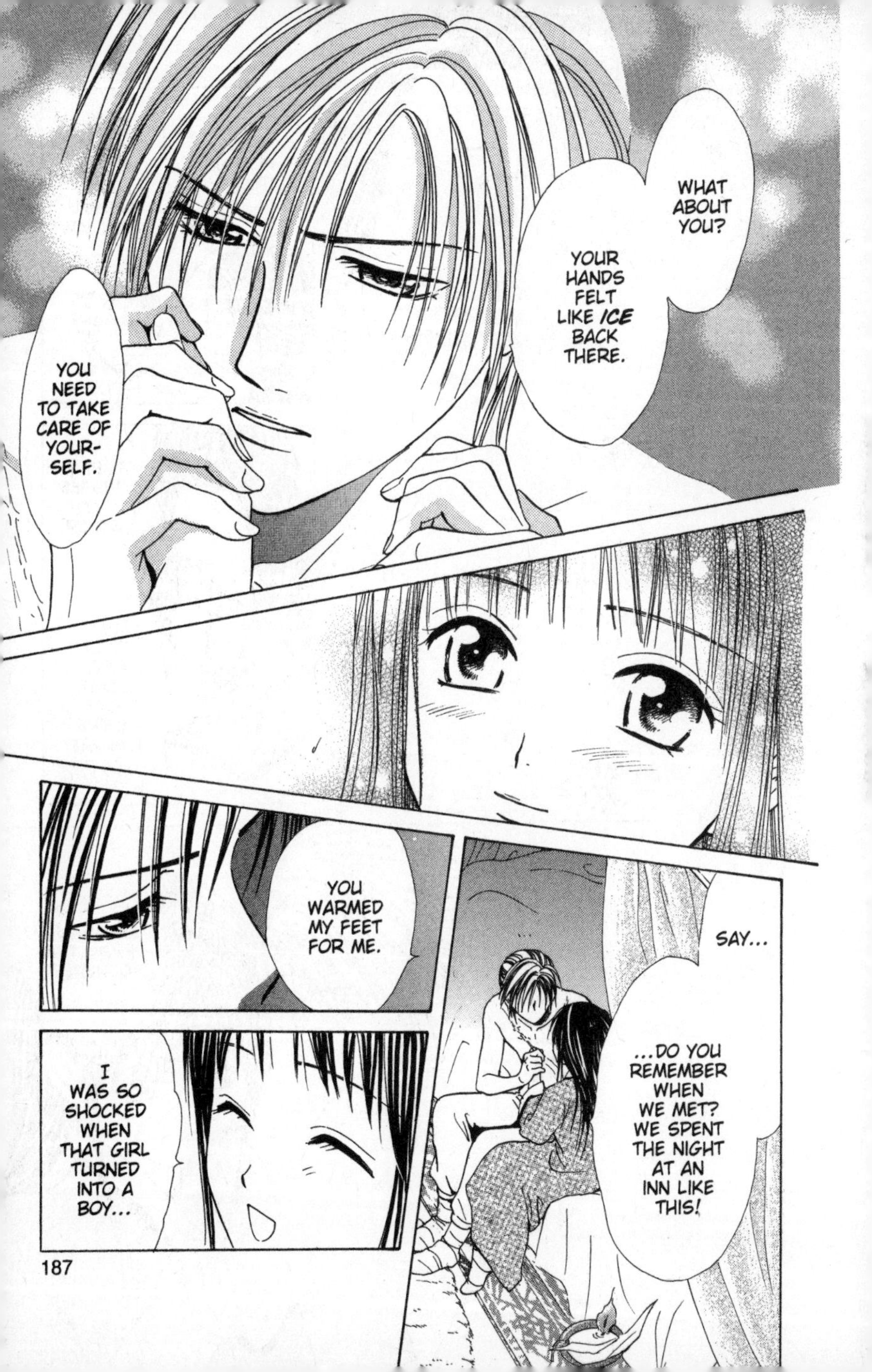
WHAT ABOUT YOU?
YOUR HANDS FELT LIKE *ICE* BACK THERE.
YOU NEED TO TAKE CARE OF YOUR-SELF.
SAY...
...DO YOU REMEMBER WHEN WE MET? WE SPENT THE NIGHT AT AN INN LIKE THIS!
YOU WARMED MY FEET FOR ME.
I WAS SO SHOCKED WHEN THAT GIRL TURNED INTO A BOY...

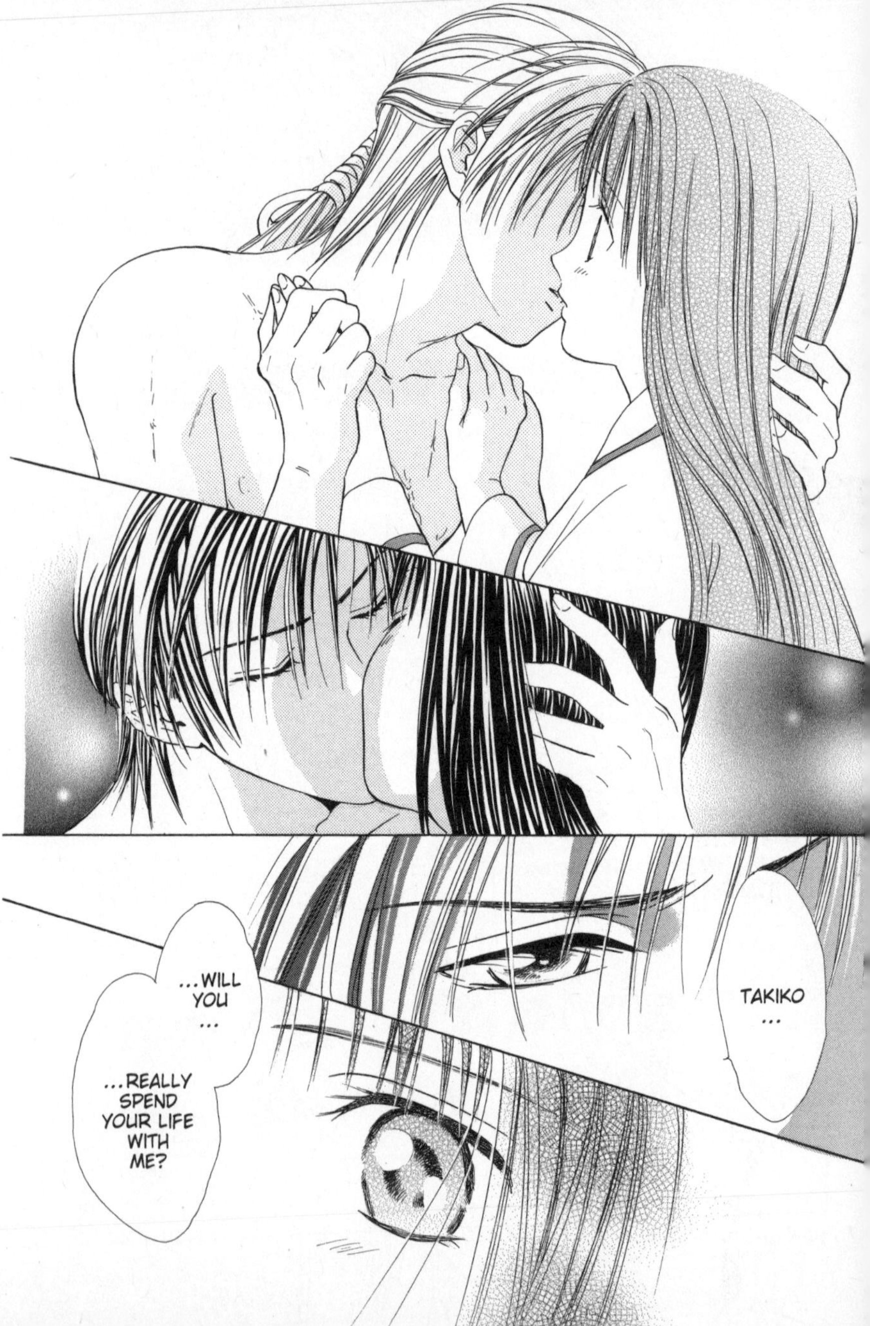
TAKIKO ...
...WILL YOU ...
...REALLY SPEND YOUR LIFE WITH ME?

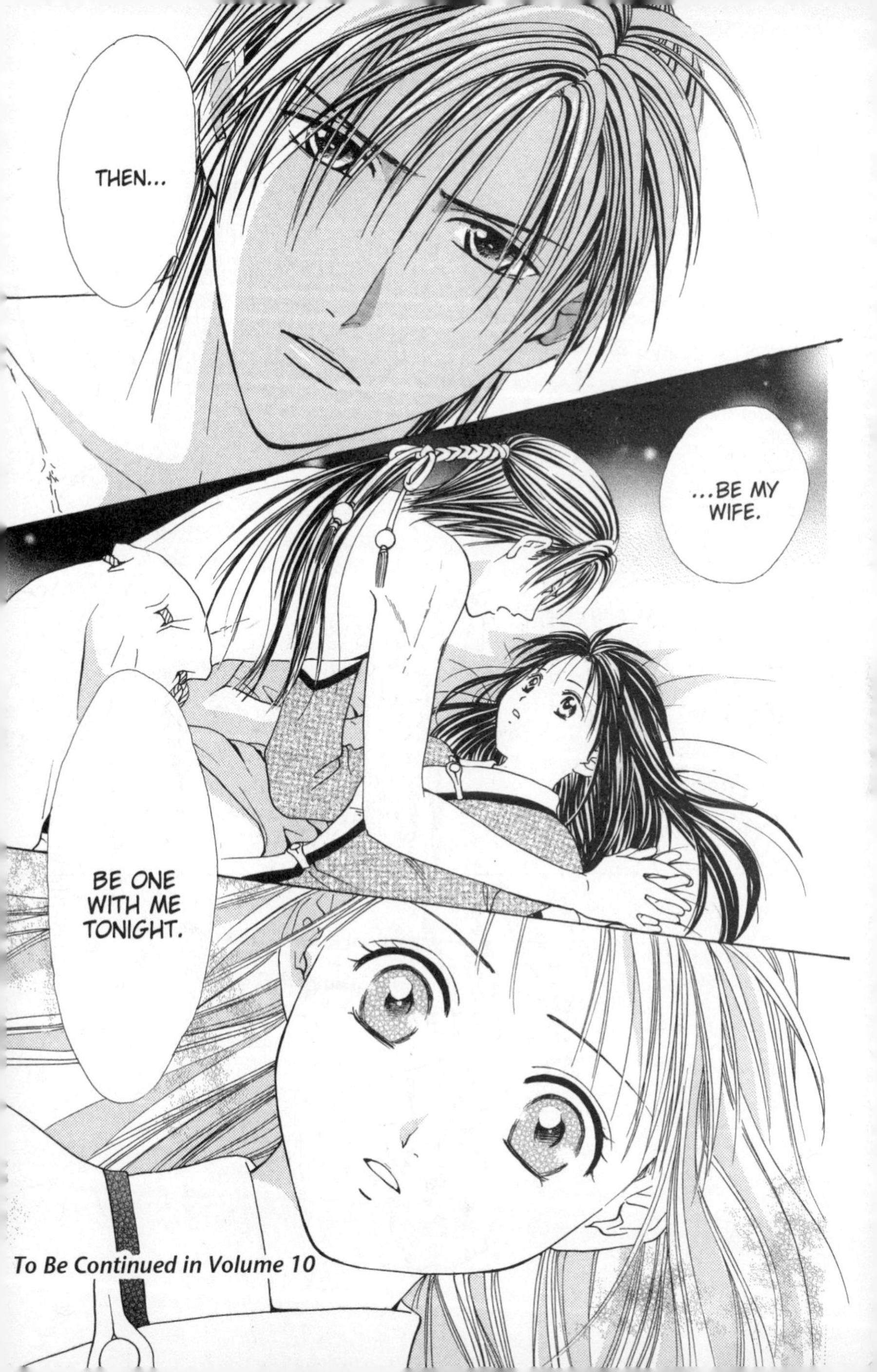
THEN...
...BE MY WIFE.
BE ONE WITH ME TONIGHT.

To Be Continued in Volume 10

Yuu Watase was born on March 5 in a town near Osaka, Japan. She was raised there before moving to Tokyo to follow her dream of creating manga. In the decade since her debut short story, *Pajama De Ojama* (An Intrusion in Pajamas), she has produced more than 50 volumes of short stories and continuing series. Her latest work, *Absolute Boyfriend*, appeared in Japan in the anthology magazine *Shôjo Comic*. Watase's other beloved series, *Alice 19th*, *Imadoki!*, and *Ceres: Celestial Legend*, are available in North America in English editions published by VIZ Media.

Fushigi Yûgi:
Genbu Kaiden Vol. 9

Shojo Beat Manga Edition
STORY AND ART BY
YUU WATASE

Translation/Lillian Olsen
Touch-up Art & Lettering/Rina Mapa
Design/Hidemi Sahara
Editor/Shaenon K. Garrity

FUSHIGI YUGI GENBUKAIDEN Vol. 9
by Yuu WATASE
© 2003 Yuu WATASE
All rights reserved.
Original Japanese edition published by SHOGAKUKAN.
English translation rights in the United States of America, Canada, the United
Kingdom and Ireland arranged with SHOGAKUKAN.

Printed in Canada

Published by VIZ Media, LLC
P.O. Box 77010
San Francisco, CA 94107

10 9 8 7 6 5 4 3 2
First printing, November 2009
Second printing, July 2016

www.viz.com

www.shojobeat.com

SURPRISE!

You may be reading the wrong way!

It's true: In keeping with the original Japanese comic format, this book reads from right to left— so action, sound effects, and word balloons are completely reversed. This preserves the orientation of the original artwork—plus, it's fun! Check out the diagram shown here to get the hang of things, and then turn to the other side of the book to get started!